Cults and New Religions

Sources for Study of Nonconventional
Religious Groups in Nineteenth-and
Twentieth-Century America

A collection of
reprinted books, pamphlets, articles, and ephemera
documenting the development of nonconventional religion in America

Edited by
J. GORDON MELTON

Director
Institute for the Study of American Religion
Santa Barbara

A Garland Series

Jehovah's Witnesses I

The Early Writings of J. F. Rutherford

Edited with an introduction by
JERRY BERGMAN

65126

GARLAND PUBLISHING
New York   London
1990

Library of Congress Cataloging-in-Publication Data

Rutherford, J. F. (Joseph Franklin), 1869–1942.
Jehovah's Witnesses I : the early writings of J. F. Rutherford / edited with an introduction by Jerry
Bergman.
p. cm. — (Cults and new religions)
Reprints of books originally published 1915–1929.
Includes bibliographical references.
ISBN 0-8240-4369-3 (alk. paper)
1. Watch Tower Bible and Tract Society—Apologetic works. I. Bergman, Jerry. II. Title. III. Title:
Jehovah's Witnesses I. IV. Title: Jehovah's Witnesses one. V. Series.
BX8525.55.R87 1990
289.9'2—dc20   89-3967

Printed on acid-free, 250-year-life paper.

Manufactured in the United States of America

Contents

INTRODUCTION

A GREAT BATTLE IN THE ECCLESIASTICAL HEAVENS,
AS SEEN BY A LAWYER
J. F. Rutherford

MILLIONS NOW LIVING WILL NEVER DIE
J. F. Rutherford

CAN THE LIVING TALK WITH THE DEAD?
J. F. Rutherford

THE BIBLE ON OUR LORD'S RETURN
J. F. Rutherford

THE STANDARD FOR THE PEOPLE
J. F. Rutherford

FREEDOM FOR THE PEOPLES
J. F. Rutherford

JUDGMENT
J. F. Rutherford

INTRODUCTION

The Challenge to Religious Freedom
Introduction to Rutherford's Works

Joseph Franklin Rutherford, the second president of the Watchtower Bible and Tract Society, led the movement during its stormiest years. During his presidency, the Witnesses were severely persecuted in virtually every country in the world and banned in many. Although never officially banned in the United States, even here they have chalked up the record of being one of the most persecuted religious groups in modern times.

In this volume, a representative selection of the Rutherford pamphlets are reprinted including, *The Great Battle in the Ecclesiastical Heavens* (1915); *Millions Now Living Will Never Die; Can the Living Talk With the Dead?; Our Lord's Return* (1925); *The Standard for the People* (1926), *Freedom for the People* (1927); and *Judgment of the Judges* (1929). This selection of Rutherford's pamphlets which, although important historically to the movement, have long been out of print and are available only in specialized private collections. They well illustrate the writings which typified what is termed "the Rutherford era" of the Watchtower Society. Rutherford managed to arouse the ire of just about everyone; the political leaders and clergy alike, and in just about every denomination. These works cover both the political controversies as well as elucidate some of the major doctrines originally developed by C.T. Russell, the founder of the Watchtower Society, and modified by Rutherford. Many of these works were probably written in the palatial mansion home that the Society owned called Beth Sarim, in which Rutherford lived and worked during most of his presidency.

Rutherford was born on a Morgan County, Missouri farm near Boonev- ille, on November 8, 1869. He was the son of James Calvin and Leonora (Strickland) Rutherford. His parents were farmers, and Rutherford was evidently raised a nominal Baptist, although his interest in religion at this time is not known. It was known that he valued education, and won his parents consent to contribute to the wages of a hired hand to replace him on the family farm so that he could go away to school. In college Rutherford learned shorthand and became a court stenographer. Later, at age twenty-two, after two years of tutoring by a local judge, he was admitted to the Missouri Bar. After studying law, he began his first practice in Booneville, Missouri, then later in Kansas City and St. Louis. He accompanied Williams Jennings Bryan on his first presidential campaign in 1896, and even though his views of politics later radically changed, in honor of Bryan, Rutherford wore his collar up for the rest of his life. He died at Beth Sarim on January 8, 1942, at the age of 72. Rutherford's wife, Mary Ann Rutherford, died in December of 1962 and his only son, Malcolm C. Rutherford, died in 1989.

Rutherford was first introduced to the teachings of Russell when two women members of the group visited his office in 1894. He evidently put the books that he had purchased from them aside until a decade later. At this time, "one night in 1904, I wondered into a meeting of one-hundred-fifty Bible students on Grand Avenue and came out so impressed and delighted that I returned to Booneville, Missouri, where I was practicing law and formed a Bible study group there." By 1906 he wrote his first book "Man's Salvation From a Lawyer's Viewpoint" wherein he discussed his new beliefs. Four years later, he was associated with the Witnesses as a lecturer and an attorney. Rutherford was soon sharing the public platform with Russell, who he proved invaluable to because of Russell's continual involvement in various forms of litigation, and Rutherford was one of the few lawyers in the movement at the time. A skilled court room defender, he soon became prominent in both the business and legal matters of the society. In January of 1917, soon after Russell's death in 1916, Rutherford was elected president of the society by the four remaining directors, of whom he was one. The other four directors had left after a bitter political struggle, and evidently with the support of the members of the Watchtower Society.

Because Russell taught political neutrality, and also that the millennial reign of Christ began in 1914, war was considered not only unchristian, but fruitless and counter-productive in view of the soon ushering in of God's Kingdom on Earth. The Watchtower's publications expounding this belief were judged seditious by a Federal court and, on June 21, 1918, Rutherford and several of his co-workers were convicted of violating the Espionage Act and sentenced on sedition charges to long terms in the Federal Penitentiary in Atlanta, Georgia.

In prison, Rutherford continued his religious activities, even developing a new journal, *The Golden Age*, which later became *Awake!* In March of 1919, the defendants were released pending the outcome of their appeal. Their case appeal was accepted and a new trial was ordered in May, but because of several clear irregularities and biases in the trial, it was decided to drop all charges. Rutherford became a hero, and this negative experience understandably set him against not only both the judicial and political systems, but also the religious systems which were openly instru-

mental in helping to put him behind bars.

Probably much of his life long fire against the political authorities and clergy of his day was rooted in his experiences of prison. While serving his twenty year sentence, he contracted pneumonia resulting in the loss of one lung. After continued problems, his doctors advised him to move to a climate warmer than Brooklyn, New York where the world headquarters was at that time. On January 13, 1930, he moved into 440 Braeburn Road in Kensington Heights, a suburb of San Diego, California. How this twenty room palatial Spanish style house with its two car garage complete with a twelve cylinder Lincoln automobile was acquired is still the subject of much controversy. The deed shows that a Watchtower official, Robert J. Martin, "for the consideration of ten dollars ($10.00) does hereby grant, bargain and sell unto Joseph F. Rutherford of 124 Columbia Heights, Brooklyn, New York, for and during his life on Earth. . ." the house, which was evidently custom built for Rutherford. The deed put the property in trust for several Biblical characters, namely David, Gideon, Barak, Sampson, Jepthae, Joseph and Samuel, "and all of the other faithful men who were named with the approval of the Bible at Hebrews the eleventh chapter." Called *Beth Sarim*, Hebrew for "house of the princesses," Rutherford planted trees indigenous to the Holy Land (including olive and palm trees) to make the prophets feel at home when they arrived. His confidence that the millennium was coming soon was reflected both in this action and in Rutherford's writings, most notably in his booklet *Millions Now Living Will Never Die*.

Among his continued conflicts and scraps with the law was an appeal to the judges of the St. Louis Court of Appeals, presided over by

Honorable Judge Charles C. Bland (69 *Missouri Appeals Reports,* October term, 1896, page 441-447) concerning the matter of "fraudulent conveyance" involving Rutherford's highly questionable legal practices in protecting a client. Actually, Rutherford was involved in much controversy for most of his life, and even his death was surrounded by problems. On his deathbed, Rutherford voiced his last wish: that his disciples would bury him at dawn after his death in a hillside crypt at Beth Sarim. After what the local papers described as a "bitter legal battle" which lasted more than three weeks, the San Diego Board of Supervisors on February 3, 1942 turned down an application to bury Rutherford on his "house of princesses" estate. The supervisors essentially sustained a ruling made two weeks previously by the county planning commission after hundreds of residents in the vicinity of the estate protested the proposed burial. W. P. Heath, Rutherford's personal secretary, claimed that prejudice and misunderstanding were responsible for the refusal; the local residents claimed that such a burial was inappropriate, and may effect property values in their highly exclusive residential district.

An incredibly bureaucratic, charismatic, and effective organizer, he utilized modern methods of advertising to spread his message. One of his his first steps as president of the Watchtower was to develop in 1921 a pithy slogan, namely "Millions now living will never die." Soon this slogan appeared on billboards throughout the country. In 1937, at an estimated cost of $100,000, one-hundred and thirty-five radio stations were paid to broadcast Rutherford's Columbus, Ohio convention speech. This hook-up, one of the first in the world, provided the nation a glimpse of the new instant news that we now take for granted.

He wrote scores of books and pamphlets, all of which received a wide distribution, primarily through the efforts of his devoted followers who hawked them from door to door. He initiated a radio station, and even designed and manufactured a phonograph that could be easily carried to private houses. This invention, one of the first workable portable models, was used to play four minute sermons by Rutherford, and occasionally other prominent individuals in the movement. Rutherford stressed that each individual Witness was a minister, responsible to spread the group's message in the local congregation and in the community itself. Often still called Russellites (and Rutherfordites) by opposers, his political astuteness forced him to realize that a new label was needed for his movement; and in 1931 at the Columbus, Ohio convention, it was announced: Jehovah's Witnesses, based on *Isaiah* 43:9. Although many of the important decisions that Jehovah's Witnesses fought and won in the United States Supreme Court and other levels were handed down after Rutherford's death, he established both the doctrine and the procedures of rationalizing their actions which eventually led to the supportive decisions.

An extremely tall, large man (6 feet-4 inches), Rutherford is said to have appeared dignified and self confident, looking "more like a senator than most senators." Having the reputation of a coarse personal style, he tended to alienate many of those that he worked with, and during his last dozen years of his life remained aloof from his followers, typically spending most of his time only with his house keeper and select individuals at Beth Sarim.

Ever critical of what he called the evil trinity, the political, business commerce, and the religious systems, his opinions of these is adequately reflected in the booklets reprinted here. They also help one to partly understand the opposition that his movement faced. His most well known struggle was with the flag salute issue. Saluting the American flag and pledging allegiance to it have been rituals in American schools for decades. Few Americans object to these exercises because they saw them as instilling in children a sense of loyalty and devotion to their country.

Jehovah's Witness opposition to the flag salute actually did not begin until 1935, or over fifty-four years after the movement was founded. Up till the mid 1930s, most Witnesses saluted the flag without much question. If they had any personal objections to the rite, few evidently made an issue of it. The topic was carefully researched by the Watchtower Society only when Nazi Germany and Fascist Italy forced their subjects to give nationalist salutes to their leaders—*der Furher* and *il Duce*. This development caused the Witnesses in those countries to examine the matter. Not surprisingly, because of their devotion to God and negative feeling of secular governments, they came to question the propriety of such acts.

After the Witness administration concluded that to *heil Hitler* was morally wrong, they were forced to ask, "If it is not proper to salute Hitler, would it be proper to salute his flag? And if it was wrong to salute his flag, what about the American flag?" Thus, the issue of saluting the American flag was raised among Jehovah's Witnesses for the first time. To be consistent, the Watchtower headquarters ruled that total neutrality required that they not salute *any* ruler, nor the flag of *any* nation—America's included. If it was wrong to salute Hitler and his flag, it was likewise wrong to salute Roosevelt and "his" flag. Of course, Americans argued that there was a great deal of difference between saluting the Swastika and the Stars and Stripes. After all, one might object to saluting Hitler and his flag on the grounds that one disapproved of this totalitarian government. The Witnesses, however, were not concerned with judgments regarding the relative quality of governments. To them all human governments were evil, and they were determined to *consistently* apply their religious principles. This issue struck at the foundation of Jehovah's Witnesses' allegiance to the Supreme Sovereign. The Witnesses first "officially" condemned saluting on Monday, June 3, 1935, in answer to a question on the flag salute issue at an assembly. Shortly thereafter, on September 20, 1935, the first incident of many occurred in what was to become the Witnesses' seven-year struggle not to salute, a struggle which was widely publicized throughout the United States and much of the rest of the world.

Soon after this first pronouncement, Witness statements against saluting became stronger. The *1936 Yearbook of Jehovah's Witnesses* (page 22) stated that, to those who "know and serve God . . . saluting of any flag by those who are in covenant with Jehovah God to do his will constituted the breaking of that covenant with God and such covenant breakers are guilty of death." As a result, many individual Witnesses were subjected to terrible persecution.

On November 6, 1935, two children of Walter Gobitis were expelled from school in Minersville, Pennsylvania, and their father was arrested. Believing that the school board's action was unjust, Gobitis decided to go to court. The case, first heard in Federal District Court, was decided in favor of the Witnesses. It was then appealed by the Minersville School District, and the Witnesses again prevailed. Finally, in 1940, the Supreme Court ruled on the matter with disastrous results for Jehovah's Witnesses. That court reversed the lower courts' favorable judgments, and the Witnesses lost in a crushing eight to one decision. Justice Harlan Stone was the lone dissenter. This decision precipitated a wave of persecution in the United States unprecedented since the nineteenth-century persecution of Mormons. So intense was the violence that United States Solicitor General Francis Biddle and first lady Eleanor Roosevelt made public appeals to the American people to discontinue their vicious onslaught against the Witnesses. The Attorney General, in a coast to coast NBC broadcast, said on June 6, 1940:

... Jehovah's Witnesses have been repeatedly set upon and beaten. They have committed no crime; but the mob adjudged they had, and meted out mob punishment. The Attorney General has ordered an immediate investigation of these outrages. The people must be alert and watchful, and above all cool and sane. Since mob violence will make the government's task infinitely more difficult, it will not be tolerated. We shall not defeat the Nazi evil by emulating its methods. (Whalen 1962:183)

After the Witnesses lost in the Supreme Court, their only alternative was to bring another case before that court. They soon settled upon *West Virginia State Board of Education v. Barnett*. The Attorney General of West Virginia felt that he could rely on the *Gobitis v. Minersville School District* case, and thus he did not bother to prepare arguments. In an unexpected move, presiding Judge Parker, Fourth Circuit United States Court of Appeals, stated: "Mr. Attorney General, if you are relying on that opinion you [had] better argue this case." Taken by surprise, the attorney general made a feeble, unprepared attempt, but the three-judge court unanimously refused to obey the Supreme Court's mandate.

When the case again reached the Supreme Court, that body reversed its previous position by a vote of six to three, holding that the Minersville School Board did not have the right to deny the children their education for not saluting. The court concluded:

To sustain the compulsory flag salute, we are required to say that a Bill of Rights which guards the individual's right to speak his own mind ... One's right to life, liberty and property, to free speech, a free press, freedom of worship and assembly, and other fundamental rights may not be submitted to vote; they depend on the outcome of no elections ... [and] no official, high or petty, can prescribe what shall be orthodox in politics, nationalism, religion, or other matters of opinion or force citizens to confess by word or act their faith therein ... the action of the local authorities in compelling the flag salute and pledge transcends constitutional limitations on their power and invades the sphere of intellect and spirit which ... is the purpose of the First Amendment of our Constitution.

Ironically, the *Barnett* decision was handed down on Flag Day, June 14, 1943. The reaction of the press was almost universally favorable. Headlines such as "Supreme Court Abdicates as the Nation's School Board" and "The Supreme Court Hands Down an Educationally Significant Decision" were typical of hundreds which appeared in journals and newspapers.

Those most often hurt by compulsory flag salute laws were the children, although many adults suffered as well. The children were often totally innocent victims, caught between the rigid demands of their parents' faiths on one hand and the attitudes of school authorities on the other. In the case of Jehovah's Witnesses, their religious leaders, acting through the parents, pressured children not to salute, while teachers, fellow students, school boards, and governmental authorities pressed them to disobey both their parents and their own consciences and salute. Unfortunately, in what were essentially adult confrontations, those on both sides showed a callous disregard for the welfare of the children, who sometimes suffered terribly. But it was the secular authorities who were generally the most cruel. In the United States—as in Canada and the many other countries where the flag salute has been an issue—they were often ruthless in their efforts to force the children of non-saluters to comply with flag salute regulations.

In most cases, acting largely in response to home training, the children sincerely objected to saluting. Those raised in the Witness faith firmly believed that if they saluted, they would be guilty of a gross sin against God which could result in their everlasting destruction. An indication of the seriousness of saluting for Jehovah's Witnesses is found in a *Consolation* article which states that Jehovah's Witnesses are "... in a covenant to do the will of God and they sincerely and conscientiously believe that if they break that covenant they must suffer complete loss of life. Neither the government of ... United States, nor any other ... can give [everlasting] life to man ... respondents thus sincerely believe [they] have no alternative. If they would live they must obey God [and not salute] because disobeying means their destruction."

This belief is foreign to many, but if a child's parents, relatives, and friends belong to a religion that teaches saluting is wrong, the child will ordinarily accept this view. Hence, if the child believes that to salute is a gross sin before God, forcing him to do so is a serious matter. To go against one's conscience in a deeply felt religious matter is, in the minds of many children, similar to forcing someone to murder his mother. Thus, even without direct pressure, the flag salute issue was very traumatic for most non-saluting children. Barbara Grizzuti Harrison, in explaining what it was like to grow up as a "non-saluter," notes:

> [I spent] ... a lot of time in the offices of principals ... explaining why I didn't salute the flag; and the Witnesses' admonition not to *"make friends with the world"* was, for me, almost entirely gratuitous: very few children wanted to make friends with me.

Partly because of this and similar issues, of all modern religions, the group which has received by far both the most persecution and martyrdom from citizens of their own country are the Jehovah's Witnesses. As Murphy concluded "no chapter in human history has been so largely written in terms of persecution and intolerance as the one dealing with religious freedom ... and the Jehovah's Witnesses are living proof of the fact that even in this nation, conceived as it was in the ideals of freedom, the right to practice religion in unconventional ways is still far from secure." (Sorauf, 1984: 336) In the United States, a country that claims to have religious freedom, according to the well known jurist Archibald Cox (1987: 189) the Witnesses were "the principle victims of religious persecution in the United States in the twentieth century ... Although founded earlier, they began to attract attention and provoke repression in the 1930s, when their proselytizing and numbers rapidly increased". As King (1982: 248) concludes:

Many of the teachings have led the sect into bitter conflict with civil authorities all over the world, in democratic as well as in totalitarian states. . . . [The major reasons are because the] Jehovah's Witnesses will not fight or undertake war-related work in a time of national emergency. They are not pacifists, they simply believe that they are already enlisted in the army of Jehovah and cannot give allegiance to another power, that of the civil state. Thus, whilst they are exemplary citizens in matters of tax payment and obedience to moral and criminal laws, they will not undertake civil duties which they see as conflicting with their duty to Jehovah—God. Witnesses will not vote . . . salute a national flag or recognize a national anthem, and they refuse to enlist. In peace time they are normally tolerated in democratic countries, but in war-time and in totalitarian regimes they frequently face imprisonment.

A summary by The American Civil Liberties Union (1941: 1) concluded that "the record of violence against [the Jehovah's Witnesses] has been unparalleled in America since the attacks on the Mormons." They also concluded that "not since the persecution of the Mormons years ago has any religious minority been so bitterly and generally attacked as members of the Jehovah's Witnesses. . . Documents filed with the department of justice by attorneys . . . showed over 3,035 instances of mob violence in forty five states during 1940 involving 1,488 men, women and children." The main issue in the forties was not only their refusal to salute the flag, but also to buy war bonds and their refusal to support the war or war effort in any way. White (1968: 330) summarizes a typical event as follows:

At Klamath Falls, Oregon, the American Legion started to harass the Witnesses assembled with requests to salute the flag and buy war bonds. Then they attacked the Witnesses and be-sieged the hall, breaking windows, tossing in stink bombs, ammonia and burning kerosene rags. Some tried to get in the hall through the broken windows, only to be hit with broken benches by the Witnesses inside. The Witnesses' cars were all disabled and many overturned. Only the militia called out by the Governor of the state finally quelled the mob which reached 1,000 at its peak.

A summary of what lead to this development by Semonche (1986: 44) concluded that the religious group in American society which was more ready and willing to confront the state than any other was the Jehovah's Witnesses:

Impressively organized, pridefully evangelistic, and often scornful of the leaders of traditional religions, the members of the sect repeatedly collided with the law. Their willingness to do battle in the courts has been crowned with remarkable success. Their record in the United States Supreme Court shows they have won more than ninety percent of the fifty or so cases brought before that tribunal.

In his summary of human rights, Starr (1964:25) stated that the Jehovah's Witnesses have done more than any other religious group in America to argue before the Supreme Court certain basic questions concerning religious freedom. Professor Cushman has estimated that between 1938 and 1946 alone, the Witnesses brought twenty major cases before this court, and were victorious in a total of fourteen. By this means, they have not only forced the clarification of many freedom and human rights issues, but in at least two instances have forced the court to reverse itself. Thus, while their stand has produced a certain vindication, in spite of occasional Supreme Court victories on rather basic issues the persecution continues today. White (1968: 327-330) lists a number of separate of incidents which provides a feeling for the extent of persecution from citizens and government officials alike that has been both consistent and pervasive since their foundings:

At Biloxi, Mississippi, a Witness was likewise advertising his literature on the streets when he was heckled by a Catholic priest. He took the priest's photo. The cleric didn't like this and had him arrested. The Witness asked Chief of Police Alonzo Gabrich to see the camera as evidence. But he destroyed it and, while a policeman held him, he struck the Witness in the face with his fist.

In Connersville, Indiana, on Palm Sunday, sheriffs jailed seventy-five Witnesses on a charge of criminal syndicalism. The court set their bail at an impossible $225,000... In Topeka, Kansas, two Witnesses children of fourteen and nine refused to salute, and were made wards of the court. The judge sentenced their mothers to a year's imprisonment.

Mob rule continued unabated. On April 25th, 1942, a mob attacked three Witnesses advertising their literature on the streets. One had his arms pinned behind him while a mobster struck him almost unconscious. Police threatened to arrest—the Witness! On May 1st, 1942, a Witness was threatened with horsewhipping and jail if he remained in town. On May 23rd, a sixteen year old Witness was beaten for not saluting the flag. In Salt Lake City, Utah, two men entered the home of a Witness and inflicted cuts, bruises and a fracture on the hip of the occupant. When friends of the Witnesses tried to file an appeal bond a mob injured them. An attorney, in Sulfur Springs, Texas, who had been defending Witnesses, was attacked by five men with a knife, but fought back and broke the noses of two of his assailants.

The 1942 network of conventions was held on September 18th-20th.

Three of the extensions were attacked by mobs. In Little Rock 100 pipeline workers formed a mob and armed with guns and pipe attempted to break up the assembly. Some entered the convention grounds and chased the Witnesses away, brandishing their weapons and firing shots...dragging the occupants out, asking them if they would salute the flag and, when they refused, beating the Witnesses and tossing them into a ditch. No arrests of the mobsters were made.

These hostilities were recently resurrected in President Bush's comments during the election relative to Governor Ducakas' vetoing a bill in his state which would require mandatory flag salute by students, legislation which is contrary to the Supreme Court ruling that such is unconstitutional. Robert Maddox, executive director for Americans United for Separation of Church and State, appeared on television's Morton Downey show to discuss this issue. His summary of his experience is as follows:

. . . in my day I've endured some tough interviews under the harsh television lights. But nothing I have ever done on camera prepared me for the situation I found myself in a few weeks ago sitting on the "hot seat" of "the Morton Downey Jr. Show.". . . It all started when the Pledge of Allegiance flap broke during the presidential campaign. Americans United issued a press release tracing the history of the problem, pointing out that the constitutional questions involved in the episode stemmed from conscientious objections against reciting the pledge raised by Jehovah's Witnesses. . . .

Fortunately, Downey and his studio herd allowed me a few uninterrupted seconds to make my statement about the religious liberty and freedom of speech problems involved in *requiring* a person to recite the Pledge. My protagonist, the quintessential 'little old lady in tennis shoes,' tore into me for 'denying children the right to say the Pledge of Allegiance.' Over the tumult that broke as the audience stomped their feet and screamed its agreement with her, I insisted that no one had any notion of denying the right to say the Pledge to anyone. The "dialogue" took a decided turn from that point. . . .

I doubt that either Downey or the audience appreciated the religious freedom implications of this entire, silly intrusion into serious presidential politics. Some in the audience convinced me they would physically attack a person who refused to give the Pledge, even if saying the words violated a deeply held religious conviction. The disturbing fact that so many in the country bought into such political claptrap as the Pledge non-issue says that millions have little tolerance for dissenting views and even less understanding of the nuances of religious freedom issues. . . . The U.S. Constitution . . . protects us from the likes of Downey and his army of religious and political bullies. (Maddox, 1988: 21)

Empirical studies have confirmed that much the same attitude is still common in the United States. Lipsit concluded from his study of prejudice that the Jehovah's Witnesses were among the most disliked of all religious minorities he listed—the group average showed that Americans displayed more dislike of them than even the most hated ethnic minorities. An average of a whopping 41% expressed clear prejudice to open dislike of Witnesses. (Lipset, 1964: 435) And research by Brinkerhoff and Mackie (1986) concluded that the least acceptable religious groups were the so-called new cults, followed by the Jehovah's Witnesses, Mormons and conservative Christians. (1986)

A major cause of the violence against Witnesses was the hostility of citizens which was condoned by the lack of support of the officials who often violated the law themselves or, at the least, condoned mob violence. As White (1968: 330) summarizes:

Robert Cofer and Oscar Lawrence Pillars were told to quit their work in Winnsboro, Texas. The marshal arrested Pillars, but promised protection if he would salute the flag. When he refused he was turned over to a mob harangued by a Baptist preacher. He was beaten to unconsciousness, revived with water, beaten again, dragged by a rope around his neck to the city hall and hanged to a post. Fortunately the rope broke. At 12:30 pm he was put in jail again, and a doctor at 3:45 pm said he would have to be taken to a hospital in order to remain alive. By 9:30 pm he was in a hospital. The police chief of Greenville, Mississippi...ordered all Jehovah's Witnesses out of town by 5:00 pm. None left. So he herded fifty into jail, leaving a Witnesses's three year old child unattended in the rain outside.

In addition, the police themselves, not uncommonly, openly contributed to the violence, not just by condoning it, but by becoming actively involved. As White (1968: 330-331) noted:

witness Clarence Bradley, a Negro, was picked up in Little Rock, Arkansas. When he refused to salute, the police beat him to unconsciousness. When he came to they repeated it. He was released two days later with hemorrhaging, and permanent head and brain injuries.

The following is the sad conclusion of the failure of the United States justice system in these cases: "Out of the many thousands of cases of violations of these statutes by mobsters who have assaulted Jehovah's Witnesses in those years, the Department of Justice has found the courage to prosecute and convict but one. That was Sergeant Ellis, who severely beat Witness August Schmidt who happened to call at his door with the

Watchtower magazine. (White, 1968: 331) As Judge Henry Edgerton concluded, "the principle threat to civil liberties [at this time] came not from the federal government, but from the activities of local officials and from the terrorism practiced by private persons against unpopular groups, especially the pacifistic group called Jehovah's Witnesses. (Edgerton, 1978: 2)

The "Rutherford era" is still with us in many parts of the world today. Hefley (1979:447) in his summary of the persecution of Christians in the modern world, noted that the Witnesses in Africa were now controlled by native Africans, not foreign Whites, and concluded that the persecution now occurring there is mostly because they "refused to salute the national flag." These events led up to the development of the most recent example of a Hitler type of concentration camp:

> After persuasion failed, Dr. Banda's government banned their activities. When they disregarded the order, soldiers rounded up thirty thousand of the sect and placed them in prison camps. In December, 1975, officials of the Witnesses in other countries protested that adherents in Malawi were being beaten, tortured, and raped with official approval. Malawi is now, in effect, a police state, Dr. Banda is firmly in power for 'life'.... [A full story] about the persecution of the Witnesses [is] hard to determine. However, twenty evangelical foreign missions enjoy freedom of operation under the Banda regime. The Presbyterian Church of Zambia, to which the President belongs, has over six hundred thousand members.

The persecution has been the most consistent in the Soviet block countries. Barmenkov, (1983: 70) writing an official government sponsored propaganda work which argues that freedom of religion *does* in fact exist in the Soviet Union, openly admits that his government outright bans the Jehovah's Witnesses.

The Soviet state cannot be indifferent to any actions directed against the Soviet way of life which encroach upon people's rights, honour and dignity, even if under religious cover. The socialist state protects its citizen's interests. This is the reason why it bans certain sects which grossly violate the accepted rules of social intercourse or perform cruel ceremonies. Such associations include Jehovah's Witnesses . . . among others. Under the guise of religious rites, the leaders of these associations instigate their members to anti-social actions, and encroach upon people's personal and human rights, sometimes even commit criminal acts.

The leaders of Jehovah's Witnesses, for instance, receive slanderous publications full of malicious lies about the USSR and other socialist countries from abroad through reactionary anti-Soviet centers and try to spread them among their believers. They call the socialist system "the devil's tool" and "the world of Satan," and threaten atheists and believers with annihilation in a "holy war" (Armageddon). These fanatic sectarians urge their co-religionists to evade civic obligations, refuse to vote in elections, or to participate in censuses under threat of "punishment from God." Some Jehovah's Witnesses prevent their children from attending school, forbid them to go to the cinema, to watch television and to read fiction, newspapers and magazines.

Of the many religions practicing in Nazi Germany, *only* the Witnesses and the Jews were severely persecuted: "The Third Reich was not willing ... to tolerate [any] minority Christian sects who might prove a challenge. . . . [but] only one group, the Jehovah's Witnesses, were the victims of total persecution" (King, 1979: 213). Beckford (1975: 33-34) concluded that their persecution in Nazi Germany far surpassed that which even the

Witnesses had previously experienced, or ever expected:

Many of Rutherford's followers were already accustomed ... to campaign[s] of terror. ... Consequently, the news that Adolph Hitler had begun to persecute Jehovah's Witnesses in Germany came as little surprise. ... Yet, the brutality and ruthlessness of persecution in Germany must have shocked even the most hardened veterans of Watch Tower clashes with civil, military, and religious authorities. German Bible Students had been subject to periodic harassment since the First World War and were inured to being charged with alleged subversion. ....In February 1933, however, Hitler formally prescribed all Watch Tower activities. ... Nazi ideologists accused them of sympathizing with the Jews, being implicated in international communism and showing disrespect for the Fuhrer. [At first, Rutherford tried to placate the Nazis; possibly this accounts for his anti-semetic writing in "Declaration" see 1934 Yearbook of Jehovah Witnesses and Penton 1985: 148-149].

The laws of many countries allow the release of official records after a certain period of time. Many of these newly released records have revealed the behind the scenes activities of governments which have openly persecuted Witnesses and other groups in the so called "free world." Records recently released in Canada reveal that in the forties, "able bodied young Jehovah's Witnesses" were sent to concentration camps, and "entire families who practiced the religion were imprisoned." (Yaffe, 1984: 4).

Sallot and Yaffee, (1984: 1) add that World War II was a time of "officially sanctioned religious bigotry, political intolerance and the suppression of ideas. The federal government described Jehovah's Witnesses as subversive and offensive 'religious zealots' . . . in secret reports given to special parliamentarian committees in 1942." The report on Jehovah's Witnesses said of them that, "probably no other organization is so offensive in its methods, working as it does under the guise of Christianity. The documents prepared by the justice department were presented to a special house of commons committee by the government of William Lyon McKenzie King in an attempt to justify the outlawing of the organizations during the second world war."

Yaffee also cites instances such as "a family of fifteen—including grandparents and children who were interrupted at home during a Bible study session and taken to prison "for their prayers." The family, spent "fifteen months behind bars for 'holding a [religious] meeting." Another case involved ten men interrupted during a small social gathering in Welland, Ontario. "The men were in a room and had with them seven musical instruments. Five of the men had Jehovah's Witness literature with them. Police were not sure whether the occasion was a musical gathering or a Bible study. The men were sentenced to a month in jail, appealed and got an even harsher six months in jail. By the time the case got to the Supreme Court of Canada it was dismissed with the court concluding that there was nothing illegal about ten men being together in a room." In the committee deliberations, Yaffee noted, a committee member pointed out the irony of the the Klu Klux Klan was not yet then declared an illegal organization, yet the Witnesses were declared such, and that accusations that the Jehovah's Witnesses were affiliated with the Klu Klux Klan "may be a point in their favor." Yaffee concluded that "documents show the government feared the group for putting God before country and for refusing to salute the nation's flag."

This brief background is necessary to understand Rutherford's writings. They are very much a product not of only his theological presuppositions, but also his life experiences, and those of the movement at the time. While his hostility towards the churches and governments was extremely important in producing much of the persecution, likely also much of the hostility resulted from this persecution. Many of the booklets reprinted here focus on theological discussions, but the political reality which Rutherford and the Witnesses were involved in figures prominently, especially in the booklets *Freedom for the People, Judgment,* and *A Great Battle in the Ecclesiastical Heavens,* (the latter, an apologetic for Russell and the persecution that he had experienced the concern that Rutherford was not properly carrying the mantle of Russell). Even his *Millions Now Living Will Never Die* is to some degree a rallying call in support of his movement, and a justification for his political policies as well as the suffering (it is stressed that only a little while longer, if one simply endures till the end which is soon, these things will be a thing of the past).

The *Great Battle* booklet is especially important because it deals with virtually all of the moral charges leveled against Russell when he was alive, including the "United States Investment Company" charge, Russell's marital problems, Russell's miracle wheat scandal, and a critique of the opposition's writings such as those by Reverend J.J. Ross and others. In addition, Rutherford tried to deal with the charges that Russell's followers were ignorant, unschooled, and uneducated. He quoted educators, generals (General Hall, a brigadier general in the United States Army) and a list of "prominent business men" who testified to Russell's character and integrity (most of whom were Bible students). Interestingly, he

also includes letters from phrenologists, and even a phrenograph of Russell. The book that was published by Rutherford himself, it did not have the imprint of the Watchtower Society (listed only as Box 51, New York City, USA), is subtitled simply "an international case reviewed by J.F. Rutherford, of the New York City Bar."

The booklet, *Millions Now Living Will Never Die,* deals primarily with the prophesies relative to 1925, stating on page 97 that "1925 shall mark the resurrection of the faithful worthies of old and the beginning of reconstruction," concluding that "millions of people now on the earth will be still on the earth in 1925" and those on the earth then will never die. This is a "positive promise" relative to reconstruction, i.e., the new world. Much in this booklet deals with evidence that the events during this time period prove that we are in the last days. This booklet also contains an interesting discussion on the development of Zionism, and clear support for the movement. Rutherford felt that the Zionist's movement was a powerful sign of the last days. Of course, many of the views in this booklet have been drastically altered in current teaching today, and the book is such an embarrassment that it has been reprinted several times by opposers of the Witnesses.

The booklet, *Can the Living Talk With the Dead?* deals with the origin of spiritism. It relates numerous eye witness testimony of people who saw "opaque lights" in various places, and heard voices, and saw various "images" and similiar phenomena. Much of the material in this booklet would be similar to that typically found in the *National Enquirer* or related newspapers, although a large number of quotes from contemporary newspaper sources are used (many evidently from the late 1800s or early 1900s). Of the large number of quotes used, typically only the name of the source (such as the *Greenville Daily Piedmont*, the *McClures Magazine*, or the *St. Louis Globe Democrat)*, is given, not the date or even the year. Discussions include not only spiritism, but also clairvoyance and related topics. The conclusion is that these events are real, and most are accepted rather uncritically, but they are manifestations of demonism, not departed relatives or related.

The Bible on Our Lord's Return deals primarily with the Watchtower teachings relative to the parousia and elucidates the Watchtower teaching that Christ's return is invisible, and the purpose is to destroy Satan's kingdom, to regather Israel, and related. The booklet also goes into the Watchtower's teaching regarding the signs of the end, the harvest work, and set up God's kingdom. The booklet is quite in contrast to their teachings today. For example, it teaches that the time of the end began in 1799 (oday it is taught that 1914 is the correct date), and that the Lord's second presence was in 1874 (it is now taught to be in 1914). Much is made about the various inventions and changes from 1799 forward, utilizing these as signs of the Lord's coming much as natural and man made disasters are now used to prove the last days.

The booklets, *The Standard for the People, Freedom for the People* and *Judgment* deal primarily with the Witnesses doctrine, but also the struggle's that the Witnesses were going through at this time with the political and religious systems of the day. These three booklets clearly elucidate the Watchtower's conclusion that the governments and religious systems were the enemy of the people, and that only God can effectively deal with this problem, which he will soon do by ushering in a new world and by the destruction of the present evil trinity of commerce, politics and religion.

Jerry Bergman, Ph. D.

BIBLIOGRAPHY

American Civil Liberties Union. *The Persecution of Jehovah's Witnesses*, New York, January ,1941.

Barmintco, A. *Freedom of Conscience in the U.S.S.R* . Moscow: Progress Publishers, 1983.

Beckkford, James A. "The Trumpet of Prophecy: A Sociological Study of a Jehovah's Witness," Oxford: Basil Blackwell, 1975. *Review*, Vol. 23, No. 4, Nov., 1975: 33-34.

Bergman, Jerry. *Jehovah's Witnesses and Kindred Groups*. New York: Garland, 1984.

Brinkerhoff, Merlin B. and Marlene M. Mackie. "The Applicability of Social Distance for Religious Research; An Exploration." *Review of Religious Research*, Vol. 28, No. 2, Dec. 1986.

Cox, Archibald. *The Court and the Constitution*. Boston: Hughton Mifflin Co., 1987.

Edgerton, Henry W. *Freedom in the Balance; Opinions of Judge Henry W. Edgerton*, edited by Eleanor Bontecou. Westport, Conn: Greenwood Press, 1978.

Harrison, Barbara Grizzuti. *Visions of Glory; A History and Memory of Jehovah's Witnesses*. New York: Simon and Schuster, 1978.

Hefley, James and Marti. *By Their Blood; Christian Martyrs of the Twentieth Century, a Continuation of Fox Book of Martyrs*. Grand Rapids, Mich.: Baker Book House, 1979.

King, Christine Elizabeth: "The Nazi State and the New Religions: Five Case Studies in Non-conformity," *Studies in Religion and Society, Volume Four*, Lewiston, N.Y.: The Edwin Mellen Press, 1979: 213.

Lipset, Seymour Martin. "The Sources of the "'Radical Right'" in *The Radical Right*, Daniel Bell, ed. Garden City, N.Y.: Anchor Books, 1964.

Maddox, Robert. "Reflections On Surviving Morton Downey," *Church and State*, Dec., 1988: 21.

Sallot, Jeff and Barbara Yaffee. "Secret Files Reveal Bigotry, Suppression" *Toronto Globe and Mail*, Saturday, Sept., 4, 1984.

Semonche, John E. *Religion and Constitutional Government in the United States; A Historical Overview with Sources*. North Carolina: Signal Books, 1986.

Sibley, Mulford Q., and Philip Jacob. *Conscription of Conscience: The American State and the Conscientious Objector, 1940–47*. Ithaca, N.Y.: Cornell University Press, 1952.

Sorauf, Frank J. "Jehovah's Witnesses" in the *Guide to American Law*. St. Paul: West Publ. Inc., 1984.

Starr, Isidore. *Human Rights in the United States*, New York: Oxford Book Co., 1964.

Whalen, William J. *Armegadon Around the Corner; A Report on Jehovah's Witnesses*, New York: The John Day Company, 1962.

White, Timothy. *A People For His Name; The History of Jehovah's Witnesses and an Evaluation*. New York: Vantage Press, 1967.

Yaffe, Barbara. "Witnesses Seek Apology for Wartime Persecution." *Toronto Globe and Mail*, Saturday, September 9, 1984.

A GREAT BATTLE

IN THE

ECCLESIASTICAL

HEAVENS

———

AS SEEN BY A

LAWYER

———

AN INTERNATIONAL CASE
REVIEWED BY
J. F. RUTHERFORD, OF THE NEW YORK CITY BAR

A GREAT BATTLE

IN THE

ECCLESIASTICAL HEAVENS

AS SEEN BY A LAWYER

CATHOLICS, EPISCOPALIANS,
METHODISTS, LUTHERANS,
BAPTISTS, PRESBYTERIANS, ET AL   }

PLAINTIFFS

VERSUS

ONE MAN   *DEFENDANT*

WHY THE GREAT CONTROVERSY?   THE MOTIVE PROMPTING IT!
THE CHARGES MADE!   THE ANSWERS THERETO!
WHAT WILL BE THE RESULT?

---

*" Yet once more I shake not the earth only,
but also heaven * * * that those things which cannot be shaken may remain."— Heb. 12:26,27.*

FOREWORD.

CERTAIN leading clergymen, representing numerous church denominations, such as Episcopalian, Presbyterian, Baptist, Methodist, Christian, Lutheran, United Brethren, and certain Catholic bishops, priests and prelates, have united in their cause of action against ONE MAN. They are assailing him from every conceivable quarter, using all possible means, foul or fair, to destroy that ONE MAN'S influence and power. They seek to enlist every possible agency, willing or unwilling, to aid them in their unrighteous conflict. They have precipitated the biggest ecclesiastical disturbance ever known. The noise of their battle is heard to the uttermost parts of the earth and their dust is blinding many people. The Ecclesiastical Heavens are being shaken with great violence. Who will fall? Who will remain unshaken?

As statements of judges and attorneys have been quoted by these allied forces, and without warrant used as a pretext for their attack, and used also as a basis for peculiar newspaper stories, the writer of this booklet feels duty bound to review the case and publish the facts to the world.

A GREAT BATTLE
IN THE
ECCLESIASTICAL HEAVENS

BELLIGERENTS FORESHADOWED

THIS is the day of big things! Big enterprises, big trusts, big alliances and big fights! A big battle always creates much noise and attracts some attention. This ecclesiastical disturbance is no exception!

In every great controversy there must be at least two parties. Usually one is wrong and the other right. Each will claim to be right. Each one may be conscientious. Conscience, however, is not always a safe moral guide. It will depend on whether or not that conscience has been educated according to the Divine rule. It is sometimes difficult for even the unbiased to determine who has the right of the controversy. There is one Guide we can always safely follow.

THE SAFE GUIDE Jehovah governs the Universe by fixed laws or rules, which we call principles. The man who acts in harmony therewith is governed by principle. The one who acts contrary thereto is controlled by passion. *The parties to a great fight may be foreshadowed, and the right or wrong thereof be determined, by the application of these fixed principles.*

Most men claim to be conscientious, and we credit them with so being, but their conscience is often guided by the wrong influence. To determine the right of the controversy we must ascertain the Divine rule and apply it. The majority are measurably controlled by other men; therefore, to that extent controlled by passion and not by principle. For this reason the man who occupies an honorable position among men holds a place of great responsibility.

CLERGYMEN WHO SOIL THEIR SACRED VESTURE A Minister of the Gospel occupies a most honorable position. A good man in such a place is a power for good, but when a Clergyman uses the garb of his sacred office to accomplish a selfish purpose, or to vent his

5

spleen against one with whom he differs, he not only violates his obligation to God, but degrades himself and dishonors the cause of Christianity.

There are but two Great Masters—God and Satan. Every person serves one or the other of these Masters. God puts in operation good principles always. His Law furnishes an absolutely perfect guide. Satan exercises an evil power always. He is the father of falsehood, misrepresentation and abuse. Do all clergymen serve the same Master? "Ye are servants of him whom ye obey." "If any man have not the Spirit of Christ he is none of His." (See Appendix for further proof on this point.)

HOLY WRIT SAYS, "SPEAK EVIL OF NO MAN"

Every Clergyman is presumed to be a Christian. Sometimes this is a vile presumption. Plainly God's Word says to Christians, "Speak evil of no man." "Who art thou that judgest another!" "Thou shalt not bear false witness." "Vengeance is mine, I will repay, saith the Lord." Sad indeed it is to see professed Christians, contrary to these Divine rules, resorting to slander, misrepresentation and vilification of a Christian gentleman who is giving his life to teaching the people to follow Christ. Even if the charges made by them were true no justification could be found in the Scriptures for uttering them, but when the charges are made in utter disregard of the truth and with the avowed purpose of doing injury we are constrained to ask, Are these the servants of God or the servants of Satan?

Every great man and every good cause has mortal enemies. Great truths are dearly bought. Great reformations have had to fight every inch of the way to triumph! For nearly a half century the defendant in this case has been a shining light in the world, battling for good, that the eyes of men might be opened to a realization of the goodness of God manifested in His Plan towards mankind. He has fearlessly held forth the light of Biblical Truth, and as it has shone with increased brilliancy his assailants have become more venomous.

LIGHT ATTRACTS BUGS—BIG BUGS, LITTLE BUGS, BLIND BUGS

There is a reason for every wilful act. There is a controlling motive back of this great fight. Jesus said, "Darkness hates the Light." Error abides in darkness. The brilliancy of a light attracts blind bugs—big bugs as well as lesser ones—which vainly try to destroy the light and usually succeed in destroying themselves. As the defendant herein has held forth the light of Divine Truth and led thousands of honest Christians away from error, away from the bondage of various man-made systems and out of darkness and into the glorious light of God, his enemies have exhibited a greater degree of ferociousness toward him.

UNHOLY ALLIANCE

ENEMIES FOR CENTURIES NOW BECOME STRANGE BED-FELLOWS It is a well-known fact that for centuries Catholics and Protestants have been deadly enemies, and . the Ecclesiastical Heavens have long been in turmoil because of the mortal combat between them. In the controversy we are here examining, Catholics and Protestants have united in a campaign of persecution. Enemies for centuries now become bed-fellows —strange bed-fellows these! Doubtless many who are following their leaders, however, are blind, and verily believe they are doing God service, by assaulting the great light bearer.

The public press exercises a mighty power, either for good or for evil. It has been a marvelous factor in the education of the people; therefore a power for good. When, however, the press is used by selfish and designing men as an instrument for the destruction of the good name of a fellow-man it then becomes a power for evil. A few unscrupulous newspapers, headed by *The Brooklyn Eagle*, always willing to be used as instruments for the promulgation of sensational and scandalous matter, have joined the aforesaid alliance and taken up the cudgel against One Man, the defendant.

The vulgar and the scandal monger, eager to ply their vocation, have joined the ranks and are performing their part.

SAME OLD GAME OF THE PHARISEES AGAINST ONE MAN Back of this motley brigade, and constituting the real brains thereof, are certain keen, intellectual, far-seeing and designing men, who, without authority from the Lord, have taken the title of "Reverend," "Doctor of Divinity," "Cardinal" or "Priest." Long have these rested in ease and comfort, as the Prophet describes them (Isa. 56:10, 11), while their poor parishioners have fed upon husks until they are famished.—Amos 8:11, 12.

Long have these designing men kept their flocks in bondage by keeping them in the dark. Now God's Day of Reckoning is at hand. Seeing their berths of comfort and popularity in danger, the walls of the Babylonish systems crumbling, while many of their former supporters are hastily withdrawing in obedience to God's command (Rev. 18:4), these men, without regard to religious belief or sectarian affiliation, in sheer desperation have joined hands against ONE MAN, the defendant, and have summoned to their aid all whom they can induce, cajole or coerce, and are exerting all their power in trying to stem the tide of Truth rapidly rising against them, striving to

save their positions of ease. The ONE MAN has turned the
light upon them, exposing them to the gaze of the people.
"Darkness hates the Light." This Unholy Alliance is strain-
ing every nerve and sinew to destroy this ONE MAN, his
influence and his work. It is the same old game of the Pharisees. It is history repeating itself.

**EVEN GOOD JOHN
WESLEY'S WIFE
JOINED HIS
PERSECUTORS**
The same class assaulted St. Paul and
persecuted him to the death. Martin
Luther and other great reformers were
victims of a like element. The great
and good John Wesley was another vic-
tim—*his own wife joining his persecutors.* The same Phari-
saical class defamed the Lord Jesus when He was on earth.
They called in question the legitimacy of His birth, applied
all manner of vile epithets to Him, denounced Him as an
enemy of the government, and finally caused His crucifixion.
Having in mind that similar treatment would be meted out to
His faithful servants, Jesus said, "The servant is not greater
than his Lord; if they have persecuted Me they also will persecute you."

This case will be of special interest to lawyers and others
who have in mind the illegal trial of our Master. Verily,
human nature has not changed, even in this twentieth century
of enlightenment!

**PAPAL ROME AND
HER MONGREL
PROGENY AGAINST
ONE MAN**
In the case here we see Greek Catholics,
Roman Catholics, Anglicans, Gentiles
and Jews, Presbyterians and Metho-
dists, Baptists, Lutherans, Congrega-
tionalists, etc., etc., not only in Amer-
ica, but in Canada, in Europe, and from the four corners of the
earth, united for the avowed purpose of overthrowing this
ONE MAN.

The fight against Martin Luther seems a pigmy compared
with this one. In Luther's case it was Papal Rome against one
man. In this case it is Papal Rome and all her mongrel progeny against *One Man.*

**THE GREATEST
LIVING PREACHER**
Who is the ONE MAN, the defendant
in this case? *PASTOR RUSSELL!*
He is the most talked of preacher in
the world. He preaches to more peo-
ple than any living man. Even his enemies concede that
much. The Editor Afield of *The Continent* a member of the
unholy combine and one of its spokesmen, recently said of
Pastor Russell:

"His writings are said to have greater newspaper circulation every week than those of any
her living man; a greater, doubtless, than the

combined circulation of the writings of all the priests and preachers in North America; greater even than the work of Arthur Brisbane, Norman Hapgood, George Horace Lorimer, Dr. Frank Crane, Frederick Haskins, and a dozen other of the best known editors and syndicate writers put together."

Herein lies one of the causes for the attack by the allied forces. Some history will here be recalled with interest.

PREACHERS' UNION AND HOW ORDINATION CARDS TO PREACH ARE ISSUED

For nearly three hundred years after Martin Luther's day there was a gradual development of Protestant denominational churches. Trouble would start in one denomination; a division would result; some would withdraw, and the seceders would organize a new denomination. Each seceding class became known by some sectarian name, such as "Baptists," "Methodists," "Campbellites," "Congregationalists," "United Brethren," "River Brethren," "Christadelphians," etc. Each sect, by its own authority, authorized certain persons to preach, and seemingly no one had any special objections to this until about 1840.

The Bible teaches that THE Church is *one*, the Body of Christ, whereas the Protestant Systems, *each claiming* to be "The Church," number nearly two hundred. Because of this apparent inconsistency, they feared that all their organizations would be brought into disrepute, and therefore there should be some alliance between all of them; hence, in 1846, the "Evangelical Alliance" was formed. While allied, each sect formed its own Ordination Boards, which boards exercised the power of ordaining or authorizing others to preach.

One of the rules resulting from this Alliance has been, and now is, that no one shall be allowed to preach unless he has received an ordination at the hands of one of these "Ordaining Boards" already existing. Anyone attempting to preach without being licensed or formally ordained by one of these "Ordaining Boards" is branded as a scab preacher.

This Alliance has become virtually a Preachers' Union, and an edict has gone forth that if anyone desires to preach he must get a union card (ordination); otherwise he is irregular. Some of the independent thinkers have held aloof from this Alliance, claiming the right to worship God according to the dictates of their own conscience and to exercise the liberty of free speech.

HELL-FIRE GONE, COLLECTIONS COME SLOWLY

The defendant herein, Pastor Russell, has refused to accept such man-made ordination, recognizing the Scriptural method provided by the Lord, *and none other.* He has refused to be forced into the Combine; hence the Combine seeks to force him to quit preaching.

One of their strong men engaged Pastor Russell in debate, hoping thereby to discredit his scholarship and teaching. This acted as a boomerang to the allied forces, because the debate exposed the fallacy of the doctrines long taught by these systems, causing many of their flocks to flee from them. One honest member of the Alliance who heard that debate said to Pastor Russell, "I am glad to see you turn the hose on hell and put out the fire." Hell-fire gone, the collections come slowly.

PREACHERS' ALLIANCE, IN DESPERATION, ASSAILS "SEATS FREE AND NO COLLECTIONS" ADVERTISED BY ONE MAN

Then Pastor Russell adopted a kind of trade-mark on all of his announcements—"Seats Free, No Collection"— and the Alliance concluded that this was a reflection on their constant begging for money, and therefore another cause for anger. For some time now the poor fellows have had great difficulty in inducing the people to part with their money. Their congregations have been reduced to a handful, while thousands flock to hear Pastor Russell. The people prefer to go and hear the ONE MAN where the "seats are free and no collections," and where they can get some comforting food.

Unable to successfully combat the shafts of Bible Truths shot forth by this great modern religious reformer, his enemies have resorted to the old device of throwing sand in the people's eyes by attacking his private life and business methods.

If a bad man reforms and becomes a preacher for one of these systems his past deeds are forgotten and he is heralded as a hero in their cause, no matter what he believes, nor the character of the language used to express his belief.

But when a good man, such as the defendant herein, who has a clean private life, boldly proclaims "the faith once delivered to the saints" and exposes the errors of the Dark Ages which have long held the people in bondage, all conceivable charges are trumped up by his enemies, and these magnified, for the manifest purpose of preventing the people from seeing the Truths he is teaching.

SOME NOTABLE EXCEPTIONS IN PREACHERS' UNHOLY ALLIANCE

Do not understand me to say that all the preachers are in this Unholy Alliance. There are exceptions. Thus is the rule proven. There are some good Christian gentlemen in the ministry who are, no doubt, doing the best they know to serve the Lord, but these are taking no part in this unholy warfare.

The active members of the Unholy Alliance, however, have grown desperate. Their operations are not confined to a single community. They have carried the fight into every State in the Union; every province of Canada; throughout Great Britain; the European Continent; China; Japan; India; Australia and the Islands of the Sea.

Members of this Preachers' Union or Alliance caused thousands of extra copies of their favorite medium of slander and libel—*The Brooklyn Daily Eagle*—to be printed and sent all over the world. As soon as announcement is made that Pastor Russell is to be in a certain city to speak, this reprint of the *Brooklyn Eagle* puts in its appearance and is freely distributed.

Some people are deceived into believing that the *Brooklyn Eagle* is one of the greatest papers printed; whereas, although published in the great city of New York, its regular circulation is only about 25,000.

POPULARITY OF THIS MAN PROVOKES PREACHERS' UNION

It is a well-known fact that Pastor Russell's sermons are published each week in hundreds of newspapers in different parts of the world. This provokes the members of the Alliance, and in nearly every country of the world they have held meetings and passed resolutions denunciatory of Pastor Russell and his work; and they try to coerce the newspapers, by threats of boycotting and other means, to cease printing his sermons.

As an illustration, we cite the four-column editorial in the *Evening Journal*, of Wilmington, Delaware, December 4th, 1914, setting forth how the Ministerial Union tried to force that paper to cease the publication of Pastor Russell's sermons. There are many similar occurrences throughout the country.

OVER 9,000,000 SEE HIS CREATION DRAMA FREE

Pastor Russell, the defendant herein, is the author of the Photo-Drama of Creation. It is a wonderful production. The Bible story, beginning with creation, is set forth in an orderly manner to modern times.

This beautiful story is told to the people, assembled in public halls, by means of a phonograph, or talking machine, and illustrated by many artistically colored stereopticon views and motion pictures. It has attracted wide attention throughout the world, and I am authoritatively informed, by the manager of the Photo-Drama, *that nine million persons have seen this great exhibition, in America alone, and that, too, "Seats Free and No Collection!"*

The Photo-Drama of Creation is the greatest educational philanthropy that has been given to the world. The money to finance it was contributed by many persons who are anxious to teach the present generation the wonders of the Bible. Had the preachers done their full duty, it might not have been necessary to have the Photo-Drama, but "God moves in a mysterious way His wonders to perform," and so HE is using many untitled and humble-minded persons to spread the Message of glad tidings concerning Christ and His Kingdom of blessings, and pointing the people to the near end of Babylonish reign.

If our forefathers, who laid the foundation of the American Government as a land of religious freedom, could see the religious intolerance manifested by this combine of ministers, they would turn over in their graves. The methods adopted in their frantic endeavor to crush Pastor Russell and his philanthropic work are shocking to every fair-minded, liberty-loving person.

SAMPLE METHOD OF PREACHERS' UNION Laurel, Mississippi, is the scene of action. Mr. Nicholson, Manager in Charge of the "Drama," rented the Opera House at this place from Mr. Taylor, the owner, in which to exhibit the Photo-Drama. The two gentlemen were standing in front of the Opera House preparing for the advertisement. Mr. Taylor was delighted with the opportunity of having such a wonderful exhibition given in his house, and was congratulating himself, when along came the leading Methodist minister of the place, who is designated "The Boss of the Preachers' Union" there.

Learning what was about to take place he became enraged, shook his fist in Mr. Nicholson's face, exclaiming in angry tones, "You try to show these things in this town and you will have the biggest fight on your hands you ever saw; better get out of town, and get *quick*'" Mr. Nicholson proceeded, undaunted by this threat, to prepare for the exhibition. The Ministerial Union at once held a meeting, in which all engaged in denouncing Pastor Russell and the "Drama," except the Episcopalian minister, who stood firm for religious tolerance and common decency. The union passed resolutions against the "Drama" and Pastor Russell; then called upon the Mayor of the City and Chief of Police and induced them to notify the "Drama" Manager that it should not be exhibited in that city.

The Ministerial Union then used its power with the Electric Light Company, and induced its owners to cut off the electric current and refuse to furnish such to be used by the "Drama." Their influence was brought to bear upon Mr. Taylor, the Opera House owner, to such an extent that he tore down the advertisements which, by his own direction, had been placed upon the billboards. The Photo-Drama Manager then went to Judge Beavours, the leading attorney of the city, and appealed to him for assistance. He is a "Lawyer of

A MODERN GAMALIEL

the Old School," who is willing to fight for the right. He at once informed the Electric Light Company and the city officials that he would apply to the courts for an injunction against them, and have them restrained from unlawfully exercising their power.

This frightened the city officials and the Electric Light Company, and the preachers weakened. They decided to not further attempt to prevent the exhibition of the Photo-Drama. The Mayor sent word to the Manager, saying, "Go ahead, only don't knock us or the preachers." They feared the result when the people should see the pictures and know they had been so woefully misrepresented. The people came and were delighted, some saying, "We cannot understand the ministers' opposition!"

And thus this Unholy Alliance continues its fight against the ONE MAN, who, like a mighty ship in a storm, majestically rides the waves, keeping steadily on his course to the goal. While the storm of persecution rages, the common people crowd the halls where he goes, eager to hear, in this hour of peril, the message of comfort that he brings to their hearts. The scope of his work and his influence continue to grow, and members of the Preachers' Union gnaw their tongues, rage and imagine vain things.

CHARGES SPECIFICALLY EXAMINED AND COMPLETELY REFUTED

The defendant, Pastor Russell, is my friend. I have known him for fifteen years or more, and for several years have represented him as his legal counselor. I have carefully investigated every specific charge that has been made against him. Being familiar with the facts, especially relating to the charges against him that have been adjudicated in the courts, I deem it my duty to the public that I publish these facts.

Pastor Russell needs no defense amongst those who know him. These lines are more especially to advise the public.

Sneeringly, his opponents refer to him as a "haberdasher" and "seller of shirts." It is true that when Pastor Russell was a young man, and before reaching his majority, he was engaged in the mercantile business, selling Gents' Furnishing Goods, and his business ability was demonstrated by the fact that he soon was operating five different stores.

If it is a disgrace in the eyes of the Preachers' Union for a man to labor with his hands, then surely they are welcome to all they can get out of it. Pastor Russell was in good company. We are reminded that St. Paul was a practising lawyer for a time, and a successful one, too, and that he also made tents to provide his temporary necessities. Jesus was a carpenter. Blessed is he that labors.

His enemies charge that he has organized various corporations through which he conducts his religious work, and that

PASTOR RUSSELL INCORPORATES BIBLE SOCIETY

he uses these as a means of personal and financial gain to himself, and that the corporations are merely blinds by which he deceives the people. What are the facts?

In 1884 the WATCH TOWER BIBLE AND TRACT SOCIETY was organized, and was incorporated under the laws of the State of Pennsylvania, for the purpose of the mental, moral and religious improvement of men and women, by teaching the Bible by means of the publication and distribution of Bibles, books, papers, pamphlets and other Bible literature, and by providing oral lectures free for the people.

NO VOTE EVER CAST AGAINST PASTOR RUSSELL

This is a non-stock corporation; it pays no dividends, no salaries, and no one has ever, as its books clearly show, reaped any financial benefit therefrom. It is supported entirely by voluntary contributions made by those who are interested in the promulgation of Bible Truths. Its work is exclusively religious. For each contribution of $10.00 the contributor is entitled to one voting share. While there are nearly two hundred thousand shares, and it would be an easy matter to elect some other man as president, *there never has been cast a vote against Pastor Russell.*

At the last election he was absent, his own votes were not cast, yet more than one hundred thousand votes of others were cast for him as president. The contributors and voters are men of strong character and many of them of superior financial standing, scattered throughout America and Canada. Such loyal supporters as these testify to the high esteem in which the president of this institution is held. Like other corporations, its business affairs are controlled by a Board of Directors.

In 1909, the work of this non-sectarian religious corporation having largely increased, and Greater New York City being

ANOTHER CORPORATION NECESSARY

the most accessible place from which to direct its work, both in America and foreign lands, it was deemed, by its Board of Directors, wise to move the headquarters to Brooklyn.

I was consulted about the matter and advised that under the laws of the State of New York the WATCH TOWER BIBLE AND TRACT SOCIETY could not have the same privileges as it enjoyed under the special statute of Pennsylvania, under which it was organized, and suggested the advisability of the organization of a similar corporation in New York State.

This suggestion was followed, and the PEOPLES PULPIT ASSOCIATION was organized under the Membership Corporation Law of New York for the identical purposes for which the WATCH TOWER BIBLE AND TRACT SOCIETY exists. The PEOPLES PULPIT ASSOCIATION holds title to the property in New York wherein the work of said Society is conducted.

Later it became necessary to have a European corporation in the interests of the work, a large portion of its activities being in European countries; hence a corporation was formed

GREAT BRITAIN
CORPORATION
I. B. S. A.

under the laws of Great Britain with headquarters at London, under the name of the INTERNATIONAL BIBLE STUDENTS ASSOCIATION. It was organized for the identical purposes for which the parent corporation, the WATCH TOWER BIBLE AND TRACT SOCIETY, was originally organized, and all three of these corporations are practically one and the same. All contributions are made to the WATCH TOWER BIBLE AND TRACT SOCIETY, which finances all the work of the three corporations named.

Throughout the various countries of the world are classes of Bible Students who, independent of all sectarian creeds or systems, regularly assemble at their homes or public halls, for the purpose of Bible study, and these are known as "Associated Bible Students," because their work and study are in harmony with that conducted by the aforesaid corporations. None of these are corporations for profit; they pay no dividends, no salaries, and no one has ever reaped any financial benefit therefrom, but all funds thereof are used for the promulgation of Bible Truths.

Much ado has been made by his enemies about business

UNITED STATES
INVESTMENT
COMPANY

corporations with which Pastor Russell is connected, particularly with reference to the UNITED STATES INVESTMENT COMPANY.

The fact is that this company was never a corporation in the strict sense of the word. It was a limited partnership organized under the Statutes of Pennsylvania. Its capital stock was $1,000. Pastor Russell furnished that $1,000 out of his personal means.

This company was organized for the purpose of taking title to certain property which it did take over and afterwards disposed of, and every dollar that was received therefrom went into the treasury of the WATCH TOWER BIBLE AND TRACT SOCIETY, and was used for its religious work.

Pastor Russell did not receive one cent profit therefrom, nor has any other person ever reaped any pecuniary profit therefrom.

This company has been out of existence for more than two years, and does not own anything today, even its capital stock being expended by the WATCH TOWER BIBLE AND TRACT SOCIETY in its religious work.

There is no corporation in existence anywhere in the world in which Pastor Russell owns a single share of stock, nor in which anyone else holds any stock for his use or benefit.

PASTOR RUSSELL'S WEALTH When Pastor Russell closed out his business, many years ago, he had upwards of a quarter of a million dollars. The greater portion he freely spent in the publication of Bible literature, which was distributed *to the people without charge* for the purpose of enlightening them concerning the harmonious Plan of God as taught in the Scriptures. The remainder of his wealth he transferred to the WATCH TOWER BIBLE AND TRACT SOCIETY in harmony with and in fulfilment of an agreement between himself and wife made before their domestic troubles began.

Pastor Russell now has no money, no bank account and owns no property aside from a few personal effects, nor does anyone hold any property or money for his personal benefit.

His life for the past forty years has been devoted exclusively to religious work, during which time he has received as a monetary compensation his meals and a modest room in which to work and sleep, traveling expenses and $11 per month for incidental expenses, which amount is supplied by the WATCH TOWER BIBLE AND TRACT SOCIETY.

The charge that he has used these corporations for his personal and private gain is absolutely false, as the books of the corporations abundantly testify. Every dollar that comes into his hands he accounts to the Society for the same.

As an illustration, it was incidentally shown in a lawsuit in which the books of the Society were necessary as evidence that on one occasion Pastor Russell was on the opposite side of the continent from New York when he was handed a draft for $10,000, payable to his own order and which he could have cashed and appropriated to his own use, but, on the contrary, be sent the draft at once to the Treasurer of the Society, authorizing him to indorse his name thereon and cash it for the benefit of the work of said Society, which was done.

On the occasion of the above lawsuit a committee of five gentlemen, experts, were appointed to audit the books of the corporation, and not one penny was found as having been misappropriated by Pastor Russell or anyone else.

I know these facts because it was necessary for me, as counsel, to go over the audit.

Pastor Russell was married in 1879. For the first thirteen years of their married life he and Mrs. Russell lived happily together. They were both engaged in religious work, and had been even before their marriage. A semi-monthly religious journal, THE WATCH TOWER, was published, of which Pastor Russell was and still is the editor. She became dissatisfied with his manner of conducting this journal and attempted to dictate the policy thereof. Being the head of the house, Pastor Russell would not submit to his wife's dictating the manner of conducting his business affairs. Without notice,

DOMESTIC TROUBLES she voluntarily separated herself from him in 1897, nearly eighteen years after their marriage. For nearly seven years she lived separate and apart from him, he furnishing her a separate home.

In June, 1903, she filed in the Court of Common Pleas at Pittsburgh a suit for legal separation. They had been actually separated for nearly seven years. In April, 1906, the cause came on for trial before Justice Collier and a jury.

It has been remarked by a number of lawyers who have read the record in this case that "no court has ever before granted a separation upon so slight testimony as appears in this case." The record discloses nothing except a misunderstanding between husband and wife, and which at one time was adjusted, by mutual consent. The issue being submitted to the jury they evidently concluded that, being already *actually* separated for a period of seven years, a *legal* separation might as well take place.

There never has been an absolute divorce of either of the parties.

GREATEST FISH STORY EVER MANUFACTURED Upon the trial of this cause Mrs. Russell testified that one Miss Ball had stated to her that her husband said, "I am like a jelly-fish, I float around here and there. I touch this one and that one, and if she responds I take her to me, and if not I float on to others."

All this matter the Court struck from the record and would not permit it to go to the jury. In his charge to the jury the Judge said: "This little incident about this girl that was in the family, that is beyond the ground of the libel and has nothing to do with the case because not being put in it, and it was condoned or allowed to pass."

It is manifest that this "jelly-fish" story was entirely the product of Mrs. Russell's imagination, and other facts which appear in the record conclusively show that it could not have been true.

Pastor Russell emphatically denied that any such thing ever occurred. It would seem unreasonable that any man would make such a statement about himself.

But the most conclusive facts disclosed by the record showing her statement to be untrue are these: Miss Ball came to them in 1889, a child of ten, and was taken into the home of Mr. and Mrs. Russell. She was treated as a member of the family. She was an orphan. She kissed both Mr. and Mrs. Russell good night each evening when she retired. They treated her as their own child. (Court Record, pages 90, 91.)

Mrs. Russell testified that the "jelly-fish" incident transpired in 1894, when the girl could not have been more than fifteen years of age. (Page 15, Record.)

Mrs. Russell lived with her husband for three years thereafter and was separated from him seven years longer before suit was filed, or ten years after the alleged incident before she filed her suit for separation. In her complaint, or bill for separation, *no reference whatever is made to the Ball or jelly-fish incident.* Her husband had no notice that she intended to make such a charge, and when upon the trial it was intimated by her counsel that he expected to prove such, counsel for Pastor Russell asked for a continuance of the case, which the Court denied. Miss Ball was then living and Mrs. Russell knew where she was and could have procured her as a witness, or have had her deposition, in court. No attempt was made to procure her attendance or her deposition.

Pastor Russell could not have had her there to testify because he had no notice or intimation that his wife would attempt to bring such into the case. It is but reasonable to conclude that this jelly-fish story was manufactured for the occasion. Truly it is a great fish-story!

A CLINCHER Another point that conclusively shows that the "jelly-fish story," or Miss Ball incident, was manufactured and untrue is this fact: Three years after the alleged incident Mrs. Russell herself selected and called together a committee of three before whom she and her husband met to discuss their differences and tried to arrange them.

Two members of that committee testified at the trial that all the differences of Mr. and Mrs. Russell were discussed and that their trouble grew out of the management of the paper, or journal. The committee decided against Mrs. Russell's contention, and, in their language, the two "kissed and made up."

The Miss Ball or jelly-fish incident *was not even intimated to this committee.* (Court Record, pages 79, 113-116.)

MRS. RUSSELL TESTIFIES HER HUSBAND WAS NOT GUILTY

At the trial of this case Mrs. Russell's counsel made mention that Mr. Russell was in a room with Emily Matthews, a member of the household, and the door was locked. To this Pastor Russell at the time made answer under oath (page 92, Record of Testimony), as follows:

"I said (to Mrs. Russell), 'Dear, you understood all about that. You know that was the room in which the slops were emptied and the water was carried, and that was the morning that Emily Matthews was sick, and you told me of it and asked me to go up and see her, and when they were running out and in with water pails I turned the key for half a minute until I would have a chance to hear quietly what she had to say, and there wasn't the slightest impropriety in anything that was done. I would just as soon that everybody in this room would be present.'"

Mrs. Russell did not deny this statement in her testimony, and therefore, being undisputed, it must be taken as the true and correct explanation. It shows not the slightest impropriety on his part.

That Mrs. Russell *herself did not believe and never has believed that her husband was guilty of immoral conduct* is shown by the record in this case where her own counsel (on page 10) asked Mrs. Russell this question: "*You don't mean that your husband was guilty of adultery?*" Ans. "*No.*"

It is seen that the court properly took away from the jury the consideration of the "jelly-fish" incident to which she testified. These are the facts which Pastor Russell's enemies distort, and upon which they charge him with immoral conduct.

There was no testimony produced upon the trial of this case that had any tendency to show that Pastor Russell had been morally derelict in the slightest. No witness testified against his moral character, and no witness in any court has ever yet uttered a word of testimony tending to show anything against his morality.

PASTOR RUSSELL EXONERATED IN SEVERAL COURTS

Shortly after the trial of the above case the *Washington Post* published the aforementioned 'jelly-fish" story in connection with the name of Pastor Russell, and charged that he was guilty of immoral conduct. Thereupon Pastor Russell filed suit for libel against the *Post*, which case was tried before a jury. The instructions of the court on behalf of the defendant, the *Post*, were manifestly erroneous and prejudicial, but notwithstanding this the jury brought in a verdict exonerating Pastor Russell, but allowed him only one dollar damages.

Pastor Russell thereupon appealed to the Superior Court, which court reversed the judgment of the lower court and remanded the case for retrial, that a jury might have opportunity to assess larger damages. The case came on for trial the second time and after plaintiff had put in a portion of his testimony counsel for the *Washington Post* offered a compromise and the case was settled by the defendant, the *Washington Post*, paying to Pastor Russell a substantial sum of money, together with all costs in the case, and the *Post* thereafter published his sermons.

Thus he was completely exonerated by two different courts concerning the "jelly-fish" or immoral story.

Still his enemies persisted in trying to get this before the public. A preacher in New Jersey wrote an article to a Chicago paper, the *Mission Friend*, charging Pastor Russell with immorality, and as proof thereof cited the Miss Ball or "jelly-fish" story. Thereupon an action of libel for damages was filed by Pastor Russell's counsel against the *Mission Friend*. The case came on for hearing, and after argument of the legal questions involved the Court decided in favor of Pastor Russell. The only question that remained to determine was the amount of damages to be allowed Pastor Russell.

Counsel for the *Mission Friend* then sought a compromise or settlement. Pastor Russell not desiring "blood money," but merely that his good name might be vindicated, agreed to the compromise upon the following terms, which were carried out, to wit:

The *Mission Friend* paid all the costs and published a retraction admitting that it had wrongfully published the Miss Ball or "jelly-fish" story concerning Pastor Russell, further stating that Pastor Russell is a Christian and a gentleman of the highest integrity and moral standing and entitled to the respect and esteem of all good people.

MIRACLE WHEAT NOT NAMED BY PASTOR RUSSELL, NOR DID HE EVER REALIZE ANY MONEY FROM IT   Pastor Russell's enemies charge that he sold a great quantity of ordinary seed wheat under the name of "Miracle Wheat," at one dollar per pound, or sixty dollars per bushel, and realized therefrom an enormous sum of money which he appropriated to his own use. This is not only an exaggeration, but a glaring falsehood.

In the year 1911 J. A. Bohnet, of Pittsburgh, Pennsylvania, and Samuel J. Fleming, of Wabash, Indiana, each having a quantity of Miracle Wheat, together presented to the WATCH TOWER BIBLE AND TRACT SOCIETY the aggregate of about 30 bushels with the proposition on their part that the wheat should be sold at $1.00 per pound and all the proceeds arising from the sale thereof should be received by the WATCH TOWER BIBLE AND TRACT SOCIETY as a donation from them, to be used by said Society in its religious work. The wheat was received and sent out by the Society, and the gross receipts therefrom were about $1,800.

Pastor Russell did not get a penny of this. His connection therewith was this, that he published a statement in his journal, *The Watch Tower*, giving notice that this wheat had been contributed and could be had for a dollar a pound.

Pastor Russell did not *discover the wheat, nor did he name it, nor did he receive any personal benefit therefrom.* Nor was the Society of which he is president guilty of the slightest misconduct.

Had this same transaction occurred with some Catholic or Protestant church no one would ever have thought of making any fuss about it. But the Preachers' Union seized upon it as another means of persecuting Pastor Russell.

PREACHERS' ALLIANCE EMPLOYS BROOKLYN EAGLE FOR SYSTEMATIC ATTACK UPON PASTOR RUSSELL — It is a well-known fact that the *Brooklyn Daily Eagle* is given to making unwarranted attacks upon others. Its persecution of the late lamented Dr. T. DeWitt Talmage is an instance. It may seem the part of wisdom to divert attention by charging another with wrongdoing. The *Eagle* has not such a reputation as a good man would desire.

Pastor Russell's teaching was not interfering with *The Eagle*, but was enlightening the people and thus interfering with the Preachers' Unholy Alliance, and some of its members deemed it necessary to do something. *The Eagle* was employed as an instrument to do the job. *The Eagle* was willing and ready to begin the attack. Hence, on March 22, 1911, *The Eagle* published an article ridiculing the religious work in which Pastor Russell was engaged (fol. 936). On the same day it published another article ridiculing "Miracle Wheat" and various persons engaged in growing it. On September 23, 1911, it published an article announcing that the United States Government was about to take up the matter of Miracle Wheat, intimating that the Government Inspector would ask to be furnished with a sample of Miracle Wheat sold at Pastor Russell's Tabernacle, to be tested, "that the faithful and a waiting world may learn more fully of the *astonishing merits* of this precious grain" (fol. 981).

As a matter of fact, the Government had been experimenting with Miracle Wheat for more than three years at that time.

22   *Miracle Wheat*

which shows that *The Eagle* was trying to mislead its readers
and prejudice them against Pastor Russell by inferentially
charging that he was selling a fraudulent wheat.

On the same date *The Eagle* published a libelous cartoon,
and words in connection therewith, directed against Pastor
Russell and his alleged relationship to Miracle Wheat.
Pastor Russell sued *The Eagle* for damages. The facts given
here are taken from the record of the trial of that case in the
Supreme Court of Kings County, New York. Figures appearing in parentheses, thus (fol. 774, etc.), refer to folios of the
printed record of the case now on file in the Appellate Division
of the Supreme Court of New York.

The chief issue raised by the pleadings in this case was
whether or not the wheat in question was superior to ordinary
wheat. Eleven witnesses testified to its superior quality over
other wheat.

Following are the names and addresses of the witnesses:

Kent B. Stoner, Fincastle, Virginia; Joseph I. Knight, Sr.,
1067 38th Street, Brooklyn, New York; Isaac L. Frey, Lower
Mt. Bethel, Pennsylvania; Frederick Widener, Belvidere,
N. J.; Henry D. Ayre, Cleveland, Tennessee; William Pray,
Mansfield, N. J.; William I. Tomlinson, Kirkwood, N. J.;
Edward W. Hunt, Stratford, N. J.; Dr. Joseph A. Carlton,
Palmetto, Georgia; J. A. Bohnet, Pittsburgh, Pennsylvania;
Samuel J. Fleming, Wabash, Indiana.

The eight first named never heard of Pastor Russell or his
religious teachings prior to the trial of this case, but had been
experimenting with Miracle Wheat and found it far superior
to any other wheat.

ORIGINAL PLANT OF MIRACLE WHEAT HAD 142 STALKS
The testimony showed that in the year
1904 Mr. K. B. Stoner noticed growing in his garden in Fincastle, Virginia,
an unusual plant, which at first he mis-
took for a kind of grass known as parlor
grass, but which, upon further observation, proved to be wheat.
The plant had one hundred and forty-two stalks, each stalk
bearing a head of fully matured wheat.

Mr. Stoner had never prior to that time seen a wheat
plant bearing more than five heads.

The unusual yield from this single plant prompted him to
save the grain, which he planted the following Fall (fols. 73-
75). For several seasons he continued producing this grain,
and in 1906, about two years after discovering it, because of
its remarkable producing qualities, he named it *Miracle
Wheat* (fol. 81).

In 1908 or 1909 Mr. Stoner called the attention of the
witness, J. I. Knight, to the unusual qualities of the wheat

The above is a photograph of One Stool of Miracle Wheat grown in 1912 in the garden of Mr. K. B. Stoner, Fincastle, Va., within two feet of the identical spot where the original stalk of Miracle Wheat was discovered. It is grown from one grain and was six feet tall at the time this photograph was taken and was not then fully grown.

and it was arranged that they should grow the wheat on shares and market it after accumulating a sufficient supply (fols. 86, 127, 129). Mr. Knight received a forty-five per cent. (45%) interest in the wheat. They agreed to withhold the wheat from the market until 1912 (fol. 128), but subsequently decided to sell in August, 1911 (fols. 128, 125).

MIRACLE WHEAT SOLD BY OTHERS AT $1.25 PER POUND After making his arrangement with Mr. Stoner Mr. Knight went to Europe and exhibited the wheat in the agricultural departments of various countries (fols. 129-131). Neither Mr. Knight nor Mr. Stoner had ever corresponded with Pastor Russell, nor had any acquaintance with him or with any of his associates prior to the time of the trial (fols. 82, 154). Prior to his meeting Mr. Knight, Mr. Stoner had sold some of the wheat, *always at $1.25 a pound* (fols. 80, 83). In 1908 he sold four pounds at $1.25 a pound to Joseph A. Carlton, a dentist of Palmetto, Georgia, the owner of a 256-acre farm (fol. 162). In 1909 he sold two pounds to Frederick S. Widener, of Belvidere, N. J., for from somewhere between two and five dollars (fol. 396). Mr. Widener gave some of this to Isaac L. Frey, a farmer of Lower Mt. Bethel. Neither he nor Mr. Frey had any connection with Pastor Russell's work (fols. 395, 387, 383).

William I. Tomlinson and Edward Hunt, farmers of New Jersey, also experimented with this wheat.

All of these persons who thus bought their wheat directly or indirectly from Stoner, the discoverer of the wheat, or from Knight, his partner, found it to have remarkable reproducing qualities (fols. 385–392, 396, 470, 1, 478–480).

OVER 80 BUSHELS OF MIRACLE WHEAT TO THE ACRE The first plant found by Stoner had over 4,000 grains to the stool. In the Fall of 1904 he planted 1,800 grains, and each grain yielded an average of 250 grains. The average return from ordinary wheat in this section was about ten grains for each grain of seed (fols. 75-78). Mr. Stoner found that a peck to the acre, that is 15 pounds of Miracle Wheat, produced over forty bushels (fol. 88). *He has raised as high as 80 bushels of Miracle Wheat to the acre* (fol. 92).

Thus it is seen that Miracle Wheat produced *twenty-five* times as much as ordinary wheat in proportion to the amount sown. Mr. Stoner had experimented with Red Wonder, Fultz and Old Mediterranean wheats. The productiveness of Miracle Wheat was found to be due to its large stooling qualities (fol. 95). For these stooling qualities it needs more

room than the average wheat, requiring 16 inches between
the rows, and about four times the space of ordinary wheat.
If sown like ordinary wheat Miracle was a failure, for room
was essential (fols. 97-99, 104). A four by four-inch space,
such as the Government allows, is too small to allow for the
normal stooling of Miracle Wheat (fol. 104). When he has
observed common wheat planted in competition with Miracle,
the spaces between Miracle planting have been about four
times the space between the other wheat plantings. This
was as he recommended (fol. 155).

Widener, when he sowed Miracle, counted 22 to 28 stalks
to the grain (fols. 396, 397). Mr. Frey raised a bushel and a
half of wheat from a quart of grain (fol. 383), and the following year, 1911, raised 108 bushels from 16 to 22 quarts of seed.
He seeded about 15 pounds to the acre (fols. 383-392).

MIRACLE WHEAT TAKES FIRST PRIZE AT SEVERAL STATE FAIRS Mr. Henry A. Ayre, a farmer of Cleveland, Tennessee, with thirty-five years'
experience, bought some Stoner (Miracle) Wheat in the fall of 1909 or
1910. He sowed one-half bushel to a
scant seven-eighths of an acre and reaped a little over twenty-
six bushels per acre. His is a poor wheat section, where the
yield of ordinary wheat is about 8 bushels per acre.

Mr. Ayre found Miracle Wheat hardier than ordinary
wheat, standing the winters better and stooling much more
than any other wheat he ever saw. It stood a freezing winter
where rye had frozen out (fols. 299-402). He had the surrounding farmers raise this wheat for him under contract
(fol. 407). He raised as large as 64 stools from one plant of
this wheat.

Miracle Wheat took first prize for him in the Fall of 1910
at the Appalachian Exposition, for Tennessee, Georgia and
North Carolina, and also took first prize at the State Fair in
Tennessee, and at his county fair (fol. 406). He grew Exhibit 6, a stool of Miracle Wheat containing 49 stalks (fols.
408, 943).

MIRACLE WHEAT STOOLS BETTER THAN OTHER WHEAT William Pray, a farmer of Mansfield
Township, N. J., who was unacquainted
with plaintiff in any way, raised Stoner
or Miracle Wheat for three years. He
grew Exhibit 30, containing over 80
stalks grown from a single grain. He had been a farmer for
twenty-five years. An acre of ordinary wheat which he sowed
with two bushels yielded 17 bushels, whereas an adjoining
acre which he sowed with a half bushel of Miracle Wheat
yielded 25 bushels. He never saw any wheat stool as Miracle

Wheat did. To this is due its superior producing qualities (fols. 464-466). The usual practice of farmers in his section is to sow two bushels of ordinary wheat to the acre, and he knows of no way of getting better results (fols. 467, 468).

William I. Tomlinson, who had been a farmer for nine years, in Kirkwood, N. J., in 1909 planted Miracle Wheat in competition with ordinary wheat—16 acres with Miracle Wheat at a half bushel to the acre, which yielded 32 bushels to the acre, and 20 acres of ordinary wheat at one and a half bushels to the acre, which yielded 21 bushels to the acre. He is not a follower of Pastor Russell, nor a believer in any of his doctrines (fols. 470, 471).

Edward W. Hunt, a farmer of Stratford, N. J., for many years, who does not know Pastor Russell and was not connected with him in any way, experimented with Miracle Wheat. He first sowed a bushel of seed to an acre and a half, which produced 56 bushels, part of the crop having been destroyed. In 1911 and 1912 he planted Miracle in competition with Amber Wheat. He planted 10 acres with Miracle, three pecks to the acre, and the yield averaged 34½ bushels per acre, or 345 bushels

Miracle Wheat produced by Edward McCleery, 2403 Wabash Ave., Los Angeles, Cal. Offered as exhibit in *Eagle* libel case (fol. 152).

in all. He planted 18 acres with Amber Wheat, a bushel and a half to the acre, and the yield was 325 bushels in all, or a little more than 18 bushels to the acre. Both fields were alike, stood side by side, and the conditions were the same.

The original plant of Miracle Wheat, discovered and named by Mr. Stoner, contained 142 heads of well-matured seed, grown from one grain (fol. 74). A bunch of wheat grown near Los Angeles, California, of the same Miracle Wheat was exhibited before the jury and put in evidence (fol. 158). It contained 118 stalks and as many heads of well-developed wheat standing more than six feet tall, all grown from one grain. (See illustration.)

PASTOR RUSSELL'S FIRST KNOWLEDGE OF MIRACLE WHEAT On November 23, 1907, H. A. Miller, Assistant Agriculturist of the United States Government, filed in the Department of Agriculture at Washington, D. C., a report upon the wheat being grown upon Mr. Stoner's farm, highly commending said wheat (fols. 1185–1188). The public press throughout the country at the time took notice of this report. Pastor Russell's attention was called to it, and on March 15, 1908, he published in his journal, *The Watch Tower*, some press comments and extracts from the aforementioned Government report. *This was Pastor Russell's first knowledge of Miracle Wheat, which wheat Mr. Stoner and others had been experimenting with for three years or more.*

Dr. Joseph A. Carlton, of Palmetto, Georgia, reading in Pastor Russell's *Watch Tower* the aforementioned notice, purchased from Mr. Stoner four pounds of this wheat for which he paid Stoner $1.25 per pound, or $75 per bushel (fol. 169). He planted a pound and three-quarters to one-fifth of an acre, took accurate account of the yield, and found that it was eight bushels and 24 pounds, or 504 pounds. Georgia is not a wheat State (fols. 162, 163). Yield of ordinary wheat in that State is from 5 to 20 bushels to the acre (fol. 164). In 1910 Dr. Carlton reaped 62½ bushels of Miracle Wheat from a little over two acres (fol. 165). From one single grain in his field 71 stalks were grown (fol. 168).

Mr. Bohnet got a peck of this wheat from Dr. Carlton. He sowed 14 pounds to one-half an acre and reaped 8 bushels. One-half of this he sent to Mr. Kuesthardt, of Port Clinton, Ohio, editor of the Ottawa *Zeitung*, a German county newspaper. Samuel J. Fleming, of Wabash, Indiana, got five pounds of seed from Bohnet and 20 pounds from Kuesthardt, and sowed 25 pounds to about one acre of land, and although it was late in the season his yield was 34 bushels. Average yield of ordinary wheat in that section (sowed a bushel and a half to the acre) is about 20 bushels (fol. 234).

MIRACLE WHEAT YIELDS 12 TO 20 TIMES MORE THAN ORDINARY WHEAT Thus the testimony showed that ordinary wheat sown at the rate of six pecks to the acre produces on an average 20 bushels, whereas Miracle Wheat sown at the rate of one peck to the acre produces from 40 to 80

FIFTEEN PLANTS OF MIRACLE WHEAT. EACH GROWN FROM ONE GRAIN.
NONE YIELDED LESS THAN 1,000 GRAINS.

bushels to the acre, showing that Miracle Wheat yields from 12 to 20 times more than ordinary wheat.

Pastor Russell having no personal knowledge of the wheat, counsel did not call him as a witness. He was in court, ready and willing to testify, but counsel did not call him for the reason above stated.

The *Brooklyn Eagle*, to offset all this testimony of practical farmers and wheat raisers, produced but a single witness, namely, Mr. Ball, of the Agricultural Department of the United States Government, who was neither a farmer nor wheat raiser. Mr. Ball testified that he was "connected with the U. S. Government with the Department of Agriculture as an Agronomist and Acting Cerealist in charge of cereal investigations" (fol. 732). His imposing title was about his only recommendation. He produced a memoranda of experiments with Miracle Wheat, supposed to have been made at the Government station, by persons whom he was unable to name.

DONATION PROCEEDS KEPT A YEAR TO REFUND, BUT NO ONE WISHED MONEY BACK

There was absolutely no testimony in the case showing that Pastor Russell had induced a single person to purchase Miracle Wheat. Not a word tending to show that anyone was defrauded. On the contrary, shortly after the publication of the libel by the *Brooklyn Eagle*, the WATCH TOWER BIBLE AND TRACT SOCIETY published broadcast over the country and sent to each purchaser a notice that if anyone was dissatisfied with his purchase he might have his money returned, and the identical money arising from the sale of said wheat was held for a year for the purpose of refunding. Not a single person asked to have his money refunded.

Upon the trial of this case, counsel for the *Brooklyn Eagle* severely ridiculed the religious teachings of Pastor Russell. The jury, being largely composed of men of strong religious prejudices, and at least one of them an atheist, disregarded the testimony of the 11 practical farmers and wheat raisers, and the several exhibits of Miracle Wheat actually produced and shown to them, and decided the case in favor of the *Brooklyn Eagle*, upon the unsupported testimony of one Government official who never raised a grain of wheat in his life. The case was at once appealed and is now pending in the Appellate Division of the Supreme Court.

Much ado has been made about the WATCH TOWER BIBLE AND TRACT SOCIETY, of which Pastor Russell is president, disposing of a small quantity of seed Miracle Wheat *at one dollar per pound*, which had been donated and the price fixed by the donors, whereas the evidence conclusively shows that Messrs. Stoner, Knight, Carlton and others had been selling the same wheat *at $1.25 per pound*, which was not only considered legitimate, but a very reasonable price in view of the extraordinary quality of the wheat and the small quantity in existence.

It cannot be conceived how anyone can honestly hold up Pastor Russell to ridicule for the connection that he had with Miracle Wheat. Neither he nor the WATCH TOWER BIBLE AND TRACT SOCIETY did anything in the slightest manner reprehensible, but, on the contrary, their conduct was open and aboveboard and proper in every way.

THE HARVEST
Kansas raised in 1914 twice as much wheat as her nearest competitor, and thirteen per cent more than any other state has ever produced in a single season

Miracle Wheat Grown by W. A. Jarrett, Columbus, Kansas, Represents the State of Kansas at World's Fair, San Francisco, 1915.

I. B. S. Ass'n.

Dear Friends.—A copy of the *Chicago Daily Tribune* recently came to my notice containing articles, the object of which was an attack upon the Association, and especially upon Pastor Russell. Among other points of attack was Miracle Wheat, and thinking that some information on the subject might be of value to you in meeting this attack, I enclose herewith picture and data relative to field of Miracle Wheat I grew last year. This picture, among thousands of others, of the best fields raised in the State, was sent to the Secretary of the State Board of Agriculture, J. C. Mohler. From this collection was to be chosen the one which would represent the State at the World's Fair, which convenes the 20th of this month.

Now, the judges in this matter did not know that this was Miracle Wheat; hence they had nothing to bias their decision. So Miracle Wheat received the award.

I grew seventy acres of this wheat and planted and cared for it in the regular, ordinary way and had no trouble in disposing of it to my neighbor wheat-growers last fall for seed, at $2 per bushel.

In this section of the country we have to sow more to the acre than in some localities; hence we could not follow the twenty pounds to the acre rate of seeding, but some we seeded at the rate of one-half bushel and some at the rate of three-quarters of a bushel per acre, and we found the three pecks to be the better.

My field yielded forty-nine bushels to the acre, more than twice the average yield of wheat in this vicinity and in many instances more than three times as much. If this information is of any value to you or any of the friends who may have charge of the matter of setting these things straight before the public, I am thankful for the opportunity to furnish the same.

I am your servant,
W. A. JARRETT.

REV. ROSS IRRESPONSIBLE FINANCIALLY Rev. J. J. Ross, of Hamilton, Ontario, published a libelous pamphlet against Pastor Russell. A warrant was issued for the arrest of Ross. He evaded the officer for some time and even failed to keep his appointment at his church to prevent the officer from taking him into custody. Finally, he was taken before George E. Jelfs, Police Magistrate, on the charge of criminal libel. Upon a hearing he was committed for trial. Upon motion, the Superior Court quashed the commitment because of a technical error in the proceedings. Ross was again taken before the Magistrate.

When the case came on for hearing the second time Pastor Russell, who was a necessary witness, was away on an extended trip in Panama and other parts of the South, filling appointments previously made, and had no notice of the date of hearing. Ross and his counsel tried to make it appear that Pastor Russell was evading the trial. As soon as Pastor Russell returned to Brooklyn and heard that he was wanted he immediately notified the Magistrate that he was ready to come to Canada. He did go and gave his testimony. Again the Magistrate committed Ross to appear before the high court to answer an indictment to be preferred by the Grand Jury. When the case came on in that court the Judge of the court in charging the Grand Jury relative to its duties, among other things, said to the jury: "Unless the jury finds that this alleged libel would cause a breach of the public peace in *Canada* then no indictment should be returned, but the parties should resort to civil suit for damages." The jury returned "no bill," and it is manifest that they could not have done otherwise under this charge of the Court, for the reason that Pastor Russell lived in Brooklyn, New York, and Rev. Ross lived in Hamilton, Ontario, Canada, and it would be physically impossible for the libel to cause a breach of the public peace when the parties were so far apart.

Thus it will be seen that the issues were never tried and never determined. Pastor Russell did not resort to civil action for damages, for the reason that he was advised that such an action would be useless, since Ross is irresponsible financially and could not be compelled by such a proceeding to publish a retraction.

ROSS PAMPHLET FULL OF UNMITIGATED FALSEHOODS Thereafter Rev. Ross published another pamphlet against Pastor Russell which for unmitigated falsehoods and misrepresentations of facts certainly has not an equal. Selecting here and there isolated paragraphs from the court records, he twisted them, added to, misrep-

resented and made them appear entirely different from their
true meaning. *This could not have been accidental on his part.*
For instance, among other things, he charges: "He (Pastor
Russell) sought to evade payment fixed by the court by fleeing
from one State to another, making it necessary for his wife to
get *an extradition order*, which she did, and which led to the
condemnation of the cunning pastor by a third court, and the
increase of the alimony."

Rev. Ross probably did not know that extradition proceedings cannot be resorted to to enforce a money judgment.
No "extradition order" was made, nor were there any extradition proceedings. But probably Rev. Ross thought the
people would believe his statement, even though false, because
he is recognized as a Minister.

Upon the hearing of the question of alimony, the Court
adjudged that Mrs. Russell should receive from her husband
the sum of $100 per month. This order was made March 4,
1908. *The amount of alimony was never increased.*

In the forepart of the winter of 1908 arrangements were
made to transfer the main office of the Bible Society's work to
Brooklyn, New York, for the reasons heretofore stated. Some
time was required to accomplish this work, but the removal,
which was open and aboveboard, was completed in March,
1909. The Pittsburgh papers made mention of the removal.
Pastor Russell remained in Pittsburgh until everything was
removed that was to be removed, himself being the last one of
the office force to leave Pittsburgh. No attempt was made to
interfere with the removal, as indeed there could not have
been any successful attempt.

In December, 1908, Mrs. Russell filed certain suits to set
aside the transfer of property made by her husband to the
WATCH TOWER BIBLE AND TRACT SOCIETY, and to enforce
the payment of alimony. Prior thereto, at a hearing of the
testimony on the alimony branch of the separation case, Pastor
Russell had testified that before the organization of the WATCH
TOWER BIBLE AND TRACT SOCIETY, both he and his wife
having consecrated their all to be used in the religious work
in which they were engaged in serving the Lord, it was agreed
between them that all of his property should be turned over to
the WATCH TOWER BIBLE AND TRACT SOCIETY, FOR THAT
PURPOSE. The property was his and he had the right to do
with it as he pleased. That after their separation, acting in
good faith and in harmony with their said agreement, he had
transferred his property to said Society, and that he had not
the means with which to pay the amount of alimony allowed by
the Court. The personal property had already been exhausted
by the Society, and the real estate was incumbered.

Early in April, 1909, and after said Society and Pastor Russell had removed to Brooklyn, the aforesaid cases came on for hearing on motions, Mr. Carpenter and myself appearing on behalf of said Society and Pastor Russell. After hearing the motions, the Court took the matter under advisement and afterwards decided it, holding that Mr. Russell's transfer of the property to the Society was a fraud on his wife and that the alimony must be paid. As it is well understood, a man's act may operate *as a legal fraud* against another, even *though he acts in absolute good faith.* Besides, court decisions are not infallible, as we all know, because rendered by imperfect human beings. At the time of the rendition of this decision, Pastor Russell's residence was in Brooklyn, but he at the time was in Europe, on his semi-annual lecture tour of Great Britain. He had not been advised of the decision of the Court upon this point. He stated to me prior thereto that he would be glad to pay Mrs. Russell, but he had no money, which fact I knew to be true.

MRS. RUSSELL NEVER DEFRAUDED OF A CENT BY HER HUSBAND

During the absence of Pastor Russell in Europe, as aforesaid, five men, his personal friends, *without his knowledge,* ascertained the amount of money required to meet the judgment of alimony. They raised more than the necessary amount among themselves, placed it in my hands and sent me to Pittsburgh to pay this judgment. I went to Pittsburgh and with Mrs. Russell's attorneys settled all the litigation, paying *to her every cent,* interest included, which *the court had allowed her,* together with all the court costs. These facts appear from the court records. *Mrs. Russell has never been cheated or defrauded out of one penny by her husband, but has received everything that the court allowed her.*

We submit that the furnishing of more than $10,000 by his five friends to relieve him of a judgment as above mentioned, and that without his knowledge, is a strong testimony of the high esteem in which Pastor Russell is held by those who know him. These gentlemen are of high standing, and if necessary I will give their names and addresses to anyone upon request. I wonder how many preachers who are assaulting Pastor Russell could find five men who would voluntarily do so much for them!

The charge that Pastor Russell procured certain property worth $40,000 to be sold for $50.00 and to be bought in by said Society for the purpose of defrauding his wife out of her dower is far from the truth and is in keeping with many other false charges made.

A wife has no absolute dower right in her husband's prop-

erty while he lives and if she dies first her inchoate right of
dower dies with her.   Where the husband owns property on
which there is a valid mortgage and the mortgage be foreclosed
and property sold, and at said sale brings no more than the
mortgage debt, then of course there would be no dower for the
wife even though she survived the husband.

Pastor Russell owned a piece of property in Pittsburgh on
which there was a valid mortgage. He conveyed this property,
under previous agreement with Mrs. Russell, to the WATCH
TOWER BIBLE AND TRACT SOCIETY *subject to said mortgage.*
Thereafter a creditor levied an execution on this property and
sold it at public auction after due notice according to law.
Pastor Russell had no title to or interest in the property at that
time because he had previously conveyed it to said Society.
The Society, in order to prevent a cloud being cast upon its
title by sheriff's deed to another, bid in the property at sheriff's
sale, it being the best bidder.   This sale and the sheriff's
deed gave said Society no more title than it previously had,
but merely kept clear the title it already had.

Years later the aforesaid *mortgage* was foreclosed and the
property sold by the *owner of that mortgage* and at *this sale* the
property brought only the amount of the mortgage debt and
costs. The sale under the mortgage eliminated any dower
or other interest Mrs. Russell might ever have had in the
property. Even had her husband still owned the property at
the time of the sale under the mortgage her inchoate right of
dower would entirely have been eliminated because the purchaser at that sale got a clear and perfect title.   Neither Pastor Russell nor the Society bid at said sale.   It is therefore
clear that Mrs. Russell was not defrauded by any one.

Ross charges Pastor Russell is unlearned because he is not
a graduate of some theological school.   I venture the assertion
that I can name a hundred living men who never even saw the
outside walls of a theological school who know more about the
Bible and its teaching than is taught in any theological college
in the land.   Pastor Russell is not a graduate of a theological

**PASTOR RUSSELL
GREATEST LIVING
BIBLE STUDENT**

college.   The greatest lawyer this
country has produced—Benjamin Harrison—never attended a law school.
Theological colleges teach theology and
not the Bible. Pastor Russell knows the Bible better than
any other living man.

Upon this point we quote with hearty approval the words
of Dr. G. W. Bull in his learned treatise of "The Gospel of
John," as follows:

"AN IRREGULAR (John 7:15).   That is what they all
say.   The crime of Christ was that He had not taken a course
in their college. 'Whence hath He learning?'   There are

some professional policemen who must protect all learning; medicine, law, gospel, or what not. If you never went through their schools of learning you are a freak, and there is something suspicious about your good sense. These men thought there was only one way of learning—they would ask a certificate of the sun! There are many schools and school-masters in God's universe. Cease your criticism of any Christian scholar. Let him learn in his own way; the Kingdom of God is going to make great progress when some of these high brows are removed to Heaven. Sometimes a man's utterance of profound Truths is stated in poor grammatical form, and the philosophers are puzzled by his power. They wonder where he got it: I do not know—probably his *alma mater* was his mother's knees—then let him speak. Remember today: 'God.hath chosen the weak things of this world to confound the mighty.'"

The other charges of Ross are equally untrue and have been heretofore answered herein, except, however, with reference to Pastor Russell's ordination, which he has clearly answered through the public press and in his sermons.

Here is a sample showing the length to which ministers and certain unscrupulous newspapers will go to malign Pastor Russell:

KIDNAPING STORY COMPETES FOR FIRST PLACE WITH FISH STORY Miss Ruth Galbraith, of Atlantic City, N. J., is the owner of certain property held in trust by a Trust Company of Philadelphia, Pa. Her mother desired to use the daughter's income, which, of course, she had no right to. Through the Trust Company's Attorney at Philadelphia, Miss Ruth began an action in the Orphans' Court to have her monthly income paid over to some other person for her benefit, in order that she might live separate from her mother. The reason for living apart was because there lived in the home an elder brother who was a consumptive, and while her mother was amply able to provide a servant to look after the invalid son Miss Ruth was required to do this, and not wishing to be exposed to the disease objected.

Her half sister, Mrs. Hollister, resided on Orange Street, Brooklyn, N. Y., and Miss Ruth went there to visit her. Mr. and Mrs. Hollister accompanied her to Philadelphia, Pa., on several occasions, at the hearing in the Orphans' Court of the aforesaid case. On a few occasions while in Brooklyn, Miss Ruth, together with her half sister, had a meal at the Bethel Home.

Some of his ministerial enemies, learning of the proceeding, started the story that Pastor Russell had kidnaped Miss Galbraith and was holding her in his home, and then some of their mediums of publication, headed by *The Brooklyn Eagle*, caused to be published that Mrs. Galbraith had instituted a habeas corpus proceeding in the Orphans' Court at Philadelphia against Pastor Russell to recover her daughter, Miss Ruth, from the Bethel Home. Other newspapers, giving credence to the story, republished it throughout the country.

Anyone, upon second thought, would know that a court in Pennsylvania would have no jurisdiction to issue a writ of habeas corpus directed to a man residing in the State of New York, and this, of itself, should have been sufficient to have given the story the "earmarks" of a falsehood. In fact, Pastor Russell was never a party to any procedure in connection with this matter; no habeas corpus proceeding was ever begun against him; Miss Galbraith at no time was in the custody of Pastor Russell or anyone else at Bethel Home, and no writ of habeas corpus was ever issued for the purpose of recovering Miss Galbraith from the Bethel Home. Furthermore, Miss Galbraith was never in the Bethel Home except for a brief period while taking a meal there.

Mrs. Galbraith, the mother, who for some years has been a member of a congregation to which Pastor Russell preaches, thinking that her Pastor could render her aid, sent him a telegram requesting such. Thereupon he addressed a letter to her saying that her telegram had been received at ten o'clock at night; that he did not know where Miss Ruth was residing, and was therefore unable to render any assistance. This is all the connection that Pastor Russell ever had with the matter, and out of this the aforesaid false statements were published.

For the past forty years Pastor Russell has been pointing out Scriptural proof showing that the great International wars would be upon the earth in 1914, just exactly as they have come, and that shortly thereafter Messiah's Kingdom would be established. His teachings have emphasized the nearness of the Kingdom of Messiah. Members of the Ministerial Union scoff at this, endeavoring to keep the people from knowing about and entering into the Kingdom. It might be well for them to take heed to the words of the Master, who said, "Woe unto you, Scribes and Pharisees, hypocrites, for ye shut up the Kingdom of Heaven against men, for ye neither go in yourselves, neither suffer ye them that are entering to go in."

BECAUSE HE TEACHES THE PEOPLE

It has ever been the rule of those entrenched in error to persecute others who bring forth Light and Truth, exposing error. Why was Jesus persecuted by the Scribes, Pharisees and Sadducees? Because He taught the people! He said to them that because of their selfishness they persecuted and killed the prophets whom Jehovah had sent to teach the people.

Again has Dr. Bull well said:

"CLASSES AND MASSES (John 7:47-50). The patronage back of a man or a movement is often responsible for the prejudice against him or it. The cultured will often condemn a form of religion which is favored by the common people; in turn the common people will look in scorn upon the religion of the 'silk stocking society.' - Yet again, the blind reverence for bosses and the aping of aristocracy will make a man attach more importance to the infidelity of 'upper-tendom' than to the weighty credentials and perfect character of Jesus Christ Himself. The question here is not a form of worship, but it concerns the very person of the Son of God. About this there can be no difference without eternal issue. I can understand why those in authority wanted to silence Him; it was not because of the conservatism of scholarship, but *because He was undermining their influence and reducing their bank account*. They need not lay their opposition to the friendship of Jesus for the under world, but to *their own falseness to the upper world*. Never mind to what class you belong, follow Christ if you have to walk alone in the procession, or walk next to the man you never meet except at the Throne of Grace. Remember today: 'Behold, how pleasant it is for brethren to dwell together in unity.'"

The Apostles taught concerning Jesus and the resurrection of the dead, and the Priests, Sadducees and Pharisees persecuted them. Why? "They were grieved that they taught the people."—Acts 4:1-5.

PREACHERS CANNOT HOPE TO FOOL ALL THE PEOPLE ALL THE TIME
Is it because Pastor Russell was at one time engaged in secular business, or because he was connected with some business corporations several years ago, or because they are especially interested in his domestic relations, that the Ministerial Union persists in persecuting him? No, indeed! Why then? BECAUSE HE IS TEACHING THE PEOPLE! But the preachers cannot "fool all the people all the time." Many of them are becoming wise concerning the methods of the preachers. The time has come for the people to know the Truth! They will be taught.

BE WISE, YE PHARISEES
Some of the Apostles were restrained of their liberty and were brought before the Priests and Pharisees, who said to them, "Did not we straightway command you that ye should not teach in this Name?" Among that ancient order of Min-

isterial Unionists was one wise Pharisee, Gamaliel, who said to his brother ministers on this occasion, "Take heed to yourselves what ye intend to do as touching these men; * * * and now I say unto you, refrain from these men and let them alone; for if this counsel or this work be of man it will come to naught, *but if it be of God ye cannot overthrow it.*" (Acts 5:28-39.) Be wise, oh ye modern Pharisees! There are some wise ones amongst you who have admonished you to let your moderation be known. Would it not be well that you heed the admonition of the learned Gamaliel?

From a personal and painstaking examination of every charge that has been made against Pastor Russell, I am thoroughly convinced and confidently state that he is the most unjustly persecuted man on earth. Notwithstanding this his good work continues and thousands testify to the blessings received therefrom. For many years he has stood forth to battle for the right. He is prematurely aged from his arduous and unselfish labors in behalf of mankind. *He is loved most by those who know him best,* and while he has some relentless enemies his stanch and substantial friends are numbered by the thousands. Probably his course is almost run, but—

WHEN THE MEMORY

OF HIS TRADUCERS

HAS PERISHED

FROM THE EARTH

THE

GOOD NAME

AND

GOOD DEEDS

OF

PASTOR RUSSELL

WILL LIVE

IMMORTAL

IN THE HEARTS OF

THE PEOPLE

ers, puffed up with pride, assumed titles and offices,... began to lord it over God's heritage. Then by degrees three came into existence a special class called "the clergy," who regarded themselves, and were regarded by others, as the proper guides to faith and practice aside from the Word of God. Thus in time the great system of Papacy was developed by an undue respect for the teachings of fallible men and a neglect of the Word of the Bible, the God.

Serious indeed have been the evil results brought about by this neglect of truth. As all know, both the church and the civil ... world were almost wholly enslaved by that system, the traditions and creeds of men.

... did and blessed strike for liberty and ... what is known as The Reformation. ... champions for his Word, among whom ... Melanchthon, Wycliffe, Knox and ... attention to the fact that Papacy had ... substituted the doctrines and ... ated out a few of its erroneous teach- ... owing that they were built upon tra- ... truth, and opposed to God's Word. ... wer adherents were called Protestants, ... against Papacy, and claimed the ... only correct rule of faith and practice.

Many studied, and, in the days of the Reformation ... in the light, so far as it was then shining. But ... day Protestants have made little progress, because, instead of walking in the light ... have halted along ... their leaders, willing to see no more ... as they saw but nothing more. They set themselves to their profession in the way of truth, helping in, with ... this truth they had, a great ... of error brought along, and ... the creeds the ... found ... many years ago ... "Christian ... a superstition, never ... supposing

... the world ... separated, and ... redeemed from ... to spiritual ... (Psa. ... too) And ... "Be not ... not ye touched be ... unto the ... not of truth, cleanse ... your feet, the walk there, you to ...

... sever, after the apostles ... began to neglect the ... looseness in building; and the te...

Daniel held a high office. He interfered with the system of graft practiced by his under officers--the Princes, Presidents, Counsellors and Captains,--who conspired to have him killed. They influenced the king to decree that whosoever should pray to any God except the King should be cast into the den of lions. Daniel continued to pray to HIS God. The conspirators reported this to the King and induced him to cast Daniel into a den of lions. God sent His angel and shut the lions' mouths that they did not hurt Daniel.

The king caused Daniel's accusers to be cast into the den of lions and they were destroyed.

(Daniel 6: 1-24)

DANIEL
IN THE LIONS' DEN

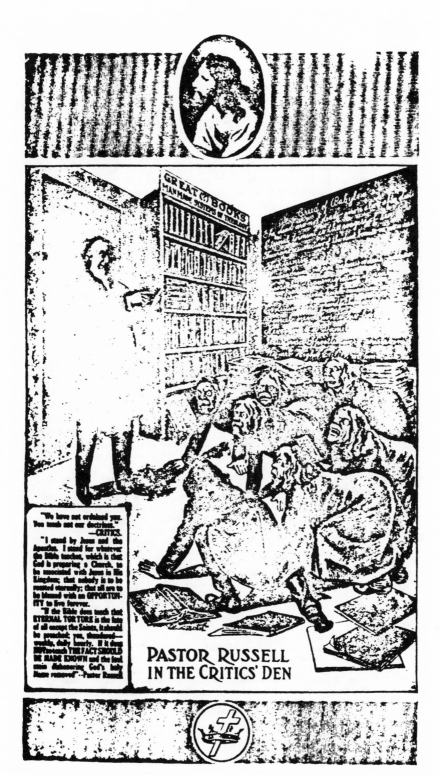

"We have not ordained you. You teach not our doctrines." —CRITICS.

"I stand by Jesus and the Apostles. I stand for whatever the Bible teaches, which is that God is preparing a Church, to be associated with Jesus in His Kingdom; that nobody is to be roasted eternally; that all are to be blessed with an OPPORTUNITY to live forever.

"If the Bible does teach that ETERNAL TORTURE is the fate of all except the Saints, it should be preached; yes, thundered—weekly, daily, hourly. If it does NOT so teach THE FACT SHOULD BE MADE KNOWN and the foul stain dishonoring God's holy Name removed."—Pastor Russell

PASTOR RUSSELL IN THE CRITICS' DEN

CHARACTER WITNESSES

It is the rule, upon the trial of a case, to introduce testimony as to the character and standing of the parties and of material witnesses, for the purpose of affecting the credibility of the witnesses on the guilt or innocence of the party charged with wrongdoing.

One of the star witnesses in this controversy, one that is always energetic and a more than willing instrument of the Preachers' Unholy Alliance, is the **"THE EAGLE" A** *Brooklyn Eagle.* It is not our purpose **WILLING TOOL** herein to assume the position of judging, but the reader will note with interest the opinion expressed by *The New York American* concerning the standing of the *Brooklyn Eagle.*

For some days the New York newspapers have been exposing a scheme engineered by ex-Senator Wm. H. Reynolds and associates to defraud the City of New York out of a large amount of property, and men prominent with the *Brooklyn Eagle* have been linked up with this matter, according to the daily press. Senator Reynolds is notorious in the City of New York as a promoter of such schemes. The *New York American*, one of the best-known papers in the United States, on April 2, 1915, editorially said:

ITS TALONS "Commenting upon the extraordinary **CAUGHT** zeal manifested by the *Brooklyn Daily Eagle* in the defense of the Marginal Railway scheme engineered by William H. Reynolds and associates, *The American* yesterday expressed these opinions:

"'The code of honor of newspapers should be, and usually is, as high as the code of honor of judges. That code forbids a newspaper man to have any private interest in any public bill he advocates or approves.

"'The editors and directors of the *Brooklyn Daily Eagle* are debarred, under this rule, from advocacy of any of the many *speculative schemes* which ex-Senator Reynolds and his Realty Associates are endeavoring to foist upon the taxpayers of New York through a too easy Board of Estimate.

"'We understand that *The Eagle* is promoting a mass meeting to push these schemes.'"

Continuing *The American* said:

"*The American* did not mention the Marginal Railway grab, although *The Eagle* is now active in *promoting it.* That is only one, though for the moment the most prominent, of Senator Reynolds' speculative schemes. As to the interest of persons connected with *The Eagle* in the series of interwoven Reynolds enterprises, the following facts drawn from the Directory of Directors are instructive:

"George F. Dobson appears in that directory as MANAGING EDITOR of THE EAGLE. He is listed also as director in the

Estates of Long Beach, OF WHICH MR. REYNOLDS IS PRESIDENT AND DIRECTOR.

"Mr. Dobson is secretary and treasurer of the Hanover Theatre Company, OF WHICH REYNOLDS IS DIRECTOR. He is secretary, treasurer and director of the Laurelton Land Company, OF WHICH REYNOLDS IS PRESIDENT AND DIRECTOR. He is secretary and director of the Metropolitan Jockey Club, OF WHICH REYNOLDS IS PRESIDENT AND DIRECTOR. And he is PRESIDENT AND DIRECTOR OF THE HARWAY IMPROVEMENT COMPANY, WHICH IS INVOLVED IN THE REALTY TRANSACTIONS COMPREHENDED IN A REYNOLDS WATER-FRONT GRAB.

"Mr. Dobson, for many years *The Eagle's* managing editor, and now its editorial writer, hardly appears as an unbiased judge of the real estate operations of Senator W. H. Reynolds.

"Again, the Bush Terminal Company is vitally interested in the Marginal Railway project, standing to profit largely if the deal is consummated. Irving T. Bush, the president, is a director in the Estates of Long Beach; Frank Bailey, director, is president of the Realty Associates, an organization already involved in real estate transactions with the city, and of three Reynolds companies besides. ASSOCIATED WITH THESE PARTNERS OF SENATOR REYNOLDS AS A DIRECTOR IN THE BUSH TERMINAL COMPANY WE FIND WILLIAM N. DYKMAN, DIRECTOR OF THE 'BROOKLYN EAGLE.'

"And finally, in the Kings County Register's Office, in section 21, of liber 19, page 124, appears the name of WILLIAM V. HESTER, SECRETARY AND TREASURER OF THE 'BROOKLYN EAGLE,' along with those of other political and real estate speculators, as a guarantor on a certain $50,000 bond given by the HARWAY IMPROVEMENT COMPANY, WHICH IS DIRECTLY AND LARGELY INTERESTED IN A REYNOLDS WATER-FRONT GRAB RECENTLY EXPOSED AND DEFEATED BY PUBLICITY."

The Brooklyn Eagle is an adept in the practice of the old scheme of throwing stones at some innocent person who is in the public eye, thereby hoping to divert the attention of the people from its own wrongful schemes.

These matters are worthy of consideration in determining the weight and credibility of the testimony given by it.

As to the character of the various ministers allied in this persecution of Pastor Russell, and the weight to be given to their testimony, we refer the reader to the APPENDIX. "By their fruits ye shall know them." Careful reading of the parallel columns of the pointed Scriptural quotations set forth in the APPENDIX will enable the reader to properly weigh the testimony of the parties hereto and the credibility to which they are entitled.

VIRGINIA'S GOVERNOR SPEAKS Mr. K. B. Stoner, of Fincastle, Botetourt County, Va., a witness on behalf of Pastor Russell in his libel case vs. the *Brooklyn Eagle*, testified that in 1904 he discovered the original stalk of wheat which he afterwards named "Miracle Wheat," growing in his garden; that it matured 142 heads all grown from one grain. He further said, "A good many names were suggested and I finally adopted the name 'Miracle' Wheat (fol. 73-81)." In answer to a question as to who suggested the name, Mr. Stoner replied, "I never saw Pastor Russell in my life until this morning, and never had any correspondence with him in any way. I had no suggestion from him at all; whoever named it (the wheat) was some person connected with me who was interested in the wheat" (fol. 82—Court Record). Mr. Stoner sold this wheat at $1.25 per lb., or $75 per bushel (fol. 162).

As to the character and integrity of Mr. Stoner, we publish the following photographic copy of a letter signed by the Governor of Virginia:

Commonwealth of Virginia
Governor's Office
Richmond

October 22, 1907.

TO WHOM IT MAY CONCERN:

K. B. Stoner, of Fincastle, Botetourt county, Virginia, the originator of the new variety of wheat, is personally known to me, and I unhesitatingly testify to his character and integrity as a man. Any and all statements of fact made by him are entitled to full faith and credit.

Very respectfully,

Governor of Virginia.

AN EDUCATOR'S VIEW

Prof. S. A. Ellis, Southern educator and writer, after review-. ing the works of Pastor Russell, prompted by the slanderous attacks of certain designing clergymen, made a voluntary examination of each of the charges, and then wrote an editorial tribute, which we clip, as follows:

I lift my pen, not in defense of any doctrine, creed or dogma, but in defense of a man, in defense of fairness, justice and righteousness. Pastor C. T. Russell, of Brooklyn, N. Y., stands out prominently as a target for the pulpit and religious press of the country today. I believe there is no one more bitterly persecuted, harshly condemned, wofully misrepresented and misunderstood than this fearless, conscientious man of God.

No infidel writer, such as Hume, Voltaire or Ingersoll, ever suffered such ruthless attacks as have been made upon Pastor Russell.

Whether this persecution and misrepresentation is due to prejudice or ignorance of this man's real character and writing is not for me to say, but I believe both are elements that play a part in the widespread criticism uttered both from the pulpit and the press.

Naturally, men will resent any attack made upon the creed of their persuasion, for they hold to their religious creed and affiliations with more tenacity than they realize, until some strong mind, backed by Scripture proof, begins to uproot their doctrines by showing their inconsistencies and errors.

This is what Pastor Russell proceeds to do. The fact is, very few of us have taken the pains to examine, critically, by the light of the Divine Word, the doctrines handed down to us by our fathers. This accounts for the fact that Methodist parents raise Methodist children and Baptists raise Baptist children, etc.

I am amazed beyond measure to read so many fallacious statements published regarding the character and writings of this man.. He has been called a "gray bearded egotist," a "bigot," a "haberdasher," and many other uncomplimentary terms have been applied to him, and statements made which I know to be without foundation.

He is charged with teaching heresy. An article by a minister was recently published in a religious paper, in which he gave a lengthy criticism of Mr. Russell's writings, referring to them as heresy (apparently forgetting that there was a time when his own denominational views were considered heretical). This article not only misrepresented Mr. Russell, but showed a lack of critical comparison of his writings with the Scriptures.

Mr. Russell was further charged in the same article with denying the Atonement made by Christ between God and man. Nothing could be further from the truth.

Mr. Russell's first sentence in his volume, entitled "The Atonement Between God and Man," is as follows:

"The Atonement lies at the very foundation of the Christian religion." He sets forth the philosophy of the Ransom in such a clear, logical way as has never been done before by any other theologian, presenting such an array of Scriptures as would satisfy any fair-minded, thinking man.

His private life also has been assailed by the same class of critics. These charges also are seen to be without foundation, when we seek the origin of such reports. No one who knows anything of his labors in theological research will ever sneer at Mr. Russell. He is not to be measured by common standards. When you look at his matchless labors, his scholarly attainments, his donations to the world, in his writings, his time, his labor and money spent for the enlightenment of others, all flippant criticism becomes contemptible and mean. Unselfish, liberal and courteous to Christians of all denominations, but fearlessly condemning, in unmeasured terms, the errors and inconsistencies in their creeds, as he sees them, Pastor Russell ranks with immortal benefactors, and is stamping his opinion on the world as no other man has done since the days of the Reformation.

The Congregations of Greater New York City, including Brooklyn and Manhattan, in order to express their disapproval of the many things wrongfully said against Pastor Russell by the nominal ministers and THE BROOKLYN EAGLE, and similar papers, recently passed the following resolu-tions

"Be it Resolved,

By the Congregation of Associated Bible Students of Greater New York, assembled at the Brooklyn Tabernacle this 7th day of April, A. D. 1915, as follows:

That we take this opportunity to unanimously and unqualifiedly express our love and esteem for our beloved Pastor, Charles T. Russell.

That now serving his 7th year as Pastor of this Congregation, we are glad to record that at no Pastoral Election has there been a vote cast against him, nor even a desire to do so.

That we express our deep appreciation of his untiring devotion, faithful service, unselfish and painstaking Pastoral oversight of this Congregation.

That we recognize in him the greatest living exponent of Scriptural Truth. He has devoted his life and all his talents to proclaiming the Gospel of the kingdom of Christ.

That we praise God for having raised him up, and we are grateful for the opportunity of having any part with him in the service of the Lord. We are thankful to bear with him the reproaches that come upon all faithful servants of God.

That we delight to testify to the purity of his life and the sweetness of spirit he always manifests. Ever dignified, but kind; amiable, but firm; sympathetic, yet determined; simple, yet wise; just, yet loving; he stands a tower of strength for Truth and righteousness. We find combined in him the highest elements of Christian character.

That we delight to uphold his hands in the great fight he is making to spread the Truth concerning Messiah's kingdom, throughout the world, and the blessings it will bring to the people.

We hereby certify that the foregoing resolution was unanimously adopted by the Congregation of ASSOCIATED BIBLE STUDENTS of GREATER NEW YORK CITY this 7th day of April, A. D. 1915.

Attest:

[signature]
Secretary.

Dr. L. E. Work
Chairman.

Foreign Speaking Deacons

FRENCH GERMAN DANISH

SWEDISH NORWEGIAN SPANISH

HEBREW GREEK COLORED POLISH

LETTISH ITALIAN SYRIAN ARMENIAN

MORE CHARACTER WITNESSES

We here present the signed testimonials of some well-known gentlemen, residing in various parts of the United States and Canada, who have known Pastor Russell intimately for several years, and whose testimony should far outweigh that of his enemies. Many hundreds more good men, tried and true, would gladly give similar testimony as to the good character of Pastor Russell and the high esteem in which he is held amongst the people who know him, but such would be merely cumulative, hence we limit the number:

Washington, D. C., April 3, 1915.

DEAR MR. RUTHERFORD:

It has come to my attention that you are receiving testimonials concerning Pastor Russell from a number of highly respected gentlemen in various parts of the country who have known Pastor Russell for years and who know his character to be above reproach, and who also are well acquainted with the manner in which he is regarded in their respective communities by people who know him. I beg the privilege of adding my hearty testimony in his favor. I was present at the trial of the libel case of Pastor Russell against the *Washington Post* and know that before that court all the charges made against him were proven untrue.

I regard Pastor Russell as a great benefactor to mankind, and to my personal knowledge he has for many years been unselfishly giving his life in faithful service.

Several years ago I became much interested in Bible study, and was anxious to find out what is the plan of God. I consulted a number of preachers, read a great deal of literature claiming to explain the Bible, but concluded that none of the explanations were satisfactory or reasonable. About the time this conclusion was reached I obtained a copy of the first volume of *Studies in the Scriptures*, never having seen the author or anyone who knew him. Before reading many pages of this wonderful book it became very clear that the writer understood his subject and possessed the faculty of making it plain to others desiring to understand. I learned that he was the author of six volumes, all of which I read. After a careful reading of these books in connection with my Bible I learned for the first time that God has a harmonious plan which He is developing in the interest of mankind, just such a plan as one would expect a great and wise God would have.

I have known Pastor Russell personally for years and have had opportunity to learn of his private life and character. I candidly state that he is the cleanest and purest man with whom I have ever come in contact, and I am sure his life is entirely devoted to the Lord and his service and that he has been and is a great benefactor of mankind.

It gives me pleasure to write this letter, and you are privileged to use it in such a manner as you see fit.

W. P. Hall

Brigadier General, U. S. Army.

52

GENERAL HALL.

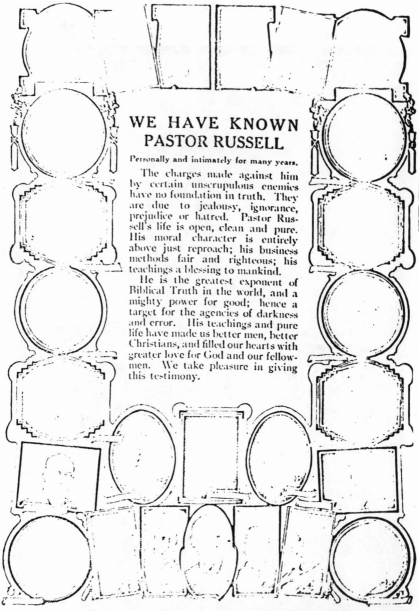

WE HAVE KNOWN PASTOR RUSSELL

Personally and intimately for many years.

The charges made against him by certain unscrupulous enemies have no foundation in truth. They are due to jealousy, ignorance, prejudice or hatred. Pastor Russell's life is open, clean and pure. His moral character is entirely above just reproach; his business methods fair and righteous; his teachings a blessing to mankind.

He is the greatest exponent of Biblical Truth in the world, and a mighty power for good; hence a target for the agencies of darkness and error. His teachings and pure life have made us better men, better Christians, and filled our hearts with greater love for God and our fellowmen. We take pleasure in giving this testimony.

1 A. C. Northrop, Agriculturist, Little Sioux, Ia.; 2. C. H. Ward, Merchant, Cumberland, Md.; 3. R. D. Strickler, Auditor, Buffalo, N. Y.; 4. N. E. Nelson, Manufacturer, Duquesne, Pa.; 5. G. F. Wison, Attorney, Oklahoma City, Okla; 6. W. M. Hizlee, Pomologist, Lima, O.; 7. C. H. Anderson, Merchant, Baltimore, Md.; 8. E. B. Henske, Publisher, Philadelphia, Pa.; 9. G. L. De Frege, Contractor, Dallas, Tex.; 10. H. A. Guepaer, Auditor, Boston, Mass.; 11. B. W. Ritchie, Real Estate, Palmerston, Ont.; 12. J. W Shorney, Manufacturer, Toronto, Ont.; 13. H. M. Litch, Sales Manager, Oakland, Cal.; 14. W. S. Scott, Contractor, Waynesburg, Pa.; 15. G. G. Smith, Secretary to Mayor, Tampa, Fla.; 16. S. T. Apollonio, Manufacturer, Providence, R. I.; 17. R. L. Streeter, Minister, Providence, R. I.; 18. C. E. Kerney, M. D., Dayton, O.; 19. F. P. Sherman, Accountant, Los Angeles, Cal; 20. E. J. Pritchard, Ins. Supt., Lawrence, Mass.; 21. F. W. Manton, Manufacturer, Toronto, Ont.; 22. A. D. Vanderveer, Merchant, Yonkers, N. Y.; 23. C. N. Stem, Stockman, Chicago, Ill.; 24. J. F. Milbourne, Teacher, Elwood, Ind.; 25. A. W. Smith, Div. Engr., Columbus, O.; 26. J. H. Hoeveler, Trav. Rep., St. Louis, Mo.

Portraits of Other Prominent Business Men Who Participated in the Above Testimonial Will Be Found on Pages 32 and 33.

PASTOR RUSSELL REGARDED BY OTHERS—HOW?

In October, 1911, Pastor Russell delivered a lecture at Motherwell, Scotland. On that occasion Professor David Dall, a noted Mental Scientist of the British Institute of Mental Science, for his own pleasure made a character sketch of Pastor Russell, afterward sending him a copy thereof, which appears from the following:

PROF. DALL'S CHARACTER SKETCH
H. M. PHRENOLOGIST

Dear Pastor Russell:

I take pleasure in sending you herewith a character sketch of yourself as a souvenir of your visit to Motherwell, which please accept with my best wishes.

It is a source of great satisfaction to me that you have been spared so long. I prize your worth and esteem you very highly. I earnestly hope that the best of Divine blessing may continue to descend upon you, and that our Heavenly Father may still grant you many useful and happy years. Yours faithfully, DAVID DALL,

(Of the British Institute of Mental Science, etc. H. M. Phrenologist).

BRIEF PHRENOGRAPH OF PASTOR RUSSELL
(Taken in Town Hall, Motherwell, Scotland, October 30th, 1911,
by Prof. David Dall, D. Ph., Mental Scientist.)

I have much pleasure in giving a sketch of the genial and fatherly head and physiognomy of Pastor Russell. He is just one of those men whose appearance, intelligence, suavity, wit, goodness of heart and soundness of head do credit to his profession. Well up in years, he has a youthful, kindly and sympathetic nature; fatherly and benign in counsel, moral and spiritual in his influence. In religion his "doxy" is broadened by the effulgent light of Bible study. His temperamental development is very even. If there is a predominance of either, it is found in the motive, which supports an intense energy of mind that cannot dream life away, but must be practical.

I find the head of Pastor Russell to be a large one, and the brain gifted with an uncommon degree of activity. A full basilar region is accompanied by the powerful endowment of the moral, intellectual and spiritual natures. His physiognomy gives a large face, a large, broad nose with ample nostrils, large mouth and chin—all that the face can indicate of a powerful constitution he has. The animal vital nature, as a whole, is amply developed; his head also is broad, which indicates general force of mind, strength of feeling and stamina of character. His eyes are large and stand out fully, which indicates a communicative disposition.

Benevolence is a leading faculty, manifesting itself in liberality of sentiment to all mankind, deep desire for the welfare of others, combining warmth of sympathy with rare simplicity of purpose. His perceptive region, as a whole, is exceedingly active, an endowment rendering his range of observation extraordinary; while his memory of faces and forms is marvelous, as is also his power to analyze, compare and draw rapid inferences. Here is a mind able to steel itself against difficulty or attack, yet full of gentleness and amiability. An intense sense of duty, together with the conviction that each moment is precious and of important value, seems to pervade his entire nature. In him dwells the soul of a patient, charitable, but equally determined reformer—a practical mind, seeing far

55

ahead, possessing large stores of philanthropy, discernment, judgment, talent and efficiency, giving him gifts as a teacher, yet also prompting him to natural desire after self-improvement. His natural refinement, taste and imagination, with large language, qualify him to express himself in a free, easy, graceful style, enabling him to present many unpleasant truths in a pleasing and acceptable manner.

As a preacher of the Gospel, his services have found a wide acceptance. As a lecturer he is especially successful. He is not a violent or enthusiastic orator. He is an effective, quiet, illustrative speaker—arresting and riveting the attention of children as well as adults. The young find in him a "guide, philosopher and friend"—the old a sage counselor whose thoughts are tinctured by experience and perfected by principle. Under such a mentor souls grow and minds expand, observation becomes keener and the perceptions sharper. He has great magnetic force, is full of electricity, and consequently he imparts life and vivacity to every word he utters, whether in public or private. Pastor Russell impresses and controls the minds of his hearers without making an effort to do so, for his utterances are like sparks that kindle a fire in the souls of those who listen to him.

PROF. C. PIAZZI SMYTH'S LETTER OF COMMENDATION.

Mr. William M. Wright, of Pittsburgh, learning that Pastor Russell was preparing a chapter of one of his books treating the Great Pyramid of Egypt, procured a copy of the manuscript and mailed it to Prof. C. Piazzi Smyth, F. R. S. E., F. R. A. S., ex-Astronomer Royal of Scotland. Prof. Smyth's reply follows and is self-explanatory:

Clova, Ripon, England, Dec. 21, 1890.

Wm. M. Wright, Esq.,

DEAR SIR:—I have been rather longer than I could have wished in looking over the MS. of your friend, C. T. Russell, of Allegheny, Pa., but I have now completed a pretty careful examination, word by word. And that was the least I could do, when you so kindly took the pains to send it with such care between boards by registered parcel, with every page flat, and indited by the typewriter in place of the hand.

At first I could only find slips of the said typewriter, but as I progressed through the pages the powers, the specialties and the originalities of the Author came out magnificently; and there were not a few passages I should have been glad to take a copy of for quotation, with name, in the next possible edition of my own Pyramid book. But, of course, I did nothing of that sort, and shall wait with perfect patience and in most thankful mood of mind for when the author of *Millennial Dawn* shall choose his own time for publishing.

So I merely remark here that he is both good and new in much that he says on the chronology of various parts of the Pyramid, especially the First Ascending Passage and its granite plug; on the Grand Gallery, as illustrating the Lord's life; on the parallelisms between the King's Chamber and its granite, against the Tabernacle and its gold; and generally on the confirmations or close agreements between Scripture and the Great Pyramid, well commented on.

In the meanwhile, it seems that I am indebted to you for your kind gift long ago of the first two volumes of *Millennial Dawn*. I did not at the time get further than the first half of the first volume, finding the matter, as I thought, not quite so new as I had expected. But after having profited, as I hope, so much by a thorough reading of this advanced Pyramid chapter of the third volume, I must take up the first two volumes again, de novo.

The parcel will go back between its boards, registered. I remain, with many thanks,   Yours respectfully,   C. PIAZZI SMYTH.

A MINISTER'S OPINION.

The Paxton, Illinois, *Daily Record* recently published the following letter addressed to that paper by Rev. W. S. Garlough, Pastor of Christian Church, Bloomington, Illinois:

"I have read a number of articles in the *Christian Standard* during the past few months concerning *Millennial Dawnism* as taught by Pastor Russell. We have all heard the criticism of the Pilgrim Fathers, how, having left their own country and endured all sorts of hardships for the sake of religious freedom, they themselves became the worst of bigots and persecutors of those who later disagreed with them. The treatment accorded Pastor Russell by the disciples of Christ is very similar to the actions of those early fathers. Since reading Pastor Russell's *Studies in the Scriptures* (the first and fifth volumes more than once), I have read all the articles and tracts against his teachings I could find. In not a single instance does the writer reply in the same Christian spirit which characterizes Pastor Russell's writings. In some instances the writer resorted to the only weapon left to the man without an argument—ridicule. Others either willingly misrepresent his teachings or do not know what he does teach. As a rule they do not touch upon the real subject matter of his *Studies*, but attack some minor subject that Russell himself would not hold as a matter of faith, but as being of a more or less speculative character.

"To my mind Pastor Russell presents the most Scriptural, clear and soul-satisfying conception of the person of Jesus I have ever heard or read. The same is true of Man, his Creation, his Experience with Sin, God's Plan for his Redemption, the Gospel of Jesus Christ, and Man's Future Destiny. Now, if any good brother feels that Pastor Russell's books are doing the Church of Christ harm let him read his books (all six *Studies*) carefully, prayerfully, once, twice or a dozen times, if it need be, until he knows he has the author's thought, challenging every doctrinal thought until it is proven by the Open Book, then just as carefully, prayerfully, and with the Christian spirit shown by Pastor Russell, let him take up his task, and in a logical, Scriptural way, step by step, show his brethren that the teaching of Pastor Russell is incorrect. Then will he have done something worth while. But so long as Pastor Russell is attacked in the present manner no one who has read his *Studies* will be convinced of the error therein, if error there be. Let no brother deceive himself into thinking that he can successfully thwart the teaching of the six volumes of *Scripture Studies* in a few articles in the *Christian Standard*, or even in a tract such as Haldeman's and others.

"One thing Pastor Russell's books will do, if carefully read by any earnest, thoughtful Christian, is that they will promote Bible study more and more. The reader will proportionately lose his interest in worldly things. It will not be necessary to preach to him that he should not go to the theatre, play cards, or dance, for he will have no desire to do those things, as well as many other things in which most Christian people indulge. It will not be necessary to solicit money from him for the Lord's work; it will be forthcoming without solicitation. It would seem that until some brother is able to present the Gospel and provide 'meat in due season' that does this work as well as Russell's *Studies in the Scriptures* it might be well to look inward for the beam, not outward for the mote, and let his *Studies* continue to do that which most preachers admit they are not able to accomplish. *Give Pastor Russell a square deal!*

"W. S. GARLOUGH, Pastor Christian Church, Bloomington, Ill."

Copy of a letter sent to Rev. Moorehead, author of a book attacking Pastor Russell and his doctrines, comes to our attention. We have not learned if it received a reply. The spirit of the letter is kind and moderate, hence we publish it. It is in marked contrast with the various slanderous attacks made upon Pastor Russell by his several ministerial enemies. The letter follows:

Rev. William G. Moorehead, D.D.

Dear Dr. Moorehead:

I read some time ago your article in the seventh volume of Fundamentals on the teachings of Mr. C. T. Russell. I felt like writing you at that time but did not. Recently I read the summary of your article in one of my religious papers and have had an increasing impression to write you. I hesitate to do so because of the high regard I have always had for you as one of my teachers of twenty years ago, and also because of the high esteem in which you are held in the company of Biblical expositors and Christian workers in general. Yet I feel also that in the interest of truth and fairness your article should have some attention.

I feel that this article from your pen is unworthy of a man like you. I cannot understand why such a careful student as yourself should make statements such as you make in this article, when they are so manifestly and greatly in error.

In addition to reading five of the six volumes of his "Studies" carefully, and the sixth volume in part, I have also read many other pamphlets, magazine articles and sermons of Pastor Russell, and also every criticism I have found or heard of in opposition to his teachings. I was one of his critics for about fifteen years, and I based my criticisms upon reading about half of one chapter of one of his books. A few years ago it occurred to me that I might not understand his full thought, so I took time to inform myself on the subject I had been criticising, and when I obtained more information I became an admirer of his work, though I do not agree with him in all his conclusions. I have reached the conclusion concerning the authors of the criticisms that I have read that they do not know any more about Pastor Russell's teachings than I did in the days when I was so liberal with my condemnation. They all remind me of the testimony of the two witnesses who offered testimony before the Jewish council when Jesus was on trial. They said, "We heard him say: 'I will destroy this temple that is made with hands, and within three days I will build another made without hands.'" Now Jesus had said something like that—though essentially different. These critics seem to have read Pastor Russell's works with the same methods and motives that Thomas Paine, Robert Ingersoll and others of their class read the Scriptures and criticised them. This seems very unfortunate since it has been done by men who have been eminent for Christian character and leaders of Christian thought.

Coming now to your article: I cannot take up all the mistakes you have made in this, but will confine myself to those lying on the surface. In the opening sentence you assure us that in the series there are "six rather bulky volumes, comprising in all some two thousand pages." On page 123 you speak of "a careful reading of these volumes," so we conclude that you have read them all carefully. (This is what you should have done before putting yourself on record in criticism of them.) I note that in your reference to and quotations from these books you confine yourself to the first three volumes, and chiefly to the first two. I note also that you quote a single sentence, or part of a paragraph, giving only a partial presentation of the author's thought, and then proceed to criticise it. This is a most unfair method. It reminds me of an article I read a few years ago in which the writer was opposing the doctrine of the total depravity of man, and as a proof text he quoted John 9:3, "Neither hath this man sinned, nor his parents," and said Jesus taught that here were at least three persons who had never sinned. Your method with Pastor Russell is identical.

Under the heading, "Ninth Error," in your article, you say: "One of these, the ninth error, essential and fundamental in Christianity, is the person and work of the Holy Spirit. There is a strange and ominous silence regarding this most important subject very apparent in the writings of Pastor Russell. A careful reading of those volumes, comprising more than one thousand pages, has discovered but one solitary reference to the Spirit; it is a casual mention of the Spirit in connection with the Day of Pentecost. The statement is simply made as a historic fact, or rather as an event which marks a stage in the development of the Christian Church. Not one word of teaching has the writer found in Pastor Russell's works as to the distinct personality of the Spirit, or as to His supreme agency in the salvation of sinners."

Now I must say frankly, though courteously, that I cannot understand how, or why, a man with your record for accuracy could be so careless or dishonest as to make such a statement. In your opening statement you say, "There are six volumes of two thousand pages;" and here you say that you have given these volumes a careful reading, and count but ONE thousand pages, and then you make a bold and erroneous statement—that the author ignores the Holy Spirit! A judge would not think of rendering a verdict with only half the evidence in, but you speak boldly in condemnation of Pastor Russell when you are only half way through his books. Now, if you have given these volumes a "careful reading," I do not see how you missed in the fifth volume, pages 163 to 300, where the author gives ONE HUNDRED AND THIRTY-SEVEN PAGES to a full presentation of the person and work of the Holy Spirit, in connection with the redemption of the race of man. How can you explain this?

It is true that Pastor Russell may teach some things concerning the Holy Spirit that you will not agree with, but he does not ignore the Spirit, as you say he does. It is evident that in making this criticism you were careless, to say the least, and this should make those who are seeking the Truth very cautious about accepting your statements without verification.

Another mistake which lies on the surface in your article is found on page 125, where, in reference to Pastor Russell's lecture on the subject of "To Hell and Back," you say: "Crowds have listened with no little satisfaction to his assertions that there is no hell, no eternal punishment, no hopelessness after death." Now I have not heard Pastor Russell speak at any time, nor have I read this particular lecture, but if he in this lecture teaches that there is no hell, and no punishment for the finally impenitent, then he in this lecture flatly contradicts what is very clear in all his writings. I have never read an expositor who speaks with more clearness and earnestness of the eternal punishment to be meted out to the finally impenitent. It is true that he does not believe in a literal lake of fire of burning brimstone, and that men are eternally tortured in this, but in this he is not out of harmony with thousands of other good, orthodox teachers.

Now, in closing, I want to say that you need have no concern about one of your pupils following Pastor Russell. I have his books in my library and consult them freely, as I do every other good expositor I can find, and afford to buy. I have passed beyond the early stage of the disciples who wanted to forbid some to teach or cast out devils because they "follow not US." I have received unlimited aid from you, and also from Pastor Russell. I do not feel like saying with you that he is "being used of the evil one to subvert the Truth of God." My church officials still regard me as sufficiently orthodox that they can go to sleep and allow me to continue preaching to the congregation.

With kindest regards for you and highest appreciation of the help I have received from you, I am,

Yours in His service,

(REV.) T. S. THOMPSON—*N. Dak*

Secretary Samaritan Institute.

APPENDIX

The Divine Measuring Rod.

To enable the reader to more completely measure the parties to the controversy hereinbefore described, and to determine the weight to be given the testimony of each, we append hereto some pertinent Biblical quotations. The Divine measuring rod is always the infallible one—"By their fruits ye shall know them."

These Scripture texts, assembled by C. J. Woodworth, compiler of the International Bible Students' Manual, show, in "deadly parallel," who are the servants of Satan and who are the servants of God.

"Know ye not, that to whom ye yield yourselves servants to obey, his servants ye are to whom ye obey?"—Rom. 6:16.

WHOSE SERVANTS ARE THESE?

Lovers of Money.

"The priests thereof teach for hire."—Micah 3:11.

"Pharisees, hypocrites! for ye devour widows' houses."—Matt. 23: 14.

"Teaching things which they ought not, for filthy lucre's sake."—Tit. 1:11.

"Shepherds that cannot understand; they all look to their own way, every one for his gain."—Isa. 56:11.

"Feed the flock . . . not for filthy lucre."—1 Pet. 5:2.

"I have coveted no man's silver or gold."—Acts 20:33.

"He that hath no money; come ye . . . without money and without price."—Isa. 55:1.

"Jesus went into the temple of God and cast out all them that sold and bought in the temple."—Matt. 21: 12.

Lovers of Titles.

"His watchmen are blind; . . . they are all D——D——s."—Isa. 56:10.

"As being lords over God's heritage."—1 Pet. 5:3.

"And love the uppermost rooms at feasts, and the chief seats in the synagogues, and greetings in the markets, and to be called of men Rabbi, Rabbi."—Matt. 23:6, 7.

"He that humbleth himself shall be exalted."—Luke 18:14.

"Praise ye Jehovah, . . . reverend is His name."—Psa. 111:1, 9.

"Call no man your father upon the earth; for one is your Father, which is in Heaven. Neither be ye called masters; for one is your Master, even Christ."—Matt. 23:9, 10.

Lovers of Church Federation.

"Behold, they shall surely gather together, but not by Me."—Isa. 54:15.

"For a certain man named Demetrius, a silversmith (typifying the money-loving clergy), ... brought no small gain unto the craftsmen; whom he called together with the workmen of like occupation, and said, Sirs, ye know that by this craft we have our wealth."—Acts 19:24, 25.

"Associate yourselves, O ye people, and ye shall be broken in pieces."—Isa. 8:9.

"Gird yourselves and ye shall be broken in pieces. Take counsel together and it shall come to naught; speak the word and it shall not stand. . . . Say ye not a confederacy, to all them to whom this people shall say, A confederacy; neither fear ye their fear."—Isa. 8:9, 10, 12.

Lovers of Ignorance.

"I will send a famine in the land, not a famine of bread, nor a thirst for water, but of hearing the words of the Lord."—Amos 8:11.

"My people are destroyed for lack of knowledge; because thou hast rejected knowledge, I will also reject thee, that thou shalt be no priest to me; seeing thou hast forgotten the Law of thy God."—Hos. 4:6.

"And the vision of all is become unto you as the words of a book that is sealed, which men deliver to one that is learned, saying, Read this, I pray thee; and he saith, I cannot; for it is sealed."—Isa. 29:11.

"If ye continue in My Word, then are ye My disciples indeed; and ye shall know the truth and the truth shall make you free."—John 8: 31, 32.

"In that hour Jesus rejoiced in spirit, and said, I thank Thee, O Father, Lord of Heaven and earth, that Thou hast hid these things from the wise and prudent, and hast revealed them unto babes."—Luke 10:21.

"But God hath revealed them unto us by His Spirit; for the Spirit searcheth all things, yea, the deep things of God . . . the things that are freely given unto us of God, which things also we speak."—1 Cor. 2:10, 12, 13.

Lovers of Human Ordination.

"Which receive honor one of another, and seek not the honor that cometh from God only."—John 5:44.

"Nor of men sought we neither of you, nor yet of o:.—1 Thessalonians 2:6.

Lovers of Long Prayers.

"Pharisees, hypocrites! ye for a pretense make long prayers."—Matt. 23:14.

"God is in Heaven, and thou upon earth; therefore let thy words be few."—Eccl. 5:2.

Lovers of Slander.

"Whosoever hateth his brother is a murderer."—1 John 3:15.

"They shall reproach you and cast out your name as evil."—Luke 6:22.

"Deceit is in the heart of them that imagine evil."—Prov. 12:20.

"An evil man, out of the evil treasure, bringeth forth evil things."—Matt. 12:35.

"Speak not evil one of another, brethren." "Speak evil of no man."—Jas. 4:11; Tit. 3:2.

"He that hideth hatred with lying lips, and he that uttereth a slander is a fool."—Prov. 10:18.

"A wicked doer giveth heed to false lips; and a liar giveth ear to a naughty tongue."—Prov. 17:4.

"Doth a fountain send forth at the same place sweet water and bitter?"—James 3:11.

"Full of envy, murder, debate, deceit, malignity; whisperers, back-

"We ought to lay down our lives for the brethren."—1 John 3:16.

"But I say unto you, love your enemies, bless them that curse you."—Matt. 5:44.

"Love suffereth long and is kind; . . . thinketh no evil."—1 Cor. 13:4, 5.

"A good man ,out of the good treasure of the heart, bringeth forth good things."—Matt. 12:35.

"I will take heed to my ways, that I sin not with my tongue."—Psa. 39:1.

"We know that we have passed from death unto life, because we love the brethren."—1 John 3:14.

"The tongue of the wise is health. The lip of truth shall be established forever."—Prov. 12:18, 19.

"He was oppressed, and He was afflicted, yet He opened not His mouth."—Isa. 53:7.

"Love rejoiceth not in iniquity, but rejoiceth in the truth; beareth all

biters, haters of God, despiteful, proud, boasters."—Rom. 1:29, 30.

"Their throat is an open sepulchre; with their tongues they have used deceit; the poison of asps is under their lips."—Rom. 3:13.

"Whoso privily slandereth his neighbor, him will I cut off; him that hath a high look and a proud heart will not I suffer."—Psa. 101:5.

"Report, say they, and we will report it. All my familiars watched for my halting, saying, Peradventure he will be enticed, and we shall prevail against him and we shall take our revenge."—Jer. 20:10.

things . . . endureth all things."—1 Cor. 13:6, 7.

"My doctrine shall drop as the rain, My speech shall distil as the dew, as the small rain upon the tender herb and as the showers upon the grass."—Deut. 32:2.

"Let the words of my mouth, and the meditations of my heart, be acceptable in Thy sight, O Lord, my strength and my Redeemer."—Psa. 19:14.

"Lord, who shall abide in Thy tabernacle? He . . . that speaketh the truth in his heart, he that backbiteth not with his tongue nor taketh up a reproach against his neighbor."—Psa. 15:1-3.

Lovers of Self.

"They are greedy dogs, which can never have enough."—Isa. 56:11.

"All their works they do for to be seen of men."—Matt. 23:5.

"Having men's persons in admiration, because of advantage."—Jude 16.

'His watchmen are blind . . . sleeping, lying down, loving to slumber."—Isa. 56:10.

"They bind heavy burdens and grievous to be borne, and lay them on men's shoulders, but they themselves will not move them with one of their fingers."—Matt. 23:4.

"Woe be to the shepherds of Israel that do feed themselves! Should not the shepherds feed the flocks? Ye eat the fat, and ye clothe you with the wool, ye kill them that are fed; but ye feed not the flock. The diseased have ye not strengthened, neither have ye healed that which was sick, neither have ye bound up that which was broken, neither have ye brought again that which was driven away, neither have ye sought that which was lost."—Ezek. 34:2-4.

"Be content with such things as ye have."—Heb. 13:5.

"Let not thy left hand know what thy right hand doeth."—Matt. 6:3.

"Hath not God chosen the poor of this world?"—James 2:5.

"Therefore, let us not sleep, as do others; but let us watch."—1 Thess. 5:6.

"Ye remember, brethren, our labor and travail; for laboring night and day, because we would not be chargeable unto you, we preached unto you the Gospel."—1 Thess. 2:9.

"Take heed therefore unto yourselves, and to all the flock . . . to feed the Church of God . . . I have coveted no man's silver, or gold, or apparel. Yea, ye yourselves know that these hands have ministered unto my necessities, and to them that were with me. I have showed you all things, how that so laboring ye ought to support the weak, and to remember the words of the Lord Jesus, how He said, It is more blessed to give than to receive."—Acts 20:28, 33-35.

Lovers of Nightmares.

"Because ye have said, We have made a covenant with death, and with hell are we at agreement."—Isa. 28:15.

"O death, I will be thy plagues; O Sheol (hell), I will be thy destruction."—Hosea 13:14.

"Lying children . . . which say, Prophesy not unto us right things, speak unto us smooth things, prophesy deceits."—Isa. 30:9, 10.

"His watchmen are blind, they are all ignorant; they are all dumb dogs, they can not bark, talking in their sleep."—Isa. 56:10 (margin.)

"Pharisees, hypocrites! for ye shut up the Kingdom of Heaven against men; for ye neither go in yourselves, neither suffer ye them that are entering to go in."—Matt. 23:13.

"In the latter days ye shall consider it perfectly. I have not sent these prophets, yet they ran; I have not spoken to them, yet they prophesied . . . Behold, I am against them that prophesy false dreams, saith the Lord, and do tell them, and cause My people to err by their lies and by their lightness."—Jer. 23:20, 21, 32.

"And the heads of the horses (hobby horses—creeds of the dark ages) were as the heads of lions; and out of their mouth issued (sermons on) fire and smoke and brimstone. By these three was the third part of men killed (stupefied, asphyxiated) by the (threats of) fire and by the smoke and by the brimstone which issued out of their *mouths,* for their power is in their *mouth.*" "If any man worship the (papal) beast and his (protestant) image, and receive his mark in his forehead (mind) or in his hand (pocketbook) the same shall drink of the wrath of God, which is poured out without mixture into the cup of His indignation, and he shall be tormented with (nightmares of) fire and brimstone."—Rev. 9:17-19; 14:9, 10.

"If any man speak, let him speak as the oracles of God . . . that God in all things may be glorified."— 1 Pet. 4:11.

"The prophet that hath a dream, let him tell a dream, and he that hath My Word, let him speak My Word faithfully."—Jer. 23:28.

"What is my reward then? Verily that when I preach the Gospel, I may make the Gospel of Christ without charge . . . that I might by all means save some."—1 Cor. 9:18,22.

"From a child thou hast known the Holy Scriptures, which are able to make thee wise unto salvation through faith which is in Christ Jesus, . . . profitable for doctrine, for reproof, for instruction in righteousness, that the man of God may be perfect, thoroughly furnished unto all good works."—2 Tim. 3: 15-17.

"Beloved, let us love one another; for love is of God; and every one that loveth is begotten of God, and knoweth God. He that loveth not, knoweth not God; for God is love. In this was manifested the love of God toward us, because that God sent His only begotten Son into the world, that we might live through Him. Herein is love, not that we loved God, but that He loved us, and sent His Son to be the propitiation for our sins. Beloved, if God so loved us, we ought also to love one another . . . There is no fear in love; but perfect love casteth out fear; because fear hath torment. He that feareth is not made perfect in love. We love Him because He first loved us."—1 John 4:7-11, 18, 19.

Lovers of Czars, Popes and Kaisers.

"The kings of the earth who have committed fornication (union of church and state) and lived deliciously with her."—Rev. 18:9.

"Saying peace, peace, when there is no peace." "Come ye, say they . . . tomorrow shall be as this day and much more abundant." "She saith in her heart, I sit a queen, and am no widow, and shall see no sorrow." "And thou saidst I shall be a lady forever; so that thou didst

"I have espoused you to one husband, that I may present you as a Chaste Virgin to Christ."—2 Cor. 11:2.

"Prepare war, wake up the mighty men." (Joel 3:9.) "For thus saith the Lord God of Israel unto me: Take the cup of this fury at My hand and cause all the nations, to whom I send thee, to drink it. And they shall drink and be moved, and be mad, because of the sword that

not lay these things to thy heart ... thou that art given to pleasures, that dwellest carelessly, that sayest in thy heart, I am, and none else beside me: I shall not sit as a widow, neither shall I know the loss of children."—Jer. 8:11; Isa. 56:12; Rev. 18:7; Isa. 47:7, 8.

I will send among them . . . all the kings of the north, far and near, one with another and *all* the kingdoms of the world, which are upon the face of the earth . . . Drink ye, and be drunken, and spue, and fall, and rise no more, because of the sword which I will send among you."—Jer. 25:15, 16, 26, 27.

"Yea, the stork in the heaven knoweth her appointed times; and the turtle and the crane and the swallow observe the time of their coming; but My people know not the judgment of the Lord . . . The pen of the scribes is in vain. The wise men are ashamed, they are dismayed and taken; lo, they have rejected the Word of the Lord; and what wisdom is in them?"—Jer. 8:7-9.

"Let us be glad and rejoice and give honor to Him, for the marriage of the Lamb is come, and His Wife hath made herself ready. And to her was granted that she should be arrayed in fine linen, clean and white; for the fine linen is the righteousness of saints; and He saith unto me, Write, blessed are they which are called unto the Marriage supper."—Rev. 19:7-9.

No one who is familiar with the work Pastor Russell is doing can read the foregoing Scriptures thoughtfully without understanding why he is most cordially hated (and lied about) by those whose shortcomings, as a class, are being exposed. It is a case of ONE MAN against the crowd. Probably, in due time, the crowd will succeed in securing his measurable defeat; any other outcome would be strange; but, BUT! B-U-T !.

"Speak, history! who are life's victors? Unroll
    thy long annals and say,
Are they those whom the world called the
    victors, who won the success of a day?
The martyrs, or Nero? The Spartans who fell
    at Thermopylae's tryst,
Or the Persians and Xerxes? His judges, or
    Socrates? Pilate, or Christ?"—
                    W. W. Story.

This pamphlet postpaid to any address:—
Ten Cents per Copy.
Eight Dollars per Hundred
By freight or express collect Five Dollars per Hundred.   Address:
J. F. RUTHERFORD, Box 51,
New York City, U. S. A.

MILLIONS NOW LIVING WILL NEVER DIE!

!   !

Published by International
Bible Students Association
Brooklyn, New York, U.S.A.

THIS BOOK IS
DEDICATED
TO THE PEOPLE
NOW LIVING ON EARTH
WHO DESIRE
LIFE, LIBERTY AND HAPPINESS

J. F. RUTHERFORD

PREFATORY

Judge J. F. Rutherford,
Brooklyn, N. Y.

Dear Sir:

The advance proof pages of your brochure, "Millions Now Living Will Never Die," which you kindly allowed me to read, have proved to be even more interesting than hoped for, and I embrace this early opportunity to express to you my sincere appreciation of the work.

The admirable way in which you have marshalled the sayings of the Lord Jesus, of the apostles, and of the prophets of old, and supported them by abundant secular evidence, all going to show that a time would come when millions then living would never die—and that we are now living in that time—will inspire hope and confidence in the mind of every honest, truth-seeking reader.

As the one who had the esteemed privilege of syndicating Pastor Russell's sermons in thousands of newspapers in many lands, I was naturally anxious to know how you would treat the prophecies so often referred to in Pastor Russell's sermons. I am glad, indeed, to note that you treat the major part of your evidence from the standpoint of *fulfilled* prophecy. For one, I am glad that you gathered such an array of evidence to substantiate your claims and to show the people, as a basis for a worth-while hope, how they may live for ever. It will not be necessary for anyone to consider your statements as a guess.

Again thanking you and wishing you rich eternal blessings for your labor of love, I subscribe myself as
    Yours in the best of bonds,
        G. C. DRISCOLL

Santa Monica, Calif., May 17, 1920.

TABLE of CONTENTS

Divine Plan for Human Redemption 8

Human History Divided into Three Great Epochs 9

Second Epoch, or World, Now Passing Away 12

Times of the Gentiles 13

Our Lord's Testimony as to the Signs of the End 16

Corroborative Testimony from the Old Testament 19

Period of Israel's Exile from Palestine 22

Zionism, Its Origin and Purpose 29

The Balfour Declaration 33

Jews Rebuilding Palestine 34

Other Evidences that the World Has Ended 39

The Interchurch World Movement 45

Distress and Perplexity World-Wide 57

Spiritism's Part in Current Events 59

The League of Nations 62

Ecclesiastical Remedy for Human Woes 63

The Divine Remedy and Promised Redemption 68

The Ransomer and the Ransom Price 73

What It Means to be a Christian 77

Religious Persecution from the Serpent's Seed 82

The Incoming Messianic Kingdom 85

Israel's Jubilee System a Type of the Kingdom 87

Beginning of Reconstruction Work of the New Order 90

Why Millions Now Living Will Not Die 92

How to Live Forever 94

Evidences of Restoration Work 100

An Appeal to the Clergy 103

Millions Now Living Will Never Die

THE emphatic announcement that millions now living on earth will never die must seem presumptuous to many people; but when the evidence is carefully considered I believe that almost every fair mind will concede that the conclusion is a reasonable one.

For nearly nineteen hundred years Christians have been looking forward to a time coming when life everlasting will be offered to all the peoples of earth. Their expectations and hopes have been based upon the combined testimony of the inspired prophets of old—from Moses to John—upon the testimony of Jesus of Nazareth, the Son of the living God, and upon the testimony of his inspired apostles.

About 4,000 years ago God made a promise to Abraham in which he said that he would bless Abraham and through his seed all the families of the earth should be blessed. Not only did he make this promise, but he bound it with his oath; and St. Paul plainly tells us that these two things, God's word and oath, are unchangeable, and that his promises must be fulfilled. Based upon that oathbound promise and subsequent like promises made to the offspring of Abraham, devout Jews of the world have since looked forward to the time coming when bless-

ings of life and happiness eternal will be offered
to mankind.

Today the eyes of orthodox Jews of earth are
fixed upon Palestine. They are looking up and
lifting up their heads and the hope is springing
into millions of hearts that the time is at hand
for the regathering of the Jews to Palestine
and the establishment there of a state or government of the Jews and for the Jews, according
to the divine arrangement. Since the time of
Abraham they have looked for the Messiah,
but have not yet discerned who constitutes the
Messiah.

Life everlasting in a state of happiness is the
greatest desire of all men. Whether men have
faith or not in the divine promises, each one
would be glad to know for a certainty that there
was before him life everlasting in a happy state.
In view of this strong desire, and of the cumulative evidence given by the holy men of old concerning such coming blessings, it seems strange
that more people have not tried to inform themselves upon the subject. The reason, as assigned
by the Apostle Paul, is that "the god of this
world [Satan, the invisible ruler of the present
social order of things] hath blinded the minds
of those who are perishing, lest the glorious
glad tidings of Christ Jesus, who is the image
of God, should shine into their hearts".—2 Corinthians 4:4.

Many men of ability in the past centuries
have entered the Christian ministry. The great

adversary, knowing their vulnerable points, has used others to flatter and cajole them and to turn their minds toward worldly things; and by far the greater number of these clergymen, yielding to the baneful and seductive influence of the adversary, have themselves turned away from the Bible, and have blindly led the people in the wrong direction. They seem to have lost sight entirely of the fact that God has a great plan which he is causing to work out in an orderly, majestic manner. But the hour has struck when the people shall know the truth, and they that know the truth shall be made free from the bondage of ignorance and superstition and their minds shall be turned into the channels leading to unending joy.

It is the purpose of the writer to try to turn the minds of the people to a careful and prayerful consideration of the divine promises. It is to be deeply regretted that the clergymen would oppose an effort to teach the people the Bible truths; nevertheless, we find much opposition everywhere, and many clergymen will attempt to prevent the people from reading what is here written. We, therefore, assure the reader that we have no ulterior motive in putting out this message. It is not propaganda. There is no desire nor effort to induce the reader to join anything. The motive for this publication is wholly unselfish. The writer has but one desire and that is to induce the people to read and rely upon the divine promises and thus fix their hearts and minds in this hour of distress upon mankind; to comfort those that mourn and point them to a better day which is near at hand.

We should have in mind that the great, all-wise Creator has been now for more than 4,000 years dealing with certain people, preparatory to bringing to every man an opportunity for life everlasting. If he whose wisdom is perfect would devote so much time and energy to the outworking of a great plan, then surely it is worthy of the careful and painstaking examination and consideration of every man, without regard to his creed, religious training, or his political view.

Since the days of Abraham many men of unusual intellect not only have diligently studied the divine plan, but have devoted their lives to having a part in making it known to others. There were twenty-four holy prophets, whose messages are recorded in the Bible. All of these foretold a coming time of great blessings to the human race. Their utterances were not their own, but they spake as the spirit of Jehovah moved upon them. It was impossible for a human mind to look down through the corridors of the ages and to foretell what the future would bring forth; but these various prophets, guided by the all-wise Creator who knew the end from the beginning, wrote and spake merely as the instruments of God. God never failed in one of his promises. He says, "For I am the Lord, I change not". (Malachi 3:6) "There hath not

failed one word of all his good promise." (1
Kings 8:56) All students of the Bible agree
that the time must come when every promise of
Jehovah will be fulfilled. Jehovah does everything orderly and on time and exactly in *his own*
due time, and not man's due time. One day with
him is as a thousand years and a thousand years
as one day; and what might seem to man a long
deferred fulfillment of a promise would be to
God only a question of a very brief space of time.

All students of the Bible also agree that it has
pleased Jehovah to divide the social order of
things existing from the beginning of the world
into epochs, which epochs we call worlds, and
which the Lord speaks of as worlds—such a use
of the word "world" meaning a social order of
things existing within a given period of time.
For nearly nineteen centuries students of divine
prophecy have expected and looked for the world
to end, because Jesus taught it would end. Many
Christian men, however, failing to recognize
the distinction between the symbolic and literal
phrases of the Bible, have been confused concerning the end of the world. For instance, the
great John Calvin taught that upon the happening of that event Jesus, reappearing near the
earth, would cause fire to be emitted from the
clouds, setting the earth aflame and totally
destroying it and everything on it. He being a
clergyman of great renown was supposed to
have based his conclusions upon a proper
interpretation of the Bible, and great numbers

believed his teaching; and for this reason, with
fear and trepidation, many have looked forward
to the ending of the world.

Reason would lead us to the conclusion that
Jehovah would not create a wonderful earth
like this, permit man to bring it to a high state
of cultivation in many places, and then completely destroy it. Such is wholly out of harmony with his character. Likewise such is
wholly out of harmony with the plain teachings
of his Word, which says: "The earth abideth
forever". (Ecclesiastes 1:4) "For thus saith
the Lord that created the heavens; God himself
that formed the earth and made it; he hath
established it, he created it not in vain, he formed it to be inhabited." (Isaiah 45:18) When the
Bible speaks of the *world* ending it does not
mean the literal earth, but it does refer to an
epoch or dispensation of time during which a
certain arrangement of things or social order
exists. In proof of this the Scriptures disclose
that there was a "world" which existed from the
time of Eden until the great deluge: "Whereby
the world that then was, being overflowed with
water, perished." (2 Peter 3:6) At the end of
the flood a new "world" began, and the promise
is made by the same Scriptural writer that it
shall end. The period of that world is from the
flood until the coming of Messiah's kingdom,
and his kingdom is to mark the beginning of
another new world or new order of things.

The first world, then, began with the creation

of man and ended with the flood. At the time of
the deluge began the second world, which the
Scriptures speak of as "the present evil world";
and God clearly foretold that the second world,
or social order of things, visible and invisible,
would pass away during a fiery time of trouble;
and then would follow the world to come, the
social order or arrangement of things. St. Paul
instructs us to "rightly divide the word of truth";
and this means, amongst other things, to apply
the texts of Scriptures within the period or epoch
to which they belong; and applying these in
their proper place, one can discern the orderly
and majestic forward movement of the divine
arrangement.

All students of the Bible further agree that
just before Jesus was crucified he told his disciples that he was going away, but that he would
return again and receive them unto himself, and
that his second coming would mark the end of
the world, i. e., the social order of things existing at the time he was on the earth. Other
Scriptures show that at that time the great
blessing long promised, viz., life, liberty and
happiness, would be offered to the entire human
family.

All students of divine prophecy agree that the
promises of God made through the prophets
must have a fulfillment some time, and that the
time for fulfillment relating to the restoration
of the human race to life, liberty and happiness
has its beginning at the end of this world and at

the beginning of the new world, i. e., at the time
when the social order of things existing in
Jesus' day shall pass away and the new order be
established. By faith the prophets of old looked
for that time and hailed its coming as the
Golden Age, because during that age the Messiah shall reign and establish righteousness in
the earth.

It must be conceded, then, by all that the first
important question for our determination is,
When does this world end? If we can definitely
fix this period, then it is an easy matter to determine when the divine promises with reference to
life everlasting will be opened to the world in
general. We therefore propose to prove in this
argument that the social order of things, the
second world, legally ended in 1914, and since
that time has been and is passing away; that the
new order of things is coming in to take its
place; that within a definite period of time the
old order will be completely eradicated and the
new order in full sway; and that these things
shall take place within the time of the present
generation and that therefore there are millions
of people now living on earth who will see them
take place, to whom everlasting life will be
offered and who, if they accept it upon the terms
offered and obey those terms, will never die. If
these facts can be established by competent testimony to the satisfaction of the reasonable
mind, then every man should hail it with gladness, every one should be delighted, even though

it upsets his preconceived opinions, formed from
the study of the creeds and plans of men. We
invite the reader, therefore, to examine each
point carefully as here made, compare the argument with the Scriptures cited; and view the
same in the light of present day events which
are discernible to all eyes, and upon all this evidence reach a conclusion. Every man should be
persuaded in his own mind and no man should
permit himself to be deterred from examining a
question based upon the Bible because a clergyman or any one else makes the unsupported assertion that it is dangerous or unworthy of consideration. Error always seeks the dark, while
truth is always enhanced by the light. Error
never desires to be investigated. Light always
courts a thorough and complete investigation.
Light and truth are synonymous. They are
progressive, and "the path of the just is as the
shining light, that shineth more and more unto
the perfect day". (Proverbs 4:18) The Psalmist plainly tells us: "Thy word is a lamp unto
my feet, and a light unto my path".—Psalm
119:105.

GENTILE TIMES

The term *Gentile times* as used in the Scriptures designates a period of time during which
the Gentiles were to govern the peoples of earth.
At the death of Jacob God organized Israel into
a nation and dealt with that nation, to the exclusion of all other nations of earth, for a specific
time. Time and again they departed from their

covenant with Jehovah and he punished them.
Time and again he warned them against a punishment of greater duration unless they profited
by previous experiences. They had many kings
—some good, some wicked. Zedekiah was the
last king, and he became so very wicked that
God issued this decree against him, saying:
"Therefore thus saith the Lord God; Because ye
have made your iniquity to be remembered, in
that your transgressions are discovered, so that
in all your doings your sins do appear; because,
I say, that ye are come to remembrance, ye shall
be taken with the hand. And thou, profane
wicked prince of Israel, whose day is come, when
iniquity shall have an end, thus saith the Lord
God; Remove the diadem, and take off the
crown: this shall not be the same: exalt him that
is low, and abase him that is high. I will overturn, overturn, overturn, it; and it shall be no
more, until he come whose right it is; and I will
give it him."—Ezekiel 21: 24 - 27.

It is a well-known historical fact that Zedekiah at the time here mentioned was taken
prisoner by King Nebuchadnezzar and carried
away to Babylon. Afterward the Israelites were
permitted to maintain a national existence by
other nations exercising a supervisory control
over them, and this condition continued until
the year A. D. 73. What happened at the time
of the dethronement of Zedekiah was that the
crown, or dominion, or ruling authority over
the peoples of earth, was taken away from the

Jews and permitted to be assumed by the Gentiles. The first universal empire was that of Babylon, followed by Medo-Persia, then by Greece, and later by Rome; and out of the Roman empire have grown all the Gentile nations of Christendom. As to how long this punishment should be inflicted upon the Jews, and therefore how long God would permit the Gentiles to have the dominion, is fixed by the Scriptures as seven symbolic times. (See Leviticus 26:18) A *time* in the Scriptures is used to represent a symbolic year.· According to the Jewish method of calculation a year is 360 days. A day for a year, then, would make each *time* 360 years in duration. The seven times would be a period of 2520 years, during which the Gentiles should have the lease of power, and at the end of which their lease of power would legally cease to exist.

The date of Zedekiah's overthrow and the establishment of Nebuchadnezzar's Gentile dominion, which was the first Gentile world government, is definitely fixed both by secular history and the Scriptures as B. C. 606. In the year A. D. 1, 606 years of the whole period had expired. Adding 1914 years to the 606 would make a total of 2520 years, therefore bringing the period of the Gentiles' lease of power or dominion to an end in the year 1914. This date corresponds with the circumstantial evidence proving conclusively when the world would begin to end, i. e., when the old order would begin to pass away, and fixes the time for the manifestation of Messianic power and the bringing in of the new order of things.

By way of illustration, if a man purchases a piece of property on which is situated a decayed building and upon which lot he expects shortly to erect a new structure, the first work in which the new owner engages is to clear the lot of the decayed building, preparatory to erecting the new. By analogy, then, if the old order began to pass away in 1914 and Messiah began to exercise his power, preparatory to setting up the kingdom of righteousness, then we should expect that his first work would be the destruction of the old systems of unrighteousness.

We here introduce the testimony of a witness whose competency cannot be questioned and whose testimony must be accepted as absolutely true. This witness is Jesus of Nazareth. To orthodox Jews he was a great teacher amongst the Jews. To Christians he was not only a great teacher, but by them is accepted and recognized as the Son of God, the Redeemer of mankind, the Savior of the world, the King of glory. He testified that the Jews should be trodden down of the Gentiles until the times of the Gentiles be fulfilled. (Luke 21:24) He gave to John the Revelator instruction as to what would take place when that time should arrive and when he, the Messiah, should begin to exercise his kingly power. He pictures the prophets, the mouthpieces of Jehovah, as saying con-

cerning himself, the Messiah: "We give thanks,
O Lord God Almighty, which art, and wast, and
art to come; because thou hast taken to thee thy
great power, and hast reigned [exercised regal
authority]. And the nations were angry, and
thy wrath is come."—Revelation 11:17, 18.

Here, then, we definitely see that the Gentile
times ended in the fall of 1914. At that time,
true to the prophetic statement, the nations did
become angry and God's wrath has been upon
the nations since. Every nation under the sun
has been growing weaker.

END OF THE WORLD

Fully corroborative of this testimony, we
direct attention to the further testimony of
Jesus set forth in the 24th chapter of Matthew
only a few days before his crucifixion, to wit, in
the spring of A. D. 33: "As he sat upon the
mount of Olives, the disciples came unto him
privately, saying, Tell us, when shall these
things be? and what shall be the sign of thy
presence, and of the *end of the world?*" After
giving them warning not to be deceived by other
testimony, the Lord plainly answers their question: "Nation shall rise against nation and kingdom against kingdom; and there shall be
famines, and pestilences, and earthquakes, in
divers places. All these are the beginning of
sorrows." (Matthew 24:7, 8) In other words,
he stated that a great world war would ensue,
in which the nations and kingdoms of the earth

should be involved. That great war began exactly on time, at the end of the Gentile times; and there the old order began to pass away. The war, involving nearly all the nations of earth, continued for about four years, and its destructiveness of treasure and human life is unparalleled in any other time of man's history.

It will be noticed that Jesus said this would be accompanied by famine. Since the coming of the war there has been great distress in the world because of the shortage of food. In many of the countries of Europe thousands have literally starved to death. The food shortage in every country on earth is very apparent and the cost of living mounts higher and higher. This is not due to the fact that the earth is less productive, nor is it due to the fact of man's inability to plant and produce more; but it is due to the unsettled conditions resulting from the world war, which conditions Jesus clearly foretold would accompany the war; and it is another evidence that 1914 marked the beginning of the end of the world; for Jesus plainly said, "These are the beginning of sorrows".

Furthermore, it is observed, Jesus said that the war and famine would be accompanied by a pestilence. This has been literally fulfilled. The Spanish influenza swept over the earth and in less than twelve months the victims from that dread pestilential disease outnumbered two to one of those who died during the great world

war in four years; and now this is being followed in the European countries by the direful
pestilence of typhus, against which the people
are being warned.

Again Jesus said that the war, famine and
pestilence would be followed by earthquakes.
It was not unusual for Jesus to use symbolic
language; in fact, he often used symbolic language or dark sayings to conceal the real meaning until the due time should come. In Biblical
symbology earthquake means revolution. Following the war have come famine, pestilence and
revolutions in many countries—some bloody
and some bloodless. Russia has experienced her
revolution and there the Babylonish systems
have fallen. The same thing has occurred in
Germany, in Austria and Hungary; and the
spirit of revolution is rife everywhere. This
does not mean the end of the trouble, but it does
mean, according to Jesus' words, that the old
world legally ended in 1914 and the process of
removing the worn out systems is now progressing, preparatory to the inauguration of Messiah's kingdom.

CORROBORATIVE TESTIMONY

It will be interesting here to examine a picture
that Jehovah caused to be made centuries ago.
The prophet Elijah was used as a type of the
true followers of Christ Jesus. His journey to
Mount Horeb pictures the journey of the true
Christians down to the time of the end of the

world. The Lord directed him to go forth and
stand on the mountain, picturing the church in
such a position as to obtain a clear vision of the
events about to transpire and transpiring. To
Elijah the Lord said: "Go forth, and stand upon
the mount before the Lord. And, behold, the
Lord passed by, and a great and strong wind
rent the mountains [symbolically representing
kingdoms], and brake in pieces the rocks [strong
parts thereof] before the Lord; but the Lord
was not in the wind [symbolic of war]: and
after the wind an earthquake [symbolic of rev-
olution]; but the Lord was not in the earthquake: and after the earthquake a fire [symbolic
of greater troubles]; but the Lord was not in the
fire: and after the fire a still small voice."—
1 Kings 19:11, 12.

In 1898 Pastor Russell, the greatest Bible
student of modern times, commenting on the
above Scripture, said:

"The four exhibitions of the Lord, given to Elijah,
represent, we believe, four manifestations in which the
Lord is about to reveal himself to mankind. the first
three of which will prepare men for the final one, in
which will come the desired blessing to all the families
of the earth. These are:

"(1) The *mighty winds* rending the very rocks.
Blowing winds seem to be used in Scripture for wars.
The wars, whose dark clouds have threatened the civilized world so ominously for the past thirty years, have
been miraculously hindered to give opportunity for 'sealing' the Lord's consecrated people in their foreheads

(intellectually) with the present truth. We are therefore to expect that when these winds of war shall be let loose, it will mean a cataclysm of warfare which shall divide kingdoms (mountains)—prefigured by the mighty wind shown to Elijah (1 Kings 19:11), which rent the rocks. But God's Kingdom will not follow the epoch of war; the world will not thus be made ready for the reign of Immanuel. No; a further lesson will be needed and will be given. It is represented in

"(2) An *earthquake.* Throughout the Scriptures an earthquake seems always to represent revolution; and it is not unreasonable to expect that an era of general warfare would so arouse the lower classes of Europe and so discontent them with their lot (and especially with the conditions which would follow such a war) that *revolution* would be the next thing in order. (Revelation 16:18) But, severe though those revolutionary experiences will be to the world, they are not sufficient to prepare men to hear the voice of God. It will require

"(3) The *fire from heaven*—an epoch of divine judgments and chastisements upon a maddened but unconverted world, wild in anarchy, as other Scriptures show us. The results of their wars, revolutions and anarchy, in the failure of their schemes, will have a humbling effect, and will prepare mankind for God's revelation of himself in

"(4) The *still small voice.* Yes; he who spoke to the winds and the waves of the sea of Galilee will, in due time, 'speak peace to the peoples'. He will speak with authority, commanding the observance of his long neglected law of love. 'And whosoever will not hear that prophet shall be cut off from among the people.'—Acts 3:23."—*The Finished Mystery.*

Every close observer will witness that this

prophecy has been partially fulfilled and is still in course of fulfillment.

ISRAEL'S DOUBLE

The Jewish people God used as a typical people. Their law foreshadowed better things to come in the future. (Hebrews 10:1) Keeping in mind that prophecy means history written in advance, i. e., that the divine mind foreknew from the beginning the end and caused the salient points to be recorded for the benefit of those living at the times when they should happen, let us now examine further the testimony of Jesus on this point. He said: "Now learn a parable of the fig tree; When his branch is yet tender, and putteth forth leaves, ye know that summer is nigh: so likewise ye, when ye shall see all these things, know that it is near, even at the doors". (Matthew 24:32, 33) The fig tree here is symbolic of the Jewish nation. We reach that conclusion from what Jesus himself said in cursing the fig tree a few days before he gave utterance to the words above quoted.—Matthew 21: 19, 20.

Jehovah, through Jeremiah his prophet, foretold to Israel that the climax of their punishment would come when he would drive them out of the land of Palestine into a strange country, where they would have to serve others and be oppressed for the same length of time that he had shown them his favor, the words of the prophet here being: "Therefore will I cast you

out of this land into a land that ye know not,
neither ye nor your fathers; and there shall ye
serve other gods day and night; where I will not
show you favor. Therefore, behold, the days
come, saith the Lord, that it shall no more be
said, The Lord liveth, that brought up the children of Israel out of the land of Egypt; but,
The Lord liveth, that brought up the children
of Israel from the land of the north, and from
all the lands whither he had driven them; and
I will bring them again into their land that I
gave unto their fathers. Behold, I will send for
many fishers, saith the Lord, and they shall fish
them; and after will I send for many hunters,
and they shall hunt them from every mountain,
and from every hill, and out of the holes of the
rocks. For mine eyes are upon all their ways:
they are not hid from my face, neither is their
iniquity hid from mine eyes. And first I will
recompense their iniquity and their sin double;
because they have defiled my land, they have
filled mine inheritance with the carcases of their
detestable and abominable things."—Jeremiah
16:13-18.

Here it is to be seen that God not only foretold
driving them out and punishing them, but that
he would ultimately bring them back into Palestine; and the length of their punishment would
be an exact double—a counterpart or duplication—of the time during which he had bestowed
his favor upon them. "First I will recompense
their iniquity and their sin double." The word

double here means duplication or exact counterpart. If we can get the proper location of these
time features, ascertain where the double began,
we can very easily determine when God's favor
should be due to return to the Jews and what
relation that has to the budding of the fig tree,
as above stated.

God is his own interpreter and will make plain
his plan to those who study to understand it.
Through the mouth of another prophet he gives
us the key to the location of the very day of
the beginning of this double. The prophet
Zechariah records concerning Jerusalem these
words: "Rejoice greatly, O daughter of Zion;
shout, O daughter of Jerusalem; behold, thy
king cometh unto thee: he is just, and having
salvation; lowly, and riding upon an ass, and
upon a colt the foal of an ass". "Turn you to
the strong hold, ye prisoners of hope: even
today do I declare that I will render double
unto thee." (Zechariah 9:9,12) This prophetic statement of the Lord must have a fulfillment at some time and it is quite evident that
its fulfillment would mark the date from which
the double counts.

PROPHECY FULFILLED

On the 10th day of Nisan, A. D. 33, corresponding practically with our month of April,
Jesus of Nazareth rode into Jerusalem upon an
ass and offered himself as king to the Jews. St.
Matthew records the incident in the following

words: "And when they drew nigh unto Jerusalem, and were come to Bethphage, unto the
mount of Olives, then sent Jesus two disciples,
saying unto them, Go into the village over
against you, and straightway ye shall find an
ass tied, and a colt with her: loose them, and
bring them unto me. And if any man say ought
unto you, ye shall say, The Lord hath need of
them; and straightway he will send them. All
this was done that it might be fulfilled which
was spoken by the prophet, saying, Tell ye the
daughter of Zion, Behold, thy King cometh unto
thee, meek, and sitting upon an ass, and a colt
the foal of an ass. And the disciples went, and
did as Jesus commanded them, and brought the
ass, and the colt, and put on them their clothes,
and they set him thereon. And a very great
multitude spread their garments in the way;
others cut down branches from the trees, and
strawed them in the way. And the multitudes
that went before, and that followed, cried, saying, Hosanna to the Son of David: Blessed is he
that cometh in the name of the Lord; Hosanna
in the highest."—Matthew 21: 1 - 9.

Here, then, is a positive statement of the fulfillment of Zechariah's prophecy, and the very
day of it is fixed; and so the Lord said, "Today
I declare that I will render the double unto
thee". That very day, then, marked the middle
point in the history of the Jews. It is exceedingly important, then, to find out how long they
had been in God's favor. The death of Jacob,

when he called his twelve sons before him and
blessed them, is the beginning of the nation of
Israel; therefore the date of the beginning of the
favor upon Israel. From the death of Jacob
until the 10th day of Nisan A. D. 33 was 1845
years. That is to say, on the 10th day of Nisan
A. D. 33 the double began to count, and from
that day Palestine began to disintegrate, the
Jewish nation began to melt away; and exactly
forty years from that date Palestine was completely depopulated. In other words, a period
of forty years was occupied by Jehovah from
the time he began to execute the double until
Palestine was completely depopulated. As evidence of this, we cite the following historical
accounts:

"It may be proper to mention also what things
occurred that show the benignity of that all-
gracious Providence, that had deferred their
destruction for forty years after their crimes
against Christ." (Eusebius' *Ecclesiastical History*) "On the 15th day of Nisan, i. e., of April,
in the year 73 A. D., the first day of the Easter
festival, the same day on which, according to
tradition, the God of Israel had led his people
out of Egyptian bondage into freedom, the last
bulwark of Israel's liberty had fallen, and Israel
was delivered into bondage." (Cornil's *History
of the People of Israel*) "Masada attained great
importance in the war with the Romans. . . .
With the fall of Masada the war came to an end,
on the 15th of Nisan, 73." (*The Jewish Encyclo-*

pedia) "The capture of Masada, a Jewish for-
tress on the southwestern shores of the Dead
Sea, put a termination to one of the fiercest
struggles recorded in history (73 A. D.)." (Mor-
rison's *Jews Under Roman Rule*) "Judea was
not entirely subjugated; for three strong for-
tresses were still in arms: Herodium, Machae-
rus, and Masada. . . . The heroes agreed to this
proposal (of their leader Eleasar) even with
enthusiasm, and on the first day of the great
Feast of the Passover (A. D. 73), after slaying
their own wives and children, they all perished
on their own swords." (Graetz's *History of the
Jews*, Vol. 2) "Eleasar accordingly persuaded
all his people during that night to kill their
wives and children and then themselves, but to
burn all their treasures first. The next day the
Romans found only 960 dead bodies, whilst but
two women and five children hid themselves in
caverns and were discovered. The Easter of the
year 73, just seven years from the beginning of
the great movement and forty years after
Christ's crucifixion, saw this end of the whole
tragedy." (Ewald's *History of Israel*, Vol. 7),
The historian Josephus corroborates these dates.

DOUBLE BEGINS TO END

The double began to count, as stated, in the
spring of the year A. D. 33; and since the period
of favor had been 1845 years, the period of punishment should likewise be 1845 years. Then
adding 1845 years to A. D. 33 brings us to 1878;

and on the latter date, if our calculations be correct, we should find, according to the parallel or double, that some time during the year 1878 there should be some marked beginning of God's favor returning to the Jew. In other words, here should begin the budding of the symbolic fig tree, which ought to be specially marked forty years later, viz., in 1918, if this parallel is carried out.

FAVOR BEGINS TO RETURN

In the summer of 1878, exactly on time and when we should look for God's favor to return to the Jew, we find there transpired a certain event of the greatest importance that had happened to Jewry in more than 1800 years. I quote from the Jewish Encyclopedia, which is a recognized authority: "Russia, at war with Turkey, was successful, and by the treaty of San Stephano practically effaced Turkey from Europe. Lord Beaconsfield, a Jew, came into power in 1874. As Premier of Great Britain Beaconsfield sent the English fleet into the Dardanelles and brought Indian troops to Malta and made a demonstration against Russia. She yielded and agreed to a discussion of the whole affair at Berlin. Accordingly from June 13 to July 13, 1878, the Berlin Congress was held. Beaconsfield compelled Russia to greatly modify her treaty. Turkey was enfranchised and made independent, but *upon condition that civil and religious rights be granted to the Jews.* This

had an important bearing on the history of the
Jews."

Other authorities state that Beaconsfield presided at that Congress, wrote the treaty and
was the leading factor. As you well know, his
real name was D'Israeli, a thorough, full-blooded
Jew, the first and only Jewish prime minister
Great Britain has ever had. From that time on
the favor of the Lord began to be shown again
to the Jewish people. According to the parallel
we should expect God's favor to increase toward
the Jews from 1878, and should have some special climax in the year 1918.

ZIONISM

For many centuries there have been repeated
efforts to destroy the Jews, all of which have
failed. God never intended that they should be
destroyed and they never shall be destroyed.
Their persecutions have held them together as
a people and increased their longing desire for
a home in the land of their fathers. In dealing
with his people God always raises up a man at
the opportune moment and often the man who
proves his faithfulness to the task imposed upon
him dies a martyr to the cause. In times past
Jehovah has proven his purpose of making the
wrath of man to praise him, and every one who
has suffered for a righteous cause will in due
time receive a reward for his faithfulness to the
principles of truth and righteousness.

In 1860 there was born in Budapest a Jewish

child who grew to manhood's estate. Choosing
first the law as a profession, he soon embraced
journalism and forged to the front amongst the
journalists and writers of the world. His heart
was torn and bleeding because of the wicked and
unjust persecution of his kinsmen, the Jewish
people, which led to the formation in his mind
of a scheme for their relief. In 1896 he gave
expression to this scheme in his splendid paper,
A Jewish State; and there many Jews of the
world began to awaken to the fact that their
cause had found a champion in this man. When
first *A Jewish State* appeared, his office assistant
wept, because he thought the author had lost his
mind; but as the import of this paper was considered, it was hailed as a message of deliverance by many of the oppressed Jews of the
world. He spent his life in the interest of the
cause and his last words were: "Greet Palestine
for me; I have given my life for my people."

Today the name Theodor Herzl is a household
word amongst the Jews of earth and the time
will come when the peoples of earth, Jew and
Gentile, will recognize that Theodor Herzl was
raised up at the opportune moment to give birth
to Zionism, which is destined to succeed beyond
the dreams of its originator.

CAUSE FOR ZIONISM

What was the inducing cause for the formation of Zionism? Was it due to the prosperity
of the Jews? No, indeed. Let the beloved Herzl

answer: "The scheme in question [Zionism] included the employment of an existent propelling force. Everything depends on our propelling force. And what is our propelling force? *The miseries of the Jews.*"

If we find that God foreknew the condition of misery of the Jews and permitted it to prepare the Jews for the Zionistic movement in order that they might be turned back to their homeland, will not that strengthen faith in the promises of Jehovah concerning what will be the ultimate result? "And I will cause them to pass over with thy enemies into a land which thou knowest not; for a fire is kindled in my anger, over you shall it burn." "Therefore will I hurl you out of this land into the land of which ye had no knowledge, neither ye nor your fathers; and there shall ye serve other gods by day and by night; so that I will not grant you any favor. Behold, I will send for many fishermen, saith the Lord, and they shall fish them; and after that will I send for many hunters, and they shall hunt them from every mountain, and from every hill, and out of the clefts of the rocks." "And thou shalt become an astonishment, a proverb, and a by-word, among all the nations whither the Lord will lead thee."—Jeremiah 15: 14; 16:13, 16; 24:9; Deuteronomy 28:37.

DEVELOPMENT OF ZIONISM

Officially organized in 1897, Zionism has advanced year by year. The first congress held in

Basle, Switzerland, in that year was attended
by 206 delegates, only a handful of Jews;
whereas today Zionism has its organization in
every part of the world where there are Jews
and there are some of them almost everywhere.
Large sums of money have been raised and
expended in the establishment of many agricultural settlements. Scientific methods have been
employed in agriculture. Schools have been
established, and the foundation of the great
Hebrew University has been laid on the Mount
of Olives. The organization of colonies is progressing. Jews are acquiring the land in Pales-
time and building houses; waste lands are being
reclaimed and gradually the nation is rising.

DOUBLE FULFILLED

When Zionism was organized, among other
things the first congress declared that its aim
was and is the procuring of such government
sanctions as are necessary in the achievement
of the objects of Zionism.

As above noted, the favor of God began to
return to the Jews in 1878 and according to the
prophetic double foretold by the Lord's prophets, forty years later, or in 1918, there should be
some marked and special manifestation of God's
favor toward the Jew. The Jewish year begins
in the autumn; therefore November, 1917, would
be in fact the beginning of 1918. In 1917 the
Allied armies drove back the Turk and took possession of Palestine. On November 2, 1917, or

about the second month of the Jewish year
1918, Great Britain officially recognized Zionism, as appears from the following:

"Foreign Office, Nov. 2nd, 1917.

"Dear Lord Rothschild:

' "I have much pleasure in conveying to you on behalf
of His Majesty's Government, the following declaration
of sympathy with Jewish Zionist aspirations, which has
been submitted to, and approved by, the Cabinet:

" 'His Majesty's Government view with .favor the
establishment in Palestine of a National Home for the
Jewish people, and will use their best endeavors to facil-
itate the achievement of this object, it being clearly
understood that nothing shall be done which may prejudice the civil and religious rights of existing non-Jewish
communities in Palestine, or the rights and political
status enjoyed by Jews in any other country.'

"I should be grateful if you would bring this declaration to the knowledge of the Zionist Federation.

"Yours sincerely,

"ARTHUR JAMES BALFOUR."

Within the year 1918 ten nations of earth, including Great Britain and the United States,
gave official endorsement of the establishment of
a Jewish homeland in Palestine. It was in the
spring of 1918, about the anniversary of the
deliverance of the children of Israel from Egypt,
exactly forty years from the time when the favor
began to return to the Jew, that a commission in
charge of Dr. Chaim Weizmann, with full
authority from the British Government, sailed
from London to Palestine, clothed with authority

looking to the establishment of a Jewish commonwealth in Palestine. Thus we see that the
double was fulfilled exactly on time, as God had
foretold through the mouth of his prophets.

PURPOSE OF ZIONISM

The first Zionist congress, convened at the in•
stance of the much beloved Theodor Herzl, made
a clear declaration as to its purpose and that
program has never been altered. The purpose
is thus stated:

"Zionism aims to create a publicly secured, legally
assured home for the Jewish people in Palestine.

"In order to attain this object, the Congress adopts
the following means:

"(1) The promotion of the settlement in Palestine of
Jewish agriculturists, handicraftsmen, industrialists,
and men following professions.

"(2) The federation and association of entire Jewry
by means of local and general institutions in conformity
with the local laws.

"(3) The strengthening of Jewish sentiment and
national consciousness.

"(4) The procuring of such government sanctions as
are necessary for achieving the objects of Zionism."

JEWS REBUILDING PALESTINE

The Jews are not only laying a foundation of
a state in Palestine, but they are putting in
operation great schemes for improving the country by means of rapid transit systems, systems
of irrigation, the building of houses, establishing
of schools, and a great university at Jerusalem,

and many other things. We cite a few of these events that have appeared in the public press:

Special Bulletin No. 469, issued by the Zionist Organization of New York City, states that the average rainfall in Palestine is twenty-six inches, and that this water stored up in Palestine would be sufficient to support a population of 15,000,-000 people. The present population is 600,000. It further states that from the spring sixteen miles south of Jerusalem great quantities of water are flowing into the city. The public press announces gigantic irrigation schemes which, if carried out, will supply all Palestine with an abundance of water for irrigation and other purposes.

The Zionist Bulletin, under date of February 25, 1920, says:

"One million seven hundred thousand eucalyptus and other kinds of forest trees are to be planted on an area of 21,125 dunams.

"In Merchavia 20,000 eucalyptus trees are to be planted, in connection with the sanitation of the settlement, on 200 dunams.

"In Kinereth and Daganiah 42,000 eucalyptus and other kinds of forest trees are to be planted on 175 dunams on the slopes of the mountain, the farm of Kinereth, the banks of the Jordan and the shores of Lake Kinereth.

"In Benschemen about 70,000 trees are to be planted on 230 dunams.

"In Hulda 425,000 trees are to be planted on 140 dunams.

"In Ber-Tobiah (Kastinie) 27,000 trees are to be

planted on 380 dunams, apart from those already
mentioned above.

"In the surrounding of the colony of Chederah 50,000
trees in all, mostly eucalyptus trees, are to be planted
on 1,000 dunams."

A special bulletin dated March 1, 1920, says:

"Three thousand school children of Jerusalem, cele-
brating the Jewish Arbor Day recently, planted 500
trees in the suburbs of the Holy City, inaugurating the
afforestation program of the Zionists to plant one million
trees this year in Palestine, according to a report from
the Zionist Commission in Jerusalem.

"During 1919, 369,000 trees were planted in the
effort to restore Palestine's forests, wantonly destroyed
by Turkish misrule and by the war. The afforestation
of Palestine, because of its importance in the agricultural rejuvenation of the country and in providing lum-
ber for construction work of the future, is considered
one of the biggest reconstruction projects that the Zionists are attempting in the Holy Land."

Another special bulletin, under date of March
26, 1920, says:

"For ten years this struggle was kept up, entirely by
Jewish labor. Today this once barren soil is covered
with forests of olive and almond trees, 150,000 olive
and 10,000 almond trees. Last year 100,000 pounds of
almonds were sold, which together with the proceeds
obtained from the sale of hides and wool from the exten-
sive raising of cattle and sheep, produced a net profit of
15 per cent. on the original investment."

It is of the keenest interest to all thoughtful
persons to note that these activities of the Zionists were foretold by God's prophet more than
2,500 years ago, who wrote: "I will open on

naked mountain-peaks rivers, and in the midst
of valleys fountains; I will change the wilderness into a pool of water, and the dry land into
springs of water. I will place in the wilderness
the cedar, the acacia, and the myrtle, and the oil-
tree; I will set in the desert the fir-tree, the pine
and the box-tree together; in order that they
may see, and know and take (it to heart), and
comprehend together, that the hand of the Lord
hath done this, and the Holy One of Israel hath
created it."—Isaiah 41:18 - 20, *Leeser*.

"THEY SHALL BUILD HOUSES"

At the Zionist Executive Council held February 16, 1920, at London, Dr. Ruppin in the
debate proposed the founding of a large society
which should begin to build houses for workers
as rapidly as possible. And even now in parts
of Palestine houses are rapidly undergoing construction for the benefit of the constant flow of
Jewish population returning to the land. Again
we find that this is clearly in fulfillment of
prophecy written long ago for the purpose of
encouraging the Jews to have faith in the promises of the Lord. The houses now built are not
in the interest of profiteers, nor will the owners
be permitted to oppress those who live in them;
but the owners shall live in them as their own
homes, as the prophet of the Lord foretold:
"They shall build houses, and inhabit them; and
they shall plant vineyards, and eat the fruit of
them. They shall not build, and another in-

habit; they shall not plant, and another eat;
for as the days of a tree are the days of my
people, and mine elect shall long enjoy the work
of their hands. They shall not labor in vain,
nor bring forth for trouble; for they are the
seed of the blessed of the Lord, and their offspring with them."—Isaiah 65: 21 - 23.

Thus the testimony definitely establishes the
fact that God's favor has returned to the Jew;
that the parallel is fulfilled; that the fig tree is
putting forth its leaves, according to the promise
—all of which Jesus said would take place at the
end of the world.

EVENTS OF NOAH'S DAY

Jesus did not leave us to make a decision
upon the happening of one event, but he enu-
merated several things that would transpire
during the period when the world is ending. He
stated that as it was in Noah's day, so would it
be at the end of the world. "As the days of
Noah were, so shall also the coming of the Son
of man be. For as in the days that were before
the flood they were eating and drinking, marrying and giving in marriage, until the day that
Noah entered into the ark, and knew not until
the flood came, and took them all away; so shall
also the coming of the Son of man be."—Matthew 24: 37 - 39.

The first world ended with the flood. One
hundred and twenty years before the flood God
instructed Noah to prepare for it, that he might

save himself, and to preach to the people concerning the approaching end. In Noah's day the
people pursued their usual and customary
course of action and were wholly indifferent and
oblivious to the fact that the old order of things
was about to pass away in a great flood. So
likewise today the mass of humanity, pursuing
its usual way, is wholly oblivious to and entirely
ignorant of the great transition period we are
now in.

In Noah's day while he was preaching to the
people concerning the coming end of the world
many scoffed at him, jeered him and mocked
him, and thereby testified to their ignorance
concerning the events that were about to occur.

Mark the parallel in events now transpiring.
Shortly after the capture of Palestine by the
Allied armies a number of good ministers of the
gospel met in London and issued the following
manifesto, as appears from a London press
report:

"The following manifesto was recently issued by a
number of England's most noted ministers:

" 'First—That the present crisis points toward the
close of the times of the Gentiles.

" 'Second—That the revelation of the Lord may be
expected at any moment, when he will be manifested as
evidently as to his disciples on the evening of his resurrection.

" 'Third—That the completed church will be translated, to be "forever with the Lord".

" 'Fourth—That Israel will be restored to its own

land in unbelief, and be afterward converted by the appearance of Christ on its behalf.

" 'Fifth—That all human schemes of reconstruction must be subsidiary to the second coming of our Lord, because all nations will be subject to his rule.

" 'Sixth—That under the reign of Christ there will be a further great effusion of the Holy Spirit on all flesh.

" 'Seventh—That the truths embodied in this statement are of the utmost practical value in determining Christian character and action with reference to the pressing problems of the hour.'

"This remarkable statement was signed by A. C. Dixon and F. B. Meyer, Baptists; George Campbell Morgan and Alfred Byrd, Congregationalists; William Fuller Gouch, Presbyterian; H. Webb Peploe, J. Stuart Holden, Episcopalians; Dinsdale T. Young, Methodist.

"These are well-known names, and are among the world's greatest preachers. That these eminent men, of different denominations, should feel called upon to issue such a statement is of itself exceedingly significant."

It is to be regretted that the ministers above mentioned do not represent the sentiment of the majority of clergymen in the world. To all people who think, it is apparent that there are two classes of ministers in the world: the good and the bad, the honest and the dishonest, the faithful and the unfaithful. This same rule applies to almost any profession. But amongst all the professions of the world, the man who occupies the position of a minister of the gospel is honored above all others from the divine standpoint, because he is supposed to deal with things pertaining to the Word of God. A faithful fulfill-

ment of his commission, then, puts him in the
honorable roll from God's viewpoint. On the
other hand, a man who assumes the title of a
minister of the gospel and who yields to the
flattery of the world and for this reason disre-
gards the plain teachings of the Bible and leads
the people into error is himself a dishonor to the
ministry and a menace to the welfare of humanity. No honest minister will take issue with
me upon this point. Any one who insists that
this is not true at once puts himself in the cate-
gory of the bad class. Let each one, then, apply
the measuring rod to himself and see which
class he is in. And if he sees he is in the wrong
one, he will if he is honest get into the right
class as quickly as possible.

An enterprising newspaper man presented a
copy of the foregoing manifesto to all the leading clergymen of one of the metropolitan cities
of America; and their action is an illustration
of how the majority have regarded the matter.
Invariably they scoffed at the thoughts therein
expressed; and many of them answered, "It is
nonsense to talk about the world coming to an
end. That event will not happen for 50,000
years or more. This war is like any other war
and these troubles upon earth signify nothing."

For more than forty years Pastor Russell, a
faithful, consecrated Christian, proclaimed to
the people by word of mouth, through the public press and through his books, that 1914 would
mark the end of the Gentile times; that the

world would begin to end at that time, and that
Messiah's kingdom would shortly follow. A few
ministers here and there joined with him in the
proclamation, but the majority of them scoffed
at him and said all manner of evil against him
because of his faithful proclamation of the message. The inspired witness of the Lord corroborated his statement that there would be scoffers at this time who would oppose the testimony
divinely provided, saying: "There shall come in
the last days scoffers, walking after their own
lusts [selfish desires], and saying, Where is the
promise [proof] of his coming? for since the
fathers fell asleep, all things continue as they
were from the beginning of creation. For this
they willingly are ignorant of, that by the word
of God . . . the heavens [invisible ruling pow-
ers] and the earth [social order of things], which
are now, . . . are kept in store, reserved unto
fire [destructive trouble] against the day of
judgment and perdition of ungodly men."—2
Peter 3:3-7.

The clear fulfillment of the above prophetic
statement ought to be sufficient to convince any
reasonable and thoughtful mind that we are now
passing through the transition period from the
old to the new order of things.

Concerning this same subject, the great Master further said: "The sun [shall] be darkened,
and the moon shall not give her light, and the
stars shall fall from heaven, and the powers of
the heavens shall be shaken". (Matthew 24:29)

These dark sayings or symbolic words of Jesus,
as shown in the light of other Scriptures, mean
this: The sun represents the gospel of Jesus
Christ and him crucified, the philosophy of the
great ransom sacrifice. The moon pictures or
symbolizes the Mosaic law covenant arrangement, which foreshadowed the development of
God's plan in both the Gospel and Millennial
ages. And the stars symbolize exalted ones,
teachers of the divine Word.

In fulfillment of this prophecy of the Lord
everybody has witnessed during the past decade
a great falling away of clergymen from the
plain gospel of Christ Jesus and him crucified.
In November, 1917, there assembled in Carnegie
Hall, New York, ministers of the Jewish, Protestant and Catholic faiths, to discuss a common
basis for action. In all that meeting the name of
Jesus as the great Redeemer was not mentioned.
There was a decided tendency to unite upon
questions relating to civil or political affairs,
but the great doctrines of the truth taught by
the apostles and prophets became darkened and
were ignored. One speaker at that convention
said: "Here are three steps which we may take:
(1) the preparation of a book of selections from
the Bible by an interdenominational commission
appointed by the legislature or by the Board of
Regents for use in the schools; (2) the formula-
tion of a plan for non-proselyting coöperation
between the schools and the various denominations, to the end that every child may have its

democratical and its religious instruction; (3)
the granting of Regents' credits for serious
work and Bible study outside of the schools."

This plan was enthusiastically adopted.
Another speaker, Dr. Finley, at that convention
said, as appeared in the public press: "The time
is come for Protestants, Catholics, Jew and Gentile, to coöperate to the end that every child
may have an intimation at least of his moral and
religious inheritance".

As further evidence, the Interchurch World
Movement has united in action but absolutely
ignored the doctrines of the truth. Their statement, which appeared in a bulletin issued in
January, 1920, says: "We believe the time is
fully ripe for such unity of action on the part
of united Protestantism that, without attempting to solve the problems arising from divergent
and conscientiously held points of view *on matters of doctrine and policy,* the churches are
ready for a common program of activity".

In other words, they are ignoring the *great
fundamental truths* of Christianity foreshadowed by the typical sacrifices and made certain
by the one great sacrifice of Jesus, the selection
of the church and through the church the restoration of the world during the reign of Christ—
clearly in fulfillment of the Master's words.

The stars, here representing the teachers of
spiritual things, are pictured as falling; therefore representing that men who have claimed to
teach the divine Word have fallen to the com-

mon level of ordinary world politics. As to the character of the Interchurch World Movement and showing that the purpose is not in harmony with the divine plan and that it is ignoring the plain purpose of Jesus and the apostles, we quote language recently uttered by some of the leading figures in it. Dr. J. Campbell White, Associate General Secretary of the Movement, according to the public press recently said: "To carry out the new program of the coöperative churches it will require 100,000 new employed leaders during the next five years. They must be college graduates. An outlay of from $250,-000,000 to $300,000,000 will be required to finance this program during 1920, and it is proposed to raise it during the week of April 25 to May 2; one-third of the money to be devoted to education, another third to Americanization and a third to reaching the billion persons in the non-Christian world. The world will be ruled by the forces of Christianity in twenty years."

This Interchurch World Movement is what its name really implies, to wit, the world moving the churches, or the churches moving in the way of the world. The movement is really organized in the interest of big business and political forces. As evidence of this we cite the following from the *Interchurch Bulletin* of recent date:

"George W. Wickersham, formerly United States attorney general, says in an interview that there is nothing incompatible between Christianity and modern business methods. A leading lay official of the Episcopal Church

declares that what the churches need more than anything
else is a strong injection of business methods into their
management.

"To the missionary China owes her expertness in
printing, as well as cotton and fruit agriculture.

"Siam has become proficient in tanning leather
through the scientific aid of missionaries.

"Brazil and India have increased the food production
of their soils through the guidance of men of the missions.

"Japan is richer through the introduction of American fruit trees by the advance agents of Christianity and
progress.

"Natives of South Africa, formerly unemployed, now
earn wages in sugar plantations and in the cultivation of
cocoa beans, introduced by missionaries."

The Reverend David Carnegie in the Toronto
Globe says:

"The Church, on this side of the Atlantic, at any rate,
has taken sides with the employing and governing classes
because of self-interest. She has been disloyal and
faithless to the charge committed to her, but, in spite
of all, she remains the one great avenue through which
all that Christianity stands for is expressed. She alone
has the spiritual message for the regeneration of in-
dustry.

"How can the Church discover and use the secret of
her power? She has to discover that society and indus-
try are inseparably linked together, that underlying
both are fundamental principles of which she is the
exponent."

Why do men who claim to be ministers of the
divine Word so dishonor the profession and
link hands with big business and politics? The

real reason is that they have lost their faith
in God and in his Word, the Bible. They are
seeking prestige and power from human sources
and not divine approval. As evidence of this
we quote from the Chicago *Herald and Examiner* of recent date:

"Methodist ministers were told yesterday that the
theological schools of America are drifting away from
the teachings of Christ, and that the Bible is no longer
regarded by many preachers as the standard of faith.

"Dr. Henry Paul Sloan of the New Jersey annual
conference of the Methodist Episcopal Church spoke at
the ministers' meeting held at First Church, Clark and
Washington streets, on the course of study required by
the church for every minister. He said twenty-five annual conferences had sent a petition to the coming general conference to be held at Des Moines next May,
demanding the course be revised.

" 'Many Methodist ministers disbelieve some of the
fundamental conceptions of Christianity and teach the
higher criticism, which is destructive of the foundations
of evangelical belief,' said the speaker."

Occasionally we find a minister of the gospel
who has the courage to tell some of his brethren
of the ministry the truth concerning the present
condition. We quote the Reverend William
Allan, as reported by the New York *American*:

" 'One reason why there is so much cause for complaint about poor attendance at most churches is because
the Lord is not among us. In too many cases Christ is
on the outside seeking to get in, while we are proud of
the large sums of money we are able to raise by our

great mass movements, acting all the time as if silver
and gold could take the place of spiritual power and
the grace of God, both of which only come when the
Lord is among us. When he is among us "it will be
noised abroad that he is in the house" and the world will
once more flock to the place where Jesus is.

"'Oh, for a return of the old days, with the Lord in
the midst of the assembly of his people, directing and
dominating the manifold activities of the church!'"

It is gratifying to see now and then some
Christian paper courageously telling the truth.
In an article concerning the Interchurch World
Movement, the *Christian Leader* of Cincinnati
editorially says:

"Any effort to secure apparent unity in sentiment and
organization apart from the *doctrine of Christ* is wholly
unworthy of the indorsement of any one who professes to
acknowledge the sovereignty of our Lord and Savior.
Neither the unity for which he so fervently prayed, nor
the organization which meets his approval, nor the spirit
of his life, can be obtained by rejecting the *doctrine of
Christ*. The spirit and life of the Christ can not be manifest in the individual or in the organization of individuals unless there first be the doctrine of Christ. All talk
therefore about accomplishing a union in spirit and organization without appealing to all to obey the gospel of
Christ, is a cheat, a fraud, a deception, a device of Satan
to deceive the unwary. It is a conglomerate farcical
union for the purpose, chiefly, to bring the church of
Christ into a compromising position and thus break the
force of the distinctive gospel which she preaches, or to
make her so odious in the sight of all denominationalists
for not uniting in the Movement that all will shun her."

WALL STREET'S SUNDAY CLOTHES

It will be interesting to note the names of some men mentioned in the public press as prominently connected with the Interchurch World Movement and the corporations in which these gentlemen are officially interested and the capital represented by the corporations. Under the name of each we mention the names of the corporations with which connected, opposite which are set the assets of the respective corporations, as far as known:

ALFRED E. MARLING
President, New York Chamber of Commerce....
Horace S. Ely & Co...........
Chairman, Board of Directors of Advisory
  Council of Real Estate Interests...........
Associates Land Co...........
Bond & Mortgage Guarantee Co...........
President, Chamber of Commerce of the State
  of New York...........
Columbia Trust Co...........$121,100,000
Commercial Union Assurance Co........ 1,607,578
Fifth Avenue Bank of New York........ 21,306,000
Fulton Trust Co. of New York........ 8,780,000
Hanover Fire Insurance Co........ 5,840,184
Mutual Life Insurance Co. of New York........ 673,714,204
New York Life Insurance & Trust Co........ 33,958,000
Sailor's Snug Harbor...........

GEORGE W. WICKERSHAM
Law firm of Cadwalader, Wickersham & Taft..
American Hawaiian Steamship Co........ $5,000,000

ALEXANDER R. NICOL
Agwi Oil Co....
Agwi Pipe Lines Co...........
Agwi Refining Co...........
Atlantic Gulf & West Indies Steamship Lines.. $39,754,800
Atlantic Gulf Oil Corporation........ 20,000,000

Carolina Terminal Co.	100,000
Clyde Steamship Co.	7,000,000
Clyde Steamship Terminal Co.	100,000
International Shipping Corporation	100,000
Mallory Steamship Co.	7,000,000
Mexican Navigation Co.	5,000,000
New York & Cuba Mail Steamship Co.	10,000,000
New York & Porto Rico Steamship Co. of New York	50,000
New York & Porto Rico Steamship Co. of Maine	5,000,000
San Antonio Co.	50,000
San Antonio Docking Co.	1,000
Santiago Terminal Co.	
Scandinavian Trust Co.	34,264,000
Seventy-Sixth Street Co.	
Southern Steamship Co.	90,000
Summit Estates Co.	
United States & Porto Rico Navigation Co.	2,000
Wilmington Terminal Co.	100,000

CLEVELAND H. DODGE

Phelps Dodge Corporation	$45,000,000
Alamogordo & Sacramento Mountain Ry.	3,900,000
Alamogordo Lumber Co.	740,000
American Brass Co.	15,000,000
Atlantic Mutual Insurance Co.	16,823,491
Burro Mountain Ry. Co.	400,000
Commercial Mining Co.	
Dawson Fuel Sales Co.	
Dawson Railway & Coal Co.	3,100,000
El Paso & Northeastern Co.	16,792,000
El Paso & Northeastern Railroad Co.	5,400,000
El Paso & Rock Island Ry.	5,000,000
El Paso & Southeastern Co.	25,000,000
El Paso & Southwestern Railroad Co.	19,055,000
Golden Hill Corporation	
Morenci Southern Railway Co.	1,250,000
Nacozari Railroad Co.	1,000,000
National City Bank of New York	887,193,000
National City Co.	
New York Life Insurance & Trust Co.	33,958,000

North Star Mines Co...   2,500,000
Old Dominion Co. of Maine.................................   7,426,775
Russell Sage Foundation.......................................

FLEMING H. REVELL
Fleming H. Revell Co...
Board of Home Missions of the Presbyterian
    Church of the U. S. A.................................
Missionary Review Publishing Co...........................
New York Young Men's Christian Association..
New York Life Insurance Co...........................$995,087,285
Northfield Schools...
Wheaton College, Norton, Mass..........................

JOHN D. ROCKEFELLER, JR.
Bureau of Social Hygiene...................................
China Medical Board..
Colorado Fuel & Iron Co..................................... $76,262,200
University of Chicago...
General Education Board......................................
International Health Commission.......................
Manhattan Railway Co................................... $60,000,000
Merchants Fire Assurance Corporation of New
    York   2,786,431
Rockefeller Foundation..
Rockefeller Institute for Medical Research........

Mr. John D. Rockefeller, Jr., is also listed in
Who's Who in America, 1920, as "looking after
his father's interests"—the well known John D.
Rockefeller, with wealth once said to exceed a
billion dollars. Since 1899 the son has been, off
and on, director of the following in addition to
the foregoing:

Chicago Terminal Transfer Railroad Co...........
Delaware, Lackawanna & Western Railroad Co...$42,597,000
Lake Superior Consolidated Iron Mines............
New York Produce Exchange Safe Deposit and
    Storage Co... ......
American Linseed Co............   33,445,678
National City Bank of New York.....................   887,193,000

Puget Sound Reduction Co....................................
United States Steel Corporation.....................1,452,229,760
Missouri Pacific Railway Co............................... 345,632,400
Federal Mining & Smelting Co............................ 18,000,000
Standard Oil Co. of New Jersey.......................... 98,338,300

From the Los Angeles *Times* we quote:

"In short, religion has decided to adopt the methods of big business and brilliant financial coöperation, whatever its other multitudinous differences may be. Our Christian pastors and masters tell us, vide the advertisements, that 'business associations, governments and the leaders of the great religious bodies have surveyed world conditions, and their verdicts all agree' that nothing but millions can buy salvation for a 'world torn with war'. And they are probably right, since that same world which, we are told 'a great shaft of light has struck', boasts few humble carpenters and fishermen to renounce all worldly comforts—disciples to follow a possessionless Master today.

"Those expensive advertisements teem with ironical truths. 'The least pretentious business concerns now train their sales forces: can the churches do less?' they demand. 'In America we must have Sunday School experts, Bible teachers, skilled fishers of men.' How very far we have traveled from the simplicity of Jesus, from the Sermon on the Mount, from that sublime doctrine, free and gratis for all who cared to take. 'The realization of humanity's need for Christ at this time has followed with sudden, blinding brilliance, not unlike that which came to Saul of Tarsus,' we are told. But Sauls of Tarsus seem to be peculiarly rare. Rather are they forsaking the ministry on all sides because of the meager worldly reward entailed. Nothing but millions can lure them back, or create new Sauls. Our modern Sauls don't

accrue without expert training and the promised reward of high salaries.

"Every item in those expensive advertisements is
quite logical. One cannot take issue with a single
assertion. They all reek of efficient promise, of indubit-
able statements as to conditions and needed reforms.
And yet, somehow, they leave us with a feeling of irony
that Christianity should have come to such a pass. Perhaps it is the glaring omission of exhortation to our
spiritual duty—only our financial duty is emphasized.
We are not asked to each and every one of us constitute
ourselves a personal missionary without pay. We are
not asked to examine the condition of our own souls,
our own lives, our own spiritual practices; we are only
exhorted to pay for the religious education of others, the
religious improvement of others. There are numerous
paragraphs beginning, 'Your money will,' etc., explaining just how much *other people's* service it will buy.
There are paragraphs referring to our 'duty', but they
all appertain to providing the money for *other people's*
duties. In fact, there is a general impression of buying
ourselves off from personal duties other than money and,
as the advertisements themselves declare, 'It were folly
to think that money alone could carry Christianity forward; the main problem has always been leaders.' 'We
must continue to send out men and women who will
carry the Christ-life into their businesses, their recrea-
tions, and their homes.' Send *other people* out—you
seem not necessarily to be those people yourselves. 'Unless you falter, a generation of trained Christian leaders
will make your children bless your name,' is another
form of exhortation—our faltering strictly taking the
form of failing with the shekels.

"They will raise their hundred millions, . . . but

unless most of us take our Christianity more personally
and individually, unless we recognize a few other requirements in ourselves besides furnishing the money,
our deputed Christianity isn't going to do the world
much good, and our financial credit won't cut much ice
in heaven."

WALL STREET WITH A PIOUS FACE

Roger W. Babson, statistician-in-chief of
Wall Street, in a letter dated January 27, 1920,
and given limited circulation, says concerning
the churches:

"The value of our investments depends not on the
strength of our banks, but rather upon the strength of
our churches. The underpaid preachers of the nation
are the men upon whom we really are depending rather
than the well-paid lawyers, bankers and brokers. The
religion of the community is really the bulwark of our
investments. And when we consider that only 15% of
the people hold securities of any kind and less than 3%
hold enough to pay an income tax, the importance of the
churches becomes even more evident.

"For our own sakes, for our children's sakes, for the
nation's sake, let us business men get behind the
churches and their preachers! Never mind if they are
not perfect, never mind if their theology is out of date.
This only means that were they efficient they would do
very much more. *The safety of all we have is due to the
churches, even in their present inefficient and inactive
state. By all that we hold dear, let us from this very
day give more time, money and thought to the churches
of our city, for upon these the value of all we own
ultimately depends!"*

Again the money-changers are operating in the house of the Lord, and again seem appropriate the words of the Master: "It is written, My

A MORE HONORABLE WAY

house is the house of prayer; but ye have made it a den of thieves."—Luke 19:45, 46.

Of course "big business" will raise the required money because it thinks this necessary.

Do the people wish to trust their spiritual interests with a class of men whose god is gold?

Occasionally yet very rarely you will find
some denominational minister who sees the sub-
tlety of this movement and who has the courage
to speak out. Dr. A. T. Peterson, an Illinois
Baptist preacher, says: "It is a super-league
of nations".

Dr. Conant, an evangelist, in a published discourse involving the Interchurch World Movement, says:

"Mergers are the order of the day in every line of
human activity, and the latest and most menacing is the
Interchurch World Movement. By this movement the
whole Christian Church is being unconsciously merged
into a great union church which will be headed by
liberals [infidels, higher critics, evolutionists, opposers
of the interests of both God and man].

"This movement is shot through and through with
fundamental error. Our Lord tells us that the mission
of the church is to preach the gospel to every creature
—just that and nothing more. But the leaders in this
movement tell us that the mission of the church is to
'establish a civilization, Christian in spirit and in passion, throughout the world'. Those two conceptions will
not mix any more than oil and water will.

"And by their social service program they are seeking
to capture the functions of the state, and are thus uniting church and state."

GOSPEL AS A WITNESS

Jesus further stated as an evidence of the end
of the world: "This gospel of the kingdom shall
be preached in all the world for a witness unto

all nations; and then shall the end come".—
Matthew 24:14.

If the leaders of the Interchurch World
Movement claim that their purpose is the conversion of the world to Christianity, then we say
to them that they are too late. They are not
doing it the Lord's way. In the first place, they
are not preaching the gospel of the kingdom.
They frankly state they are ignoring the doctrinal truths of the gospel. In the second place,
the preaching of the gospel of the kingdom is
not for the purpose of converting the whole
world, but for taking out from the world "a
people for his name". (Acts 15:14)   And
thirdly, this has already been done and we are
at the end of the old order and the new is coming in.

DISTRESS AND PERPLEXITY

The conditions which have arisen in the world
since 1914 are distressing and perplexing. All
the rulers of earth are perplexed. The financiers are in perplexity; the business men are in
perplexity; the people are in perplexity; and all
are in distress. Why is this so, and what does
it mean? Jesus further answered concerning
the end of the world, and in proof of it, that there
would be "upon the earth distress of nations,
with perplexity; the sea [restless humanity]
and the waves [organized radical movements]
roaring; men's hearts failing them for fear and
for looking after those things which are coming
on the earth; for the powers of heaven shall be

shaken". (Luke 21:25, 26) This is daily in course of fulfillment.

As a sample of how the rulers of earth view the matter, President Wilson, in his speech before Congress after the great war began, said: "These are days of great perplexity, when a great cloud hangs over the greater part of the world. It seems as if great, blind, material forces,have been released which had for long been held in leash and restraint." .

Fear has taken hold of men in all walks of life. Selfishness seems to pervade every line of business. The landlord, feeling that he may not get another such chance to reap a harvest, increases the rent upon his tenant. The groceryman, the dealer in other foodstuffs, clothing, etc., seem to fear that another opportunity will not come and that now advantage must be taken of this opportunity to get all the money possible. The spirit of distrust exists everywhere. All of this is but in fulfillment of the words of Jesus.

MAN'S DESIRE

Amidst all of this trouble, sorrow and distress, there is a longing desire in the hearts of the people; and that desire is for life, liberty, and the pursuit of happiness. Almost every one would prefer to dwell in peace with loved ones and to avoid strife and controversy; but conditions seem to be such that man's difficulties are insurmountable. They cannot do what they would like. Seemingly there is an unseen

force or power controlling them. And what is
that power?

DEMONS ACTIVE

Again we refer to the fact that as it was in
Noah's day, so shall it be at the end of the world.
The Scriptures clearly teach that in Noah's day
the world had been overrun by fallen angels.
As set forth in the sixth chapter of Genesis,
these had assumed the forms of men and, in
violation of their obligation to Jehovah, had
selected wives from amongst the human race,
and there resulted an offspring which was
wicked to the last degree, and the whole earth
was filled with violence. God.brought on the
deluge. The Apostle Peter, answering as to
what became of these demons, said: "God
spared not the angels that sinned, but cast them
down to *tartarus,* and delivered them into chains
of darkness, to be reserved unto judgment".
"Christ also hath once suffered for sins, the
just for the unjust, that he might bring us to
God, being put to death in the flesh, but quickened in the spirit; by which also he went and
preached unto the spirits in prison; which some-
time were disobedient, when once the longsuf-
fering of God waited in the days of Noah, while
the ark was a preparing." (2 Peter 2:4; 1 Peter
3:18-20) "The angels which kept not their
first estate, but left their own habitation, he
hath reserved in everlasting chains under darkness unto the judgment of the great day."—
Jude 6.

These demons, restrained in the atmosphere
about the earth, have had power to communicate with the living ones of the human race
through the instrumentality of mediums. These
matters are fully discussed in my book, "Talking
With the Dead", and I do not here go into detail.
I merely call attention to the fact that the clear
inference to be drawn from the above texts is
that when the end of the world is reached the
demons would have greater power and would
exercise that power over men. The Czar of
Russia was constantly in communication with
the demons through a medium whom he kept
in the royal palace. Emperor William of Germany claimed to have an "inner ear" and averred
that he heard "voices" from beyond and was
guided largely by these. The course of the demons is that of wickedness, and without a doubt
the great world war which started in 1914 was
chiefly induced by the influence of these demons.

The Scriptures tell us of a great whirlwind
that will be raised up from the coasts of the
earth. (See Jeremiah 23:19; 25:32, 33; 30:23,
24) A whirlwind is a symbol of a great war.
The great war created an interest in spiritism
such as the world has never known; and some
of the leading minds of the world have become
devotees of it and are proclaiming the spiritualistic doctrine to the confusion of mankind.
These demons are otherwise described in the
Scriptures as the "four winds"; and Jesus,
speaking through the Revelator, said: "I saw

four angels standing on the four corners of the
earth, holding the four winds of the earth, that
the wind should not blow on the earth, nor on
the sea, nor on any tree, . . . till we have sealed
the servants of our God". (Revelation 7:1-3)
These winds, or powers of the air, are not powers of natural air, but are the powers referred
to by St. Paul when he speaks of "the prince of
the power of the air". (Ephesians 2:2) These
demons are exercising power over the minds of
the people, causing distress, discontent, rest-
lessness, hatred, ill-will, malice, strife, and all
kinds of controversy and trouble.

All of the elements, as the Lord foretold
through the Apostle Peter, are thus melting
away amidst fervent heat.—2 Peter 3:10.

REMEDIES—HUMAN

What remedies do men offer to bring order
out of chaos and establish peace and prosperity
amongst the people? The financiers desperately
struggle to hold the present financial systems in
order; but they have no remedy and know of
none to bring about a better condition.

After centuries of effort, political parties
have proved their inadequacy to meet the present conditions and to solve the distressing problems. Economists and statesmen, studying the
question diligently, find that they are able to do
nothing. And this applies to all political parties
and organizations, for the reason that all are
composed of selfish, imperfect men: and therefore cannot bring about an ideal condition.

LEAGUE OF NATIONS

With the cessation of hostilities, statesmen representing the leading nations involved met in conference and (giving them credit for the desire. to establish peace and prosperity) the result of their deliberations was a covenant known as the League of Nations. This is offered as a remedy for present evils. Will it succeed? A league formed amongst all the nations of earth and based upon the principles of justice and righteousness, and in which all the contracting parties would honestly carry out the purpose expressed, would doubtless result in great good. But where selfishness is the chief motive and controls the action of any or all, an ideal condition could not be attained. God in his wisdom foreknew and foretold the formation of the League of Nations; and he likewise foretold that it must fail.—Isaiah 8: 9, 10.

The inducing cause for the formation of the League is admittedly fear. Faith in God and his promises is entirely ignored. Because of these facts the League will never accomplish the expressed desire. It is not God's way. He has plainly said: "My thoughts are not your thoughts, neither are your ways my ways, saith the Lord. For as the heavens are higher than the earth, so are my ways higher than your ways, and my thoughts than your thoughts." (Isaiah 55: 8, 9) Jehovah's great plan was entirely ignored in the formation of this League of Nations. The prophet truly wrote: "Blessed is the nation whose God is the Lord". (Psalm 33:12) But a nation that ignores the divine plan, or any league of nations formed which ignores the same, need not expect a desirable result. The Lord's prophet clearly had in mind the formation of the League of Nations, and also the league of ecclesiastical systems, when he wrote: "Associate yourselves, O ye people, and ye shall be broken in pieces; and give ear, all ye of far countries; gird yourselves, and ye shall be broken in pieces; gird yourselves, and ye shall be broken in pieces. Take counsel together, and it shall come to nought; speak the word, and it shall not stand."—Isaiah 8:9, 10.

ECCLESIASTICAL REMEDY

Ecclesiasticism relates to organized church systems, and particularly to the clergymen or priestly class operating and controlling the same. For a long time the Roman Catholic was practically the only creed extant. In the sixteenth century there was a great reformation movement and Protestant ecclesiasticism resulted. The ecclesiastics, therefore, come forward with a proposed remedy for distressed humanity; and since they do so, we are justified in a candid examination of their proposed remedy to see whether or not it is adequate. The ecclesiastical systems both Catholic and Protestant claim that their mission is to convert the world, thereby bringing the people into the churches. Let us suppose they could accomplish this expressed purpose and that the whole human race was brought into one or the other of the churches. What, then, is the hope that they hold out to the people?

The Catholic creed or teaching is that the destiny of man is fixed at death and that those who are good and faithful Catholics at death pass on to heaven, a condition of endless bliss. All other Catholics who have not been faithful in every particular go to purgatory, there to remain for an indefinite period of time (not less than a thousand years), during which time they are supposed to be cleansed and purified and made ready for the heavenly realm; that all the others, the heretics, the apostate, etc., must spend their destiny in hell fire, consciously suffering forever.

The Protestant teaching generally is that the destiny of every man is eternally fixed at death, the faithful church member passing at death into glory, a condition of bliss in heaven; and all others spending their eternity in conscious torture, eternal in duration.

It will be noticed, therefore, that if there be any real difference between these two remedies, the Protestant remedy is the worse of the two, because it offers no middle ground. It is plainly to be seen by any one that neither the Catholic nor the Protestant creed offers any remedy whatsoever for the present disorder that would lead to peace, prosperity, liberty and happiness and life everlasting on the earth. It follows, then, that if they should succeed in converting most or all of the people to their theories it would be no solution of the present problems.

The great difficulty with the systems ecclesiastical is that they ignore entirely the divine remedy. They ignore the commission given to the Christian and build their hopes upon manmade theories, creeds and institutions. They ignore completely the commission divinely given to every one who has consecrated himself to do the Lord's will. It will be admitted by both Catholics and Protestants that only a small portion of the earth's population have even pretended to embrace the teachings of their respective systems, and the most sanguine amongst them will never claim that they hope to convert everybody to their way of thinking and bring them into the church organization. The facts are that in modern times they have ignored the doctrines and do not ask the people to believe these but to unite in action; and the chief action is the solicitation and collection of money. Seizing the war spirit, the spirit of the world, these ecclesiastical systems now are engaged in raising millions of dollars, saying to the people: "If only we had the money we could convert the world". Is it not apparent to all that this is a reflection on the Lord, that he needs money to carry out his purposes; and is he pleased to use the unconsecrated funds of the worldlings to do his work? Is it necessary to solicit in the name of the Lord money from men who have no interest in the Lord's arrangement but who yield

to the importunities of the clergy and pay the
money in order that they may have a social or
political standing amongst a certain class of
people? Could it be said that the Lord must
resort to such methods in order to carry out his
arrangement? Every reasonable man must say,
Surely not. And again we are reminded of the
Lord's words through the prophet, directing
them at those who are advancing these worldly
theories: "My thoughts are not your thoughts,
neither are your ways my ways, saith the Lord.
For as the heavens are higher than the earth,
so are my ways higher than your ways, and my
thoughts than your thoughts."—Isaiah 55:8, 9.

The wise man, then, is he who seeks to know
what is the divine remedy and, finding this,
seeks to conform himself to it; for nothing
else short of divine power can bring order out
of the present chaotic condition and bring to
man that which he desires. Let us keep in mind
that it has ever been the desire of man to enjoy
life, liberty and happiness. This was so uppermost in the minds of the forefathers in laying
the foundation for the American government
that they placed this statement in the fundamental law of the land. The people, therefore,
are wasting their money, wasting their time and
energy to pursue a will-o'-the-wisp, a man-made
theory, in utter disregard of the divine remedy;
and, of course, if the people are ignorant of this
remedy which the Lord has provided, they cannot pursue it. The great masses are ignorant

and their ignorance is due to the fact that the
ecclesiastics have been unfaithful to their commission, have failed to teach the Scriptures, but
on the contrary have taught man-made theories;
and for this reason God, foreknowing that it
would be thus, recorded: "Behold, the days
come, saith the Lord God, that I will send a
famine in the land, not a famine of bread, nor a
thirst for water, but *of hearing the words of the
Lord.*"—Amos 8:11.

After many centuries of divine favor the
clergy of the church nominal as a class has
proven unfaithful to the divinely given commission. After six thousand years of laborious
effort to establish an ideal government in the
earth, the nations are now face to face with a
condition of chaos, and mankind is groping
blindly about. The people who love righteousness and truth have been without aid, advice and
comfort from those from whom they might expect it and who claim to be the messengers of
the Lord. These so-called spiritual advisers
have torn off the mask and now boldly declare
that they ignore the doctrines and unite in
action for money and power.

With the great doctrines of Christianity
ignored, upon what will the hungry souls feed?
—those souls that hunger and thirst for righteousness, from whence will they gather their
satisfying portion? (Psalm 107:1-7) Is it not
time for all such to seek the divine remedy?
Man's extremity is God's opportunity. The

whole world is being humbled by suffering and
sorrow. Let those who mourn be comforted by
the great and beneficent arrangement disclosed
by his Word.

REMEDY—DIVINE

The Holy Scriptures contain the expression of
the will of God concerning man. The Bible is the
only true source of knowledge upon which man
can base a hope for the future. The Apostle
Paul with prophetic vision, looking on down to
the time of the blessings that shall come to the
human race, wrote to the followers of Jesus:
"Eye hath not seen, nor ear heard, neither have
entered into the heart of man, the things which
God hath prepared for them that love him. But
God hath revealed them unto us by his spirit:
for the spirit searcheth all things, yea, the deep
things of God."—1 Corinthians 2: 9, 10.

It was the great Master who said: "Sanctify
them through thy truth: thy word is truth".
(John 17:17) Nothing, then, but an understanding and appreciation of the Word of God
can lead man into the right way and unfold to
him visions of the blessings that are to come;
and the understanding of the divine arrangement brings comfort and joy to the heart.

The inspired witness wrote: "Known unto
God are all his works from the beginning of the
world". (Acts 15: 18) From the very creation
of man to the full consummation of his plan
Jehovah knew everything and his great program
has been working out in a progressive and

orderly manner. In order, therefore, for us to appreciate the divine remedy we must first ascertain the real cause of the present condition of strife, turmoil, trouble, wars, revolution, etc., in the earth.

THE CAUSE

The first man was created perfect and given a perfect home in Eden, endowed with life as a human being, with happiness, with peace, and with all the blessings incident to a perfect life and a perfect home. He was endowed with the power and authority to produce perfect children and to fill the earth with a perfect race of people. His enjoyment of those blessings eternally depended upon his obedience to the divine law; and his disobedience of that law he was informed would lead to the forfeiture of his right to life as a human being, as well as his right to happiness and peace. Man violated the law. This account is briefly set forth in the third chapter of Genesis. Man was sentenced to death, driven out from his perfect home, and the judgment executed by causing him to subsist upon the poisonous elements of the unfinished earth. As long as he existed he was caused to eat his bread in sorrow. In all these centuries he has been under the bondage of the evil effects of sin, waiting and hoping for liberation.

It must be observed that Adam did not lose a home in heaven. He was not offered a home in heaven; but what he did possess was a home on earth, with human life in perfection, as a man;

and his violation of the law forfeited these. Therefore, if man is ever restored to his original favors and blessing it must be to that which he first enjoyed—perfection of life as a human being, a perfect home, and peace and happiness on earth.

The disobedience of Adam entailed upon all of his offspring sorrow, sickness, suffering and death. The perfect pair did not bear children while in Eden; but they exercised this function after the condemnation and after man was earning his bread in the unfinished earth. He was gradually undergoing the sentence of death. He was imperfect, and it follows as a logical and reasonable conclusion that he could not produce a perfect race of people. The result was that his offspring were born in a dying condition. And this is what the prophet meant when he wrote: "Behold, I was shapen in iniquity; and in sin did my mother conceive me". (Psalm 51:5) This is the same thought expressed by St. Paul when he wrote: "Wherefore, as by one man sin entered into the world, and death by sin; and so death passed upon all men, for that all have sinned".—Romans 5:12.

REDEMPTION PROMISED

Jehovah had in mind from the beginning the redemption of mankind from this condition of suffering and death, and their restoration to that which was lost. Abraham, who lived in the land of the Chaldees, trusted in Jehovah; and

God called unto him and made him a promise, saying: "I will bless thee, and make thy name great; and thou shalt be a blessing: . . . and in thee shall all families of the earth be blessed". (Genesis 12: 2, 3) At the time this promise was made Abraham had no children. He was seventy-five years of age, his wife had passed the age of child-bearing; yet he had faith in God, and when Abraham was a hundred years old his son Isaac was born. When Isaac grew to manhood's estate God put Abraham to a test of faithfulness to him and directed Abraham to take his son Isaac into a mountain and offer him up as a sacrifice. It grieved Abraham's heart much to do this; but having faith in God he obeyed. Journeying to the mountain, he built an altar, bound Isaac to it, and the knife in his hand was about to strike death to his son when the Lord called unto him out of heaven, saying: "Lay not thine hand upon the lad, neither do thou any thing unto him: for now I know that thou fearest God, seeing thou hast not withheld thy son, thine only son, from me". (Genesis 22: 12) Thereupon God renewed his promise to Abraham and bound it with his oath, saying: "By myself have I sworn, saith the Lord, for because thou hast done this thing, and hast not withheld thy son, thine only son: that in blessing I will bless thee, and in multiplying I will multiply thy seed as the stars of the heaven, and as the sand which is upon the sea shore; and thy seed shall possess the gate of his enemies; *and*

in thy seed shall all the nations of the earth be blessed; because thou hast obeyed my voice".
—Genesis 22: 16 - 18.

This promise to Abraham has not yet been fulfilled. It must be fulfilled, because God is not slack in any of his promises. He changes not. (Malachi 3: 6) Clearly, the blessing here intended is life, liberty and happiness—a restoration to the very things Adam had forfeited by reason of his disobedience. All the prophets who thereafter wrote foretold the coming of such times of restoration and blessing.

The judgment of condemnation against Adam could never be reversed because that would be equivalent to God denying himself; therefore the judgment must be enforced. But it would be entirely consistent with the divine arrangement for provision to be made for satisfaction of the judgment, thus maintaining the dignity and majesty of the divine law. Hence God made promise through the prophet Hosea, saying: "I will ransom them from the power of the grave; I will redeem them from death: O death, I will be thy plagues; O grave, I will be thy destruction".—Hosea 13: 14.

This provision for the satisfaction of justice .and release of mankind from condemnation must come through the voluntary sacrifice of another perfect human. The word *ransom* means exact corresponding price. A perfect man had sinned and forfeited life, liberty and happiness. This penalty was demanded by the

divine law. Hence God could make provision
and did make provision that if another perfect
man could be found who would voluntarily permit his life, liberty and happiness to be taken
from him, all these rights could be substituted
for those which Adam had forfeited and thereby
lay the foundation or basis upon which Jehovah
could restore Adam and his offspring to liberty,
happiness and life. Of course, it follows that
none of Adam's offspring could meet these
divine requirements, for the reason that all are
imperfect. Hence the Psalmist wrote: "None of
them can by any means redeem his brother, nor
give to God a ransom for him". (Psalm 49:7)
What, then, could be done for the redemption
of the human race?

THE RANSOMER

St. John records the fact that the Word or
Logos was the beginning of Jehovah's creation,
and that he (the *Logos*) afterward became
the active agent in the creation of everything made; and that "the Word [*Logos*] was
made flesh, and dwelt among us, and we beheld
his glory, the glory as of the only begotten of the
Father, full of grace and truth". (John 1:14)
St. Matthew gives the account of the birth of
Jesus; that he was begotten not by man but by
the power of Jehovah; therefore he had none of
the inherited condemnation or contamination of
Adam. The *Logos* was transferred from the
spirit to the human plane. He became the child

Jesus. He was born "holy, harmless, undefiled,
separate from sinners" (Hebrews 7:26); he was
without sin. (1 Peter 1:19) He was born
under the law covenant, which covenant fixed the
legal majority for priestly purposes at thirty
years. Therefore when Jesus attained the years
of maturity he was perfect physically, mentally,
morally—perfect under the law, the exact counterpart of the perfect man Adam in Eden prior
to his disobedience to the divine law. Why had
Jehovah permitted his beloved Son to be transferred from the spirit to the human plane? Why
had he come to earth at all? Let Jesus himself
answer: "The Son of man came not to be ministered unto, but to minister, and to give his life a
ransom for many". (Matthew 20:28) And
again he said: "I am come that they might have
life, and that they might have it more abundantly". (John 10:10) Again, speaking in dark
saying or symbolic phrase, he likens himself
unto bread, which men eat and live, saying: "I
am the living bread which came down from
heaven: if any man eat of this bread, he shall
live for ever; and the bread that I will give is
my flesh [humanity], which I will give for the
life of the world".—John 6:51.

THE RANSOM PRICE

To ransom means to purchase, and the ransom
price means the exact corresponding price. A
perfect man had sinned and lost all. A perfect
man now, by voluntarily going into death, would

provide the corresponding price for the redemption of mankind. Jesus was not a sinner. He never committed a sin. Why, then, should he die? St. Paul answers: "Christ died for our sins according to the Scriptures". (1 Corinthians 15:3) St. John adds: "He is the propitiation [satisfaction] for our sins: and not for ours only, but also for the sins of the whole world". —1 John 2:2.

"God so loved the world, that he gave his only begotten Son, that whosoever believeth in him should not perish, but have everlasting life. For God sent not his Son into the world to condemn the world; but that the world through him might be saved." (John 3:16,17) Jesus was put to death in the flesh, a man, and was raised from the dead a spirit being, divine in nature. (1 Peter 3:18) He ascended on high as a divine being, having the right to a perfect human life, now to be given in the place of that which Adam had forfeited; and by this perfect human life and all the rights incident thereto he had provided the ransom or purchase price for the redemption and deliverance of all mankind from death. As surely as God has made this provision, so surely then he will carry it into full force and effect.

THE SEED

It will be noticed that in the promise God made to Abraham he said: "In *thy seed* shall all the families of the earth be blessed". (Genesis 28:14) The blessing here promised is life ever-

lasting. (Romans 6:23) It follows, then, that
before the blessing of life everlasting and the
blessings incident thereto could be extended to
mankind *through the seed, the seed* itself must
first be developed. The seed according to the
promise was the mystery for ages and generations. It is yet a mystery to all except those
who have given their hearts to the Lord and diligently sought to understand what constitutes
the seed. The Apostle Paul under inspiration
defined the seed: "Now to Abraham and his seed
were the promises made. He saith not, And to
seeds, as of many; but as of one, And to thy
seed, which is Christ." (Galatians 3:16) The
word Christ here means anointed one. The
word Messiah means the same thing. The Christ
consists of Jesus glorified, the head, and the
members of his body, which constitutes the
church. "For as many of you as have been baptized into Christ have put on Christ. And if
ye be Christ's, then are ye Abraham's seed, and
heirs according to the promise." (Galatians
3:27, 29) "And he is the head of the body, the
church: who is the beginning, the firstborn from
the dead; that in all things he might have the
preëminence."—Colossians 1:18.

SELECTION OF BODY MEMBERS

Clergymen as a class, particularly of modern
times, seem to misconceive entirely the commission of a Christian and the purpose that God
has in developing that class. They have conceived the thought and advance it to the people

that everybody must join some denominational system in order to be saved; whereas the Scriptures plainly teach that God's purpose and plan, during the time elapsing from the crucifixion of the Lord to the setting up of his kingdom, is to select from amongst men his church. The word church means called-out class. It does not mean any denominational system. It means the true followers of the Master who continue faithful unto death. The Apostle Paul speaks of the church when he refers to the "church of the firstborn, which are written in heaven". (Hebrews 12:23) He does not say, Whose names are written on church books, or who have signed pledges to contribute so much money—not the names of those who are recorded by men, but who are recorded by the Lord in the heavenly records, based upon their consecration and faithful service to him. The divine purpose is clearly set forth: "God at the first did visit the Gentiles, to take out of them a people for his name. And to this agree the words of the prophets; as it is written, After this I will return, and will build again the tabernacle of David, which is fallen down; and I will build again the ruins thereof, and I will set it up; that the residue of men might seek after the Lord, and all the Gentiles, upon whom my name is called, saith the Lord, who doeth all these things."—Acts 15:14-17.

In the Scriptures a pure virgin is used to symbolize the bride of Christ, the true church;

and an unchaste woman, or harlot, is used to
symbolize the false system; and the Lord showed
that these two would be in development side by
side and that the pure virgin class would be
persecuted by the unchaste class.   The Lord
Jesus gave a parable, likening these two classes
unto wheat and tares, the true church being designated as wheat, whereas the others are designated as tares. (Matthew 13:24-39) He said:
"Let both grow together until the harvest: and
in the time of harvest I will say to the reapers,
Gather ye together first the tares, and bind them
in bundles to burn them: but gather the wheat
into my barn". The great apostate systems are
binding themselves together in bundles and the
Lord is gathering his true saints unto himself.
Defining this parable Jesus said: "The good
seed are the children of the kingdom; but the
tares are the children of the wicked one; the
enemy that sowed them is the devil; the harvest
is the end of the world". (Matthew 13:38,39)
Further answering the question as to what
would happen at the end of the world, he said
he would send forth his messengers with the
"sound of a trumpet .[proclamation of the
truth], and they shall gather together his elect
from the four winds, from one end of heaven
[ecclesiastical systems] to the other". (Matthew
24:31) For the past forty years or more the
true Christians have been gathering themselves
together without regard to creed or denomination, while the denominational systems are bind-

ing themselves into great compacts or leagues,
and making much fuss about converting the
world.

A CHRISTIAN'S TRIBULATION

It has become a popular matter to become a
member of some church system or to join the
Interchurch World Movement; and the man or
woman who contributes the greatest amount of
money is the one who receives the greatest
honor.

On the contrary, it has never been popular to
be a true Christian, a true follower of Jesus;
and this is due to the fact that the divine program is: "We must through much tribulation
enter into the kingdom of God". (Acts 14:22)
Jesus said: "If any man will come after me, let
him deny himself, and take up his cross, and
follow me".(Matthew 16:24) Jesus consecrated
himself fully to do the Father's will. His foot-
step followers must do likewise. Jesus suffered
indignities and persecution at the hands of the
religionists of his time. His followers must
have a similar experience. "For even hereunto
were ye called: because Christ also suffered for
us, leaving us an example, that ye should follow
his steps." (1 Peter 2:21) Jesus said: "The
disciple is not above his master, nor the servant
above his lord. It is enough for the disciple to
be as his master, and the servant as his lord. If
they have called the master of the house Beelze-
bub, how much more, shall they call them of his
household?" (Matthew 10:24, 25) Again he said

to his followers: "If the world hate you, ye know
that it hated me before it hated you. If ye were
of the world, the world would love his own; but
because ye are not of the world, but I have
chosen you out of the world, therefore the world
hateth you. Remember the word that I said
unto you, The servant is not greater than his
lord. If they have persecuted me, they will also
persecute you; if they have kept my saying, they
will keep yours also." (John 15:18-20) Suffering ignominy and persecution at the hands of
the nominal religionists and the forces that they
can bring to bear, is the course clearly marked
out for the true follower of Christ Jesus. "The
Spirit itself beareth witness with our spirit, that
we are the children of God; and if children, then
heirs; heirs of God, and joint-heirs with Christ;
if so be that we suffer with him, that we may be
also glorified together." (Romans 8:16,17) "It
is a faithful saying: For if we be dead with him,
we shall also live with him: If we suffer, we
shall also reign with him."—2 Timothy 2:11,12.

The divine arrangement makes it a condition
precedent to entering into glory that the true
Christian should be perfected through suffering.
The church is but a small number, comparatively speaking; and the church, together with
Christ Jesus, the head, is called to the high and
exalted position in heaven, constituting the seed
of Abraham according to the promise, pictured
by the stars mentioned in the promise. Hence,
because of this exaltation, God permits them to

be put through a period of trying circumstances
and sufferings in order that they might be
afforded the opportunity of proving their faithful, loyal devotion to him. "For it became him,
for whom are all things, and by whom are all
things, in bringing many sons unto glory, to
make the captain of their salvation perfect
through sufferings. For both he that sanctifieth
and they who are sanctified are all of one: for
which cause he is not ashamed to call them
brethren."—Hebrews 2:10, 11.

True to the divine arrangement, the church
has been put through a course of suffering. The
head and the body members have been unjustly
accused of crime time and again. St. Paul tells
us, as likewise does the Master, that Satan is the
god of this world. (2 Corinthians 4:4) Again
we read that the whole world lieth in the wicked
one. (1 John 5:19) The governments of earth,
therefore, have been under the dominion of
Satan, and the seed of Satan is and has been the
instrumentality he has used for the purpose of
persecution. In the days of the Master the
scribes, Pharisees, and doctors of the law, who
claimed to sit in Moses' seat and represent Jehovah, were the ones who led the persecution
against the Master. Jesus plainly told these
that they were a part of the seed of the serpent,
the devil. It would be most reasonable, therefore, to expect that Satan would inject into the
minds of his instruments the thought of charging the followers of Jesus with the crime of

sedition against his (Satan's) empire. The nominal religionists of his day charged Jesus with
the crime of sedition and caused him to be executed on that charge. St. Stephen, the first
martyr to the cause of true Christianity following the Master, was stoned to death after being
unjustly convicted upon perjured testimony on
the charge of sedition. St. Paul, because of
his faithfulness to the Lord, was confined in
prison for four years under a similar charge and
was otherwise ill-treated. St. John the Revelator, under a similar charge, was banished to the
isle of Patmos and required to don a prisoner's
garb and beat rock. The history of the world
shows that the true followers of Jesus have met
with opposition and persecution upon all hands
and at all times.

As an illustration of this fact: the church
nominal of England became a part of the political power and those who refused to conform to
the state-church were persecuted. A short distance from London stands a building erected to
the memory of men who were burned upon that
spot because of their faithfulness to the truth
and who refused to conform to man-made theories of religion. John Bunyan, a humble follower of Jesus, refused to be a conformist to
man-made theories and he was tried and convicted and placed in prison. A clergyman then
was delegated to wait upon him and tell Bunyan
words to this effect: You are going to be kept
in prison for three months. If at the end of

that time you recant and conform yourself to
the church-state you will be released; otherwise
you will be put to death. And Bunyan calmly
replied: "You might as well put me to death
now; I will never conform". He was kept in
prison for twelve years and while there wrote
Bunyan's *Pilgrim's Progress,* which has been
a great comfort and help to Christians who have
trod the narrow way from then until now.

Speaking of the evidences concerning the end
of the world, Jesus furthermore said: "Then
shall they deliver you [meaning his followers]
up to be afflicted, and shall kill you: and ye shall
be hated of all nations for my name's sake".—
Matthew 24:9.

It is often true that advantage is taken of conditions of war and strife to vent some ill-feeling
upon others. When the great world war began,
in Germany certain Christians, known as Bible
Students, who asked to be exempted from com-
batant military service because of their devotion and faithfulness to the Lord and because
of his command to them that they should not
kill, were ill-treated, placed in the front ranks
of battle, and were amongst the first to fall. In
Austria, the very stronghold of one of the great
ecclesiastical systems, a number of these same
Bible Students were killed and others imprisoned during the period of the war. In Canada
many were haled into court and summarily
tried without being given an opportunity to
offer a defense, and were fined or imprisoned,

the charge being that they had in their possession Bibles with certain comments, hymn books
which they had used for years in the worship of
God, and other literature in harmony with the
Scriptures. To the astonishment of many people in the United States there was a wide persecution of conscientious followers of the Master
in this land. No Christian permits himself to
become embittered because of this unjust treatment, but he recognizes it as a fulfillment of the
divine prophecy and one of the evidences given
by the Lord to those who yield submissively to
the divine arrangement, to assure them that
they belong to him. The inspired Apostle wrote:
"Beloved, think it not strange concerning the
fiery trial which is to try you, as though some
strange thing happened unto you: but rejoice,
inasmuch as ye are partakers of Christ's suffering; that, when his glory shall be revealed,
ye may be glad also with exceeding joy. If ye
be reproached for the name of Christ, happy
are ye; for the spirit of glory and of God resteth
upon you: on their part he is evil spoken of, but
on your part he is glorified."—1 Peter 4: 12 - 14.

Jesus and the members of his body thus developed through trial and tribulation according
to the divine arrangement will constitute the
seed of Abraham, through which seed God will
ultimately extend blessings to all the families of
the earth. The Apostle Paul with prophetic
vision looking down through the corridors of the
age, marking the suffering of mankind and the

development of the Christ class, *the seed,* exclaimed: "The whole creation groaneth and travaileth in pain together until now, waiting for the manifestation of the sons of God".— Romans 8: 19, 22.

KINGDOM COMING IN

The wars, famine, pestilence, distress of nations, etc., upon the earth are but the forerunners of the establishment of the Messianic kingdom. The Lord through his prophet said: "I will shake all nations, and the desire of all nations shall come". (Haggai 2: 7) And while this great shaking is in progress and monarchs are losing their crowns, aristocratic and autocratic thrones are tumbling to the earth, the words of the prophet ring out clearly in the ears of the followers of Jesus: "And in the days of these kings shall the God of heaven set up a kingdom, which shall never be destroyed: and the kingdom shall not be left to other people, but it shall break in pieces and consume all these kingdoms, and it shall stand for ever".—Daniel 2: 44.

Elijah was a type of the followers of Christ Jesus; and the Lord used him to picture the events transpiring in the end of the world, as we have heretofore mentioned. (See pages 19-22) In fulfillment of the antitype, the Elijah class knew that the war was coming and one of them, the Lord's faithful servant, Pastor Russell, for forty years pointed out from the prophecies that

it would come in 1914. The Lord is not in the
war, meaning that the Lord's kingdom is not
yet in full sway. Then follows the earthquake,
symbolic of revolution, which has already swept
some of the countries. Then shall follow the
anarchy—destructive troubles. Anarchy means
a disregard of all law, certain classes assuming
to exercise power and authority where it is not
granted, causing indescribable suffering and
sorrow. In this the Lord is not, but it is another
means of clearing away the ground preparatory
to establishing the kingdom. Then Elijah heard
the still small voice. This still small voice is
a message from the Lord. The voice is used to
symbolize a message or messenger. The Lord
has long ago put the message in his Word the
Bible for the benefit of those who should live
in this hour of stress. The multitudes of earth
are clamoring everywhere. They are confused;
they are distressed. They are in sorrow, in
tears of bitterness. They are almost at their
wits' end. But if they could be heard to express
their hearts' sincere desire now, without a doubt
there would come up from every quarter of the
earth this request: Give us a government of
righteousness with a wise ruler who will administer the laws in behalf of all; give us peace and
not war; give us plenty and not profiteers; give
us liberty and not license; give us life and not
suffering and death. Back from the past comes
the sweet small voice of the Lord saying that
this request shall be fulfilled: "For unto us a

child is born, unto us a son is given: and the
government shall be upon his shoulder: and his
name shall be called Wonderful, Counseller, The
mighty God, The everlasting Father, The Prince
of Peace. Of the increase of his government
and peace there shall be no end, upon the throne
of David, and upon his kingdom, to order it,
and to establish it with judgment and with
justice from henceforth even for ever. The zeal
of the Lord of hosts will perform this."—Isaiah
9: 6, 7.

THE JUBILEE

An understanding of the jubilee system which
Jehovah inaugurated with Israel throws a great
light upon the immediate future events. The
Scriptures clearly show that Israel, while God
dealt with them for more than eighteen centuries, was a typical people. Their law was typical, foreshadowing greater and better things to
come. The Lord commanded Moses to institute
the Sabbath system the year that Israel entered
the land of Canaan, which was 1575 years before
A. D. 1 (Leviticus 25: 1 - 12), and that every
fiftieth year should be unto them a year of
jubilee. This was done on the tenth day of the
seventh month, the day of atonement. "And ye
shall hallow the fiftieth year and proclaim freedom throughout the land unto all the inhabitants
thereof; it shall be a jubilee unto you and ye
shall return every man unto his possessions and
ye shall return every man unto his family."
Other Scriptures show that there were to be

seventy jubilees kept. (Jeremiah 25:11; 2
Chronicles 36:17 - 21) A simple calculation of
these jubilees brings us to this important fact:
Seventy jubilees of fifty years each would be a
total of 3500 years. That period of time beginning 1575 before A. D. 1 of necessity would end
in the fall of the year 1925, at which time the
type ends and the great antitype must begin.
What, then, should we expect to take place? In
the type there must be a full restoration; therefore the great antitype must mark the beginning of restoration of all things. The chief
thing to be restored is the human race to life;
and since other Scriptures definitely fix the fact
that there will be a resurrection of Abraham,
Isaac, Jacob and other faithful ones of old, and
that these will have the first favor, we may expect 1925 to witness the return of these faithful
men of Israel from the condition of death, being
resurrected and fully restored to perfect humanity and made the visible, legal representatives of the new order of things on earth.

Messiah's kingdom once established, Jesus
and his glorified church constituting the great
Messiah, shall minister the blessings to the
people they have so long desired and hoped for
and prayed might come. And when that time
comes, there will be peace and not war, as the
prophet beautifully states: "In the last days it
shall come to pass, that the mountain of the.
house of the Lord shall be established in the top
of the mountains, and it shall be exalted above

the hills; and people shall flow unto it. And
many nations shall come, and say, Come, and
let us go up to the mountain of the Lord, and to
the house of the God of Jacob; and he will teach
us of his ways, and we will walk in his paths:
for the law shall go forth of Zion, and the word
of the Lord from Jerusalem. And he shall judge
among many people, and rebuke strong nations
afar off; and they shall beat their swords into
plowshares, and their spears into pruninghooks;
nation shall not life up a sword against nation,
neither shall they learn war any more. But they
shall sit every man under his vine and under his
fig tree; and none shall make them afraid; for
the mouth of the Lord of hosts hath spoken it."
—Micah 4:1-4.

EARTHLY RULERS

As we have heretofore stated, the great jubilee cycle is due to begin in 1925. At that time
the earthly phase of the kingdom shall be recognized. The Apostle Paul in the eleventh chapter
of Hebrews names a long list of faithful men
who died before the crucifixion of the Lord and
before the beginning of the selection of the
church. These can never be a part of the heavenly class; they had no heavenly hopes; but God
has in store something good for them. They are
to be resurrected as perfect men and constitute
the princes or rulers in the earth, according to
his promise. (Psalm 45:16; Isaiah 32:1; Matthew 8:11) Therefore we may confidently expect that 1925 will mark the return of Abraham,

Isaac, Jacob and the faithful prophets of old, particularly those named by the Apostle in Hebrews chapter eleven, to the condition of human perfection.

RECONSTRUCTION

All the statesmen of the world, all the political economists, all the thoughtful men and women, recognize the fact that the conditions existing prior to the war have passed away and that a new order of things must be put in vogue. All such recognize that this is a period now marking the beginning of reconstruction. The great difficulty is that these men are exercising only human wisdom and have ignored the divine arrangement. We are indeed at the time of reconstruction, the reconstruction not only of a few things, but of all things. The reconstruction will not consist of patching' up old and broken down systems and forms and arrangements, but the establishment of a new and righteous one under the great ruler Christ Jesus, the Prince of Peace. The Apostle Peter at Pentecost, speaking under divine inspiration, and referring to that time, said: "Times of refreshing shall come from the presence of the Lord; and he shall send Jesus Christ, which before was preached unto you: whom the heaven must receive [retain] until the times of restitution of all things, which God hath spoken by the mouth of all his holy prophets since the world began". —Acts 3: 19 - 21.

Examination of the prophecies from Moses to John discloses the fact that every one of the prophets foretold the time coming for restitution blessings. Reconstruction and restitution mean the same thing—i. e., the restoration of mankind to the things which were lost. The reward of the church in heaven is not that which man originally had; but is given as a great reward for faithfulness to the Lord under trying conditions and circumstances. Restitution means the blessings that will be given to mankind in general through the divine arrangement and therefore restoring him to life, liberty and happiness on the earth, once enjoyed by the perfect man Adam and which was included in the promise made to Abraham. This blessing comes to the world through the seed, the exalted, elect class, the Messiah, the Christ.

The Scriptures clearly show that this great time of blessing is immediately preceded by a great time of trouble. This trouble is now on the world. The word Michael used in the following text means "who as God", or representing God—Christ Jesus, the great captain of our salvation. His second coming and the establishment of his kingdom has been the hope and desire of Christians for centuries past. In referring to this time, then, the prophet Daniel under inspiration wrote: "And at that time shall Michael stand up, the great prince which standeth for the children of thy people: and there shall be a time of trouble, such as never was since there was a nation even to that same time: and at that time thy people shall be delivered, every one that shall be found written in the book. And many of them that sleep in the dust of the earth shall awake, some to everlasting life, and some to shame and everlasting contempt."—Daniel 12: 1, 2.

MILLIONS WILL NEVER DIE

Every part of the divine arrangement must be fulfilled; not one jot or tittle shall pass away unfulfilled. Every portion of the divine promise, therefore, is important. Answering the question as to the conditions prevailing at the end of the world, Jesus quoted the above prophetic statement from the Book of Daniel, or used words similar, saying: "Then shall be great tribulation, such as was not since the beginning of the world to this time, no, nor ever shall be. And except those days should be shortened, there should no flesh be saved: but for the elect's sake those days shall be shortened." (Matthew 24: 21, 22) Thus he shows that the distress upon the earth will end with a time of tribulation such as the world has never known and that this will be the last. There will never be another. Then he adds that for the sake of *the elect* those days shall be shortened; and much flesh shall be saved.

We ask, Why would the Lord carry through this time of trouble a large number of people, sparing them from death in the time of trouble, unless he intended to minister unto them some

particular blessing? And since God has promised
a blessing of restitution to that which Adam
lost, and since these promises point to a beginning of fulfillment immediately following this
trouble, and since the promise clearly is that the
elect, constituting the seed of Abraham, according to the promise, shall be the instruments
through which the blessings shall flow, then this
statement of Jesus clearly and conclusively
proves that many peoples living on earth at the
end of the trouble will be the first ones to be
offered the blessings of restoration, which blessings will be offered through the elect, the Messiah. It follows as a matter of course that those
accepting the offer as made and rendering themselves in obedience to it shall be restored to that
which was lost in Adam, viz., life, liberty and
happiness.

The prophet of God offers other testimony in
corroboration of this: "And it shall come to
pass, that in all the land, saith the Lord, two
parts therein shall be cut off and die: but the
third shall be left therein. And I will bring the
third part through the fire, and will refine them
as silver is refined, and will try them as gold is
tried: they shall call on my name, and I will hear
them: I will say, It is my people: and they shall
say, The Lord is my God." (Zechariah 13:8, 9)
Here, then, is a clear statement to the effect that
one part God will spare in this time of trouble
and that these shall ultimately be his people and
he will be their God.

Having in mind that it was an earthly home, human life and attendant blessings, that Adam lost, and that these are the blessings God promises shall be restored to man, we can understand the words of the prophet David when he wrote: "Blessed is he that considereth the poor: the Lord will deliver him in time of trouble. The Lord will preserve him, and keep him alive; and he shall be blessed upon the earth; and thou wilt not deliver him unto the will of his enemies." (Psalm 41:1, 2) Here he plainly states that those who deal righteously in this time of trouble shall be blessed upon the earth.

HOW TO LIVE FOREVER

The church systems would have the people believe that only those who become church members can be saved. The Bible never taught any such doctrine. The Lord never organized the nominal systems, and the true church is but a little flock, who shall inherit the kingdom of heaven, and the others of the world do not inherit it. To the church Jesus said: "Fear not, little flock; for it is your Father's good pleasure to give you the kingdom". (Luke 12:32) Jesus died not only for those who will constitute the members of the church, but for all. St. John plainly stated: "He is the propitiation [satisfaction] for our sins: and not for ours only, but also for the sins of the whole world".—1 John 2:2.

The Apostle Paul, discussing the great Redeemer and his office, said: "We see Jesus, who

was made a little lower than the angels for the
suffering of death, crowned with glory and
honor; that he by the grace of God should taste
death for every man. For it became him, for
whom are all things, and by whom are all things,
in bringing many sons unto glory, to make the
captain of their salvation perfect through sufferings." (Hebrews 2: 9, 10) Thus we see that
Jesus died for every man, not only for a few.
Again says the Apostle: "There is one God, and
one mediator between God and men, the man
Christ Jesus; who gave himself a ransom for
all, to be testified in due time". (1 Timothy 2: 5,
6) By this Scripture it is clearly seen that in
God's due time every creature must hear the
testimony as to what Jesus has done for him
and know of the plan of salvation. Again says
the Apostle Paul: "The gift of God is eternal
life through Jesus Christ our Lord". (Romans
6: 23) There can be no gift without both a giver
and a receiver, and this could not operate without knowledge on the part of both. In other
words, the giver must intelligently offer the gift
to another, and the other must intelligently know
of this fact before he can receive it. It would
be impossible for the human race, therefore, to
accept the gift of life everlasting before it is
offered. It will be offered only in God's due
time and the divine plan shows that his due time
is after the seed of promise is developed; after
the kingdom is set up; and then each one in his
order will be brought to a knowledge of the fact

that a plan of redemption exists and that the
way is open for him to accept the terms of it
and live. Knowledge being essential, it precedes
the reception of blessings from the Lord; and
knowing this fact, it is easy to be seen why the
adversary, the devil, and his agencies so diligently strive to prevent the people from knowing the truth. But when Messiah's kingdom is
established we are definitely informed (Revelation 20:1-4) that Satan will be restrained of
his power that he might deceive the nations no
more; and then the people shall know the truth
and nothing shall hinder them from knowing it.

POSITIVE PROMISE

The words of Jesus must be given full force
and effect because he spake as never man spake.
His speech was with absolute authority. And in
God's due time his words must have a fulfillment, and they cannot have a fulfillment until
that due time. Jesus plainly said: "Verily, verily, I say unto you, If a man keep my saying,
he shall never see death". (John 8:51) As
above stated, no one could keep the saying of
Jesus until he hears it, until he has a knowledge
of God's arrangement. Throughout the Gospel
age none but Christians have had this knowledge
and all who have kept this saying and keep it
faithfully until the end will receive life everlasting on the divine plane. (Revelation 2:10) The
remainder of mankind have not heard it; therefore could not keep it. They will hear, however,

in due time after the establishment of the kingdom. Then it shall come to pass that every one who will keep the saying of the Lord shall never see death. This promise would not have been made by Jesus if he did not intend to carry it into full force and effect in due time.

Again he said: "Whosoever liveth and believeth in me shall never die". (John 11:26) Do we believe the Master's statement? If so, when the time comes for the world to know, then they who believe and, of course, render themselves in obedience to the terms have the absolute and positive statement of Jesus that they shall never die.

Based upon the argument heretofore set forth, then, that the old order of things, the old world, is ending and is therefore passing away, and that the new order is coming in, and that 1925 shall mark the resurrection of the faithful worthies of old and the beginning of reconstruction, it is reasonable to conclude that millions of people now on the earth will be still on the earth in 1925. Then, based upon the promises set forth in the divine Word, we must reach the positive and indisputable conclusion that millions now living will never die.

Of course, it does not mean that every one will live; for some will refuse to obey the divine law; but those who have been evil and turn again to righteousness and obey righteousness shall live and not die. Of this we have the positive statement of the Lord's prophet, as follows:

"When the wicked man turneth away from his wickedness that he hath committed, and doeth that which is lawful and right, he shall save his soul alive. Because he considereth, and turneth away from all his transgressions that he hath committed, he shall surely live, he shall not die."
—Ezekiel 18: 27, 28.

RETURNING YOUTH

The Lord, in the exercise of his loving-kindness toward man, has graciously given many illustrations and pictures of the outworkings of his great plan. In the book of Job he gives us a picture of the perfection of man, of his fall, of the redemption by the great Ransomer, and then the subsequent restoration. When the times of restoration begin there will doubtless be many men on the earth who will be very old and almost ready for the tomb. But those who learn of the great ransom-sacrifice and who accept the Ransomer shall return to the days of their youth; they shall be restored to perfection of body and mind and live on the earth forever. We note the words of the prophet:

"He [Jehovah] keepeth back his [man's] soul from the pit, and his life from perishing by the sword. He [man] is chastened also with pain upon his bed, and the multitude of his bones with strong pain: so that his life abhorreth bread, and his soul dainty meat. His flesh is consumed away, that it cannot be seen; and his bones that were not seen stick out. Yea, his soul draweth near unto the grave, and his life to the destroyers."

Thus is given a vivid description of the dying human race, individually and collectively. Then the prophet shows how the message of truth will be brought to him and he will learn of the great ransom-sacrifice. Continuing, he says: "If there be a messenger [one who brings a message of glad tidings] with him [man], an interpreter [one who expounds and makes it clear], one among a thousand [the Lord will provide here and there teachers for the benefit of others], to show unto man his [the Lord's] upright-ness: then he [the Lord] is gracious unto him [man], and saith, Deliver him from going down to the pit [grave; and the man joyfully says:] I have found a ransom. His flesh shall be fresher than a child's: he shall return to the days of his youth."—Job 33: 18 - 25.

When God expelled Adam from Eden he said: "And now, lest he [Adam] put forth his hand, and take also of the tree of life, and eat, and live for ever: therefore the Lord God sent him forth from the garden of Eden, . . . and he placed at the east of the garden of Eden cherubims, and a flaming sword which turned every way, to keep the way of the tree of life". (Genesis 3: 22 - 24). Thus the Word shows that had Adam remained in Eden, feeding upon the perfect food it afforded, he would have continued to live. The judgment was executed against him by causing him to feed upon imperfect food.

Perfect food, therefore, seems a necessary element to sustain human life everlastingly. When
the kingdom of Messiah is inaugurated, the
great Messiah will make provision for right
food conditions.

Thus, when restoration begins, a man of seventy years of age will gradually be restored to
a condition of physical health and mental balance. The Lord will teach him how to eat, what
to eat, and other habits of life; and above all, the
truth, and how to think and how to fix his mind
upon holy things. And by the gradual process
of restoration he will be lifted up by the great
Mediator and restored to the days of his youth
and live on the earth forever and never see
death.

RESURRECTION

Not only will those living on the earth when
restoration begins have the opportunity of life,
but all the dead shall be awakened and brought
back in their regular order and likewise be given
an opportunity for life. It was the great Master
who declared: "Marvel not at this: for the hour
is coming, in the which all that are in the graves
shall hear his voice, and shall come forth".
(John 5:28,29) St. Paul plainly says: "There
shall be a resurrection of the dead, both of the
just and unjust". (Acts 24:15) In his clear,
forceful and logical argument set out in 1 Corinthians 15, St. Paul conclusively proves that
the resurrection of Jesus Christ is a guarantee
that every one of the dead shall be awakened

and brought to a knowledge of the truth. Then he says: "He [God] hath appointed a day, in the which he will judge the world in righteousness by that man whom he hath ordained; whereof he hath given assurance unto all men, in that he hath raised him from the dead" (Acts 17:31); thus showing that during the reign of the Messiah every one shall have one fair and impartial opportunity for the blessings of life, liberty and happiness.

The brave young men who went to war and died upon the battlefield have not gone to heaven, nor to eternal torture, as the creeds of Christendom would make their loved ones believe. They have not shed their bodies and gone floating about in space, as the spiritists would make men believe. They are dead, waiting for the resurrection; and in due time they shall be brought back to the condition of life and restored to their loved ones and be given a full opportunity to accept the terms of the new order of things and live forever.

Many a good mother has spent sleepless nights and wept tears of bitterness because of her loved one that died upon the battlefield. Many a sweetheart, many a father, many a child, has likewise been bowed down in sorrow because of the great suffering that the war, trouble and death entailed upon the people.

CLERGY'S OPPORTUNITY

What a wonderful opportunity the clergy have

had and neglected during the past five years of distress! Instead of misleading the people into erroneous ways, where they have found sorrow reigning in the home because of the death of loved ones, because of the loss upon the battle-field of some dear one, what a splendid opportunity to call attention to the precious promises of the Scriptures! For instance, to say to the weeping mother: "Thus saith the Lord: . . . Refrain thy voice from weeping, and thine eyes from tears; for thy work shall be rewarded, saith the Lord; and they shall come again from the land of the enemy. And there is hope in thine end, saith the Lord, that thy children shall come again to their own border." (Jeremiah 31:15-17) The land of the enemy is the land of death, because death is the great enemy; and the Lord will call back all who have gone into that condition, and during his reign he will destroy death.—1 Corinthians 15:25, 26.

APPEAL TO THE CLERGY

It is not my thought to hold up the clergy to ridicule, but rather would I appeal to them that they fulfill their duty and obligation to the people in this hour of distress. I would remind them that the commission given to all followers of Jesus is not to convert the world and bring them into some organized system. Their commission is not to collect money from the people to carry out these purposes. Their commission is not to persecute others. But their divinely given commission is plainly set forth by the Lord in these words: "The Spirit of the Lord God is upon me; because the Lord hath anointed me to preach good tidings unto the meek; he hath sent me to bind up the brokenhearted, to proclaim liberty to the captives, and the opening of the prison to them that are bound; to proclaim the acceptable year of the Lord, and the day of vengeance of our God; to comfort all that mourn; to appoint unto them that mourn in Zion, to give unto them beauty for ashes, the oil of joy for mourning, the garment of praise for the spirit of heaviness; that they might be called trees of righteousness, the planting of the Lord, that he might be glorified."—Isaiah 61:1-3.

Never was there such a time to bind up the brokenhearted; never such a time to comfort those that mourn, as now. Why not tell the people the beautiful, wonderful truths contained in the Bible and thereby enable them to look beyond the distress that afflicts mankind, to the new day that is coming in when life, liberty, happiness and blessings will be offered to all mankind!

GREAT JOY COMING

It was life, liberty and happiness that Adam possessed and lost. These things Jesus purchased by his own blood. In the time of his reign he will give liberty to all the prisoners in the prison-house of death and under the domination of the adversary, as beautifully declared by the prophet, thus establishing full liberty in the

earth: "Behold my servant, whom I uphold;
mine elect, in whom my soul delighteth; I have
put my spirit upon him: he shall bring forth
judgment to the Gentiles. He shall not cry, nor
lift up, nor cause his voice to be heard in the
street. A bruised reed shall he not break, and
the smoking flax shall he. not quench: he shall
bring forth judgment unto truth. He shall not
fail nor be discouraged, till he have set judgment in the earth: and the isles shall wait for his
law. Thus saith God the Lord, he that created
the heavens, and stretched them out; he that
spread forth the earth, and that which cometh
out of it; he that giveth bread unto the people
upon it, and spirit to them that walk therein: I
the Lord have called thee in righteousness, and
will hold thine hand, and will keep thee, and give
thee for a covenant of the people, for a light of
the Gentiles; to open the blind eyes, to bring out
the prisoners from the prison, and them that sit
in darkness out of the prison-house."—Isaiah
42:1-7.

We have heretofore set forth how the Lord will
minister life everlasting to all the obedient ones
under his glorious reign. And when these favors are returned it will indeed be a time of
happiness—a happiness that will come to stay.
God's prophet, looking down to that time, under
inspiration of the Holy Spirit, wrote: "The ransomed of the Lord [the whole human race] shall
return [from the condition of bondage to sin and
death], and come to Zion [the Messiah] with

songs and everlasting joy upon their heads: they shall obtain joy and gladness, and sorrow and sighing shall flee away".—Isaiah 35:10.

Then the prophet in beautiful phrase pictures how the earth itself shall become a fit habitation for man. The wilderness and the solitary place will blossom as the rose, and streams shall break forth in the desert; the earth will yield its increase, and everything in the earth give praise to God for the fulfillment of his wonderful promises.

This is the Golden Age of which the prophets prophesied and of which the Psalmist sang; and it is the privilege of the student of the divine Word today, by the eye of faith, to see that we are standing at the very portals of that blessed time! Let us look up and lift up our heads. Deliverance is at the door!

GLORIOUS CLIMAX

The Messiah, the Christ in glory, will constitute the new invisible ruling power; therefore designated in the Scriptures as the new heaven. The righteous government organized in the earth will constitute what the Scriptures symbolically speak of as the new earth—the earthly phase of the Lord's kingdom. St. Peter stated that the faithful ones, according to God's promise, look for such "new heavens and a new earth, wherein dwelleth righteousness".—2 Peter 3:13.

When John the Revelator was serving his sentence on the isle of Patmos, our Lord showed

approval of him and visited him and graciously
granted to him a marvelous vision, which is recorded as a part of the Holy Scriptures. With
ecstasy that inspired witness of the Lord wrote:
"And I saw a new heaven [invisible ruling
power] and a new earth [organized society]:
for the first heaven and the first earth [the old
order] were passed away; and there was no
more sea. And I John saw the holy city [the
kingdom of Messiah], new Jerusalem, coming
down from God out of heaven, prepared as a
bride adorned for her husband. And I heard
a great voice out of heaven, saying, Behold, the
tabernacle of God is with men, and he will dwell
with them, and they shall be his people, and God
himself shall be with them, and be their God.
And God shall wipe away all tears from their
eyes; *and there shall be no more death,* neither
sorrow, nor crying, neither shall there be any
more pain: for the former things are passed
away. And he that sat upon the throne said,
Behold, I make all things new. And he said
unto me, Write: for these words are true and
faithful."—Revelation 21:1-5.

No one can gainsay this positive and conclusive promise that under the Messiah's reign
death shall be destroyed, and sorrow, sighing
and crying shall cease, and that all who are
obedient shall be restored to life, liberty and
happiness. And since the old order is passing
away and the new is coming in, we can with confidence proclaim the glad message that millions

now living on the earth will be granted the opportunity for life everlasting and those who obey shall never die, but shall be restored and live in happiness, joy and peace upon the earth forever.

Reader, have you found the foregoing pages of interest? Would you like to have further detailed and corroborative proof establishing beyond a doubt that the war, profiteering, famine, pestilence, the falling away of the clergy and their union with the financial powers and professional politicians to oppress mankind, were long ago foretold in the Bible? If so, at once supply yourself with a copy of "The Finished Mystery".

"The Finished Mystery" is the first and only book that has ever made clear the prophecies of Revelation and Ezekiel. It supplies additional detailed and abundant proof that the present unrighteous systems must be shortly supplanted by Messiah's government of righteousness in the earth, in which every honest man is interested. Your personal interest and that of your family demand that you read "The Finished Mystery".

It is obtainable from the International Bible Students Association, Brooklyn, New York, U. S. A., at the nominal cost of $1.00. See advertisement on page 126.

Bible Citations in Substantiation

Compiled by C. J. Woodworth

GENESIS

1:26. God designs that man shall have the dominion of earth. He does not have that dominion yet, as explained in Hebrews 2:8, 9, and he cannot have it until the Life-Giver returns and gives it.

1.28. If it is God's purpose to fill the earth with a race that shall be all righteous, as declared by the prophet, Isaiah 60:21. The basin of the Amazon is so rich that nothing but a population of swarming billions could ever subdue the rank vegetation.

2:2, 3. It was the divine plan that man should have six one-thousand-year days of toil under the great taskmaster, Sin, to be followed by a seventh one-thousand-year day of rest from it. This is here foreshadowed.

2:8, 9. This is a picture of what the whole world is to become. The work we now see everywhere going on about us, of beautifying the earth, is part of the preparation for Messiah's reign.

3:15. The Messiah is to have the power to destroy Satan and all the works of Satan, one of which is death. When Messiah reigns, Satan will no longer have power to lead men into sin and death.

3:21. This looks forward to the sacrifice of the Lamb of God, and thus to provision for redeeming man from the curse of death.

3:22-24. God purposes that man shall live forever upon earth.

4:4. Abel's sacrifice looked forward to the all-sufficient one.

4:8. Abel's death represented the death of the Christ; it is the death of these that makes the future blessings sure.

8:21. In the passing over from "this present evil world" to "the world to come" God will not smite all, but will save some alive.

9:11. All flesh shall not be cut off again.

9:15. Again "Millions now living will never die".

12:3. When the due time comes for blessing all the families of the earth, those then living will be due for a blessing also.

13·15, 16. Some are promised an everlasting earthly inheritance.

13.17. Abraham's promised inheritance is to be on the earth.

15:7-21. The word here renderea "whereby" conveys the thought of, "Please give me all the information available on the subject." The Lord answered in signs which we summarize:

Eleven symbolic years, the combined ages of these animals, equal 3,960 literal years. They begin to count, as appears from Genesis 16:3, "after Abram had dwelt ten years in the land of Canaan" and this, as the Bible chronology shows, was about October 1, 2,036 B. C. 2,035¼ years brings us down to the A. D. period and 1,924¼ brings us to the full end of the 3,960. 1,924 full years of the A. D. period will end December 31, 1924 A. D. and ¼ years more ends about October 1, 1925 A. D., at which time there is reason to believe that Abraham will come into possession of his inheritance.

The attendant phenomena seem to suggest that the vision will be fulfilled during the time of trouble, pictured by the "smoking furnace"; at a time when the Lord Jesus will be present in his second advent as the light of the world, pictured as a "burning lamp". As ten is a symbol of national completeness the ten nations here mentioned seem to represent all the nations of the earth.

17:8. The everlasting inheritance of Abraham and his posterity is to be on earth. As some will never die and the time for them to appear is near it is reasonable to infer that co-inheritors now living, will never die, and there are millions of them.

17:17-19. The name of Isaac, meaning "laughter"; the fact that he typified the Christ, as explained in Galatians 4:28; and the fact that he was the blesser of all his brethren, as here prophesied, prove that there will come a time when millions will never die.

18:18. All the nations of the earth, including the dead nations are here promised a blessing, implying their resurrection. When that time comes the living will be blessed with opportunities for life also.

19:17-22. As Lot and his two daughters were delivered from the destruction of literal Sodom and given a little city to live in, so it may be that many will be delivered from the destruction of churchianity, "that city which is spiritually called Sodom", Revelation 11:8, and permitted to live on into the new order of things.

21:14-19. The hopes of the world are knit up with the hopes of fleshly Israel, whom Ishmael represented, even as Isaac represented spiritual Israel.. The hopes of Zionists were revived at the great Hippodrome meeting in 1910 when Pastor Russell delivered his address on Zionism in Prophecy to 5,500 Jews. Here the antitypical Ishmael, ready to die of thirst, was supplied with just the water of life most needed. This is a sign of the early approach of returning favor to the Jew, now manifest in Zionism.

22:7, 8, 13. The lamb caught in the thicket represented Jesus, the blesser of all the living and the dead.

22:18. The living nations will participate in these blessings.

25:1-4. Keturah represented the New Covenant, God's means for fulfilling the Abrahamic Covenant and blessing all mankind. She had six sons, representing that her offspring, at first, are imperfect. But she had ten grandsons, symbol of national completeness, symbolizing that, in the end, the whole world will own the New Covenant as their source of life, and by it will reach perfection.

26:3. The living nations will participate in these blessings.

28:12. A vision of our Lord Jesus in his capacity as the Savior of mankind, bringing blessings of life to all, living and dead.

28:14. The living families will participate in these blessings.

35:18. The fact that we now see the time of nominal Zion's travail argues that the time for the blessing of mankind is near. Benjamin, in a way, brought blessings to his other brethren.

45:3-5. This revelation of Joseph to his brethren prior to his blessing of them represents the second advent of our Lord now being gradually revealed to the world to their ultimate joy.

49:10. Shiloh is Christ, the Prince of Peace, the peacemaker between heaven and earth. When he begins to draw all men unto himself it will include the millions now living as well as the dead.

50:17. This represents the spirit of prayer and supplication as it will shortly be poured out upon millions now living.

50:20. As God was pleased to save much people alive at the hands of Joseph, so there is reason to believe he will be equally pleased to save alive millions now living at the hands of Christ.

EXODUS

3:8. This represents the purpose of the second advent of Christ.

4:4. This represents God's purpose to lay hold upon present evil conditions, banishing sin and death and every evil thing.

5:17. This sign preceding Israel's deliverance from Egypt we now see preceding mankind's deliverance from Satan's empire.

7:12. This sign preceding Israel's deliverance shows how our clear comprehension of the reason for the permission of evil completely obliterates by its greater power previous explanations.

7:20.   This sign shows how the millions of tracts setting forth the blessed harvest tidings would seem to churchianity. This sign, fulfilled, shows that the time for earth's deliverance is near.

The succeeding chapters of Exodus, down to 12:30 inclusive, narrating the plagues successively of frogs, lice, flies, murrain, boils, hail, locusts, darkness and the death of the firstborn, represent successive manifestations of God's power in setting forth the truth. Among the antitypes of these plagues we see the seven volumes of Studies in the Scriptures. The fact that these have all been published shows that the deliverance of the world is nigh.

14:29,30.   The passage of Israel through the Red Sea may represent that some will pass through the time of anarchy alive.

15:13.   This applies to the whole world of mankind.

15:26.   This promise to fleshly Israel applies also to the world of mankind in the end of the gospel age.

16:21.   As the Israelites gathered the manna fresh every morning so the world in the new age will need to seek supplies of grace to live. This will apply to those living when the day of grace dawns.

16:23.   It was the divine plan that man should have a great Sabbath day for recovery of living and dead from sin and death.

19:10, 11.   This third day represents the early morning of the third thousand-year day beginning with the thousand-year day in which the ransom was provided for the living as well as the dead.

20:8-10.   The Sabbath day typified the great thousand-year Sabbath day of restitution for the living as well as the dead.

28:33.   The bells of gold represent that when the King shall come the fruits of his redemptive work will be manifest to all.

32:34.   This leading of the people into the promised land represents the leading back of all who will into harmony with God.

34:30.   The bright-shining of which Israel was afraid represents the time of trouble which the world will not be able to endure. Following this the greater than Moses, Christ, will speak to the living and the dead through the medium of the vail, the Ancient Worthies.

LEVITICUS

9:23.   This appearance of the glory of the Lord unto all the people represented the time soon coming when "the glory of the Lord [his love for all men, living and dead] shall be revealed" to all.

13:2.   This represents the arrangement of the Lord for the healing of all mankind, living and dead, from sin, in the new age.

14:4.   The cedar wood represents the everlasting life that may be obtained by living and dead in the Millennial age, the scarlet the blood of the ransom, the hyssop the cleansing Word.

14:12.   The trespass offerings represent the means of reconciliation shortly to be opened for the living as well as the dead.

18:5.   Those who will keep the new laws may live everlastingly.

23:3.   The Sabbath day typified the great thousand-year Sabbath day of recovery of the living and dead from sin and death.

25:10.   This represents the coming deliverance of all, living and dead.

26:18, 24, 28.   The seven Gentile times ended in the fall of 1914.

26:34, 35, 40-45.   A reference to the seventy jubilees which must pass over Israel before they really enter the promised land. These 3,500 years began with the entrance into Canaan in the spring of 1575 B. C., 1574½ years before the A. D. era and will come to their full end in 1924½, or about April 1, 1925, at which time we may expect the resurrection of the Ancient Worthies and the beginning of the blessing of all the families of the earth, living as well as dead. The last year of the 3,500 years will be itself a jubilee year witnessing the antitype, the great jubilee of restitution.

27:24.   Another reference to the coming deliverance of all men.

NUMBERS

14:31-34. The last verse of this citation is one of the keys that unlock the time prophecies and one, therefore, by which we discern that the world has ended. There seems to be a parallelism in the preceding verses between the experiences of the professed people of God in this harvest time and the experiences of fleshly Israel there. We may see that the forty years wandering of spiritual Israel began in the fall of 1881. The ten unfaithful spies, the worldly clergy, rejected the restitution message as an awful message, a devilish message, and the people heeded them instead of heeding the truth, but it may well be that, literally, they and their systems shall fail to enter in, while their children, literally, shall have the promised inheritance. It may be that these worldly systems will go down in the fall of 1921. Or the forty years may be viewed as beginning with the proclamation of the harvest message in 1878 and ending with the beginning of the downfall of ecclesiasticism, which took place in Russia in 1918.

19:9. These ashes of the red heifer, kept for the cleansing of the people from sin, represent the remembrance of the faithfulness of the Ancient Worthies which will be available for all ere long.

21:9. The serpent of brass represented sin, Satan's agent in luring our first parents into condemnation, hence our Lord Jesus who took the place of the sinner, living and dead.

DEUTERONOMY

4:9-11. These words, applicable to Israel at the inauguration of the old Law Covenant, will be applicable to all mankind, living and dead, at the inauguration of the new Law Covenant. The fulfillment of these symbols we now see going on about us.

4:40. Under the new Law Covenant Israel and, by extension, all mankind, living and dead, may, if obedient, live forever.

5:12-14. Fleshly Israel's day of rest typified the coming time in which the whole world, living and dead, shall rest from sin.

5:16. Those may live forever who honor Jehovah and the New Covenant, represented here by father and mother.

18:15-18. A prophecy of the coming offer of life to all.

28:1-14. Representing the blessings coming upon all the world, living and dead, with the advent of the new Law Covenant.

30:15,19. These words apply to all the world, living and dead, in the dawn of the new age. They have never yet had fulfillment; never yet has a real offer of *life* for the living been held out to any.

32:43. This rejoicing of the nations of earth with Israel has not yet taken place, but it will take place for both living and dead.

JOSHUA.

1:11. The three days' preparation of victuals represent the thousand-year day in which Christ was crucified and the two succeeding ones in which the church is gathered out. Upon this food the world, living and dead, will feed in the age almost at hand.

5:12. Representing new offers of life to millions now living.

6:20. This represents the utter overthrow of the powers of sin, and the end of all necessity for any man to die. Already we see the walls of the antitypical Jericho, churchianity, tottering.

14:10. This keeping of Caleb alive from the time Israel left Egypt until the promised land had been conquered and divided represents how some will go over into the new age without dying.

JUDGES

3:9. The judges of ancient times were not only rulers but deliverers. The present commotion in the earth is due to the fact that the Judge is here and the judgment day is under way. The Judge not only will suppress all wrong but will hold out life for all.

1. SAMUEL

2 : 6. Soon none will need longer to go into the grave.
11 : 12, 13. In some senses of the word the first king of Israel represented earth's new king—"not willing that any should perish".

2. SAMUEL

7 : 10. When the time has come that Israel shall "dwell in a place of their own and move no more" the time will also have come when "millions now living will never die".
19 : 21, 22. David was a type of earth's coming king—"not willing that any should perish".

1. KINGS

1 : 51, 52. Solomon similarly was a type of earth's coming king.
8 : 56. The rest from their enemies which came upon fleshly Israel represents the real rest coming upon all the living and dead.

2. KINGS

4 : 5, 6. This pouring out of the oil represents the pouring out of the holy spirit upon all flesh, living and dead. Every vessel fitted for its reception shall be filled to the full with God's spirit.

1. CHRONICLES

16 : 31 - 34. The judgment day, which we have already entered, is a time of hope and blessing for all mankind, living and dead.
17 : 9. A permanent dwelling place signifies the end of death.

2. CHRONICLES

36 : 21. A reference to the seventy jubilees beginning in the spring of 1575 B. C. and ending in the spring of 1925. When these jubilees are complete the time will have come for blessing all.

NEHEMIAH

8 : 5 - 12. This reading of the law by Ezra and the aid rendered by his thirteen assistants, followed by the rejoicing of the people, seems to represent the coming unfolding of his Word by the Lord, the coöperation of the twelve tribes of spiritual Israel and the great company, and the subsequent joy of all, living and dead.

JOB

33 : 14 - 30. Elihu, not one of the three contenders with Job that were reproved by the Almighty, but a fourth one whose utterances seem to have been guided by the Lord, calls attention to the fact that God has repeatedly warned mankind during this night time of evil ; that man has seen strange visions upon his creed bed throughout this period, but now that we are in the day of wrath he is getting his eyes and ears open. No longer shall men be permitted to follow their own plans. Then follows the history of a man that is sick, his pains, his failing appetite, his loss of flesh, all suggesting his speedy dissolution. Then he explains that if the time has come for the second advent of the Lord, the Messenger of the Covenant, God's interpreter of his own character, the fairest among ten thousand, God is gracious unto the sick one and says, in substance, "He need not die, the ransom has been applied for him ; if he will repent of his sins he may grow young again and live forever."
38 : 11 - 15. Evil is permitted only to a certain extent. Here its coming end is shown as associated with the fixed time for the coming of the Dayspring from on high. When he comes, in the language of verse 14 (Leeser) "She is changed as the sealing clay and all things stand as though newly clad". All things shall be made new; death shall be no more.

42:12. Job's experiences picture the experiences of those of mankind that shall live through the time of anarchy.

PSALMS

2:1-12. This entire psalm has particular reference to our day.

4:3. The kind of people that will be spared in the day of wrath.

5:3-7. Here is a prayer that the world of mankind may well pray in their morning, a prayer that they may not be destroyed.

5:11,12. Those whom the Lord defends and blesses in the time of trouble need not pass into death.

6:4,5,9. David's prayer to be delivered out of death, and its favorable answer afford encouragement to millions now living.

7:9,10. In the Millennial age the wickedness of the wicked will come to an eud and the just shall be established, defended, saved.

8:1-9. God's original purpose to have man as the lord of his earthly dominion is here stated, and there is also a reference to the divine determination to visit him, which will mean his life spared.

9:9,10. This promise would seem to be particularly appropriate to those living in the greatest of all times of trouble.

10:16. When the heathen are perished out of the earth there will be no occasion for anybody else to perish, but all may live.

11:6,7. When the wicked are destroyed others will be preserved.

13:3-6. A prayer especially appropriate to those now living.

15:1-5. After the time of trouble there will be only one mountain or hill left, the kingdom of God, represented by Mount Moriah. This Psalm shows who alone may dwell permanently in it.

16:11. The parable of the sheep and the goats, Matthew 25:31-46 shows that those on the right hand of earth's new king need never die, even as here suggested.

17:4. Words peculiarly appropriate for some of the world at this time.

18:12-14. These signs that the world has ended are here.

22:27,28. When all the kindreds of the nations worship before the Lord none will need to die. The Lord, as governor, is at the door.

24:3-5. Shows who may permanently dwell in the kingdom.

25:12,13. A promise for millions now living that will never die.

27:1-14. This entire Psalm seems to be one in which the poor world can take special comfort in this evil day.

30:1-12. This Psalm of rejoicing will be appropriate to the millions now living that are carried through the time of trouble.

31:22-24. Words appropriate for those who are spared.

32:6-11. Other words appropriate to the world now.

33:18-22. A promise that millions now living will never die.

34:11-22. Words addressed to millions now living.

35:9,10. With the close of the time of trouble the Lord will deliver man from the power of "him that is too strong for him".

36:7-10. Words appropriate for millions now living.

37:1-40. This entire Psalm is filled with direct evidence that there are millions now living that will never die.

41:1-3. A promise that millions now living will never die.

45:16,17. There are to be princes in all the earth and a people there that shall praise the Lord for ever and ever without death.

46:1-11. This Psalm shows that the world has ended.

47:7,8. When God is king over all the earth, reigning over the (now) heathen nations, there will be blessings of life for all.

49:7. But God provided one who could give a ransom price.

53:6. This rejoicing will be on the part of the living.

55:22,23. The destruction of the bloody and deceitful, coupled with the statement that the righteous shall not be moved, is evidence that there will be a time when some will not need to die.

59:16. God's mercy and power to deliver from the grave are to be made manifest in the Millennial morning.

60:2-4. Evidences that the world has ended.
65:5. God is not yet the confidence of the ends of all the earth but when he is, death will be no more.
66:4. When all the earth worships God death will be at an end.
67:1-7. God's saving health is to be made known among all nations. This whole Psalm is appropriate to this, our day.
68:1-3. The destruction of the wicked implies that the righteous will not be destroyed; indeed, the text says they shall be glad.
69:35, 36. This language seems to imply that certain Jews will have a permanent inheritance in the land, and that inheritance will be shared by others, including some now living.
72:2-7. The breaking in pieces of Satan, the great oppressor, implies that his reign of death shall end. The condition of man now is like that of mown grass. He is on the way to death, but the return of Christ will bring life as showers to dying grass.
72:12-14. The poor world needs life and redemption from the violence of death and their cry shall be heard.
72:16. Here is promised prolonged life for those who dwell in the cities, now admittedly the hardest places to sustain life.
76:8, 9. Now, in the judgment day, God will save the meek.
82:1-5. Evidence that the world has ended.
84:11. Now that the due time has come God will not withhold the gift of continued life from those that walk uprightly.
86:9. When the due time comes for the dead nations to come forth and worship God millions then living will never die.
89:15. The joyful sound is that the King has come, bringing life not only to the dead but to the living.
90:3. Shortly none will need to continue going into destruction.
92:9-12. When the enemies of the Lord perish those who are not his enemies may continue to live, to flourish like the palm tree.
94:20-23. When the Lord cuts off the wicked in their iniquity, especially those who frame their mischief into laws for the suppression of his truth, the innocent will be spared from like fate.
96:1, 10-13. The new song is that the King has come to bring life to the dead and the living.
97:1-6. Evidences that the world has ended. When all the people see (understand) the Lord's glory none will longer need to die.
98:2. Here the complete evangelization of the world is shown and when this time arrives none will longer need to die.
100:1-5. When all lands unite in praise of the Lord's mercy death will be at an end.
101:5-8. When the slanderers, the proud, the deceitful and the wicked are cut off, the faithful and perfect of heart may live on.
102:19, 20, 28. Evidence that millions now living will never die.
103:19. When the Lord's kingdom rules over all none need die.
104:5. The earth is designed to be the home of an everlasting race. God did not design to fill the earth with dying creatures.
104:35. When the wicked are no more the righteous may live on.
107:11-16. Our parents in Eden rebelled against God's Word, set at naught his counsel and fell down, in labor, under the curse of death. Out from this curse they are shown here as emerging, the hands which have been hastening them toward the brass gates and iron bars of the tomb having been sundered.
107:24-31. Here we have a picture of present conditions indicating that the world has ended, and accompanying it is the statement that the Lord will bring peace and life out of the turmoil.
110:3-6. Here is represented the submission of earth's peoples to the Lord in the day of his power and such submission will bring life. The last verse supplies evidence that the world has ended.
112:4. The greatest light that can arise upon man in this land of darkness is the Sun of Righteousness, bringing compassion and life.
113:3-8. Here is evidence that the Lord shall be praised

everywhere and that in that day some of the poor and needy of mankind will be given life and a place with the Ancient Worthies.
115:16-18. Words appropriate for millions now living.
116:6-9. The Lord will preserve some from going into death.
118:15-23. "I shall not die, but live" is a theme for today.
119:119. The putting away of the wicked implies life to others.
119:144. An assurance of continued life to the wise toward God.
125:4, 5. The crooked and the workers of iniquity are to go into death but good (life) is to be to the upright.
139:24. The righteous may be led in the way everlasting.
140:11-13. The violent will be overthrown along with the evil speakers, but the upright will be privileged to live on.
145:9-21. The twentieth verse is direct evidence that those that love the Lord need not die when the wicked are destroyed, and the balance of the context is all appropriate to that thought.

PROVERBS

2:20, 21. Direct evidence that some will continue to live on.
3:1, 2. Here some are promised long life and peace and this life and peace may be everlasting.
3:13-18. Length of days and the tree of life promised to some.
11:31. Some of the righteous will be rewarded with everlasting human life. When that time comes millions now living need not die.
29:2. All will rejoice over Christ's righteous rule and live on.

ECCLESIASTES

1:4. God designed the earth to be the permanent home of man, and although now the generations succeed one another in death yet death shall cease, as other Scriptures show.

CANTICLES

2:8-13, 17. Here is evidence that the world has ended and that the world's springtime of hope and of life has come.
4:6. A reference to the dawn of the day of life for the world.
5:9. Inquiry is the first step to hearing, and hearing is the first step toward life. This text is located in the immediate future.

ISAIAH

1:9. Since Brother Russell applies verse 3 to nominal Christendom, this verse may apply to the millions who will not die, but who will be a very small remnant compared to the billions of dead.
1:19. Continued life will be the reward of willingness.
1:24-31. Evidence that the world has ended, the transgressors are to be destroyed and the judges (life-givers) restored.
2:2-4. When the time comes that many nations and peoples desire to join themselves to the Lord death will cease.
2:7, 8. An evidence that the world has ended.
2:11. When Jehovah is exalted in the hearts of men there will be no occasion for death to continue.
2:20. Evidences of the end of the world.
3:5. Evidences that the world has ended. Compare 2 Timothy 3. "In the last days perilous times shall come", etc.
3:10. The righteous shall eat the fruit of their own doings.
3:12. In the end of the age preachers cause the people to err.
4:2-6. Direct evidence that millions now living will never die.
5:7. An evidence of the end of the age.
6:13. A hint that possibly one-tenth will live on forever.
8:21 to 9:7. Evidence that the world has ended and an everlasting era of peace is at hand. In this era death shall cease.
11:4-9. Nothing shall hurt nor destroy. Death will cease.
11:12-16. An evidence that the world has ended.

12:1-6. When the world of mankind is joyfully drawing water out of the wells of salvation they will appreciate this prophecy.

14:7. Rest from every foe, including death, is here promised.

16:5. When lasting righteousness prevails in the earth none will longer need to die.

18:3. The seventh trumpet marks the jubilee of earth, the end of death and of dying.

19:21-25. Here is pictured the healing of the sin-sick world.

21:12. Earth's time of inquiry after God is after her trouble.

24:6. A direct statement that there will be some men left after the time of trouble has swept the earth.

24:16-23. Evidences that the world has ended. The glorious reign of the Prince of Life also made known.

25:6-12. A feast of fat nourishing things provided; death is condemned to be swallowed up in victory.

26:9. The inhabitants of the world, living and dead, will learn righteousness when the Lord's judgments are in the earth.

26:19. When the earth casts out her dead none will longer need to go into death.

27:1-6. Evidences that the world has ended.

27:12,13. The seventh trumpet marks the end of death.

28:18. Agreement with the grave to be ended; none to go there.

29:19-24. The meek shall increase their joy in the Lord, not gradually lose it, pogroms will be at an end and even sneaking provocateurs will come to know something of justice and truth.

30:26. Jehovah will *bind up* the hurt of his people.

32:8. In noble things shall the noble continue.

32:15-18. God's people shall *abide* in a *sure* dwellingplace.

33:2. The Lord will be the salvation of some in the evil time.

33:6. In the Lord's times there will be stability and salvation.

33:16. Seek peace, seek righteousness; ye may never die.

33:22. Jehovah will save us. This may now be said by some.

33:24. The inhabitant shall not say, I am sick.

34:16,17. Men shall dwell from generation to generation following the time when the Word of the Lord becomes understood.

35:1-10. This includes the thought of physical restoration of those now feeble, blind, deaf, and lame and their progress from the dying condition to that of everlasting joy.

40:1-5. Here are mirrored stupendous social changes and the straightening out of all earth's crooked and rough places. All flesh, the living, no less than the dead, shall see the glory of the Lord, come to know his glorious attribute of love.

41:1. The people shall renew their strength. They need not die.

41:17-20. The perfection of the earth as the everlasting home of man is here visioned, with its blessings of life for the needy.

42:1-7. When the time comes for the Lord to bring the prisoners out of death's prison house none need longer die.

42:16. This way of restitution will be a new way for the world, a way of life and not a way of death.

45:8. Salvation, life, shall spring forth from the earth under the beneficent reign of the new heavens.

45:17-19. Israel shall not be ashamed nor confounded, world without end. God made the earth to be man's permanent home.

45:22-24. All the ends of the earth shall be saved, in righteousness and strength.

49:6. When the Lord is for salvation unto the end of the earth that salvation will be for the living as well as the dead.

49:8. The earth is to be established and its desolate heritages inherited. God's covenant is to bless the people with life.

49:13. The Lord will have mercy upon the mourning people.

50:2. Who is able to prove that the Lord has no power to deliver man from going down into the tomb?

51 : 6. God's salvation shall be forever.
51 : 11. Sorrow and mourning shall be at an end.
51 : 21 - 23. The afflicted shall no more drink of God's wrath.
52 : 10. When all the ends of the earth see the salvation of our God it will include the living as well as the dead.
52 : 15. The sprinkling of many nations with the blood of the New Covenant will mean their healing, their life.
53 : 11. Christ would never be satisfied unless the time should come when those for whom he died that they might live should have the opportunity to live which he bought for them.
54 : 3. The seed of the Christ, i. e., Israel, is to possess the nations. It is not God's purpose that this shall be a dead inheritance.
55 : 3. Hear and your soul shall live—shall never die.
55 : 7 - 13. God will abundantly pardon the wicked who turn to him after the day of wrath is ended.
56 : 6 - 8. Here is pictured the reconciliation of all the world, living and dead—the gathering of the outcasts.
58 : 11. The righteous shall be like a spring of water.
60 : 1 - 13. This entire passage speaks of the glory of ransomed Israel and the gathering of the forces of the redeemed race under their banner. This includes the living and the dead.
60 : 18. There shall be no more destruction in the land.
60 : 21. The people will all be righteous and not need to die.
61 : 1 - 3. A part of the church's commission is now to help the stricken world to put on beauty for ashes, to rejoice instead of mourn, to put on the garments of praise for the spirit of heaviness, by declaring that millions now living will never die.
62 : 10. The way is now being prepared for the people, a way by which they may go up to everlasting life without dying.
65 : 8. For the elect's sake God will not utterly destroy man.
65 : 17. There shall be a new earth, one in which men do not die.
65 : 20. The houses and vineyards of the people will be their permanent possession. They need not die and leave them.
66 : 18, 19. When all nations see God's glory, there will be millions then living that will see it likewise and will not need to die. The glory of God is his mercy, his love, his pity.

JEREMIAH

3 : 12 - 18. Israel shall have knowledge and understanding and no more walk after the imagination of an evil heart. This will be true of all others, living and dead, who become Israelites.
4 : 1, 2. All nations shall bless themselves in becoming Israel's seed and all shall see God's glory, and not need to pass into death.
8 : 14. An evidence that the world has ended.
15 : 19 - 21. Fleshly Israel will stand before the Lord in the time of trouble and be delivered from all her enemies. By extension this will include millions of others now living.
16 : 15, 18. Evidence that the world has ended.
16 : 19. The nations will all come to Israel to learn the truth in the new age, that they may live.
18 : 7, 8. Any nation that shall repent may be spared from the evil prophesied against it.
23 : 3, 4. Evidences that the world has ended.
24 : 6, 7. Israel (and others with him) shall be builded and not pulled down, planted and not plucked up.
25 : 11, 12. A reference to the seventy jubilees that must pass over Israel before they really enter the promised land. These 3,500 years began with the entrance into Canaan in the spring of 1575 B. C. and will end in the spring of 1925 A. D. That is to say, the last year will be a jubilee year and the last year of the 3,500 years will witness the antitype, the great jubilee of restitution.

29:14. Evidences that the world has ended.
30:3. Evidences that the world has ended.
30:18. Evidences that the world has ended.
30:23. Evidences that the world has ended.
31:6-12. Evidences, that the world has ended.
31:15-17. When Rachel's children return from the land of the enemy there will be millions of other children that need not die.
31:29, 30. None will die except those who sin wilfully.
31:34-37. All shall know the Lord. The nation of Israel shall never cease from being a nation. ·
32:39, 40. The people will have one heart and one way and God will not cease to do them good.
33:1-14. Millions now living will never die.
46:16. Evidence of the end of the world.
46:27, 28. Israel, and by extension the world, shall be in rest, at ease and no longer afraid of going into death.
49:11. Certain ones are to be preserved alive in the evil time.
50:4, 5. God's perpetual covenant with Israel, and by extension the world, looks to the time when death will end.

LAMENTATIONS

3:52-56. Evidence that the world has ended.

EZEKIEL

1:16. Evidence that the world has ended.
2:3, 9. Evidence that the world has ended.
3:15, 21. Evidence that the world has ended.
4:5, 6. Evidence that the world has ended.
7:16, 19. Evidence that the world has ended.
8:3. Evidence that the world has ended.
9:2. Evidence that the world has ended.
11:17-19. Evidence that the world has ended, also of God's purpose to recreate fleshly Israel, and by extension the world, in righteousness to the end that they need not die.
14:21. Evidence that the world has ended.
16:53-63. God's promised recovery of the Sodomites out of death and to righteousness argues that millions living need never die.
18:1-32. This entire chapter contains direct evidence that the time will come when none will need to die.
20:33-44. Evidence that the world has ended, also of God's purpose to turn his smile of favor and hence of life to fleshly Israel and, by extension, to the world.
21:15, 25-27, 31. Evidence that the world has ended.
24:16. Evidence that the world has ended.
28:26. The people are to dwell with no fear of death.
33:11-16. Direct evidence that the time will come when men shall live and not die.
33:22. Evidence that the world has ended.
34:25-28. The people shall dwell safely and not fear death.
36:26-30, 35-38. When the people receive their new hearts and the attendant blessings none will longer need to go into death.
37:21-28. Evidence that the world has ended, because we see the regathering progress; also of God's purpose to bless the Israelites with everlasting peace from all their enemies, including the greatest of enemies, death. This, by extension, goes to all the world.
38:23. When the nations know God they will no longer die.
39:13-16, 29. When the Lord is exalted in the end of Jacob's trouble the remnant will not need to go into death.
47:9. This story about the river of life shows that when it flows the people then living need never die.

DANIEL

2:34, 35. Evidences of the end of the world.
2:44, 45. The kingdom of life, when established, will be unending. None living then need ever die.
5:25, 26. Evidence that the world has ended.
7:26, 27. The dominion of papal power has been taken away and is being consumed, and about to be destroyed. To take its place we are shortly to have an everlasting dominion *under* the whole heavens which will bless all the obedient with life everlasting.
8:25. The papal beast is now standing up against the Prince of princes and is immediately to be broken without hand. The world has ended; his power is forever at an end.
12:1, 4, 12. Evidence that the world has ended.

HOSEA

2:13. Evidence that the world has ended.
2:14, 15. A door of hope is opened that the world may not die.
2:18-23. When the people are betrothed to the Lord in faithfulness they will no longer go into death.
3:5. When men fear the Lord and his goodness it shows such a heart relationship as will make their continuous life assured.
6:1, 2. Chronological evidence that the world has ended, and that the time for continuous life is here.
6:9. Evidence that the world has ended.
8:8-10. Evidence that the world has ended.
10:12. When the Lord rains righteousness upon the people it will reach the living of mankind first.
13:14. Death is to be destroyed out of the earth.

JOEL

1:15. Evidence that the world has ended.
2:2. Evidence that the world has ended.
2:23-32. When the Lord pours out his spirit upon all flesh none then living need ever die.
3:9, 10. Evidence that the world has ended.

AMOS

5:4. A direct statement that some need never die.
5:8 A direct statement that God will turn the shadow of death into the morning and that hence many now living need never die.
5:14, 15. A remnant is promised the gift of continued life.
8:11, 12. Evidence that the world has ended.
9:11-15. Israel (and so the world) is to plant vineyards and eat the fruit and not to be pulled up any more, not even by death.

OBADIAH

17-21. When the saviors come up on Mount Zion they will save Israel and all the world from death and every evil thing.

JONAH

3:4. An evidence that the world has ended.
3:10. Repentance is the way to life. Some may find this way.
4:11. This preservation of Nineveh from destruction fitly represents the passing over of some in the end of this age.

MICAH

1:2-4. Evidences that the world has ended.
3:6, 7. This prophetic blindness of the clergy has come to pass.
4:1-8. They shall sit under their own vines and fig trees, no longer afraid even of death, for it shall not come near them.

MICAH

7:16-20. God will pass by the transgression of the remnant of the heritage; they need not die; a direct statement.

NAHUM

1:15. When the wicked are cut off others will be spared.
2:8-6. Evidence that the world has ended.

HABAKKUK

1:12. "We shall not die."
2:1. Evidence that the world has ended.
2:14. When the earth is thus filled with the knowledge of God none will longer need to die.
3:2-6. In the day of wrath God will remember mercy.
3:12-16. When the earth is filled with the knowledge of the love of God none will longer need to die.

ZEPHANIAH

1:14-17. Evidence that the world has ended.
2:2,3. Some will be hid in the day of the Lord's anger.
2:11. All false gods will be destroyed; the people will all serve the true God and not need to go into death.
3:8-20. This entire passage is all in sympathetic harmony with the thought that millions now living will never die.

HAGGAI

2:7. The desire of all nations is life; and it will come.

ZECHARIAH

2:10-13. The Lord will dwell in the midst of the people, bringing the blessing of life for which they long.
3:10. When every man loves his neighbor as himself none will need to die.
8:3-15. Blessings promised to the remnant of the people.
8:21-23. Evidence that the world has ended.
9:9-12. Chronological evidence that the world has ended.
9:16,17. When the prisoners of hope are saved the salvation will also extend to those in the prison yard as well as in the tombs.
10:8-12. Israel (and so all the world) is redeemed and is to be restored and strengthened and to live with her children.
13:8,9. The third part is to be brought through the fire.
14:8-11. When the Lord is king over all the earth none will longer need to die. There shall be no more utter destruction.
14:16-20. When holiness is so general in the earth that men are glad to travel with signs on their harnesses "Holiness unto the Lord" the time for death will have passed.

MALACHI

1:11. When in every place heart adoration is offered unto the Lord none will longer need to die.
3:1-3. Evidence that the world has ended.
3:7,16-18. There is coming a day when the world will turn about and see things from the divine viewpoint, and cease dying.
4:1-6. Evidence that the world has ended and that millions now living will "grow up as calves of the stall".

MATTHEW

5:1. The meek shall inherit the earth; they shall not die.
7:27. Evidence that the world has ended.
8:11. The living shall participate in the kingdom.
8:26. Representing the great calm following the time of trouble.

11:28. The weary, heavy laden world will find rest in the new king. They will be no longer burdened by the fear of death.
12:20. The work of the judgment day, now begun, is for the very purpose of preventing the utter extinguishment of life.
13:48. Evidence that the world has ended.
17:11. Evidence that the world has ended.
18:11. The Son of man came to save the dying world, not to destroy. When he reigns death is no more.
19:16. The privilege of living on into the new era will be possible for those who take advantage of the means then open.
19:30. Many who are last upon the earth prior to the kingdom will be first to be blessed.
20:8, 16. Evidence that the world has ended.
20:28. A ransom for all means an opportunity for all and this will be granted to both the living and the dead in his due time.
22:11, 13. Evidence that the world has ended.
22:32. God is a god of the living and when his time comes to give life to the dead he will surely not overlook those then living.
24:1-51. Entire chapter is evidence that the world has ended.
25:5. Evidence that the world has ended.
25:19. Evidence that the world has ended.
25:31, 32, 46. The living, as well as the dead, will share in this classification and in the promised reward of eternal life.
26:28. When the blood is applied on behalf of the many, millions now living need never die.

MARK

3:26. Evidence that the world has ended.
9:12. Evidence that the world has ended.
10:31. Many who are last upon earth prior to the kingdom will be first to be blessed.
13:10. Evidence that the world has ended.
13:19. Evidence that the world has ended.
13:20. The days will be shortened and some flesh will be saved.

LUKE

2:10, 14, 22. The glad tidings of life will be to all people, living and dead, when the due time has come.
3:7-11. These warnings to fleshly Israel are appropriate to be given now to nominal spiritual Israel in the end of *their* age.
11:2. The doing of God's will on earth as it is done in heaven implies that death will some time be no more.
12:32. Those who are to be saved with the heavenly salvation will be but a little flock, but they shall have myriads of subjects.
13:28-30. The living shall participate in the kingdom.
15:11-32. The parable of the prodigal son shows the world's recovery from sin and death, beginning with those now living.
17:26-30. Evidence that the world has ended; also, Noah and Lot did not die in their times of trouble.
18:8. Evidence that the world has ended.
19:10. The Lord comes at his second advent to give life to those he redeemed at his first advent.
19:27. Those who are willing the king shall reign over them will not be slain.
21:24, 25, 29-33. Evidence that the world has ended.

JOHN

1:4, 9. Every man that ever lived is to be enlightened and, appropriately, this enlightenment will begin with the living.
3:15, 16. It is not God's will that any should perish.
4:36. Evidence that the world has ended.

5:25-29. When all that are in their graves hear his voice and come forth none will longer need to die.

6:5, 47-51, 58. This great multitude that was fed with literal bread represents the world, living and dead, that will be given life.

8:51, 52. Some will never taste of death.

10:10. Christ has come that they may have life, not death.

11:25, 26. At the proper time, those believing shall never die.

12:32. All men, living and dead, are to be drawn to the Lord.

17:2. Christ's power over all flesh will result in eternal life to living as well as dead.

21:4, 5, 6. In the morning of the Millennial day there will be a great ingathering, both of the living and the dead.

ACTS

1:6. When the kingdom is restored to Israel death will end.

2:16-21. Evidence that the world has ended and that millions who call upon the name of the Lord shall be saved from death.

3:19-21. Times of refreshing accompany the times of restitution.

7:23, 30, 36. Chronological evidence that the world has ended.

7:37. A reference to the great Deliverer of living and dead.

10:42, 43. During the judgment day, now here, the Lord will judge (uplift and bless) both the living and the dead.

13:38, 39. The forgiveness and justification here referred to will be operative toward both the living and the dead.

13:47. The Lord will be the salvation of all, living and dead.

15:13-18. After the people for the Lord's name have been selected and his ruined kingdom has been reëstablished in the earth, the ultimate purpose, the blessing of the residue of men, living and dead, with the gift of life, will be manifested.

17:30, 31. A blessed assurance to the living and the dead.

24:15. This restanding of the unjust for which the apostle hoped will be operative toward the living as well as the dead.

ROMANS

2:10. These blessings coming to the Jews and afterwards to the Gentiles will be for the living as well as the dead.

3:26. The Lord Jesus will be justifier of living as well as dead.

5:17-19. When the "many" are made righteous it will include the living as well as the dead.

6:23. This gift of God will be extended to the living as well as the dead when the New Covenant goes into operation.

8:5. The law could not give life to the weak Jews but Jesus can do so, and, by extension, to all, living and dead.

8:19-23. When the creation ceases to groan, as a result of the manifestation of the sons of God, Jesus and his body-members, the blessings then due will be for both living and dead.

10:13-21. When the message of the gospel does go into all the world and when Israel does know the truth, as herein prophesied, all who shall call upon the name of the Lord shall be saved.

11:26-32. When all Israel is saved the salvation will extend to others, living and dead, as they come under the New Covenant.

16:20. When Satan is bruised under the feet of the Christ, salvation will follow to all the living and the dead.

1. CORINTHIANS

6:2. When the saints judge the world (for their uplifting) this judging work will begin with the living and, in a sense, now is.

15:20-23. When the due time for all to be made alive is here it will not be longer necessary for any to go into death.

2. CORINTHIANS

5:15. Christ died for all and the blessings of his ransom price will be extended to all, living and dead.

5:18-20. When, as a result of the world's trespasses being imputed to our Lord, he offers them the gift of life under the New Covenant, that gift will be for the living as well as the dead.

GALATIANS

3:8. When all the nations are blessed the living will participate.
3:29. The promise is that all the nations shall be blessed.

EPHESIANS

1:10-14. When Christ gathers together all the earthly things in himself it will include the living as well as the dead. All mankind are his purchased possession.

PHILIPPIANS

2:9-11. When every knee bows and every tongue confesses that Jesus Christ is Lord of his heart death will be no more.
3:21. When God subdues all men, bringing them unto himself, his work will include the living, as well as the dead.

COLOSSIANS

1:20. It is God's purpose to reconcile to himself all men.

1. THESSALONIANS

4:16. This is a shout of encouragement for both living and dead.
5:3, 4. Evidence that the world has ended.

2. THESSALONIANS

1:9, 10. The Lord will be admired by the whole world, living and dead, in his Millennial day, now at hand.
2:3-9. Evidences that the world has ended.

1. TIMOTHY

2:3-6. When Christ Jesus' due time has come that his ransom be testified to all men, it will reach the living first.
4:1-3. Evidence that the world has ended.
4:9-11. God is the savior of all, living and dead.

2. TIMOTHY

2:20. When the earthen vessels in God's great house of the universe are being put in order the work will begin with those living.
3:1-5, 9. Evidence that the world has ended.
4:1-4. Evidence that the world has ended.

TITUS

2:11-14. When God's grace that brings salvation to all men appears to the world it will come first to the living.

HEBREWS

2:7-9. The original plan is to be carried out. The first feature or step toward the carrying out of the plan is the death of Jesus as man's ransom price. The return of the dominion will follow.
6:2. During the "age-lasting judgment" day referred to in this text the first to be blessed will be the living.
7:19-27. The old Law Covenant brought perfect life to none, but the new Law Covenant will accomplish what the first could not.
8:6, 10. Another reference to the better covenant. See above.
9:7. The typical offering on behalf of all the people of Israel represented Christ's offering for all the people, living and dead.
9:26-28. The first to "look for him" will be the living, followed, every man in his own order, by all the dead.
10:16. The rewriting of the law of love in the hearts of men will begin with the living first.

11:39,40. An earthly salvation is provided for some, and obviously will be first presented to those living when it has arrived.
12:22-27. Evidence that the world has ended.

JAMES

5:1-5. Evidence that the world has ended.

1. PETER

2:12. The day of visitation of the world will be the Millennial day and the first ones thus "visited" will be the living.

2. PETER

3:1-13. Evidence that the world has ended.

1. JOHN

2:2. Inasmuch as Jesus' death was the propitiation or satisfaction for the sins of the whole world it follows that the whole world, living and dead, have a direct interest in it and will share the gift of life thereby purchased. These blessings will be available to both the living and the dead, and to the living first.
2:17,18. Evidence that the world has ended.

JUDE

6,17,18. Evidence that the world has ended.

REVELATION

1:18. Our Lord has the key of death for a purpose, and that purpose is to unlock the prison-house, both for those already in the prison itself and those in the courtyard of the prison, those in the grave and those on the way thither.
4:10. These elders may now be discerned in this very act.
5:10. God's kingdom is to be reëstablished in the earth and its subjects will be the living and the dead—the living first.
6:12-17. Evidence that the world has ended.
8:1. Evidence that the world has ended.
10:3,7. Evidence that the world has ended.
11:17,18. Evidence that the world has ended.
14:6,10,20. Evidence that the world has ended.
15:3. Evidence that the world has ended.
15:4. This promise to all nations will be to the living first.
15:6. Evidence that the world has ended.
16:13-21. Evidence that the world has ended.
17:12-18. Evidence that the world has ended.
18:1-24. Evidence that the world has ended.
20:3. Evidence that the world has ended.
20:12. This trial of the world will be for the benefit of those dead in trespasses and sins as well as those actually dead.
20:13. The sea here apparently is a symbolic sea, and seemingly offers direct evidence that the first to be reached by the kingdom blessings will be those who have been through the time of trouble.
21:1-7. Evidence that the world has ended and that millions now living will never die.
21:24. This bringing of the nations into light and life will be for the living nations first.
22:2,3. The healing of the nations will be for the living nations first. When the curse is removed none will longer need to die.
22:17. When the spirit and the bride say, Come, they will say it first to those then living and subsequently to all mankind. There is every reason to believe that, when the due time has come for the bride to extend this message to mankind, none of those who hear and heed the message need longer go into death.

Every
other week

$2.00
Canada & Foreign $2.50
per year

A·JOURNAL·OF·FACT
HOPE·AND·CONVICTION

A magazine with the
unique object of inter-
preting world events in
the light of divine pro-
phecy, of chronicling
the birth-pangs of the
nascent age of bliss?

The
Golden
Age

Thirty-two pages

Ten departments:

Labor & Economics · Social & Educational · Fi-
nance, Commerce, Transp'tion · Political · Agriculture
Science & Invention · Housewifery & Hygiene · Travel and
Miscellany · Religion & Philosophy · Manufacturing & Mining

The Golden Age, 35 Myrtle Ave., Brooklyn, N.Y. City.

The WATCH TOWER

and

Herald of Christ's Presence

This journal, founded by the author of SCRIP-TURE STUDIES, should regularly visit all who have the slightest interest in the topics discussed in this and the other treatises of the SCRIPTURE STUDIES series, booklets, etc. It is issued twice a month, 16 pages, at $1.00 a year, in advance for the United States, or $1.50 a year to Canada and foreign countries.

That *none* of the interested may be without it, the arrangement is that those who need may have it on credit on application while those too poor to pay may receive it regularly *free* by stating the facts and making request each year.

Published by:

WATCH TOWER BIBLE & TRACT SOCIETY

BROOKLYN, N. Y., U. S. A.

BRANCHES: LONDON, W., MELBOURNE, CAPE TOWN, TORONTO, OREBRO, BARMEN, ZURICH, BERNE, ETC.

This Society never solicits donations, but it uses voluntary contributions as wisely and economically as possible in the propagation of Christian knowledge along the lines presented in SCRIPTURE STUDIES. It yearly circulates tons of tracts and papers free, through the mails and through voluntary agents.

It justifies that portion of its name which relates to the Bible (not by publishing Bibles, nor by circulating them gratuitiously, but) by supplying Bibles and Bible-study helps at wholesale prices; and often below the usual wholesale rates. We mention a few of these on accompanying pages, of course ranking SCRIPTURE STUDIES as the most important helps or "Bible Keys", and THE WATCH TOWER, semi-monthly, their efficient supplement.

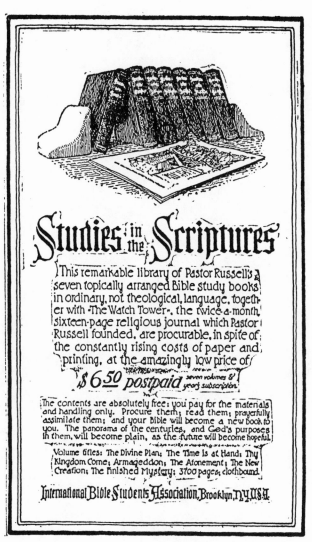

CAN ?
THE LIVING
TALK WITH
THE DEAD
? ?

Can?
THE LIVING
TALK WITH
THE DEAD
? ?

A CLEAR EXPLANATION
OF SPIRITISM

Published by
International Bible Students Association
Brooklyn, New York, United States of America

THIS little booklet is written and specially dedicated to certain inquiring friends, and to all of mankind who are sincerely interested in their departed loved ones.

J. F. RUTHERFORD

New York, N. Y., U. S. A.
January, 1920

FOREWORD

AMONG the topics of absorbing interest which are before the public mind today none can be of greater importance to men and women of every nation than "Can the Living Talk with the Dead" and "Millions now Living will Never Die".

The first of these topics is treated in this booklet in such a manner, we trust, as to satisfy the desire of all honest truth-seekers and to free them from the distress of superstition and needless fear.

"Millions now Living will Never Die," the companion piece to this booklet, now published, is helping multitudes of people to discern between truth and error.

The demand for these treatises has arisen from the fact that lectures on both of these subjects have been and still are being delivered in the great cities of Europe, Great Britain, Canada, and the United States. Judge Rutherford, of New York, probably the world's best known lawyer-Biblicist, after treating these topics orally has been urgently and repeatedly requested to put his treatises into printed form. This booklet is a response to these urgings. A more exhaustive treatment of these subjects will be found in STUDIES IN THE SCRIPTURES. See advertisement, page 128.

INTERNATIONAL BIBLE STUDENTS ASSOCIATION

Brooklyn, N. Y., January 15, 1920

Table *of* Contents

CHAPTER I
THE COLLOQUY

Three Gentlemen discuss the subject of Communication with the Dead—Two Opposing Views presented, for the purpose of convincing the third man—Strong arguments pro and con............5

CHAPTER II
PSYCHIC'S ARGUMENT

Holds that such communication is an established fact—Quotes from Professor Hyslop and Sir Arthur Conan Doyle—Demonstrates that a willing mind, a desire to penetrate into the unknown, is the first essential to conviction — Evidence produced in alleged letters from a dead soldier to his mother................9

CHAPTER III
LIGHTBEARER'S ARGUMENT

Presents negative side of the proposition — Declares that the argument stands or falls with the doctrine of the Inherent Immortality of man's soul — Cites Scriptures to prove his position — What is the soul ? — Death the penalty for sin — Satan's great deception in Eden — Origin of evil spirits or demons — Meaning of Jesus' death and resurrection — Satan's seed and their work — "The Mystery of Iniquity" — Demons in Babylon...43

CHAPTER IV
NEWDAY'S CONCLUSION

Holds to Scriptural evidence — Man's hope of future life lies in the Resurrection......................87

CHAPTER V
UNSEEN RULER

A minic god — His demon associates — The earth corrupted — Noah's flood — True religion established by Jehovah — False religion instituted by Satan—Counterfeit "seed of the woman" — Origin of all heathen worship — Israelites influenced by heathen — God's typical kingdom overthrown — True "seed of the woman" — Christendom not Christ's kingdom — False religion vs. faithless religion — Three ruling elements of devil's organization — Symbolic beasts of Scripture — The overthrow of Satan's empire in progress.........................89

CHAPTER VI
DEMON PHENOMENA ANALYZED

-ism as reported in the Public Press — Demon methods of manifestation — Evil spirits hate and fear the Bible — Have no real interest in humanity — Encourage loose morals — Incite to murder and other crimes — Have power to inject thoughts into men's minds — Deceive the senses by supposed materializations —Actual materializations have occurred, but at cost of suffering to the medium —Downward tendency of all spiritist phenomena — Victims frequently driven insane.....................103

Can the Living Talk with the Dead?

CHAPTER I

THE COLLOQUY

MR. PSYCHIC: Good morning, Mr. Newday. I read in the paper that your son has fallen in the great World War while fighting in France. Permit me to extend my condolence and deep sympathy.

MR. NEWDAY: Yes, it is true. My beloved son, the idol of my life, is gone and my heart is almost broken.

PSYCHIC: But be of good courage, Mr. Newday; I do not believe he is dead. Can you really think your son is dead?

NEWDAY: Oh yes, there is no doubt about it; the proof has been brought to me by men who saw him drop, pierced with an enemy ball. If only I could have spoken to him once before he departed.

PSYCHIC: I am sure, Mr. Newday, what I am about to tell you will bring some consolation to your heart; hence I bring this message to you. For some time I have been reading in books, papers and magazines some very remarkable facts, which seem to show that our dead friends are not really dead, but have passed on to another world, and that they are progressing in happiness; and that we on the earth, under certain conditions, can communicate with them.

NEWDAY: But is not that what is known as spiritism, which has been attended by so much fraud? How do we know that this is not some fraud practised upon us? Does not human experience show that men have been

5

dying for centuries, and why should we now think we
are able to talk with the dead; particularly why should
this be so since the war?

PSYCHIC: I know the majority of people have little
or no confidence in the ability of one to communicate
with the spirit world—those who have died and gone;
that they believe it to be fraudulent. But when so many
great men come forward with their testimony, giving
their experience—men who have no purpose whatsoever
in practising fraud upon others—the situation seems to
be changed. I know there are many who deny that
there is even such a thing as a spirit being; but did not
Jesus of Nazareth go and preach to the spirits in prison,
and does not that prove that men who had previously
died were then alive and able to hear his preaching?
And if so, is it at all unreasonable to think that they can
communicate with us? Let me encourage you to investigate this, Mr. Newday.

NEWDAY: Yes, there seems to be some force in your
argument; but it would really seem too good to believe
that my son is where I can now talk to him. Ah, but
here comes Mr. Lightbearer. I know him to be a man
of sterling honesty and a lover of the truth—one who
has given much study to the question concerning the
dead. Let us ask him what he thinks about it.

Mr. Psychic, please make the acquaintance of Mr.
Lightbearer.

PSYCHIC: I am glad to meet you, Mr. Lightbearer.
Our mutual friend, Mr. Newday, lost his only son in this
great war and I have just been telling him that I am
sure his son is not dead and I believe he can talk with
him if he desires; and he proposed that we ask your
opinion about this matter. May we be favored with
what you think upon this subject?

MR. LIGHTBEARER: I do not believe we can communicate with the dead, for the reason that they are dead. I do not believe that Mr. Newday can communicate with his dead son. To my mind such a conclusion is wholly illogical, unreasonable, and above all it is un-Scriptural. By this you will understand that I believe in the Bible.

PSYCHIC: Ah, but we all believe in the Bible.

NEWDAY: Yes, indeed, I have been a Christian all my life and believe the Bible is God's word of truth, given to us for our instruction.

LIGHTBEARER: Well, gentlemen, it is gratifying to know that all of us believe in the Bible. We have now some reasonable point from which to view this question; and, according to my way of looking at the matter, the Bible is the only true and reliable source of knowledge concerning it. I consider this a great and vital question to the people today and believe that a wrong conclusion upon it will have much to do with wrecking society.

Since we all believe in the Bible as God's inspired word of truth, we will surely all agree that the Bible must be the final arbiter of this great question. Do we all so agree? Thank you, gentlemen; I am glad that you indicate your assent.

NEWDAY: Gentlemen, I am at this time more vitally interested in this question than either of you, seeing I have just lost my beloved son. I believe I am competent to weigh dispassionately the arguments *pro* and *contra,* and I know my desire is to have the truth upon the subject. Therefore I propose that each of you present your respective arguments and let me make up my mind at the conclusion. There can be no harm resulting from hearing both sides of the question, and all of us may be greatly blessed if we are honest in our endeavors to reach a just conclusion. Are you willing to do this?

Since you both signify your willingness, we will first hear Mr. Psychic present his side.

CHAPTER II

PSYCHIC'S ARGUMENT

PSYCHIC: The evidence now available proving that the living can talk with the dead is so cumulative and overwhelming that I attempt to present it to you, Mr. Newday, with confidence that I will convince your reasonable mind of the correctness of the claim; and if I do, then I am certain I have done you a great good and brought much comfort to your heart.

I am fully aware of the fact that for many years men of strong reasoning faculties have refused to consider any evidence on this subject, looking upon it as partaking of fraud and misrepresentation, or due to some hallucination. For a long while the ultra-ignorant and superstitious have been willing to listen to such testimony, but not so with those who 'desired to have something more substantial or tangible upon which to base a conclusion. In modern times, however, the conditions have been exactly reversed. The World War seems to have awakened many and now the greatest thinkers among worldly men have become devotees of the psychic science and phenomena—men of character, who have no desire or purpose to mislead and who would positively refuse to be parties to anything that would have a semblance of fraud or deceit. Among the great men who have testified that the living can communicate with the dead are the late William T. Stead, the greatest of modern journalists; Prof. Lombroso, the great scientist; Prof. James H. Hyslop; Crookes, the great chemist; Wallace, Darwin, Flammarion, Sir Oliver Lodge, Sir Arthur Conan Doyle, the Reverend Fielding Ould, the Reverend Arthur

Chambers, the Reverend Charles Tweedale, the late Archdeacon Wilberforce, and many others.

It will be conceded that man's greatest desire is to have and enjoy endless life. Nearly every living person has some friend or relative or loved one who has been taken away from him by death. The living, of course, are deeply interested in their loved ones who have gone. They also desire to have some knowledge themselves of what their future holds for them. This desire to communicate with their departed ones has greatly increased and especially has this been augmented by the conditions resulting from the World War. When we consider the fact that the flower of civilization, the stalwart young men of the world by the million have fallen in the last few years, we are not surprised that scientific minds have moved with greater energy and keener desire to know what there is beyond the grave. Probably this is the reason we have such a great abundance of testimony today that the dead are not dead, but are more alive than before they died; and that they can communicate with those on the earth who have a desire to communicate with them and who are willing to meet the necessary requirements to do so.

All the evidence shows, as you will observe, that the first thing essential is a *willingness* to be convinced of the truth of psychic claims—a *consent of the will* and the mind to hear, to understand and to believe that our dead friends are really alive and that we can communicate with them; and with such an open mind we are in a proper attitude to receive the proof, and without it we cannot.

I first desire to call attention to the various tested methods by which the living can communicate with the dead. I make the following quotation from the book*

---

* "Contact with the Other World", Chapter X.

by James H. Hyslop, Ph.D.,LL.D., formerly Professor
of Logic and Ethics in Columbia University:
"The popular terms for the method of communicating
with the dead are automatic writing, raps, table-tipping,
planchette writing, spelling by the ouija board, impressions, and the more technical terms of clairvoyance and
clairaudience. All but the last two take their names from
the physical instruments or the physical means employed
in the work. The last two are names for peculiar phenomena in vision and hearing, which will be more fully
described a little later.

"Automatic writing is distinguished from ordinary
writing only in being unconscious or involuntary. Only
certain tests, such as trance or anæsthesia, or the testimony of the trustworthy subject, will decide whether a
person is writing automatically. . . . .

"The methods of table-tipping, the planchette and
the ouija board are only modifications of automatic writing. Many people suppose that there is some mystery or
virtue about the ouija, which enables it to spell out
messages from other minds. They do not reflect that
the same process is involved in all the methods named.
The muscular system of the operators is in action in
each of them in the same way. The instrument or means
of expression has nothing to do with the result, when the
human organism must intervene in the phenomena.
There is no mysterious power in the ouija, the planchette,
or the table, any more than there is in the pencil. They
are all agents or media, as they are in normal action of
the same kind. The actual evidence for the supernormal
lies, not in the action of automatic writing, of the ouija
or planchette, or of the table, but in the content of the
message. If the content represents normally acquired
information, we explain the message by subconscious
action of the writer's mind. If the content is unmistak-

ably foreign to normal experience, we seek for the external stimulus or mind that may account for it. The method of delivery is of secondary importance.

"Another method of communication is by raps. They are not always connected with the motor action of the psychic. No doubt some raps are simply ordinary automatisms like automatic writing and other unconscious actions. But they are often independent of any intervention by the human organism as revealed to sense-perception. They are used as signals of answers to questions: and, being foreign to either conscious or unconscious action of the organism, another explanation must be sought for them than for automatic writing. The latter assumes at least the intervention of the physical organism with its powers and habits. But raps may involve no such intermediary and in this case they must be regarded as independent physical phenomena. They can be used only for answers to questions or for spelling out words in various ways. Their method of communication is crude, in the sense that it takes time and trouble to get intelligible messages; but they signify the possibility of communication with the outside world without the mediation of the subconscious or normal machinery of the human organism.

"Clairvoyance and clairaudience are very different processes. Clairaudience is the hearing of apparently foreign messages, by means of voices, usually 'internal voices'. Possibly they are sometimes apparently external, but since those who experience the facts are not always adept in analyzing and describing the experiences, we are not sure that the experiences are other than subjective or hallucinatory, though the stimulus may be foreign. Both clairaudience and clairvoyance are sensory phenomena, unconnected with motor action, whereas automatic writing and other forms of communication, except independent raps, are connected with the motor functions.

"Clairvoyance, however, is a term that does duty for three distinct types of phenomena. (1) It denotes generally the power of mediumship in so far as the messages are obtained by impressions or visual pictures. It is even very often used to denote any type of communication with the dead, and so is made synonymous with mediumship, excluding purely physical phenomena. (2) It is more technically used to denote the acquisition of foreign information through visual phantasms, as clairaudience is used to denote auditory hallucinations of the veridical type. (3) Lastly, still more technically, it denotes the perception of concealed physical objects whose whereabouts are not known by any living being. It represents the visual perception, transcendental in nature, of facts or things that cannot be known through telepathy. It presupposes supernormal perception at a distance, and excludes all mind-reading. This is the more technical conception of the process. Telæsthesia is probably a better term for this conception of clairvoyance."

It will be observed that in order to communicate with those in the spirit world it is necessary for a living person on the earth to be willing to be used and to be used for that purpose. In other words, there must be a medium. The word medium denotes a middle, or intermediary, between two things—a means of communication. Further quoting Dr. Hyslop:

"It was adopted to denote the agency which intervenes between the physical and the transcendental world. The only means of communicating with the dead has been found to be a *living organism* capable of connecting the two worlds."

You will observe that all the evidence tending to prove

that the living can talk with the dead is founded upon the great teaching that *the soul of man is immortal.* Is it not true that the Catholic and Protestant churches, almost without a single exception, for many centuries have taught that the soul is immortal, that it cannot die; hence when one dies it is merely the body that is dead, but the soul lives on? Have not these great religious teachers founded their teachings upon the Bible? Would any of us dare say that they do not believe the Bible? I am free to admit that, aside from the doctrine of inherent immortality of the soul, it would be impossible for us to believe that the dead are able to communicate with those who are on the earth.

But is it not also true that the best evidence that the soul is immortal is the fact that the dead do actually talk or communicate with the living? I first offer the evidence by Sir Arthur Conan Doyle, the noted author, who has recently published a book entitled, "The New Revelation". I quote here liberally from Sir Arthur:

"Apart from personal experiences, this movement must gain additional solidity from the wonderful literature which has sprung up around it during the last few years.

"Before going into this question of a new religious revelation, how it is reached, and what it consists of, I would say a word upon one other subject. There have always been two lines of attack by our opponents. The one is that our facts are not true. The other is that we are upon forbidden ground and should come off it and leave it alone.

". . . When the war came it brought earnestness into all our souls and made us look more closely at our own beliefs and reassess their values. In the presence of an agonized world, hearing every day of the deaths of the flower of our race in the first promise of their unfulfilled youth, seeing around one the wives and mothers who had

no clear conception whither their loved one had gone; I
seemed suddenly to see that this subject with which I
had so long dallied was not merely a study of a force
outside the rules of science, but that it was really something tremendous, a breaking down of the walls between
two worlds, a direct undeniable message from beyond,
a call of hope and guidance to the human race at the
time of its deepest affliction. The objective side of it
ceased to interest; for, having made up one's mind that
it was true there was an end of the matter. The religious side of it was clearly of infinitely greater importance."

The evidence seems to show with clearness that those
beings who are communicating with the living are not
so far away, but are in fact right near the earth. On
this point Sir Conan Doyle says:

"On my asking that lady to raise her hands and give a
succession of names, that table tilted at the correct name
of the head mistress of the school. This seemed in the
nature of a test. She went on to say that the sphere she
inhabited was *all around the earth;* that she knew about
the planets."

Continuing, in Chapter II of "The New Revelation",
Sir Arthur says:

"I can now turn with some relief to a more impersonal
view of this great subject. Allusion has been made to a
body of fresh doctrine. Whence does this come? It
comes in the main through automatic writing where the
hand of the human medium is controlled, either by an
alleged dead human being, as in the case of Miss Julia
Ames, or by an alleged higher teacher, as in that of Mr.
Stainton Moses. These written communications are sup-
plemented by a vast number of trance utterances, and by
the verbal messages of spirits, given through the lips of
mediums. Sometimes it has even come by direct voices,

as in the numerous cases detailed by Admiral Usborne
Moore in his book *The Voices.* Occasionally it has come
through the family circle and table-tilting. . . .

"It has been asserted by men for whose opinion I have
a deep regard—notably by Sir William Barratt— that
psychical research is quite distinct from religion. Certainly it is so, in the sense that a man might be a very
good psychical researcher but a very bad man. But the
results of psychical research, the deductions which we
may draw, and the lessons we may learn, teach us of the
continued life of the soul, of the nature of that life, and
of how it is influenced by our conduct here. If this is
distinct from religion, I must confess that I do not
understand the distinction. To me it *is* religion—the
very essence of it.

"But that does not mean that it will necessarily
crystallize into a new religion. Personally I trust that
it will not do so. Surely we are disunited enough
already? Rather would I see it the great unifying force,
the one provable thing connected with religion, Christian
or non-Christian, forming the common solid basis upon
which each raises, if it must raise, that separate system
which appeals to the varied types of mind. The Southern races will always demand what is less austere than
the North, the West will always be more critical than
the East. One cannot shape all to a level conformity.
But if the broad premises which are guaranteed by this
teaching from beyond are accepted,then the human race
has made a great stride towards religious peace and
unity. The question which faces us, then, is: How will
this influence bear upon the older organized religions
and philosophies which have influenced the actions of
men?

"The answer is, that to only one of these religions or
philosophies is this new revelation absolutely fatal. That

is to Materialism. I do not say this in any spirit of hostility to Materialists, who as far as they are an organized body are, I think, as earnest and moral as any other class. But the fact is manifest that if spirit can live without matter, then the foundation of Materialism is gone, and the whole scheme of thought crashes to the ground.

"As to other creeds, it must be admitted that an acceptance of the teaching brought to us from beyond would deeply modify conventional Christianity. But these modifications would be rather in the direction of explanation and development than of contradiction. It would set right grave misunderstandings which have always offended the reason of every thoughtful man, but it would also confirm and make absolutely certain the fact of life after death, the base of all religion. It would confirm the unhappy results of sin, though it would show that those results are never absolutely permanent. It would confirm the existence of higher beings, whom we have called angels, and of an ever ascending hierarchy above us, in which the Christ spirit finds its place, culminating in heights of the infinite with which we associate the idea of all-power or of God. It would confirm the idea of heaven and of a temporary penal state which corresponds to purgatory rather than hell. Thus this new revelation, on some of the most vital points, is *not* destructive of the beliefs, and it should be hailed by really earnest men of all creeds as a most powerful ally, rather than a dangerous devil-begotten enemy.

"On the other hand, let us turn to the points in which Christianity must be modified by this new revelation.

"First of all I would say this, which must be obvious to many, however much they deplore it: Christianity must change or must perish. That is the law of life— that things must adapt themselves or perish. Christian-

ity has deferred the change very long, she has deferred it
until her churches are half empty, until women are her
chief supporters, and until both the learned part of the
community on one side and the poorest class on the
other, in both town and country, are largely alienated
from her. Let us try to trace the reason for this. It is
apparent in all sects, and comes, therefore, from some
deep common cause.

"People are alienated because they frankly do not
believe the facts as presented to them to be true. Their
reason and their sense of justice are equally offended.
One can see no justice in a vicarious sacrifice, nor in the
God who could be placated by such means. Above all
many cannot understand such expressions as the 'redemption from sin', 'cleansed by the blood of the Lamb,' and
so forth. So long as there was any question of the fall
of man there was at least some sort of explanation of
such phrases; but when it became certain that man had
never fallen— when with ever fuller knowledge we could
trace our ancestral course down through the cave-man
and the drift-man, back to that shadowy and far-off time
when the man-like ape slowly evolved into the ape-like
man—looking back on all this vast succession of life, we
knew that it had always been arising from step to step.
Never was there any evidence of a fall. But if 'there
were no fall, then what became of the atonement, of the
redemption, of original sin, of a large part of Christian
mystical philosophy? Even if it were as reasonable in
itself as it is actually unreasonable, it would still be
divorced from the facts.

"Again, too much seemed to be made of Christ's
death. It is no uncommon thing to die for an idea.
Every religion has equally had its martyrs. Men die
continually for their convictions. Thousands of our lads
are doing it at this instant in France. Therefore the

death of Christ, beautiful as it is in the Gospel narrative, has seemed to assume an undue importance, as though it were an isolated phenomenon for a man to die in pursuit of a reform. In my opinion, far too much stress has been laid upon Christ's death, and far too little upon his life. That was where the true grandeur and the true lesson lay. It was a life which even in those limited records shows us no trait which is not beautiful— a life full of easy tolerance for others, of kindly charity, of broadminded moderation, of gentle courage, always progressive and open to new ideas, and yet never bitter to those ideas which he was really supplanting, though he did occasionally lose his temper with the more bigoted and narrow supporters. Especially one loves his readiness to get at the spirit of religion, sweeping aside the texts and the forms. Never had any one such a robust common sense, or such a sympathy for weakness. It was this most wonderful and uncommon life, and not his death, which is the true center of the Christian religion.

"Now, let us look at the light which we get from the spirit guides upon this question of Christianity. Opinion is not absolutely uniform yonder, any more than it is here; but reading a number of messages upon this subject, they amount to this: There are many higher spirits with our departed. They vary in degree. Call them 'angels', and you are in touch with old religious thought. High above all these is the greatest spirit of whom they have cognizance—not God, since God is so infinite that he is not within their ken—but one who is nearer God and to that extent represents God. This is the Christ Spirit. His special care is the earth. He came down upon it at a time of great earthly depravity—a time when the world was almost as wicked as it is now, in order to give the people the lesson of an ideal life. Then he returned to his own high station, having left an example which is

still occasionally followed. That is the story of Christ
as spirits have described it. There is nothing here of
Atonement or Redemption. But there is a perfectly
feasible and reasonable scheme, which I, for one, could
readily believe.

"If such a view of Christianity were generally accepted,
and if it were enforced by assurance and demonstration
from the New Revelation which is coming to us from the
other side, then we should have a creed which might
unite the churches, which might be reconciled to science,
which might defy all attacks, and which might carry the
Christian faith on for an indefinite period. Reason and
faith would at least be reconciled, a nightmare would
be lifted from our minds, and spiritual peace would
prevail.

"When I read the New Testament with the knowledge
which I have of Spiritualism, I am left with a deep
conviction that the teaching of Christ was in many most
important respects lost by the early church, and has not
come down to us. All these allusions to a conquest over
death have, as it seems to me, little meaning in the
present Christian philosophy, whereas for those who
have seen, however dimly, through the veil, and touched,
however slightly, the outstretched hands beyond, death
has indeed been conquered. When we read so many
references to the phenomena with which we are familiar,
the levitations, the tongues of fire, the rushing wind, the
spiritual gifts, the working of wonders, we feel that the
central fact of all, the continuity of life and the communication with the dead, was most certainly known.
Our attention is arrested by such a saying as: 'Here he
worked no wonders because the people were wanting in
faith'. Is this not absolutely in accordance with psychic
law as we know it? Or when Christ, on being touched
by the sick woman, said: 'Who has touched me? Much

virtue has passed out of me,' could he say more clearly
what a healing medium would say now, save that 'he
would use the word 'power' instead of 'virtue'? Or when
we read: 'Try the spirits whether they be of God,' is
it not the very advice which would now be given to a
novice approaching a séance? . . . Two examples have
already been given. One which convinced me as a truth
was the thesis that the story of the materialization of
the two prophets upon the mountain was extraordinarily
accurate when judged by psychic law. There is the fact
that Peter, James, and John (who formed the psychic
circle when the dead was restored to life, and were
presumably the most helpful of the group) were taken.
Then there is the choice of the high pure air of the
mountain, the drowsiness of the attendant mediums,
the transfiguring, the shining robes, the cloud, the words:
'Let us make three tabernacles,' with its alternate reading: 'Let us make three booths or cabinets' (the ideal
way of condensing power and producing materializations)—all these make a very consistent theory of the
nature of the proceedings. For the rest, the list of gifts
which St. Paul gives as being necessary for the Christian
disciple, is simply the list of gifts of a very powerful
medium, including prophecy, healing, causing miracles
(or psychical phenomena), clairvoyance, and other powers. (1 Corinthians 12:8,11) The early Christian church
was saturated with spiritualism, and they seem to have
paid no attention to those Old Testament prohibitions
which were meant to keep these powers only for the use
and profit of the priesthood."

You will see that this witness bases much of his
conclusion upon the Bible. I further quote from him:

" . . . Communications usually come from those who
have not long passed over, and tend to grow fainter, as
one would expect. . . . There is, in Mr. Dawson Roger's

life, a very good case of a spirit who called himself
Manton, and claimed to have been born at Lawrence
Lydiard and buried at Stoke Newington in 1677. It
was clearly shown afterwards that there was such a man,
and that he was Oliver Cromwell's chaplain. So far as
my own reading goes, this is the oldest spirit who is
on record as returning, and generally they are quite
recent.

" . . . It may be remarked in passing that these and
other examples show clearly either that the spirits have
the use of an excellent reference library or else that they
have memories which produce something like omnis-
cience. No human memory could possibly carry all the
exact quotations which occur in such communications
as *The Ear of Dionysius.*"

The powers of those beyond the grave seem to be
limited, as Sir Conan Doyle says: "The spirits seem to
know exactly what they impress upon the minds of the
living, but they do not know how far they carry their
instructions out". There also seem to be lying and
wicked ones beyond the grave who seek to deceive those
on this side, according to Sir Arthur, who says:

" . . . We have, unhappily, to deal with absolute
cold-blooded lying on the part of wicked or mischievous
intelligences. Every one who has investigated the matter
has, I suppose, met with examples of willful deception,
which occasionally are mixed up with good and true
communications."

"The conclusion, then, of my long search after truth,
is that in spite of occasional fraud, which Spiritualists
deplore, and in spite of wild imaginings, which they
discourage, there remains a great solid core in this movement which is infinitely nearer to positive proof than
any other religious development with which I am acquainted. As I have shown, it would appear to be a

rediscovery rather than an absolutely new thing, but the result in this material age is the same. The days are surely passing when the mature and considered opinions of such men as Crookes, Wallace, Flammarion, Chas. Richet, Lodge, Barratt, Lombroso, Generals Drayson and Turner, Sergeant Ballantyne, W. T. Stead, Judge Edmunds, Admiral Usborne Moore, the late Archdeacon Wilberforce, and such a cloud of other witnesses, can be dismissed with the empty 'All rot' or 'Nauseating drivel' formulæ. As Mr. Arthur Hill has well said, we have reached a point where further proof is superfluous, and where the weight of disproof lies upon those who deny. . . .

" . . . The situation may, as it seems to me, be summed up in a simple alternative. The one supposition is that there has been an outbreak of lunacy extending over two, generations of mankind, and two great continents—a lunacy which assails men or women who are otherwise eminently sane. The alternative supposition is that in recent years there has come to us from divine sources a new revelation which constitutes by far the greatest religious event since the death of Christ (for the Reformation was a re-arrangement of the old, not a revelation of the new), a revelation which alters the whole aspect of death and the fate of man. Between these two suppositions there is no solid position. Theories of fraud or of delusion will not meet the evidence. It is absolute lunacy or it is a revolution in religious thought, a revolution which gives us as by-products an utter fearlessness of death, and an immense consolation when those who are dear to us pass behind the veil."

As to who may be able to communicate directly with their dead friends, Sir Conan Doyle says:

" . . . We cannot lay down laws, because the law

works from the other side as well as this. Nearly every woman is an undeveloped medium. . . .

"The clear call for our help comes from those who have had a loss and who yearn to re-establish connection. This also can be overdone. If your boy were in Australia, you would not expect him to continually stop his work and write long letters at all seasons. Having got in touch, be moderate in your demands. Do not be satisfied with any evidence short of the best, but having got that, you can, it seems to me, wait for that short period when we shall all be re-united. I am in touch at present with thirteen mothers who are in correspondence with their dead sons. In each case, the husband, where he is alive, is agreed as to the evidence. In only one case so far as I know was the parent acquainted with psychic matters before the war.

"Several of these cases have peculiarities of their own. In two of them the figures of the dead lads have appeared beside the mothers in a photograph. In one case the first message to the mother came through a stranger to whom the correct address of the mother was given. The communication afterwards became direct. In another case the method of sending messages was to give references to particular pages and lines of books in distant libraries, the whole conveying a message. The procedure was to weed out all fear of telepathy. Verily there is no possible way by which a truth can be proved by which this truth has not been proved."

Sir Conan Doyle's testimony also shows that this phenomenon of communicating with the dead was known centuries ago. Upon this point we quote:

" . . . Then or afterwards I read a book by Monsieur Jacolliot upon occult phenomena in India. Jacolliot was Chief Judge of the French Colony of Crandenagur, with a very judicial mind, but rather biased against spiritualism. He conducted a series of experiments with native fakirs, who gave him their confidence because he was a sympathetic man and spoke their language. He describes the pains he took to eliminate fraud. To cut a long story short he found among them every phenomenon of advanced European mediumship, everything which Home, for example, had ever done. He got levitation of the body, the handling of fire, movement of articles at a distance, rapid growth of plants, raising of tables. Their explanation of these phenomena was that they were done by the Pitris or *spirits*, and their only difference in procedure from ours seemed to be that they made more use of direct evocation. They claimed that these *powers were handed down from time immemorial* and traced back to the Chaldees."

I now present some testimony which to me is unusual and seems to prove conclusively that the living communicate with the dead. In November, 1919, *The Ladies' Home Journal* published a manuscript, concerning which the Editor of that journal says: "The manuscript was received from a known author. Convinced of the sincerity of the author, and realizing that these messages from an American soldier were no ordinary spirit communications, the publishers asked for further information. The author replied: 'I ask you to regard the book as truth, unaccompanied by proofs of any sort, making its own explanation and appeal'."

Briefly epitomized, this testimony is to the effect that a mother and her only son were much devoted to each other. The son was interested in wireless telegraphy. The war came on and the son received word from Washington to dismantle the wireless apparatus immediately. The son was very much disappointed, saying that he believed he was just on the verge of hitting a plan to do away with a lot of unnecessary paraphernalia with reference to wireless. The son was sent to France, assigned to an engineers' corps and became a second lieutenant. In one of the battles in France he was killed. Immediately thereafter the mother received a wireless message in the Morse code as follows:

"Mother, be game. I am alive and loving you. But my body is with thousands of other mothers' boys near Lens. Get this fact to others if you can. It's awful for us when you grieve, and we can't get in touch with you to tell you we are all right. This is a clumsy way. I'll figure out something easier. I'm confused yet.   Bob."

When they lived together in the United State both mother and son were familiar with the use of the wireless instrument. Soon after the death of her son upon the battlefield the mother claims to have received a wireless message from him, and thereafter almost daily communication by wireless telegraphy for many days. Later the wireless instrument was abandoned for the better known method of communication, viz., automatic writing. The use of cabinets and like paraphernalia was done away with, some unseen power moved the mother's hand and she wrote the messages herself. There followed from the son what are supposed to be, and what the mother claims to be, many communications in the nature of letters produced by automatic writing. These letters are quite lengthy and I shall not ask you to read them all, but I will here state in substance what they contain and refer you to the *Ladies' Home Journal* above mentioned for the full text of these letters.

The son supposed to have been killed on the battlefield, had a friend named Lieut. Wells, who had been killed also and whom the son claims to have met on the other side shortly after he was shot upon the battlefield. These messages from the son to the mother begin by attracting her with the words "Attention, get

this across"; and then the son proceeds to tell her that
there is no horror in death; that one minute his
company was in the thick of the fight and he heard the
command of the officer, and the next minute his friend
Wells touched his arm and said: "Our command has
crossed; let us go". The son, whom the letters speak of
as Bob, claims to have followed Wells, not in his human
body, but states that the human body lay dead upon
the battlefield, while with a new body and a new kind
of uniform and with no gun he followed his friend
Wells. He states that his friend Wells told him he
was dead and yet he says that he felt all right.

The son then proceeds to tell his mother that according to Wells his company is assigned for duty in the
other world. He then adds that there is much talk on
that side about the presence of one supposed to be the
Savior, amongst the dying. He claims that the best
young men of the world are selected for the army and
are killed on the battlefield in order that they might
form an ideal democracy on the other side.

He then tells his mother not to be deceived into believing that he is a mere ghost, but to believe that he is
his real self; and if she will, that they will be able to
start something worth while. He tells his mother that
in order to communicate with him she must concentrate
her mind upon him, and then adds that if he and his
mother together can convince folks that this communication is true, they can go a long way toward wiping
out sorrow. He tells his mother that if she wants to get
in communication with him to get into a quiet corner
and listen with her inner ear or finer perceptions; that
any one who has a will to do so can put out a mental
wire that will be picked up, i. e., can send out a message
and receive a message from the unknown.

He then adds that on that side there are scallawags

who are ready to jump into all conversations and mix
them up, and warns his mother against such. He advises that the best way to rid herself of them is to say:
"I will not entertain mischievous spirits".

He then proceeds to tell his mother that he has been
out on duty and that he has just returned to headquarters; that they go and come and serve, but are
not seen; that they do not need food or sleep.

Permit me now, Mr. Newday, to diverge for a moment
from stating the substance of these letters to call your
attention to a doctrine which has for many centuries
been taught in our churches, both Catholic and Protestant, and which clergymen of almost all denominations yet
hold and teach, viz., that man has an immortal soul
and that this soul is separate and distinct from the
body and cannot die. It will be seen by the examination
of the communications of the son to the mother hereinafter referred to that it is upon this doctrine of inherent
immortality that these communications are made possible. I will now proceed with an abstract of the statements in these communications from the son to the
mother.

He begins his other communication with this statement: "For we must *start on the fact that the soul is
immortal; that there is no death to the individual*".
His communication in substance then continues, that the
earth is but a preparatory planet; that the human race is
here developed and advanced to a certain point of existence, and then a change comes, which is called death;
that the new existence begins where the old left off.

But one of the strange things about this communication is (and it seems rather remarkable) that he states
that on the other side there are many dogs with him
and his friends. He does not know whether they are
astral dogs or not; but they look just like any other

dogs. They go about and help in the work, and the boys are delighted to see them.

To strengthen her confidence in his communications, the boy advised his mother not to let herself be led into a maze of reasons why, not to argue with any one, but simply to believe and to do what she is told.

He then says to his mother that he is able to estimate the speed and determine the course of shells while the battle is going on on this side; and that he has been able, while on the other side, to protect men in battle on this side. He advises his mother to encourage others who have lost loved ones to try to get into communication with them, saying, "If you could just make them understand there is no death".

Another important thing appears in the examination of this evidence, Mr. Newday, that *those beyond cannot read our thoughts against our own will.* This would seem to indicate that we can keep our secrets only by not telling them to any one, and that before others can read our thoughts we must be willing for them to read them. Upon this point I call attention to the substance of the further communication of the son to his mother:

"I cannot read your mind yet. Speak to me as you would if you could see my face." Then the son assures his mother of his great love for her. He tells her that his appearance on the other side is just as she saw him last, only clothed in a cloudlike vapor, and that he is able to cover many miles without fatigue. No one is required to rest from labor. He tells his mother that he thinks the Savior is on the battlefields and urges her to tell this to other mothers, that they may be comforted. His mother asked him where he is; and his reply was that he is in and about Verdun, France, and has still remained near his division in the army, and that when boys come across (meaning when they are

killed) those on the other side guide them across the
invisible line; that the boys when they come are all
right. Then he instructs his mother to say that the
mothers should not mourn for their sons; that the
tears torture those who have passed over.

He then states to his mother: "I want to start this,
whole propaganda of comfort on the one sure thing,
There is no death".

I call your attention to the fact, Mr. Newday, that
those soldiers who have died upon the battlefield, as did
your son, are anxious to spread this news of their ability
to communicate with their loved ones on this side, and
evidently this is the reason why you see so much in
the magazines and public press today about communicating with the dead. Continuing to analyze this testimony
you will see that the son says to his mother that she
should get some of the sanest women she knows who
have lost their dear ones and persuade them to try to
communicate with their loved ones. He then tells her
that the thing which troubles the men who have gone
on the other side is the fact that their loved ones on
this side are in agony, and advises that they should not
be in agony because all tears shed on earth greatly
affect those on the other side. He asks his mother not
to weep for him, assuring her that he is still her son,
and that he and she are yet pals and will be always.

Now, Mr. Newday, if we are to believe this evidence
of the mother and the son, it seems to warrant the
conclusion that your son may now be right at your side,
or at least very near you. In this evidence that I am now
presenting to you the soldier boy says to his his mother:
*"I am still in the atmosphere about the battlefields in
France"* (where he fell). He also tells his mother that
he hopes soon to be able to visit her. Then he tells his
mother that what he is really trying to do now is to

have her hear him as well as he can hear her. He then
advises h r to read a book on communication with the
dead, written by Swedenborg. He assures his mother
that he receives all of her messages, but that he cannot
yet answer them all.

He then tells his mother that recently in his service
while on the battlefield, invisible to others, he was easing
in his arms a boy who was crying for his mother and
that he could not comfort the lad. But some other one
by his side succeeded in bringing comfort to the boy.
He assures his mother that he is still in the atmosphere
about the earth, but that he may pass on to some other
sphere later. He then relates instances of others on the
battlefield being comforted by those who have gone over;
and adds that beyond is a great receiving camp, a kind
of model cantonment. He assures his mother time and
again that they are alive and not dead.

I call your attention, Mr. Newday, to the fact that
this corroborates the teaching of our clergymen, which
they now teach and have taught for many years. The
son says to his mother: "All who have passed over are
alive and progressing toward fuller life. *Harp on that
string. Keep at it.* Do not let your mind become discouraged or confused."

And now, Mr. Newday, I further emphasize the fact
that my efforts to convince you that your son is alive
will avail nothing if you stubbornly *set your will against
believing* that he is alive; nor could you have communication with your son or from your son unless *you are
willing to receive it.* I base this conclusion upon what
this young soldier says to his mother and upon other
evidences which I have here to present to you.

Continuing to examine the son's evidence, you will
note that he says to his mother: "*We cannot convince
any one against his will*". Then he expresses to his

mother regret that she is unable to convince some of her friends and urges her to continue to try to induce them to believe.

His testimony further shows, Mr. Newday, that the method of communicating with the dead is progressive, especially since the war. He speaks of communication formerly being by knocks and jumpings of tables, but declares that now a more advanced and better suited method of communication has been established. He assures his mother that his friend Wells even now visits the place where his earthly relatives live.

In brief, Mr. Newday, the testimony I here submit of the communication of the soldier boy to his mother shows that when he fell on the battlefield he did not really die, but passed on to another realm in the atmosphere, still near the battlefield, yet not visible; and that in the atmosphere about the battlefield, invisible to others, he still is able to see what goes on and send messages of comfort to his mother. This is so fully corroborated by the teachings of our clergymen that you must be convinced that your son is living and not dead.

I now submit some further testimony corroborative of the foregoing. I submit a copy of the Oakland (Calif.) *Tribune* of December 14, 1919, in which is published a letter written by C. W. Shaw, 3108 College Avenue, Berkeley, Calif., in which he claims to have had a communication with a soldier that died upon the battlefield. This appearance and the voice that spoke to him directed him to communicate with the parents of the young man that was killed. I insert his letter here, as follows:

"Berkeley, Calif., Dec. 5, 1917.

"Mr. H. D. Hay, Glidden, Ia.

"Dear Sir: Just a word of explanation for this letter to a stranger, which is written by request.

"I am a business man and have resided here for over twenty years, owning property and am very well known. I am not what is called a religious man, using the term of the churches, but am deeply interested in all things that pertain to the 'Human God', which to me includes not only those who live in this our life, but also the life to come.

"I am deeply concerned with the fact of the spirit return, and that there is no death, only a step into a broader and better life, and as much better as one's desires and inclinations here may uplift and broaden our lives.

"This is not written as an apology, and whether the impression appeals to you or not does not change the result.

"On the night of December 3, 1917 (last Monday), I returned to my home after attending a meeting of the Berkeley Defense Corps, of which I am a member, and retired about 11 p. m. A few moments after retiring and saying my prayers (I always do that), I saw a large opaque light over my bed, and watching it closely I saw come from it a perfect American flag, perfect in stripes but not in color. This shortly disappeared; and I heard a voice say, 'My name is Hay; I must speak to you,' and then I saw a young man in uniform (hard to give detail of height and weight), but a clean-looking and -talking man whom I should say anyone would be glad to meet and know. I am sure I was, and shall be glad for him to come again. He asked me to write his folks and tell them he was not dead and was not unhappy.

"I find it impossible to give you in his own words what he told me, but this is the substance of it: That he knew you missed him and were sad over his death. He smiled and said: 'Tell them I am not dead but alive in

another life, where I can still not only help and cheer
you at home but, more than all else, help the boys carry
on this great struggle for justice and right, and with
them win the victory that shall make our homes sacred,
the world better to live in'. To tell the boys at home
what a glorious feeling it is when you know the truth,
to give one's life for others. The full horror of this
war has not yet been told or you at home cannot even
comprehend what defeat would mean, but that will
never be; for justice and right will conquer and the
stars and stripes will always wave over the homes and
in the hearts of the free and brave.

"The only expression of regret he gave was that he
might have been spared a little longer to help the boys
at the front.

"He also said his mother had an impression when he
left home that she would not see him again, but that
she was loving and brave through it all and was trying
to be the same now. If I could only express to you, who
love him so deeply, the words he spoke and the manner
in which he spoke them. I am sure no sadness would
come to you and only gladness would fill your hearts, to
think that you have a son like him; for as he says, you
still have him, and after the great struggle is ended
you will know surely that he is not only in your hearts
but in your home also.

"I am deeply grateful I have met him and consider
the privilege a great one that I am able to send you his
love and this little message of cheer. To me it is a
beautiful thought that there is no death, and somehow
and somewhere we shall meet again with a full knowledge of what has been. These brave soldier boys of
ours need all our help, and I am sure you and yours will
go out with loving hearts and tender hands to help
some of them on their way. Tell them for him [that]

it is grand and noble to feel one has done his best in a cause as glorious as this, and with head erect and eyes keen, he is still marching on to victory with the boys he loves.

"My one wish is that the angel world will come close in your lives and show you the great truth for his sake, a truth because it cannot be denied, and in these days of separation and sadness bringing strength and hope to aching hearts. We may never meet here but we shall there. I sympathize with you for the material loss and am glad with you that you have such a son.

"Very sincerely yours,

"C. W. SHAW."

I submit further evidence, which was published in the Denver (Colo.) *Post* Sunday, April 25, 1920, which speaks for itself:

"The distance between the living room of a ranch house at Tollberg, Colorado, and Concord, Massachusetts, is something more than twenty-five hundred miles.

"The distance between the Argonne forest of France and the living room of a ranch house at Tollberg, Colo., in many thousand miles more, yet, according to Mrs. A. H., of Tollberg, the distance was negotiated by the spirit of one giving his name as John Henypecker, killed in the Argonne an evening in January. In sending an account of her experience to the *Post*, Mrs. A. H. says:

"My daughter is a natural automatic writer; a fact we discovered some years ago. To pass away the time several neighbors who were visiting us suggested a 'sitting', and we gathered about the table. Two of my sons had come home from war, and were of the party.

"Very soon after we had become quiet my daughter's hand began to write: 'At your service. My name is John Henypecker. My body lies in the Argonne forest. It is one of many that never were buried. I just want

to come and say that my mother still has hopes that I am
living and will return home. She lives at Concord,
Mass. Her name is Elizabeth Henypecker. Could you
write and tell her that I have passed on to a better
world? Goodbye.'

"We did not pay much attention to this, imagining
that the presence of my sons so recently returned from
France affected our imagination. But every day for
three weeks my thought would turn unexpectedly to that
message. And one day, perhaps to rid my mind of a
persisting duty, I addressed an envelope as directed by
the spirit, enclosed the message as received by my daughter's hand, and mailed it to Elizabeth Henypecker,
Concord, Mass.

"After about a month my amazement was complete
when I received my letter back with a note from the
postmaster at Concord telling me that Mrs. Elizabeth
Henypecker had recently died and that the letter being
unclaimed he returned it according to directions written
on my envelope.

"I am sure had I written to Mrs. Henypecker the
day after the receipt of the message from her son she
would have received it and been comforted by the assurance that he was waiting for her in a better world.
Because so many fail to understand, I ask that my name
be withheld, also the names of the witnesses to the
occurrence."

I submit also a communication by Westbrook Pegler,
published in the St. Paul (Minn.) *Daily News* on
December 24, 1919, which shows how these spirits communicate with those on this earth:

"American soldiers who perished in the war are banded together in a spirit army 'behind the veil', according
to messages claimed to have been received by gold-star
mothers through spirit media, using various devices.

"Miss Gertrude Tubby, assistant secretary, American Society for Psychic Research, today declared that in response to 'hundreds and hundreds' of requests for word from departed heroes, communication has been established with members of the spirit army.

"SPIRIT AMERICAN LEGION

"They are banded together, Miss Tubby said, by the same ties that united them into an army on earth—a sort of American Legion of heroic shades.

"Mothers and other relatives of dead soldiers are writing to the society from all sections of the country, seriously inquiring as to whether they can be placed in spiritual contact with boys who lost their lives in the war. The séances have proven, according to Miss Tubby, that the spirits themselves hunger for tidings of their families.

" 'When a boy's spirit is brought into communication with his mother and father through a medium,' said Miss Tubby, 'it frequently happens that all his spirit friends will crowd around him behind the veil so that they will not miss being introduced to the parents of their comrades.'

"HOW THEY MINGLE

"Spirits are not bound to neighborhoods by the same considerations that cause earth-bound people to become neighbors. A mortal chooses a location to suit his physical comfort and his purse, although his neighbors may be uncongenial. But in the spirit world there is no locality as we understand it—spirits colonize through community of interests, tastes and customs.

"Miss Tubby said that relatives of slain heroes may establish communication with their loved ones by means of ouija boards or planchettes or by 'automatic writing',

the latter process being the simplest. The person desiring to receive the message must approach the task with
a serious, though not unduly solemn purpose, and in a
mental state of passivity. The hand holding a pencil is
placed on the paper. The writer looks away and gradually, Miss Tubby said, the hand begins to write under the
impulse of the departed spirit.

"SPORTIVE BAD SPIRITS

"Sometimes, Miss Tubby said, a *vigorous evil spirit*
will 'steal the wire' of communication, and the writer
is astonished upon perusing the message his own hand
has written to read off-color and risque stories, dictated by the bad spirit.

"The American Society for Psychic Research includes
in its membership Sir Oliver Lodge, Arthur James
Balfour and David Starr Jordan, president of Leland
Stanford University.

"So great is the interest in psychic matter under the
impetus of recent alleged phenomena and because of the
desire of soldiers' relatives to communicate with d parts-
ed heroes that the organization is now preparing further
to extend its work throughout the country."

A MESSAGE FROM ABRAHAM LINCOLN

The New York *World Magazine* of November 21,
1920, published a communication written by Mr. C. B.
Fernald, who says:

"One day during the present year a friend said to me
with some diffidence that he was in the habit of receiving messages from the dead, and that he had received
one from my son, begging me to communicate with him.
My son was an American who was in England when the
war broke out and who could not wait for America to
come in. He crashed in an aeroplane of which he was

pilot, and was killed. This was over the Austrian border.

"I have always wished to preserve an open mind—even when there is something in it. I used the familiar wineglass and circular letters, in attempt to get a message from my son. At first I had only just enough result to stimulate further trials. Eventually I received messages which for length and coherence appear to rank high in the history of these things.

"After a while my son said that he had met the shade of Abraham Lincoln, who wished to speak to me. I was sceptical. I am now. Any one else may judge as well as I the reality of what followed.

"Abraham Lincoln began in characteristic style a discourse on the present relations of capital and labor in the United States. As it went on I began to receive it by automatic writing. All this was written by me in two sittings."

Then Mr. Fernald begins to quote the message from Lincoln as follows:

"I am Abraham Lincoln. I believe that there is now an omen in the sky which portends a great disaster. I can only hope that it will have proved a false omen. But I am of the opinion that in the near future we shall witness what will ill mix with the huge self-satisfaction with which we view the vast inventory of our almighty and immense Republic. In the near future I expect to see a change of greatest meaning in our national life."

The communication is too lengthy here to insert it all. Mr. Fernald gives the full text of what purports to have been a communication from Abraham Lincoln, and says that he took this up and got into communication at the instance of his son, who he states had some time before fallen in the World War.

The Terre Haute (Ind.) *Post* of December 23, 1919,

published a communication written by Hereward H.
Carrington, Ph. D., and which purports to be a communication received by Mrs. L. M. Ackerman, a medium
living in a suburb of Newark, N. J., from Theodore
Roosevelt. Mrs. Ackerman claims to have received many
messages from Mr. Roosevelt on the ouija board. The
writer says:

"We sat down at the ouija board, Mrs. Ackerman and
I, and after a few minutes' wait, the following message
was given: 'I am Theodore Roosevelt. How are you
today?' Mrs. Ackerman replied: 'Well. How are you?'
'I am always well!' Mrs. Ackerman said he replied."

The communication then states that Mrs. Ackerman
sent some of these messages to the Roosevelt family,
thinking that they would be interested in them; but
they refused to accept them or to reply to the letters.
When this was stated to the spirit, Mrs. Ackerman says
Colonel Roosevelt replied:

"My Dear Archie: I cannot tell you how disappointed
your father, who loved you so dearly, and who has
never lost that love for you and never will, is because
you will not try to communicate with me. Remember,
Archie, I have been here only seven months and I am
as strong as spirits who have been here for years, as
you reckon time."

The New York *World* recently published an interview
with Bishop Fallows, of the Reformed Episcopal Church,
in which he is quoted as saying:

"Telepathy is an established fact. In recent years
great strides have been made in the explanation of
psychic phenomena and in the years to come the science
of communication with the dead will be made a part
of the curriculum of great educational institutions. I
have called the new science 'Immortalism' because it
depends for its existence upon the immortality of the

soul, in which we all believe, and the preservation of identity beyond the grave."

And now, Mr. Newday, I think I have submitted ample evidence to sustain my position. I have here a great abundance of cumulative testimony, experience upon experience, of men in various walks of life, particularly the testimony from some of our leading clergymen. You will see that all these distinguished writers, scientists, savants, theologists, stand by the teaching which we have heard from our youth up, that the soul of man is immortal; and believing this, we must believe that our dead beyond are alive, and it is wholly consistent, then, that they can communicate with the living. If the living cannot communicate with the dead, then our time-honored doctrine of the immortality of the soul must get a terrible shock, if not be completely upset. And you, Mr. Newday, as a consistent member of the church for many years, would not wish to repudiate that doctrine. I submit, then, that from all this evidence we have much reason to rejoice that your son is alive and that you can communicate with him if you will do so.

Mr. Newday: You have made a very strong presentation of your side of the case, Mr. Psychic. I must concede the fact that you offer the testimony and experiences of some of the greatest of modern scientists, savants and clergymen; and this together with the doctrine which all the churches, Catholic and Protestant, have taught and teach, that the soul is immortal and cannot die, makes out a very strong case. I cannot escape that fact. But before I reach a final conclusion, I must hear the argument of our friend, Mr. Lightbearer.

CHAPTER III

The testimony and the argument presented by Mr. Psychic is very subtle and calculated to convince almost every mind except the mind of him who insists on squaring all teachings by the great truths which are definitely and conclusively settled.

In the very outset I perceive that I am confronted with the public opinion, educated largely against my position. In this connection we are reminded of the trite but truthful saying of the poet:

> "Truth forever on the scaffold,
> Wrong forever on the throne;
> But that scaffold sways the future
> And within the dim unknown
> Stands the form of Christ the Savior,
> Keeping watch around his own."

Truth ultimately must prevail and I am confident that truth in God's due time will prevail and that error will be forever annihilated.

My abiding faith in Christ Jesus and in the Word of God, which is the truth, makes me bold in presenting evidence against the theory of communicating with the dead. I am confident that the proof which I present will convince every reverent mind believing the Bible to be God's Word of truth. Every point that I can conscientiously concede I will and do concede, in order that the issue may be clearly drawn.

In the beginning all of us agreed that the Bible is God's Word of truth revealed to man for his instruction.

I agree with you that man's greatest desire is that he might have life everlasting, dwelling continually in a state of happiness. All of us must agree and do agree,

43

I believe, to the truthfulness of the Biblical statement concerning the obtaining of life everlasting through Christ Jesus, that "there is none other name under heaven given among men, whereby we must be saved".
—Acts 4: 12.

I will concede that the gentlemen whose testimony has here been presented are honorable men. I do not call in question their veracity or honesty, nor is it necessary for me to do so. If I cannot explain and account for their testimony in the light of revealed truths as contained in the Word of God, then my argument must fall flat. I invite you, Mr. Newday, and all who hear me, to suspend final judgment upon this question until you have heard me through; and then if you can truthfully say that you believe the teachings of the Word of God, you will have to say it is impossible to communicate with the dead.

I agree that the World War that has caused millions in a short time to go down in death has greatly increased the desire of the living to know of the state of the dead, and that this situation has been seized upon for the purpose of foisting upon the people the theory that their dead loved ones are alive and that they can communicate with them. If the living can talk with the dead, then all the people should know it, and it should not be necessary to conduct a paid propaganda in order to teach them. On the other hand, if from a fair consideration of all the evidence we should find that the living cannot talk with the dead, but that the testimony produced in support of the contention is deceptive and misleading and destructive of faith in God's Word, then the people should be acquainted with these facts; and all honest people, without regard to creed or denomination, ought to be willing to herald these facts broadcast among their fellow men.

I most emphatically agree with you, Mr. Psychic, that according to the testimony of all these witnesses the ability of the living to communicate with the dead depends upon the one important question: Is the soul of man immortal? In other phrase, your argument must stand or fall upon the truthfulness or falsity of the theory of the immortality of the soul. If it is true that every man has inherent immortality, then there is a basis for your argument; but if that contention is false, then there is no basis for your argument, and your argument, of course, must fail. It is of first importance, then, that we determine what the soul is; and determining that, whether it is mortal or immortal. Let the Bible be the final arbiter upon this question.

WHAT IS THE SOUL?

It is true that Catholic and Protestant clergymen for centuries have taught the people that the soul is the divine part of man which cannot die and that therefore there is no death of the soul. This is not supported, however, by the Scriptures, which read: "The Lord God formed man of the dust of the ground, and breathed into his nostrils the breath of lives; and man became a living soul". (Genesis 2: 7) The word soul means moving, breathing, sentient being; i. e., a living creature that possesses the senses of sight, hearing, touch, taste, smell. It will be conceded that the dust out of which Jehovah formed the body was not immortal, nor did it have intelligence. It must be further conceded that the breath of lives which God breathed into the nostrils of that body did not constitute the soul; but that the body, perfectly formed, and the breath which Jehovah then placed in its organism together formed a living, moving, sentient being, which we 'call a soul. Every creature that breathes *is* a soul. No creature *possesses* a soul. If

the breath is separated from the body, which stops the
action of the lungs and the circulation of the blood,
death results. Thus did God form the first man, from
whom the whole human race sprang, and we have a
clear and positive statement in the Scriptures that the
first man is of the earth, earthy, and not divine, not
immortal.—1 Corinthians 15:47.

The Word of God speaks of beasts as souls: "Levy a
tribute unto the Lord of the men of war which went
out to battle: one soul of five hundred, both of the persons, and of the beeves, and of the asses, and of the
sheep".—Numbers 31: 28; Genesis 1: 20, 30, *margin.*

Man's preëminence over the beast is in life, not in
death. They both die alike. "For that which befalleth
the sons of men befalleth beasts; even one thing befalleth
them: as the one dieth, so dieth the other; yea, they
have all one breath; so that a man hath no preëminence
above a beast: for all is vanity. All go unto one place;
all are of the dust, and all turn to dust again."—Ecclesiastes 3: 19, 20.

THE GREAT DECEPTION

That we may get the proper setting of this subject
and view it from a rational standpoint, we must take a
brief glimpse at the history of the human race. For
centuries the whole earth has been a playhouse and all
the people players. The great drama opened in Eden,
the garden of God—perfect in its appointments—with
Adam and Eve, the perfect pair, in possession, with
authority to multiply and fill the earth with a happy
race of people and establish a kingdom among men.
They were perfect human beings, but without experience. Lucifer, an angel of great beauty and wisdom,
was placed in Eden as an overseer of this perfect human
pair. Observing that Jehovah had granted authority to

man to establish a kingdom, Lucifer sought to steal the inheritance of man. God's prophet describes him in Eden as a wise and beautiful creature, and tells how he sinned and was degraded and became Satan, thus: "Thou hast been in Eden the garden of God; every precious stone has been thy covering, the sardius, topaz, and the diamond, the beryl, the onyx, and the jasper, the sapphire, the emerald, and the carbuncle, and gold: the workmanship of thy tabrets and of thy pipes was prepared in thee in the day that thou wast created. Thou wast the anointed cherub that covereth [officially appointed to act as man's overseer]; and I have set thee so; thou wast upon the holy mountain of God; thou hast walked up and down in the midst of the stones of fire. Thou wast perfect in thy ways from the day that thou wast created, till iniquity was found in thee. By the multitude of thy merchandise they have filled the midst of thee with violence, and thou has sinned: therefore I will cast thee as profane out of the mountain of God; and I will destroy thee, O covering cherub, from the midst of the stones of fire."—Ezekiel 28: 13-19.

Ambitious for a kingdom of his own, Lucifer reasoned thus! I am far greater than man. Why has not God granted me an exclusive dominion? Jealousy was in his heart and he determined to bring man under his control. He meditated a usurpation of God's authority thus: "I will ascend into heaven, I will exalt my throne above the stars of God: I will sit also upon the mount of the congregation, in the sides of the north: I will ascend above the heights of the clouds; I will be like the Most High". (Isaiah 14: 13, 14) Because of this ambition, Lucifer lost the favor of Jehovah and was thereafter designated as "that old serpent, which is the devil, and Satan" (Revelation 20: 2)—the author and instigator of all wickedness that has cursed mankind.

God instructed Adam and Eve that they must not partake of certain fruit in Eden, saying to them, "In the day that thou eatest thereof thou shalt surely die". (Genesis 2:17) Satan deceived mother Eve by convincing her that God was lying and by this means undertook to deprive her and her husband of their just rights and privileges. To Eve he said: "God doth know that in the day ye eat thereof, then your eyes shall be opened, and ye shall be as gods, knowing good and evil. *Ye shall not surely die."* (Genesis 3: 4, 5) This was the first lie ever told and from it sprang all other lies. So says Jesus.—John 8: 44.

This disobedience of Eve and of Adam, who joined her in the transgression, brought swiftly upon them the judgment of Jehovah. They were sentenced to death and driven from Eden. In pronouncing this judgment, Jehovah, addressing Satan and the perfect human pair, said: "I will put enmity between thee and the woman, and between thy seed and her seed; it shall bruise thy head, and thou shalt bruise his heel". (Genesis 3:15) Thus God definitely declared that there would be two seeds and that there would be deadly enmity between these until the seed of the serpent, Satan, should perish. The seed of the woman here mentioned is the Christ, the Messiah—Jesus the head and his faithful body members, constituting his bride. The seed of the serpent consists of his dupes and emissaries, whom he has used to defraud, deceive and blind the people for centuries.

IMMORTAL SOULS?

Immortal means not subject to death; possessed of an indestructible life. Therefore one who is immortal cannot die. Did not God speak the truth when he said to Adam: "Thou shalt surely die"? Did he not speak the truth when he sentenced man to death, saying to him, "In the sweat of thy face shalt thou eat bread, till thou return unto the ground; for out of it wast thou taken: for dust thou art, and unto dust shalt thou return"? (Genesis 3:19)   God did not sentence him to pass on to another world.   But you, Mr. Psychic, will say that sentence was on his body, which is a mere shell for the soul, and that when he died he merely shed the shell; and you cite the clergy and the savants as your authority.   I submit, Mr. Newday, that since we have agreed to take the Bible as arbiter, let us hear Jehovah answer the question.   He says: "The *soul* that sinneth, it shall die".   (Ezekiel 18:4, 20)   "What man is he that liveth, and shall not see death? shall he deliver his *soul* from the hand of the grave?"   (Psalm 89:48) If the soul be immortal, then God himself cannot destroy it, and we know that God has power to destroy the soul.   Jesus is authority for this: "Fear him which is able to destroy both soul and body".   (Matthew 10:28) There is not a single Scripture in the Bible that warrants any one in saying that the soul is immortal.

You will observe that all the testimony offered here by Mr. Psychic is based upon the conclusion that the soul is immortal and he emphasizes the question of immortality more than any other one thing.   With all due deference to him as a devotee of this theory, I must say that the conclusion of the immortality of the soul is based upon Satan's lie and is wholly unsupported by anything else except the lie of the adversary.   And from the time since he told this lie, he has sought to deceive mankind and blind men to the real truths of God's Word and he has brought forth all kinds of deceptions for the very purpose of blinding the people.—2 Corinthians 4:4.

Satan himself is not immortal, the Lord declaring that in his own due time Satan shall be destroyed.   (Hebrews 2:14)   Who, then, has immortality?   The Scriptures

answer: God "only hath immortality". (1 Timothy
6:16) He is the self-existing one, from everlasting to
everlasting, and not subject to death. When Jesus was
on earth, he said: "As the Father hath life in himself;
so hath he given to the son to have life in himself".
(John 5:26) And at his resurrection he was exalted
and granted immortality.—Philippians 2:9-11; Revelation 1:18.

All the human race was mortal, i. e., subject to death.
"As in Adam all die." (1 Corinthians 15:22) Immortality is offered as a special reward to be granted only
to those who are faithful followers in Jesus' footsteps.
"Be thou faithful unto death and I will give thee a
crown of life." "Seek for . . . immortality." (Revelation 2:10; Romans 2:7) A man does not seek what he
already possesses. "This mortal must put on immortality" was written concerning the new creature who is
begotten to the heavenly nature and is a follower of
Jesus, and the statement has no application to man in
general.—1 Corinthians 15:53.

Since it is claimed that the dead are able to communicate with the living, then of course it must follow that
the dead are conscious. In fact, all the experiences
related by the witnesses whose testimony Mr. Psychic has
here offered is to the effect that death does not mean
death but merely a "passing" to the other side of the
line, consciousness still being maintained and a full
memory of everything that had transpired in the past.

If this contention be true, then God did not mean
what he said when he sentenced man to death and told
him he must return to the dust. Subsequent Scriptures,
however, prove that God did mean what he said and that
man has returned to the dust and is not conscious. We
read: "In death there is no remembrance of thee: in the
grave who shall give thee thanks?" (Psalm 6:5) "Wilt

thou show wonders to the dead? shall the dead arise
and praise thee? Shall thy lovingkindness be declared
in the grave? or thy faithfulness in destruction?"
(Psalm 88:10, 11) "The dead praise not the Lord,
neither any that go down into silence."—Psalm 115:17.

Furthermore, the Scriptures clearly show that when a
man dies he stops breathing, ceases to think, and returns
to the dust. "His breath goeth forth, he returneth to
his earth; in that very day his thoughts perish."—
Psalm 146:4.

He is so completely dead and unconscious that he
knows nothing. "The living know that they shall die:
but the dead know not any thing." The dead have no
knowledge, they are not wise, and they do not work
where they go. "Whatsoever thy hand findeth to do,
do it with thy might: for there is no work, nor device,
nor knowledge, nor wisdom, in the grave, whither thou
goest."—Ecclesiastes 9:5, 10.

Man perishes like the beast. "Nevertheless man being
in honor abideth not: he is like the beasts that perish."
(Psalm 49:12) When Jesus was on earth, men had
been dying for four thousand years and he said that up
to that time "no man [had] ascended up to heaven".
(John 3:13) And furthermore, Jesus said that all the
dead are in their graves, unconscious, knowing nothing.
"Marvel not at this: for the hour is coming in the which
all that are in the graves shall hear his voice and shall
come forth."—John 5:28, 29.

The inspired apostle Paul, speaking of the dead, refers to them as asleep in Jesus, unconscious, knowing
nothing. "I would not have you to be ignorant, brethren, concerning them which are asleep, that ye sorrow
not even as others which have no hope. For if we believe that Jesus died and rose again, even so them also
which sleep in Jesus will God bring with him. For this

we say unto you by the word of the Lord,that we which are alive and remain unto the coming of the Lord shall not prevent them which are asleep. For the Lord himself shall descend from heaven with a shout, with the voice of the archangel, and with the trump of God: and the dead in Christ shall rise first."—1 Thess. 4 : 13 - 16.

In all the Bible there is no doctrine so plainly and emphatically taught as that concerning the resurrection of the *dead.* If Mr. Psychic's theory is correct, that the dead are alive and progressing from one sphere to another, then the doctrine of the resurrection is both untrue and a farce, and upsets the entire teaching of Christianity. Of the resurrection we will have more to say as we progress.

The eminent witnesses from whose testimony Mr. Psychic quotes at length claim to believe that Jehovah God is the great First Cause. They admit that Jesus came down from heaven, was made flesh and dwelt among men; that he spake as never man spake; that he lived on earth; that he died, rose from the dead, and ascended into heaven. They quote from the Bible as God's Word of truth, thereby admitting the authenticity of the Scriptures. Then let their case stand or fall by the Bible. They cannot blow both hot and cold.

But it is argued by our opponents that the witnesses on their side are of great eminence in the world. Look at them, they say, such men as Dr. Hyslop, Sir Arthur Conan Doyle,Sir Oliver Lodge, Bishop Fallows, the Rev. Fielding Ould, the late Archdeacon Wilberforce,etc. And we admit that they are eminent men of the world.

Then, argues Mr. Psychic, surely it cannot be possible that these eminent scholars are telling falsehoods and trying to deceive the people by making them believe that the spirits of dead men can tip tables and make them walk, can cause the hand to write, and can speak through mediums or even communicate direct!

How the people are impressed by such testimony is illustrated by an incident which has come to my attention and which is similar to that related by Mr. Psychic:

The father of Mr. A had been dead a number of years. He was met by a spiritist, who said to him: "Mr. A, would you like to talk to your father?" Mr. A replied: "Why, my father is dead". "Yes," responded his questioner, "but you can communicate with the dead." Mr. A expressed his unbelief. Then his questioner said: "Mr. A, are you willing to give the matter a trial and let me demonstrate to you that you can talk to your father? If you will go to a certain number on a certain street and call for Mrs. ——— and say to her you have come to communicate with one of your dead friends, but do not tell her whom; and then put her to the test, you will see if she can call up your dead father." Mr. A assents. He calls on the woman, who is known as a spiritualistic medium. He says to her: "I came here for the purpose of communicating with a dead friend. I am a skeptic, but I came at the instance of my friend and I want you to prove to me whether or not I can talk to some one who is dead." The medium replies: "If you will do what I tell you, I will make an effort to put you into communication with the one with whom you would like to talk. The conditions I impose upon you are these: First, you must sit quietly in that chair. You must not resist me with the power of your will, but be entirely submissive and willing to be convinced. You must then center your mind upon the person with whom you would like to talk."

Mr. A agrees to the conditions and carries them out, sitting quietly, being willing to be convinced and, therefore, submitting his will. In a short time the medium

announces the presence of some one who wishes to talk
to him. Mr. A listens and presently he hears a voice
speaking to him and he recognizes it as the voice of his
father, long since dead. The father then relates to him
certain events that transpired in Mr. A.'s boyhood and
also tells him other things which Mr A subsequently
proves from other evidence to be correct. Mr. A has been
a Christian up to this time, thoroughly believing in the
Bible. Now he goes away, however, convinced that his
father is alive and not dead and is able to talk to him.

Mr. Psychic would accept this as conclusive evidence
that the man was actually communicating with his
father. And he will ask, Did not Mr. A hear his father's
voice? We answer no, because his father was dead and
the Scriptures conclusively prove that dead men do not
talk. Can it be denied that Mr. A heard a voice? We
answer no; nor will there be any attempt to deny that.
We admit that Mr. A, Sir Arthur Conan Doyle and
every other witness offered who claims to have heard
voices did in fact hear them, and we will further admit
that these witnesses are testifying to what they believe
to be the truth. We emphatically deny, however, that
they heard the voices of, or in any other manner communicated with, the spirits of dead men. On the contrary, the voices they heard were the voices of demons,
who never were men, and their communication is with
demons and not the spirits of men. And we gladly
assume the burden of proof upon this proposition. It
will be seen that these demons are the allies of Satan,
for centuries under his domination and direction, and
that they aid him in his further attempt to foist upon
humanity his first lie, *There is no death.*

ORIGIN OF THE DEMONS

From the time Adam and Eve were driven out of

Eden until now there has been war between the seed of
the woman and the seed of the serpent, Satan, the devil.
Satan was deprived of his position as overseer of man.
Adam having lost his dominion, there was none in the
earth in authority. Horrified at the results of Lucifer's
wrongful course, the angels of heaven (sons of God)
desired to uplift man, and God permitted certain ones
of them* to undertake the task. (Hebrews 2: 5; Genesis
6: 1-5) These angels possessed the power to materialize
in human form and were permitted to assume dominion
over the affairs of earth. They likewise had power to
dematerialize. Satan determined that he would not be
thwarted in his purpose of opposing Jehovah. He had
become a liar and the father of lies and now, with a
malignant heart, he set about to seduce these angels, his
former companions in glory, and through them to retain control over man. He injected into the minds of
these spirit beings the thought to take wives from among
the daughters of men, which they did, thereby leaving
their own loftier estate. Thus Satan caused the angels
to sin and fall. The offspring resulting from this unholy alliance filled the earth with violence and God
announced his determination to destroy all flesh. He so
advised Noah and then brought on the deluge.

Noah and his family, eight in all, not having been
contaminated by these evil ones, received favor in God's
sight and were saved in the ark which Noah had built
at the direction of Jehovah. The great flood destroyed
all fleshly beings save those that were in the ark. The
angelic beings, however, exercising their power to dematerialize, were not destroyed. What became of them?
The Bible answers that they were restrained of their
liberty and confined in the darkness of the atmosphere
near the earth.* This is exactly what is claimed by

---

* See letter on page 37

Mr. Psychic. "God spared not the angels that sinned, but cast them down to *tartarus* [mistranslated hell] and delivered them into chains of darkness to be reserved unto judgement." (2 Peter 2:4) "The angels which kept not their first estate, but left their own habitation, he hath reserved in everlasting chains under darkness unto the judgment of the great day." (Jude 6) In this condition they were to be restrained until the judgment day, the inference being that at the judgment day they would exercise greater power than at any time since the flood. At no time since the flood have they been permitted to materialize in human form. We here assert that the judgment of the fallen angels is at hand and, therefore, this explains why they exercise so much more power now than at any other time. Of this we will speak later. Since the time of the deluge they have had power to communicate with the human race only through the instrumentality of willing mediums.

This is in exact accord with the testimony of Dr. Hyslop, whose words we quote: "The only means of communicating with the dead has been found to be a living organism capable of connecting the two worlds".

The communication of man with these evil spirits impersonating the dead is not a new thing. It has persisted since the flood. When God made the Law Covenant with the nation of Israel, as a safeguard against these demons he provided in the law that any one who would consult a medium concerning the dead should be put to death. (Exodus 22:18; Leviticus 19:31 20:6, 27) An attempt to communicate with them was declared by Jehovah as an abomination in his sight. "There shall not be found among you . . . a witch or a charmer or a consulter with familiar spirits, or a medium or a necromancer; for all that do these things are an abomination unto the Lord."—Deuteronomy 18:10-12.

Saul, the first king of Israel, had a séance with a medium who pretended to call up Samuel, much as is done by what the eminent witnesses above mentioned have related in modern times. (1 Samuel 28: 7-20) Samuel was a good prophet. He died. Saul, the king of Israel, became evil and God withdrew his favor from him. The king then directed his servants to find him a witch or spiritualistic medium with whom to consult. He was directed to a woman living in a cave at Endor.

It will be noted that the one selected as the medium for communication between Saul and the dead prophet was a woman. It will be noticed that in nearly every instance of testimony cited by Mr. Psychic the medium has been a woman; and in that testimony Sir Arthur Conan Doyle says: "Nearly every woman is an undeveloped medium". And here again we remind you that Satan began his nefarious work by using a woman, deceiving her, and through her caused the fall of man. King Saul in consulting a medium departed from the plain teachings that the Lord had given him through his Word.

Knowing that it was his duty to put to death all such mediums, as provided by the law; and knowing that if she recognized him as the king of Israel she would not operate for him, Saul disguised himself and then went to the cave to see the woman. .Evidently the demons revealed to this medium that the man who stood before her was the king of Israel; and horrified, she exclaimed: "Why hast thou come to take my life?" Saul then admitted to her that he was the king, but promised to preserve her life if she would obey him and call up Samuel, the dead prophet. The séance then took place. The demons caused to pass before her mind a vision of a man rising from the earth and the witch cried out; and being inquired of by Saul as to what she saw, she said she beheld an old man rising, wearing a mantle, the description being like that of Samuel the prophet. Saul fell prone upon the earth and then the medium proceeded to tell him that the message from Samuel was that on the morrow he should engage in battle with the Philistines, that he would be defeated, and that the king and his sons would be killed.

Again quoting from the testimony offered, as given by Sir Arthur Conan Doyle: "We have, unhappily, to deal with absolute cold-blooded lying on the part of wicked or mischievous intelligences. Every one who has investigated the matter has, I suppose, met with examples of willful deception, which occasionally are mixed up with good and true communications".

Surely the demons through the witch at Endor tricked Saul on this occasion and lied to both the witch and Saul. Samuel was dead and therefore could not arise. History discloses the fact that the battle between Saul and the Philistines did not take place the next day, but was fought some days later and that not all of his sons were killed; but on the contrary, two of them survived and lived for years.

From the days of the flood until now these evil spirits or demons have been unable to communicate with *any one who is unwilling* to submit to their influence, and this explains why, in the incident above recorded, Mr. A was requested to remain quiet, not to resist with his will, but be willing to be taught and to concentrate his mind upon the one with whom he would like to speak. This contention is further borne out by the testimony offered by Mr. Psychic to the effect that *only the willing can be convinced*: "Don't argue. We cannot convince any one against his will. Let him believe or deny."

While spiritists—those believing in communication with the dead—try to get away from the fact that human beings are obsessed or possessed by evil spirits or demons, evidence is unmistakable that such is the case, and even they in their argument admit that to be true. We quote from Dr. Hyslop's elaborate work entitled, "Contact with the Outer World":

"Experience has shown that mischievous personalities are desirous of concealing instead of revealing their identity. In default of evidence to the contrary, we should have to accept the orthodox verdict of medicine and psychiatry, which explain obsessions as cases of dual or multiple personality, hysteria, or some forms of insanity. . . . But in all cases it represents an influence foreign to the organism instead of within it, due to the action of a discarnate spirit or spirits, whether the influence be voluntary or involuntary. . . . In a number of cases, persons whose condition would ordinarily be described as due to hysteria, dual, or multiple personality, dementia precox, paranoia, or some other form of mental disturbance, *showed unmistakable indications of invasion by foreign and discarnate agencies.*"

If these wise scientists would only take the words of Jesus they would see and understand the matter at once. When the great Master was on earth demons possessed human beings, causing insanity, and they have done so ever since. Accounts of such experiences are found in Matthew 9:32, 33; 10:8; 12:22; Mark 5:1-20; 9:17-27; Luke 9:38-42.

These demons have minds superior to human minds and doubtless are perfect in memory. Having existed, as demons, since the time of the flood, they are familiar with the events of earth and this explains why one such can impersonate a human being who has been dead a long while. Sir Conan Doyle cites the instance of one who named himself Manton and who is said to have died in 1677 and who was Oliver Cromwell's chaplain. It

is an easy matter for a demon, familiar with the life of
Cromwell and those living at his time, to come forward
and produce such evidence and thus overreach a mind
that is willing to be convinced.

Mr. A above mentioned did not hear the voice of his
father, but he heard the voice of one of the demons,
who being familiar with his father's life and history was
able to produce facts having a tendency to convince the
son that his father was still living; and the son, being
ignorant of who these demons are, fell a ready victim to
the delusion that his father yet lives.

Thus it will be seen that these demons who inhabit the
atmosphere around the earth communicate to willing
mediums messages of divers kinds, some claiming to be
good and some evil. Naturally you ask, What would be
the motive of these demons or evil spirits in thus communicating with the human race and constantly representing to them that the dead are alive and that living
human beings are actually communicating with their
dead friends? This question is important and demands
careful consideration and when properly answered clari-
fies the whole subject and exposes the fraudulent purposes of Satan and his allies.

We refer you again to the quotations from numerous
letters offered by Mr. Psychic, which state in substance
that a propaganda by the spirits is now in progress, and
they repeatedly say to the medium: "This is our big
fact: I am really, vitally alive. All others who have
passed the change called death are alive and progressing
toward fuller life. Harp on that string. Keep at it.
Nothing that I can write you is of any importance compared to this."

We here emphasize again the point that from the time
of the disruption in Eden, Satan, the great adversary of
God and righteousness, has vigorously put forth his

efforts to bolster up his lie that the dead are not dead but alive. The real motive of Satan and the demons is to deceive the people concerning God's plan of redemption and blessing for mankind through Christ. The Scriptures state that "there is none other name . . . whereby we must be saved"; but if Mr. Psychic's theory is correct, then the death and resurrection of Jesus Christ were unnecessary and there is no salvation through him. St. Paul says that Satan "hath blinded the minds of them which believe not, lest the light of the glorious gospel of Christ, who is the image of God, should shine unto them". (2 Corinthians 4:4) In order to appreciate this point it is necessary to examine briefly the

PLAN OF REDEMPTION

The disobedience in Eden brought upon man the condemnation of death. The perfect man and woman in Eden did not beget or bring forth children. It was only after they had been driven from Eden and were undergoing the legal judgment of death, which was being enforced by their being compelled to eat of the impure food that the unfinished earth produced, that man exercised the power of producing children. It necessarily follows, then, that all of the offspring of man would be imperfect, and for this reason the Psalmist said: "Behold, I was shapen in iniquity; and in sin did my mother conceive me". (Psalm 51:5) And for the same reason St. Paul wrote: "By one man sin entered into the world, and death by sin; and so death passed upon all men, for that all have sinned".—Romans 5:12.

Approximately twenty centuries after the fall of man, God called to Abraham, who had manifested a disposition of righteousness, and promised him that in his seed all the families of the earth should be blessed. (Genesis 12:3) Thereafter God reiterated this promise, binding

it by his oath. (Genesis 22: 18) St. Paul says: "By two
immutable things [God's word and oath], in which it
was impossible for God to lie, we might have a strong
consolation, who have fled for refuge to lay hold upon the
hope set before us". (Hebrews 6: 18)   The seed of
promise made prominent throughout the Scriptures, being the offspring of the Abrahamic Covenant as typified
by his wife, Sarah (Galatians 4: 22-25), is the seed of
the woman against which God foretold Satan would war
even unto the end. This seed is the Christ, Jesus the
head and the members of his body who loyally and faithfully follow him even unto death and who have the promise of participating in the first resurrection. St. Paul
in his argument says: "Now to Abraham and his seed
were the promises made: He said not, And to seeds, as
of many; but as of one, And to thy seed, which is Christ
[Messiah]. For as many of you as have been baptized
into Christ have put on Christ. And if ye be Christ's,
then are ye Abraham's seed, and heirs according to the
promise." (Galatians 3: 16, 27, 29) "He is the head of
the body, the church." (Colossians 1: 18)   "God . . .
hath put all things under his feet, and gave him [Christ
Jesus] to be the head over all things to the church,
which is his body."—Ephesians 1: 22, 23.

Many pictures in the Old Testament foretold the coming of the Christ, the Messiah. Satan for a time thought
that the seed was a fleshly one. For this reason he
caused Cain to kill Abel. (1 John 3: 12) When the
promise was made to Abraham, Satan made an attempt
to have Sarah, his wife, debauched, that the seed might
be destroyed. When God's favor was shown to David,
Satan sought to have him killed, believing him to be the
seed. When Jesus came to earth, Satan and the demons
recognized him as the promised seed. (Mark 5: 6-8;
Acts 19: 15) Satan caused the persecution of the Lord

and his death by inciting the Pharisees—the clergy element of that time—against him.

Redemption from the judgment of death must precede the selection of the seed, because no one under the condemnation could God call to be associated with Christ. God promised redemption through his prophet, saying: "I will ransom them from the power of the grave; I will redeem them from death: O death, I will be thy plagues; O grave, I will be thy destruction; repentance shall be hid from mine eyes". (Hosea 13:14) It will be noted here that the promise of redemption is from death and from the grave and there is no intimation that the dead have gone to the spirit world.

Adam, a perfect man, had sinned and lost for himself and all of his offspring the right to life everlasting. Justice demanded the forfeiture of that life. While God cannot deny himself and therefore could not reverse the judgment of death against man, he could consistently provide a plan of redemption whereby another perfect man, exactly equal to Adam, could die and thus provide the redemptive price for Adam and his offspring. There was none perfect among the human race, because all were the children of Adam. "None of them can by any means redeem his brother, nor give to God a ransom for him."—Psalm 49:7.

In the creation of all things the Logos was Jehovah's active agent; and Jehovah offered to him the opportunity of coming to earth, and redeeming the human race. The Logos [Jesus] was made flesh and dwelt among men. (John 1:14) He was born of a woman but not begotten by a man. Therefore, in the language of the Apostle, he was " holy, harmless, undefiled, separate from sinners". (Hebrews 7:26) And when he grew to manhood's estate he was the exact counterpart of the perfect man Adam prior to his violation of God's law.

RANSOM SACRIFICE

The whole plan of redemption upon which rests *solely* the hope of man for life everlasting depends upon the great ransom sacrifice. Jehovah has graciously provided a measuring rod by which every doctrine can be measured to determine its truth or falsity. The measuring rod or key by which this is determined is the great ransom sacrifice. Any doctrine out of harmony with it is false. Sir Conan Doyle quotes this Scripture: "Believe not every spirit, but try the spirits whether they are of God: because many false prophets are gone out into the world". (1 John 4:1) It will be observed from his testimony offered that he quotes only a part of the text. Had he examined the context, he would have seen that this has no reference to the spirits of dead men. The Apostle further states:"We [the apostles] are of God:he that is not of God heareth not us. Hereby know we the spirit of truth, and the spirit of error". (1 John 4:1-6) When we are invited to try the spirits it means for us to measure the doctrines offered in support of any theory and not to communicate with some demons; and if we understand the plan of God, with this absolutely perfect measuring rod we can determine whether the spirit (doctrine or teaching) is of truth or of error, whether of God or of the devil. We try the doctrines by measuring them according to God's perfect standard given in his Word.

The theory of the living communicating with the dead is a positive denial of the ransom. Sir Conan Doyle admits as much and does not hesitate to deny the ransom. He says: "Christianity must change or must perish. . . . One can see no justice in a vicarious sacrifice, nor in the God who could be placated by such means. Above all, many cannot understand such expressions as the 'redemption from sin', 'cleansed by the blood of the Lamb,' and so forth. . . . Again, too much seemed to be made of Christ's death. It is no uncommon thing to die for an idea. Every religion has equally had its martyrs. Men die continually for their convictions. Thousands of our lads are doing it at this instant in France."

. Here is one witness who boldly denies the merit of Christ's death; and this alone should stamp his testimony as unworthy of consideration. *Falsus in uno, falsus in omnibus*—i. e., false in one thing, false in everything. I appeal to you, Mr. Newday, and to every Christian who claims to love God and the Lord Jesus and to believe the Bible, to consider carefully this point, which is really decisive of the whole question. If the theory of communicating with the dead is accepted, the vicarious atonement of Jesus Christ must be rejected; and if rejected, Christianity falls and the Bible falls with it.

Speaking of Christ, Sir Conan Doyle says: "His special care is the earth. He came down upon it at a time of great earthly depravity—a time when the world was almost as wicked as it is now, in order to give the people the lesson of an ideal life. Then he returned to his own high station, having left an example which is still occasionally followed. That is the story of Christ as spirits have described it. There is nothing here of Atonement or Redemption."

This is exactly what Satan and the demons would like to have the people believe. Shall we believe Sir Conan Doyle and his demon prompters and other like witnesses; or shall we believe the Lord Jesus Christ? Of himself Jesus says: "I am come that they might have life, and that they might have it more abundantly". (John 10:10) Again, "the Son of man came not to be ministered unto, but to minister, and to give his life a ransom for many". (Matthew 20:28) We believe that

Jesus is a better witness than any of the professors,
doctors of divinity, or demons. Again Jesus said: "God
so loved the world, that he gave his only begotten Son,
that whosoever believeth in him should not perish, but
have everlasting life". (John 3:16) Sir Conan Doyle
and his messengers would have us believe that the people
already had life and could not die. He specifically denies the fall of man and thereby contradicts the Bible,
both the Old and New Testaments. Since we have
agreed to let the Bible be the arbiter of this question,
then Sir Conan Doyle's testimony must absolutely fail.

Further, the apostle Paul corroborates the statement of Jesus, that he came to earth to die for the
human race, when he says: "Jesus . . . was made a
little lower than the angels for the suffering of death,
crowned with glory and honor; that he by the grace of
God should taste death for every man". And again,
"There is one God, and one mediator between God and
men, the man Christ Jesus, who gave himself a ransom
for all, to be testified in due time".—Hebrews 2:9; 1
Timothy 2:5, 6.

The witnesses offered by Mr. Psychic all claim that
man does not lose his life but merely loses his "shell",
meaning the body of flesh; that there is, in fact, no
death, no cessation of life. We submit that this is a flat
contradiction of the Scriptures, for "the wages of sin is
death; but the gift of God is eternal life, through Jesus
Christ our Lord".—Romans 6:23.

THE RESURRECTION

The death and resurrection of Jesus provided for the
awakening of the entire human race out of death and
the opportunity to each of them to get life everlasting.
St. Paul states: "Christ died for our sins according to
the scriptures, was buried, and rose again the third

day according to the scriptures". (1 Corinthians 15: 3,
4) He was put to death for our sins and raised for
our justification.—Romans 4: 24, 25.

Resurrection means a restanding to life, which would
be impossible if the dead were already alive. Jesus illustrated the awakening of the dead to resurrection by calling forth Lazarus. Lazarus had been dead for four
days and buried in a tomb. Jesus surely knew more
about where he was than any of the eminent witnesses
offered by Mr. Psychic. He did not build a booth and
try to get into communication with him. He did not call
some woman as a medium and try to have her communicate with him. He did not have table tippings to get
some answer from Lazarus. He did not have automatic
writing in order to get some message from him. But
we read concerning Lazarus: "Then said Jesus unto
them plainly, Lazarus is dead". (John 11: 14) Jesus
and the disciples then went down to Bethany. He was
met by Mary and Martha; and they together with others
were weeping. And Jesus said: "Where have ye laid
him? They said unto him, Lord, come and see. Jesus
wept."—John 11: 34, 35.

The demons, misrepresenting the dead, would tell us
that is is wrong to weep for those whom we lose. Did
Jesus do wrong when he wept? Jesus then went to
Lazarus' tomb. "It was a cave, and a stone lay upon
it. Jesus said, 'Take ye away the stone. Then they
took away the stone from the place where the dead was
laid." Then he prayed to God. Now mark what Jesus
did. If Lazarus was floating around in the air, able to
send a wireless or to talk through a medium or to do
some automatic writing, why did not Jesus ask him to do
it? What did he do? We read: "And when he [Jesus]
thus had spoken, he cried with a loud voice, Lazarus,
come forth. And he that was dead came forth, bound

hand and foot with grave clothes; and his face was bound
about with a napkin. Jesus saith unto them, Loose him,
and let him go." (John 11: 43, 44) If Lazarus had
been floating around with his head and body tied up,
associating with the spirits of other dead ones, why does
not the record say something about it? Because, we
answer, the Word of God is true and anything in contradiction of it is false.

Mr. Psychic's testimony, particularly that of Sir
Conan Doyle, admits that Jesus Christ died, was buried,
rose from the dead and ascended on high, but would
have us believe that there was no merit in that except
as an example. The Scriptures answer that his death
and resurrection were a guarantee that all the dead shall
be awakened out of death. Note this Scriptural proof:
"Now if Christ be preached that he rose from the dead,
how say some among you that there is no resurrection of
the dead? But if there be no resurrection of the dead,
then is Christ not risen: And if Christ be not risen, then
is our preaching vain, and your faith is also vain. Yea,
and we are found false witnesses of God; because we
have testified of God that he raised up Christ: whom he
raised not up, if so be that the dead rise not. For if
the dead rise not, then is not Christ raised: and if Christ
be not raised, your faith is vain; ye are yet in your sins.
Then they also which are fallen asleep in Christ are
perished."—1 Corinthians 15: 12-18.

St. Paul then proceeds to prove conclusively that
Jesus Christ did rise from the dead and that his resurrection is a guarantee that every one who has died shall
be awakened out of death. "But now is Christ risen
from the dead, and become the firstfruits of them that
slept. For since by man came death, by man came also
the resurrection of the dead. For as all in Adam die,
even so in Christ shall all be made alive. But every man

in his own order: Christ the firstfruits; afterward they that are Christ's at his coming."—1 Cor. 15: 20-23.

The testimony offered by Mr. Psychic would have us believe that at the very instant of death the spirit passes into another world alive. Is this in harmony with the Scriptures? On the contrary, it is positively disproven by the Scriptures. Jesus said: "I go to prepare a place for you. And if I go and prepare a place for you, I will come again, and receive you unto myself; that where I am, there ye may be also." (John 14: 2, 3) St. Paul shows that the resurrection of the dead does not take place until the second coming of Christ and that until that time the dead are wholly unconscious and know not anything. "If we believe that Jesus died and rose again, even so them also which sleep in Jesus will God bring with him. For this we say unto you by the word of the Lord, that we which are alive and remain unto the coming of the Lord shall not prevent them which are asleep. For the Lord himself shall descend from heaven with a shout, with the voice of the archangel, and with the trump of God: and the dead in Christ shall rise first." —1 Thessalonians 4: 14-16.

Again, in proof that the dead are dead, waiting for the resurrection, this Scripture says: "There shall be a resurrection of the dead, both of the just and unjust". (Acts 24: 15) "Marvel not at this: for the hour is coming, in the which all that are in the graves shall hear his voice, and shall come forth." (John 5: 28, 29) If Sir Conan Doyle and his colleagues are correct, why did not Jesus in this Scripture say, 'Marvel not; all of those who are floating around in the air shall again manifest themselves'? No one can be a follower of Christ Jesus and accept as truth the teaching of these eminent wise men that the dead are alive.

And now, Mr. Newday, choose this day whom you will

believe, the Lord Jesus and the Apostles, or the devil and his allies. The issue is squarely drawn. If one is true, the other is false.

But, Mr. Psychic will say, shall we repudiate the testi-. mony of these great wise men who have given their lives to an investigation of this important subject? In this connection we are reminded of the words of God's prophet, speaking as his mouthpiece concerning testi-. mony of men who are wise in their own conceits with reference to the condition of the dead: "And when they shall say unto you, Inquire of those that have familiar spirits, and of wizards [mediums] that whisper [clairau-dience, the hearing of apparently foreign messages, by means of voices, usually 'internal voices'—Dr. Hyslop], and that mutter [messages through mediums]: Say to them, Should not a people inquire of their God? Should we then in behalf of the living inquire of the dead? Hold to the law and to the testimony. If they [the wit-nesses] speak not according to this Word [the Scrip-tures] there is no light in them."—Isaiah 8:19, 20, see *Leeser.*

But, says Mr. Psychic, I remind you that there are distinguished doctors of divinity and clergymen who support these other witnesses who say that they can talk with the dead. And to this we answer, We admit that there are some who have called themselves doctors of divinity who thus believe and teach and to them the preaching of the fall of man and the cross of Christ is foolishness, just exactly as St. Paul said it would be. And furthermore, the Apostle in this same connection says: "I will destroy the wisdom of the wise, and will bring to nothing the understanding of the prudent". (1 Corinthians 1:18, 19) To this same class and those who follow them the Lord prophetically wrote: "Where-fore the Lord said, Forasmuch as this people draw near

me with their mouth, and with their lips do honor me,
but have removed their heart far from me, and their
fear toward me is taught by the precept of men: therefore, behold, I will proceed to do a marvellous work
among this people, even a marvellous work and a wonder: for the wisdom of their wise men shall perish, and
the understanding of their prudent men shall be hid.
Woe unto them that seek deep to hide their counsel from
the Lord, and their works in the dark [with mediums
in booths], and they say, Who seeth us? and who
knoweth us?"—Isaiah 29:13-15.

THE MOTIVE

The real motive of Satan and the demons to propagate
among the people the teaching that they can communicate with the dead is that God and his great plan might
be discredited and that the people might be turned away
from Christ, the only hope of life; and that the seed of
promise might be destroyed. It is a war of light against
darkness. God has permitted Satan and his emissaries
to carry it to the limit and in his own due time he
will destroy both Satan and all his minions of darkness.

For nearly nineteen hundred years God has been developing the seed of promise, the seed of the woman,
through which blessings shall come to all the families of
the earth, according to the promise, which blessings are
an opportunity for life everlasting. There has been
enmity between this seed and the seed of the serpent
at all times. When Jesus died upon the cross, Satan
thought he had succeeded in his purpose to destroy the
seed. Subsequently, however, Jesus arose from the dead
and ascended on high. That was a surprise and disap-
pointment to Satan, who then set about to develop a
counterfeit seed.

At Pentecost the body members of the seed of promise,

the seed of the woman, began to be selected and developed, which work has progressed until now. The body members of this seed are designated in the Scriptures under various names, such as the church, the bride of Christ, the wheat, the Lord's jewels, etc. This seed is a limited number, as the Scriptures plainly set forth.—Revelation 7:4; 14:1-3.

SATAN'S SEED

At Pentecost, or shortly thereafter, Satan observed for the first time (because the mystery was not sooner revealed) that the seed of the woman, according to the promise, is the Christ and that the body members would be selected from among men and be designated as the church. In his desperation to destroy this seed, he again resorted to fraud and deceit and proceeded shortly thereafter to organize a counterfeit system of the Christ. Civil Rome had become a world power. It was a pagan nation. Christians began to grow in number. Desiring to corrupt Christianity, Satan induced the autocratic Constantine to profess the acceptance of Christianity. It is unnecessary to cite history to show the wickedness of Constantine. Yet by his accepting Christianity in form, but not in fact, Satan accomplished a two-fold purpose; viz., the corrupting of the church nominal and the uniting of the civil and ecclesiastical powers, and there began the development of the Antichrist—Satan's own seed. In time Pagan Rome became Papal Rome, an ecclesiastical power exercising civil authority, which the Scriptures denounce as whoredom.—Revelation 17:1-5.

We quote the following from Lord's *Old Roman World*, showing how Satan corrupted the early nominal church and thereby added others to his seed, which has since warred against the true seed according to the promise:

"It was not till the Fourth Century—when Constantine was converted; when the church was allied with the state; when the early faith was itself corrupted; when superstition and vain philosophy had entered the ranks of the faithful; when bishops became courtiers; when churches became both rich and splendid; when synods were brought under political influence; when monachists [monks] had established a false principle of virtue; when politics and dogmatics went hand in hand, and emperors enforced the decrees of [church] councils —that men of rank entered the church. When Christianity became the religion of the court and of the fashionable classes, it was used to support the very evils against which it originally protested. The church was not only impregnated with the errors of pagan philosophy, but it adopted many of the ceremonies of Oriental worship, which were both minute and magnificent.

"The clergy, ambitious and worldly, sought rank and distinction. They even thronged the courts of princes and aspired to temporal honors. They were no longer supported by the voluntary contributions of the faithful, but by revenues supplied by government, or property inherited from the old [pagan] temples. Great legacies were made to the church by the rich, and these the clergy controlled. These bequests became sources of inexhaustible wealth. As wealth increased and was intrusted to the clergy, they became indifferent to the wants of the people—no longer supported by them. They became lazy, arrogant and independent. The people were shut out of the government of the church. The bishop became a grand personage, who controlled and appointed his clergy. *The church was allied with the state,* and religious dogmas were enforced by the sword of the magistrate.

"An imposing hierarchy was established, of various grades which culminated in the Bishop of Rome. The Emperor decided points of faith, and the clergy were exempted from the burdens of state. There was a great flocking to the priestly offices when the clergy wielded so much power and became so rich; and men were elevated to great sees [bishoprics], not because of their piety or talents, but by their influence with the great. The mission of the church was lost sight of in a degrading alliance with the state. Christianity was a pageant, a ritualism, an arm of the state, a vain philosophy, a superstition, a formula."

In due time there was a great effort at reformation and much progress was made. The Protestant church was established, but with its establishment the adversary again sowed the seeds of wickedness and in the course of time ambitious clergymen in all the Protestant systems were teaching Satan's first and famous lie, the doctrine of inherent immortality and the kindred doctrine of eternal torture; and mixing politics and religion, civil and ecclesiastical functions, they gradually drifted away from the Lord and his teachings; and thus Satan gathered more into his net.

In all these systems, however, both Catholic and Protestant, there have been some true Christians and are yet true Christians. But every one of their leaders that has fallen to the flattery of the adversary has become his real instrument and his seed; and they do his will, especially when they preach that the dead are alive, thus denying the fall of man, denying the ransom sacrifice, and denying the resurrection and restitution of the human race.

Who is the seed of Satan? Jesus answers: "Ye are of your father the devil, and the desire of your father ye will do. He was a murderer from the beginning, and

"OUR FRIEND IS NOT DEAD.
HIS SOUL IS NOW HOVERING NEAR."

abode not in the truth, because there is no truth in him.
When he speaketh a lie, he speaketh of his own; for he
is a liar, and the father of it." (John 8:44) Then we
ask, Is it the will of God or the will of Satan that the
doctrine of inherent immortality—there is no death—be
taught? The answer is obvious. It is Satan and his
emissaries that would ever keep before the minds of the
people, There is no death. "In this the children of God
are manifest, and the children of the devil; whosoever
doeth not righteousness is not of God, neither he that
loveth not his brother."—1 John 3:10.

DEMONS IN BABYLON

But, says Mr. Psychic, have not these distinguished
clergymen given their lives to a study of the Scriptures
and are they not qualified to answer, and when they say
that we can communicate with the dead shall we say
that they are working in conjunction with the demons?

A brief examination of the Scriptural account will
satisfy your mind upon this subject. The word Babylon
originally meant the gateway to God. Afterward, in
derision, it came to signify confusion, because at Babel
the language of men was confused. The ancient city of
Babylon typified mystic Babylon. Mystic Babylon is described in Revelation 17:1-6 as "Babylon the Great, the
Mother of Harlots and Abominations of the Earth".
Harlotry is the illicit relationship between church and
state. In the Scriptures a good woman is used to symbolize the true church—the bride of Christ—while a
harlot symbolizes the false church. The fact that this
Scripture speaks of one as mother of harlots indicates
that there must be daughters. The Papal system claims
to be the mother church and avers that the Protestant
systems are her daughters. The word, then, in the
larger sense applies to ecclesiasticism, Catholic and Prot-

estant systems—not to the people in them. The Lord
foretold that the seed of the serpent would spill the
blood of the true saints, saying, "I saw the woman
drunken with blood of the saints, and with the blood
of the martyrs of Jesus".

Throughout the greater part of the gospel age the
seed of the woman, the true saints, have been in captivity
to and persecuted by the Babylonish systems; and truly
the church systems represent confusion; for none of
them teaches a harmonious doctrine, in harmony either
with the Word or with each other. It is a fact too
well known that the church, Catholic and Protestant,
has become exceedingly worldly. It has become popular
for politicians to be members of a church. For instance,
in the year 1916 a governor of one state was elected
because he prayed publicly in the Baptist church and yet
it was well know that he was not a follower of Christ.
Politics and religion have become so mixed up that it
is an abomination in the sight of the Lord. The Lord
foretold it would thus be, saying, "Babylon the great is
fallen, is fallen [from God's favor], and is become the
habitation of devils [demons], and the hold of every
foul spirit, and a cage of every unclean and hateful bird.
For all the nations have drunk of the wine [doctrine]
of the wrath of her fornication [illicit relationship between religion and politics], and the kings of the earth
have committed fornication with her, and the merchants
of the earth are waxed rich through the abundance of
her delicacies."—Revelation 18: 2, 3.

And this explains why the doctrine of demons has
gotten into the church systems and why many clergymen
today who have forsaken the Word of God and who are
teaching higher criticism and their own theories are announcing that the dead are alive and that the living can
communicate with them.

But, Mr. Newday, the Lord calls to you and to every Christian who really loves him and loves righteousness and who is yet in bondage to Babylon, saying, "Come out of her, my people, that ye be not partakers of her sins, and that ye receive not of her plagues".—Rev. 18: 4.

We note, for instance, that Bishop Fallows, endorsing the talking with the dead, says: "I have called the new science 'Immortalism' because it depends for its existence upon the immortality of the soul, in which we all believe, and the preservation of identity beyond the grave". Many Catholic and Protestant clergymen adhere strictly to the doctrine thus stated by Bishop Fallows. They adopt the theory of communicating with the dead as conclusive proof of their position. By this they accept the lie that Satan told—"Ye shall not surely [i.e. really] die"—and deny God and Jesus and all the plain teachings of the apostles.

Above we quote the Scripture that there is no other name given under heaven whereby we must be saved except the name of Christ Jesus. The testimony of the eminent witness Sir Conan Doyle is to the effect that too much stress is laid on the death of Christ Jesus. Sir Conan is a very prominent man and he and the other professors named have a wide influence over the people, and the public press is open to these influential men now to sway the people; and thus Satan is blinding these great men and is blinding those who yield to them, including a large number of clergymen, just as the Apostle said it would be. (2 Corinthians 4: 3, 4) If the people can be thoroughly convinced that their dead friends are alive and not dead, then they will believe that man did not fall; that there was no necessity for a redeemer; that Jesus Christ did not die to save them; that there is no resurrection of the dead; and thus Satan and the demons would succeed in destroying the faith of the people in

God's great plan of redemption. It is easy, therefore,
to be seen that one of the greatest menaces to the human
race today, the strongest delusion, and one which threatens to destroy the very foundation of faith in God's
word and plan, is the deception held before the people
that the living can communicate with the dead.

From the Scriptures above cited (2 Peter 2:4; Jude
6) we have seen that these demons were to be restrained
in darkness until the judgment day. The clear inference
to be drawn from this is that when the judgment day
is reached they would be able to exercise greater power
than ever before because they would be in a measure at
least released from their restraint during judgment.
Other Scriptures clearly and conclusively prove that we
are in the time of the judgment upon the nations and upon
Christendom, and that this is also the time of the judgment of the evil spirits, the demons. This explains why
the World War which has just ended was used as a means
of inducing more people to turn to spiritism. The great
war was foretold by the Lord Jesus as the time when
"nations shall rise against nation and kingdom against
kingdom", and he further foretold that this would be
one of the evidences of the end of the old order of things
just preceding the inauguration of the new order, which
is the Golden Age.

The Great Master stated that a further evidence of
that time would be that this war would be followed
by general social disturbance, revolutions, and like
trouble throughout the earth; and we now see that
in progress. As an additional evidence that we are
at the end of the old order and the time for the beginning of the new, which will bring in the Golden
Age, Jesus said: "As the days of Noah were, so shall
also the coming of the Son of man be". (Matthew
24: 37) It will be remembered, referring to the Scrip-

tural account of Noah's day, that the demons then
had overreached and debauched practically all of the
human race and that the people were indifferent to the
preachings of Noah and they were going about pursuing
that which would gratify their desires. They had disregarded God and his Word, and we see exactly the same
thing now prevailing; and it is being brought about
chiefly through the ministration of demons who did the
same in Noah's day. We warn you and the people, therefore, to be not deceived by the testimony of wise men,
but turn attentively to a careful and faithful study of
the Bible, which alone contains the pure doctrine with
reference to God's provision for the salvation and blessing of mankind.

  The above Scriptural proof adduced, therefore, conclusively shows that the dead are dead and are not conscious; that the living cannot communicate with the
dead; and the testimony of the eminent wise men is
fully and conclusively explained by the Scriptures, which
show that in the time in which we are now living the
demons would exercise greater power, deceiving the
minds of many, inducing them to believe that their dead
friends are alive and by thus pretending fraudulently to
bring them a measure of comfort are in fact deceiving
them and driving them away from God's great arrangement for their own salvation.

  I perceive, Mr. Newday, that you love Jehovah, Christ
Jesus, and the Word, and I perceive an attempt on the
part of the adversary to accomplish the very thing that
Jesus foretold. You remember in some of the testimony
offered here by Mr. Psychic mention is made that Christ
appeared with the soldiers on the battlefields, which we
know is false and contrary to the spirit of Christ, because he teaches us to do good and not to do evil—not to
war against each other—and positively forbids us to

kill. In answer to the question concerning events that
would transpire at the end of the world, among other
things he said: "There shall arise false Christs, and false
preachers, and shall show great signs and wonders; in-
somuch that if it were possible they shall deceive the
very elect"—God's own people.—Matthew 24: 24.

Satan is the prince of devils, or demons. The testimony offered in order to camouflage the real purpose and
to enable deception to be practised upon Christian people
pretends to put forth Christ and claims he was a great
and mighty and good man, and that he now appears on
the battlefields to comfort those that mourn and to comfort the bereaved ones at home. We know that Satan
and the demons have no love for Christ and that their
only purpose in taking his name is to defraud. Such
action on their part marks this as the time mentioned
by Jesus in Matthew 12: 24-28—pointing to the fall of
Satan's kingdom. The demons now breaking away from
Satan's domination in a measure have produced a condition of anarchy in his realm. The Scriptures (Revelation 7: 1-4) show that they would be the cause of
great trouble in the earth; and without a doubt the
prevalency of the spirit of insubordination, the spirit
of revolution and anarchy, the spirit of wickedness
in high places throughout the earth is due largely
to the fact that the demons are influencing the minds
of the people. They are convincing many that there
is no death and then injecting into their minds all
kinds of evil thoughts. Without doubt they had much
to do with the conditions which provoked the World War;
and when the war came, they took advantage of it to
deceive the people further. And this condition will continue to grow worse and worse, resulting, as Jesus states,
in "great tribulation, such as was not since the beginning of the world to this time, no, nor ever shall be".

(Matthew 24: 21) But with the ending of this trouble will come the overthrow of Satan, his empire and all of his emissaries, to be followed by the righteous reign of Christ, bringing blessings to all the people.

I will submit with my argument and append to this copy for your perusal some of the great signs and wonders which these evil ones are working and which are calculated to deceive all except those who have their minds and hearts turned to the Lord.

The great time of stress is now on the world. The hearts of the people are made sad by so much sickness, sorrow, war, revolution, trouble and death. The fraudulent, dishonest and deceiving adversary—this he has always been—and his cohorts come forth with a pretended message of comfort, taking advantage of this time of distress. Their real purpose is to turn the minds of the people away from God and away from Jesus, the great Redeemer and Deliverer through whom only the blessings can come to mankind. It will be of interest to you to notice for a moment what God purposes to do with the seed of promise. The Scriptures announce that when this seed of promise is completed, the church being fully selected and glorified with Christ at the time of his second coming and the setting up of his kingdom, there will be a time of refreshing for the blessing of the people. The people are really waiting for the manifestation of his seed, as St. Paul puts it: "The whole creation groaneth and travaileth in pain together until now" —waiting "for the manifestation of the sons of God". (Romans 8: 22, 19) This is the seed of promise through which the blessing shall come and will come. St. Peter describes it thus: "Times of refreshing shall come from the presence of the Lord; and he shall send Jesus Christ, which before was preached unto you; whom the heaven must receive [retain] until the times of restitution of all things, which God hath spoken by the mouth of all his holy prophets since the world began". (Acts 3:19-21) This is the time of reconstruction; and with the Lord's kingdom in full sway, with Satan bound, the reconstruction and blessing of mankind will proceed. "Because he [God] hath appointed a day, in the which he will judge the world in righteousness by that man whom he hath ordained; whereof he hath given assurance unto all men, in that he hath raised him from the dead." (Acts 17:31) Then all the dead shall be awakened (John 5:25) and given a full opportunity to accept the Christ and live everlastingly in happiness.

The Lord foretold how comfort would come to those who have lost their sons, such as you and the good mothers described, good mothers whom these demons are seeking to deceive: "Thus saith the Lord: A voice was heard in Ramah, lamentation, and bitter weeping; Rachel weeping for her children refused to be comforted for her children, because they were not. Thus saith the Lord: Refrain thy voice from weeping, and thine eyes from tears; for thy work shall be rewarded, saith the Lord; and they shall come again from the land of the enemy. And there is hope in thine end, saith the Lord, that thy children shall come again to their own border." (Jeremiah 31:15-17) The land of the enemy here described is the condition of death, because death is the enemy.—1 Corinthians 15:25, 26.

That will be a time of rejoicing, as the Prophet beautifully describes it in the thirty-fifth chapter of Isaiah. There he points out that, when the Lord's kingdom is established, "the eyes of the blind shall be opened, and the ears of the deaf shall be unstopped"; and the people shall rejoice with exceeding joy because the time for blessing has come; "and the ransomed of the Lord shall return, and come to Zion with songs and ever-

lasting joy upon their heads: they shall obtain joy and
gladness, and sorrow and sighing shall flee away". Why
does he say here that sorrow and sighing shall flee away?
We answer, Because it is Messiah, the Christ, the Seed
according to the promise, the glorious kingdom, that will
bring blessings to the people.

St. John the Revelator beautifully described the
Lord's kingdom. In symbolic phrase he designates it as a
holy city, saying, "And I John saw the holy city, new
Jerusalem, coming down from God out of heaven, prepared as a bride adorned for her husband. And I heard
a great voice out of heaven saying, Behold, the tabernacle
of God is with men, and he will dwell with them, and
they shall be his people, and God himself shall be with
them, and be their God. And God shall wipe away all
tears from their eyes; and there shall be no more death,
neither sorrow, nor crying, neither shall there be any
more pain: for the former things are passed away. And
he that sat upon the throne said, Behold, I make all
things new. And he said unto me, Write: for these words
are true and faithful." (Revelation 21: 2-5) The Lord
plainly shows when death will cease. Satan is trying to
blind the people to believe that there never was any
death; and thus, you see, to accept the theory advanced
by Mr. Psychic and his witnesses means to reject God's
plan. This Scriptural testimony should be so overwhelming and convincing that Christian people everywhere would resist the efforts of the adversary and turn
their minds and hearts prayerfully to an examination
and following of the Word of God.

Now, Mr. Newday, the issue is squarely drawn; and
you must determine upon which side of it you will
stand. If you accept the theory presented by Mr. Psychic
that you can communicate with your dead son, then
you must believe that the dead are alive; you must be-

lieve that the soul of man is immortal—both of which views are contradictory of the Scriptures; you must repudiate the Bible account of sin and the fall of man; you must deny the doctrine of the great atonement sacrifice. Any doctrine or teaching out of harmony with the ransom sacrifice is absolutely false, because the ransom is the key to the understanding of God's plan of salvation. Further, you must repudiate the blood of Jesus which bought you; you must repudiate the Bible as a whole as the Word of God, and if you take this course you must believe Satan's lie instead of God's Word; and Jesus said concerning God's Word: "Thy word is truth". I feel sure you want the truth and not falsehood.

If you accept the Bible view of the question, which I have presented to you, you will find it entirely consistent with the fact that God created man perfect; that man sinned and fell and that Satan was the inducing cause; that Satan and his emissaries have attempted to blind the human race to God's plan of redemption; and that he seduced the angels, causing them to become demons, and they together are the ones now that misrepresent the dead. You will find the Bible view of this question entirely consistent with the great ransom sacrifice and God's wonderful plan for the resurrection of the dead and for the blessing of all the families of the earth in due time. Truth must be shortly taken from the scaffold and forever enthroned. The two forces are now in a desperate and final conflict. You must align yourself upon the side of one or the other. Choose you this day which you will accept, error or truth.

I am now content to submit my side of the case upon this argument; but for your convenience and that of others, I append hereto a more specific reference to operations of the demons.

CHAPTER IV

NEWDAY'S CONCLUSION

MR. NEWDAY: Gentlemen, I thank you for the presentation of this matter. I have followed your arguments with keen interest. As I listened to that of Mr. Psychic it seemed so plausible that I was almost persuaded; but when I come to compare it with the Word of God, I am constrained to use the words of St. Paul: "Let God be true, but every man a liar". (Romans 3:4) As I stated to you in the outset, I have been striving to be a Christian all my life. Many of these deep questions I have been unable to understand, but as I have listened to the presentation of this subject I have received great enlightenment. I believe in the Lord Jesus Christ. I believe that he died to save us from our sins and that he was resurrected from the dead and ascended on high; and I believe that he has been selecting his church for the past centuries, and the evidence seems clear that soon his kingdom will be established, and, as announced time and again in the Bible, that the purpose of this kingdom is to extend blessings to all the families of the earth. And this being true, the theory that the dead are alive somewhere and can communicate with the living cannot be true. On the contrary, I see that Satan for many centuries has held before the people that which Jesus denounces as the first lie, viz., *There is no death.*

And all this testimony presented here on behalf of or by Mr. Psychic, even as claimed by him, is based upon the theory that there is no death; and since this theory is supported only by Satan's falsehood, I reject it most

emphatically. I rejoice that the Lord has permitted me
to see this clear distinction between truth and error;
and as thus I try the spirits (doctrines), and measure
them by the great ransom sacrifice, I am convinced of
the truth as taught by Jesus and the apostles; namely,
that the dead are dead; that Jesus has provided a redemption price; that in God's due time there will be a
resurrection of the dead and that all will have an opportunity for life everlasting who will render themselves in
obedience to his righteous arrangement. And while I am
convinced of the correctness of your position,I shall be
pleased, Mr. Lightbearer, if you will attach to your argument the answer to the points that you have indicated.

CHAPTER V

UNSEEN RULER

The ambition of Lucifer was to become a ruler. This ambition led to his downfall and thereafter he is designated in the Bible as the dragon, that old serpent, Satan, and the devil. (Revelation 20:2) He is a spirit being, therefore invisible to the eyes of men. He is more powerful than men and exercises power for a wrongful purpose over men. When the holy spirit gives a name to any creature or thing, the name signifies much. The name dragon means devourer; serpent means deceiver; devil means slanderer; Satan means adversary. Each of these names properly applied to the devil represents his characteristics.

Primarily all dominion belongs to Jehovah. He is the great God of the universe. None properly have dominion without his permission. He created man, placed him in Eden, and gave him authority to rule the earth and to have dominion over it and to fill it with a perfect race of people. Lucifer had access to Eden. He conceived in his heart the ambition to take possession of the first man and woman, alienate them from God, and thereafter control their posterity to his own glory.

Standing over against Jehovah and his kingdom of righteousness is this mimic god, the usurper, the devil. He attained control over our first parents by deception, thus using the quality which the word devil implies. When God sentenced man to death and expelled him from Eden man began to propagate his children, who were born imperfect; and Satan saw therefore that

Jehovah's sentence was not an idle threat, but would ultimately lead to the destruction of the human race. Jehovah subjected the human race then to other spirit beings or angels. (Hebrews 2:5) These angels God gave power to materialize as human beings. Satan the devil now conceived the thought of seducing a host of these angels. He caused them to take wives from amongst the human race with the evident purpose of producing a progeny in earth that would survive the shock of the death sentence pronounced by Jehovah. (Genesis 6:1, 2) Those angels or spirit beings did debauch mankind. For this reason the Bible says of them that they "left their own estate".—Jude 6.

In the symbology of the Bible *heaven* means invisible ruling power; while *earth* symbolically means the social and political order in the earth. These demons had the power to materialize and dematerialize. Satan and the wicked angels became the invisible ruling power over men, hence properly designated "the heaven"; and the social and political order existing amongst the human race on earth under Satanic influence constituted the "earth" or social order that then was. Satan's dominion, both visible and invisible, became so wicked, and the earthly arrangement was so filled with violence, that God brought the great deluge and destroyed all the human beings. Hence the heavens and the earth, being overflowed by water, perished. (2 Peter 3:5, 6) Every human being except the eight in the ark died. After the flood Noah and his children began to propagate the race on earth.

Noah was a godly man and was faithful to Jehovah, as were also some of his descendants. The race increased, and in due time Abraham came upon the scene. To him God made a promise, saying, "In thy seed shall all the families of the earth be blessed". (Genesis 12:3)

Thereafter God organized the Jewish people into a nation, an earthly organization formulated after just rules and principles. Jehovah established amongst them the true religion, directing that they should worship him and him alone. (Exodus 20: 3) The promise made to Abraham was renewed to that people time and again, and they looked forward to the coming time when their nation would constitute "the seed" which would deliver all other peoples from the influence of Satanic power. These people clearly understood that Satan and the demons were ruling the other nations round about. God instructed them to hold themselves entirely aloof from the heathen nations. In his law he provided that they should have no fellowship with any one who attempted to communicate with the unseen world through mediums, necromancers, etc., and that anyone who did so must be put to death. (See Exodus 22: 18; Deuteronomy 18: 9-14) The Lord here expressly says that the other nations have gone after such evil ones.

Satan, the great adversary and mimic god, established the false religion, inducing the other nations aside from Israel to worship various objects representing himself and the other devils as gods. Satan and the fallen demons therefore constituted the heaven or invisible ruling power, ruling by influencing the minds of those nations aside from Israel. These nations, which are designated as heathen, constituted Satan's earthly organization.

Thereafter the Israelites from time to time yielded to the influence of Satan and the demons, exercised in a subtle and deceptive manner, and turned to devil worship. In the Scriptures we read: "They forsook the Lord God of their fathers, which brought them out of the land of Egypt, and followed other gods, of the gods of the people that were round about them, and bowed

themselves unto them, and provoked the Lord to anger.
And they forsook the Lord, and served Baal and Ash-
taroth." (Judges 2:11-13) These were names of their
unseen gods.

In Genesis 10: 8-12, we find the account of the birth
of Nimrod, who "began to be a mighty one in the earth.
He was a mighty hunter before the Lord." Nimrod
builded Nineveh, an idolatrous city. Nimrod was used
by the devil to fasten upon the people a false religion.
He was a mighty man, a great hunter, who destroyed
wild beasts which preyed upon the people, and therefore
became a great man amongst them, which necessarily,
because of his wicked course, tended to destroy reverence
for Jehovah and led to the worship of the creature
rather than the Creator. Josephus, the historian, writes:
"The multitude were very ready to follow the determination of Nimrod, and to esteem it a piece of cowardice
to submit to God".—Ant. 1:4:3.

Nimrod was an exceedingly wicked man. His mother
Semiramis was a beautiful but very depraved woman.
Nimrod married his own mother; and because of their
wicked lives the patriarch Shem caused Nimrod to be
tried before the tribunal of 72 supreme judges of Egypt.
This court condemned him to death, and his body was
dismembered and sent to various other cities as a warning, according to the then well-known judicial custom.
(See Judges 19:29; 1 Samuel 11:7; Wilkinson's History, Vol. 5, page 17) Ancient history discloses that
Semiramis made the claim that her son Nimrod was
none other than the "seed of the woman", as promised
in the Scriptures, who had been destined to bruise the
serpent's head. Thus did the devil again resort to deception by inducing them to believe that Semiramis
represented God instead of the devil. She therefore

declared that her son had risen from the dead and had been deified, and that hence he should be worshiped as a god. This could have been suggested by none other than Satan. Thereafter Semiramis was deified as the mother of this one; hence the false worship of mother and son, from which emanates the false heathen worship of the various heathen nations of the world, instigated by Satan, largely through which influence he has controlled the minds of the rulers of the earth, as well as the peoples. In time Semiramis became known as the queen of heaven, while Nimrod was worshiped as the seed of the woman, with evident purpose to draw away the minds of men from the "true seed" according to the promise.

Jeremiah recognizes this idolatrous condition in writing his prophecy to the Israelites. Those who refused to hear his admonition to return to righteousness are recorded as saying: "As for the word that thou hast spoken unto us in the name of the Lord, we will not hearken unto thee. But we will certainly do whatsoever thing goeth forth out of our own mouth, to burn incense unto the queen of heaven, and to pour out drink offerings unto her, as we have done, we, and our fathers, our kings, and our princes, in the cities of Judah, and in the streets of Jerusalem; for then had we plenty of victuals, and were well, and saw no evil. . . . And when we burned incense to the queen of heaven, and poured out drink offerings unto her, did we make her cakes to worship her, and pour out drink offerings unto her, without our men?"—Jeremiah 44: 15-17, 19.

The wickedness of Israel continued until it reached its climax under the reign of one of the kings. God then speaks to the wicked ruler of Israel through his prophet Ezekiel, saying: "Because ye have made your iniquity to be remembered, in that your transgressions are discovered, so that in all your doings your sins do appear; because, I say, that ye are come to remembrance, ye shall be taken with the hand. And thou, profane, wicked prince of Israel, whose day is come, when iniquity shall have an end, thus saith the Lord God: Remove the diadem, and take off the crown; this shall not be the same; exalt him that is low, and abase him that is high. I will overturn, overturn, overturn it; and it shall be no more, until he come whose right it is; and I will give it [to] him."—Ezekiel 21: 24-27.

This dethronement of Israel's king occurred in the year 606 B. C., and was followed by the immediate establishment under Nebuchadnezzar of the Babylonish world-empire. God, having here taken away the right of the Israelites to rule until such time as the Messiah should come, for a time withdraws from the field of action and Satan takes possession of all nations. There he became the "god of this world", by which title he is designated by the Apostle (2 Corinthians 4: 3, 4) ; and also called by the Lord Jesus the "prince [ruler] of this world" or order of things (John 14: 30) ; and again by St. Paul, the "prince of the power of the air" (Ephesians 2: 2) ; thus showing that he is the ruler of an invisible empire as well as of a visible one.

Thereafter the nobles of Israel, the scribes, Pharisees and doctors of the law, claimed to be obedient servants of God; yet they were dishonest and practised fraud and deceit. In the eyes of the people they stood for the true religion; yet Satan had overreached their minds. When Jesus came to earth these same scribes and Pharisees without a doubt were used as instruments of Satan. Jesus plainly told them that they were the offspring of the devil, their father, and that they would do their father's will and not the will of God.—John 8: 44.

The apostle Paul is authority for the statement that

God's dealings with the Jews were typical, foreshadowing better things to come. (Hebrews 10:1; 1 Corinthians 10:11) Therefore we may expect to find and do find, a counterpart in the gospel age of the things that occurred during the national existence of the Jews.

Jesus, the true seed of promise, at the age of thirty years began his ministry, teaching concerning the kingdom of heaven, and taught his disciples to pray to Jehovah: "Thy kingdom come; thy will be done on earth as it done in heaven"; and thus continued to teach concerning his kingdom as long as he was on earth. And during all his ministry Satan resisted him as his adversary.

That Satan regarded himself as the king or ruler of the nations of the earth is clearly evidenced by the Scriptures. He appeared to Jesus to tempt him, concerning which we read: "The devil taketh him [Jesus] up into an exceeding high mountain, and showeth him all the kingdoms of the world, and the glory of them; and saith unto him, All these things will I give thee, if thou wilt fall down and worship me. Then saith Jesus unto him, Get thee hence, Satan; for it is written, Thou shalt worship the Lord thy God, and him only shalt thou serve." (Matthew 4:8-10) Thus Jesus by his answer tacitly admitted that Satan was then the god of the world. Subsequently Jesus spoke to his disciples concerning Satan, calling him the "prince of this world". —John 12:31.

Time and again Satan sought to destroy Jesus, because he is the "seed of promise"; and to this end he incited the Pharisees to take our Lord's life. They entered into a conspiracy with Judas to have Jesus taken and put to death; and it is plainly stated in the Scriptures that Satan had taken possession of the mind of Judas. "And the chief priests and scribes sought how they might kill him; for they feared the people. Then entered Satan into Judas, surnamed Iscariot, . . . and he went his way, and communed with the chief priests and captains, how he might betray him unto them."—Luke 22: 1-4.

After the death and resurrection of the Lord Jesus and his ascension on high, God began the selection of his church, the members of the body of Christ. From Pentecost forward this work progressed. It was the belief and teaching of all the early Christians that Satan and the demons ruled an invisible kingdom, as well as in the earth. From a well-known historian we quote concerning the early Christians: "They simply declared the truth, warned the people against all Satanic temptations and dangers, held to and realized angelic ministrations, experienced wonderful visions, cast out demons, and preached a final victory over all the powers of darkness. . . . They held and taught the reality of a vast spiritual world with various regions of abode suitable for the habitancy of different classes of angels, spirits and demons, and that there all were associated more or less for the time being according to their respective kinds, congenialities, whether higher or lower. . . . They held and taught that among these demons there is an order of governmental rank, authority and subordination analogous to what is universal among mankind."—*Primitive Christianity*, pages 130, 131.

From another well-known English writer on primitive Christianity we quote the following: "The gods of the gentiles were at best but demons, impure and unclean spirits, who had imposed upon mankind, and by their villlany, sophistries and arts of terror had so affrighted the common people, who knew not really what they were and who judge of things more by appearance than by reason, that they called them gods, and gave to every one of them that name, which the demon was willing to take to himself; and that they really were nothing but devils, fallen and apostate spirits."— *Primitive Christianity,* by William Cave, page 5.

FAITHLESS RELIGION

A false religion is that which worships other than Jehovah. A faithless religion is one which claims Jehovah as God and Jesus as the Redeemer, yet acts under the influence of Satan and his emissaries. In the early stage of Christianity, Satan and his allies began to inject into the minds of the leaders in the church an ambition to rule; and soon it was that these men united politics and religion, introduced heathenish· or demon· doctrines as a part of the ritual of the Christian church, and formed an alliance between Christianity, in name, and commercialism and professional politicians. From this springs the Papal system, which has been devilish in all of its various machinations; and likewise comes an apostate Protestantism. Therefore nominal Christianity or, better named, "Churchianity", has become and is "a faithless religion".

When Jesus stood before Pilate he plainly said: "My kingdom is not of this world". (John 18:36) His followers in earth had been commissioned to preach his kingdom and hold themselves aloof from this world; yet we find that practically all the clergy of all denominations, Catholic and Protestant, have abandoned their high position, participate in the politics and big business schemes of this world, and the larger portion of them even deny the inspiration of the Scriptures, the fall of man, and redemption through Christ; and thus nominal Christianity has become an instrument of Satan's hands, and that is why so many clergymen are turning to spiritism and teach the devil's first lie: "There is no death"—the doctrine of inherent immortality of all souls. His influence has become so complete throughout the earth that St. John wrote: "The whole world lieth in the wicked one".—1 John 5:19.

The allies of Satan in his realm, invisible and visible, are the demons or devils which kept not their first estate and which were incarcerated in *tartarus* at the time of the flood. Satan is the chief amongst these devils; therefore called a prince. (Matthew 25:41; Ephesians 2:2) The apostle Paul removes all doubt about the organization invisible influencing visible things when he writes that the Satanic organization is made up of despotisms, empires, and hosts of evil spirits which war against all representatives of truth and righteousness.—Ephesians 6:12.

The main point to prove here is this: that Satan has an empire invisible, as well as visible; and that the demons, the fallen angels, are his associates in that empire; and that this must continue until it is finally destroyed; that the existence of this unseen or invisible empire centuries ago proves that it is still in existence, unless it has been destroyed; and we will show that it has not yet been destroyed but that its destruction is in the near future.

Hence upon the Scriptural authority above quoted, the governments of this world constitute the kingdom of Satan, and these governments or controlling factors in what is nominated "Christendom", are made up of three ruling elements; viz., commercialism, professional politicians, and apostate clergy, or faithless religion. This ruling power or earthly organization of the devil is designated in the Scriptures by the term "beast". Thus God's prophet Daniel describes the four universal empires, to wit: Babylonia, Medo-Persia, Greece, and Rome. The latter is described as "dreadful and terrible". The word "beast", then, is a symbol for an earthly ruling power or rule by violence. By this we mean a ruling factor that controls the consciences of men and resorts to violence to control mankind. The Book of Revelation in symbolic phrase refers to the same rule by violence as a "beast". ₁ The thirteenth chapter describes the "beast" rising up out of the sea, which means the devil organization taking form out of a disorganized society. This took place about the third century, at which time ecclesiasticism joined forces with commercial and political power, forming the then Roman empire. This "beast" is shown in Revelation to receive a deadly wound, which it did in 1799 at the hands of Napoleon; and for a time it goes into oblivion. The Revelator then pictures a "two-horned beast" rising on the scene, which revives or gives life to an "image of the beast" which received the deadly wound. The "two-horned beast" is clearly recognizable in the light of history as the British empire; whereas the "image of the beast" or the last of the devil's earthly organization, is the association of nations under a compact or agreement in the nature of a league or other agreement or association, which is now formed and is trying to strengthen itself. This is the last desperate effort of Satan to fasten his power upon the nations and peoples of earth.

THE FINAL CONFLICT

The gentile times ended in 1914, and there it was that the true ruler of the new heavens, Christ Jesus, began to exercise his kingly authority. (Revelation 11:18) The Apostle plainly states that these demons were reserved in restraint until the judgment day. (2 Peter 2:4; Jude 6) The judgment day began in 1914 and thereafter it is to be expected that the demons would exercise a greater power. It is a well-known fact that the Russian government was directed by the demons

through the mediumship of Rasputin. It is also a
well-known fact that the Kaiser of Germany heeded
the voice of the unseen, which led him into the World
War.

Upon the evidence above cited from the Scriptures,
it is clearly seen that Satan and the demons are now
desperately striving to control mankind by turning the
minds of men away from God and from the Lord Jesus
and the true kingdom. It is also well known that the
Versailles peace treaty does not mention the Lord or
his kingdom; and that at the opening of the disarmament conference at Washington the name of Jesus
was not mentioned.

What, then, should we expect to transpire when the
gentile times end? St. Peter speaking of this says:
"The heavens and the earth which are now, by the same
word are kept in store, reserved unto fire against the
day of judgment and perdition of ungodly men. . . .
The heavens shall pass away with a great noise; . . .
the earth also and the works that are therein shall be
burned up. Nevertheless, we, according to his promise,
look for new heavens and a new earth, wherein dwelleth righteousness."—2 Peter 3: 7-10, 13.

The Lord through his prophet speaking of the same
Satanic empire said: "Lift up your eyes to the heavens,
and look upon the earth beneath; for the heavens shall
vanish away like smoke, and the earth shall wax old
like a garment, and they that dwell therein shall die
in like manner; but my salvation shall be for ever, and
my righteousness shall not be abolished". (Isaiah 51: 6)
"And all the host of heaven shall be dissolved, and the
heavens shall be rolled together as a scroll." (Isaiah
34: 4) The holy spirit makes no mistakes in its pictures. A scroll is rolled up when its usefulness is over.
A thing goes up in smoke when it is destroyed; thus pic-

turing that Satan's invisible empire shall be destroyed.
A garment when it is worn out is thrown away. And
the figure here shows that the earth when it is worn out
shall be cast away as a garment, marking the end of
Satan's visible empire. This is the day of God's vengeance upon Satan's empire, visible and invisible.
(Isaiah 34: 8) It is the judgment time of the demons.

The promise long ago made by Jehovah, that the
seed of the woman should bruise the serpent's head,
was a symbolic picture of how the Christ, the true
"seed of promise" (Galatians 3: 16, 27, 29), will destroy
Satan's empire and set up a righteous kingdom. The
Apostle plainly states that that wicked one the Lord
will consume with the spirit of his mouth and shall
destroy with the brightness of his presence.—2 Thessalonians 2: 8.

The judgment of Satan and the demons is now on.
This is the day of their judgment; and this explains
why Satan and his wicked allies plunged the nations
into the World War, and now take advantage of the
great suffering to induce the living to believe that they
can talk with the dead, and thus divert their minds
from the King of glory and his kingdom which shall
shortly bring the long-promised blessings. But within
a short time the Lord will destroy this wicked regime
and establish "a new heaven and a new earth", as St.
Peter plainly shows is now due to come, and which St.
John pictures as being fully established by the reign
of the Messiah.—2 Peter 3: 13; Revelation 21: 1-6.

Since the Lord is now present, and dashing to pieces
Satan's empire, we know that the time has come for the
setting up of his kingdom, for which Christians have
long hoped and prayed. And since the Scriptures
plainly teach that his coming and his kingdom is for
the purpose of restoring to mankind that which Adam

lost (Acts 3: 19-24), and that those who hear and keep
his sayings shall live (John 8: 51), and that those who
live and believe upon him shall not die (John 11: 26),
it can be confidently said at this time that MILLIONS
OF PEOPLE NOW LIVING ON THIS EARTH WILL NEVER DIE.
For full and conclusive Scriptural proof as to why
millions now living · will never die see "The Harp of
God", a book of 384 pages, published by the International Bible Students Association, Brooklyn, N. Y.

CHAPTER VI

DEMON PHENOMENA ANALYZED

The Book of Revelation is written in symbols. The "four winds of the earth" of Revelation 7:1 symbolize the demons inhabiting the atmosphere around the earth. The conclusion must be drawn from this text that a period of time would come in the world's history in which the demons would have their restraint in a measure removed and there would be a great time of distress and trouble in the world, for which they would be largely responsible. Certain Scriptures tell of a whirlwind that will be raised up from the coasts of the earth. (Jeremiah 23:19; 25:32, 33; 30:23, 24) These words are also symbolic, used evidently to convey the thought of a time of great activity of the demons. Satan, the chief of devils, the Apostle mentions as "the prince of the power of the air". (Ephesians 2:2) The letting loose of these winds or air powers (devils) would seem' to show that God would remove his restraining hand and then there would follow a great trouble. For years these demons have been exercising their power to the extent granted. Had they been permitted to exercise unlimited power they would have wrecked the world long ago.

Without doubt the great revival of so-called communication with the dead, which in fact is demonism, that came with the World War is another proof of the time in which we are living and proof that the demons are exercising greater power because of their time of judgment. The Scriptures indicate that all people, being overreached by their sinister influence, will suffer greatly. In order that the reader might see the many inconsistent things they do, and in order that the reader might appreciate the baneful influence of these evil ones, we give herein a statement of many so-called phenomena that the public press has recently recorded. A brief statement is made in the analysis, followed immediately by a number enclosed in parenthesis, which corresponds with the number of the subhead set forth in this chapter; and by referring to that the facts can be ascertained. For instance, we say concerning these demons, "They hate and fear the light (9)"; and by reference to this number the proof of the statement here made can be found.

SPIRITISM IN THE PUBLIC PRESS

THE NATURE OF THE MESSENGERS
For substantiation see items on following pages as indicated by numbers.

They are liars and deceivers (1, 2, 3, 4, 5, 6, 22, 45,) ; they hate and fear the Bible (7, 12), and ridicule it (8, 11) ; they hate and fear the light (9) and hate the thought of Jesus as man's ransom (10, 11, 12) ; they encourage prayers for the dead (14).

They claim to speak as the voice of the Almighty (13, 45), yet they encourage and advocate loose morals (15, 16), have no interest in mankind (17), have done nothing for mankind (18, 20), supply neither wisdom nor comfort (19), and produce evil and only evil effects (20).

They insult and scold (4), curse and swear (21, 22, 23), create discord and confusion (38), take advantage of the weak (39), frighten dumb animals (24) and have frightened soldiers into insanity (25). They do acts of malicious mischief (26), commit arson (27), lead to suicide (28, 29) and incite to violence and murder (5, 30, 31, 32). They are fraudulent and malignant (33, 34). They pretend to have high moral principle but are sinister, depraved and obscene, and convinced of their own immorality (6, 23, 35, 36, 37, 38). They are the spirits of devils (39) and delight to hinder God's work (40). They deny the existence of Satan in some spiritistic cults (41) and worship him in others (42).

THE METHODS BY WHICH THEY MANIFEST THEMSELVES

They are made of the finest gas, held together by electricity (43) and are countless myriads in number (48, 63). They sometimes impress the brain from without, and sometimes from within (5, 6, 29, 31, 32, 44). They have the power to inject thoughts into the mind (45, 46), and if for any reason the will is weak or not wholly in harmony with God's will they may even read the mind (32, 34, 37, 68). They fill the mind with wonderful illuminations (47, 48), produce strange lights (25, 48, 65), cause dreams (30), and impress upon the mind pictures which the eye does not see (29, 45, 49, 59).

They deceive the senses by supposed but not actual materializations (51, 52, 53, 54). There are, however, actual materializations, composed of living material drawn from the medium's body for the purpose (9, 55, 56, 57, 58, 59, 60). The method by which the demons invade and use the medium's person (61, 62, 63) is of an electrical or galvanic nature (45).

The first step in the road to ruin by these evil agents is the use of the ouija board or planchette now to be found everywhere (2, 22, 40). The next step is to use the medium's hand in writing (29, 67, 68, 69), and the next is possession, described above. Demons have power over the voices of those they obsess and have vocal powers of their own (30, 45, 64). They can imitate the scent of roses (65, 66).

They draw and paint pictures (29, 70, 71)) and produce pictures on sensitized plates (72, 73). They do various lifting feats (9, 45, 57).

HOW THEY AFFECT THEIR VICTIMS

By their seizure of the base of the brain of mediums they shatter the nerves and break the spirit (20). Al-

though they may, to gain a point, temporarily heal a
disease (48. 69), yet in the end they drive their victims to
insanity (37).

THE REWARDS WHICH THEY PROMISE

These demons admit that their habitat is in tartarus, the
atmosphere of this earth (43). They teach that in it is a
heaven unknown to the Bible wherein, besides other attrac-
tions, there are cats (15), dogs (15), lawlessness (69), liars
(1, 2, 3, 4, 5, 6, 22, 45), liquor (15), murderers (5, 30, 31,
82), sexual delights (15), and tobacco (15).

THE OMINOUS SITUATION

Demonism is sweeping the earth. While it has not deceived THE WATCH TOWER (40, 45, 46, 50, 59, 67, 68) and
a few other theologians (20, 39), yet there are many
ministers who have been totally deceived by it (14, 16, 51,
52, 54, 65, 71). This spiritism craze is nothing more or less
than a revival of the necromancy denounced in the Bible
a return to the witchcraft practised in the days of King
Saul.

THE REMEDY

The remedy for demonism lies in a resolute fixing of the
mind upon good and useful things, a hearty interest in
doing all that is done as unto the Lord, determination to
resist everything akin to spiritism or occultism, avoiding
them as you would the plague, and as you value your happiness here and your salvation hereafter.

THEY ARE LIARS AND DECEIVERS

(1) The New York *Times* quotes Dr. J. H. McMahon, the
Roman Catholic theologian, as saying:

"The testimony is unanimous that you can't always believe the
spirits."

(2) The Pittsburgh *Press* contains a dispatch from New
York stating that a woman's apartment was robbed of gems
worth $15,000. Detectives were called in. While there the
woman asked a ouija board whether the thief was still in
the house. The board lied and said yes. He was not there.

(3) The Woodhaven *Leader-Observer* narrates an incident
where a woman whose son was drowned by the sinking of

the Tampa in Bristol Channel, on the west coast of England,
September 26, 1918, is said by his mother to have told her
through a ouija board that the ship was bombed by a
Zeppelin. This was not the case as the ship is known to have
been torpedoed by a submarine.

(4) Rubert Hughes in the Cleveland *Plain Dealer* says
of a noted spirit medium:

"Mrs. Piper's wonderful hand was controlled by Dean Bridgman
Conner, who wrote from Mexico that he was in prison and wanted
to be rescued. It was proved afterward that his body had been in
its grave all this while. It sickens my soul to be asked to plod
back along the same old ruts with the same old insolent and
insulting liars, swindlers, lovers of the dark and practicers of
legerdemain that have made a Coney Island out of sacred territory
since the first contemptible magician hoodwinked the first hungry
dupe."

(5) Of a woman, who was lured by the spirits into killing
her child, the Chicago *Tribune* says:

"Mrs. G. explained that she had been told at the spiritualistic
meetings that she was a medium. She attended meetings for a
year before the voices told her to kill Eleanor. She was told to sit
for development and the messages would come to her. They did.
They were whispered to her all the time. One voice told her it
belonged to a man she did not know who had lived and died in
that neighborhood and was still lingering around in spirit. The
voices at times became confused. They told her once to go to
Danville. When she packed up to go they told her not to go.
She did not know what to do, which voice to obey."

(6) Of another refined and educated woman, who was
gradually led by the spirits to the belief that she had been
married on the spirit plane, the same paper gives the
following sad story:

"She became greatly exalted and told her friends that she could
communicate with the next world. She found many spiritual
friends beyond, and one day they told her she had been appointed
to be married to a certain man. She had only met this man once.
Her spiritually-led fiancé did not appear, but this made no difference
with her preparations. She prepared her wedding supper for July
31, in spite of the protests of her family. When the man did not
come to the supper she consulted the spirits again and was told
he would come the next day. This was continued day after day
for several weeks. Finally she was convinced that she had been
married on the spiritual plane. She talked to her brother in Mars
and he told her how to live. She was told to become a vegetarian;
that a form of magnetism was to do away with the old conception
of child-bearing. She learned one day that her spiritual husband
would be at the Blackstone. She went to meet him, but the clerk
said he was not in. Then 'the voices' began to bother her. They
came from evil, she thought. She found that her 'husband' was
being detained at a sanitarium at Lake Forest. So she went out
there, too. Later she was sent to a sanitarium at Milwaukee. She
was convinced that her 'husband' was shot and she tried to kill
herself."

THEY HATE AND FEAR THE BIBLE

(7) The *Watchman* records the experience of a Korean woman possessed with five demons who went to Christian missionaries to have them pray for her deliverance from their power.

"While sitting with her face to the floor, with eyes shut, muttering to herself, an open Bible was placed on the back of her head. She at once snatched it away, saying that she was afraid of it. But when a song book was likewise placed, she laughed, saying it could not hurt her."

THEY RIDICULE THE BIBLE

(8) The *Progressive Thinker*, a leading spiritist paper, says:

"The writer of Genesis starts out by saying: 'In the beginning God created the heavens and the earth,' and he mentions three distinct days before the sun was created; then he tells us how God made man and never thought about making woman until he saw that his man was tired associating with animals; then he made the first woman out of man's rib. Later, a devil got into a snake and defeated all God's plans. In this more enlightened age of the world, clear thinkers do not believe that the universe had a beginning, but that it always existed and always will exist."

THEY HATE AND FEAR THE LIGHT

(9) The New York *Evening Telegram* narrates that at a private séance, while a table was being turned on end and lifted by the spirits:

"The writer, becoming nervous over where they might attempt to put the table, flashed on light, which revealed table directly in my line of vision back of medium, its lower end fully two feet from floor. Alas! I did not consider result. The table fell with a crash that jarred the whole house and frightened the women of the party so that it broke up our sitting."

THEY HATE THE THOUGHT OF JESUS AS MAN'S RANSOM

(10) The *Progressive Thinker*, spiritist, says:

"The dogmas of vicarious atonement and the forgiveness of sins are overthrown by Spiritualism."

(11) The *Weekly Journal*, spiritist, says:

"It is an absurd idea that Jesus was a perfect man.... Jesus had defects and imperfections like all other men. He was a simple Jewish enthusiast and religious reformer, foolishly supposing himself the Messiah, thereby coming to an untimely death."

(12) *Moral Philosophy*, a spiritist book, says:

"Slaughtered oxen, hecatombs of human victims, or ten thousand bleeding Christs will not atone for the least transgression of the laws of our being. . . . The true redemption is not through the . . . efficacy of Christ's blood. . . . Terrible is the significance, and humiliating . . . are the words, 'peace with God' 'reconciled unto God,' 'atonement,' 'salvation through the blood of the Lamb,' . . . an endless vocabulary which is fossilized ignorance, credulity, fear and rascality."

THEY CLAIM TO SPEAK WITH THE VOICE OF THE ALMIGHTY

(13) A writer in *Cosmopolitan*, whose little daughter is a medium, reports these beings as saying through his daughter:

"We are expressions of him; but do not forget that it is he who speaks through us, and that we are the reflections of his glory."

THEY ENCOURAGE PRAYERS FOR THE DEAD

14) At the Congress of the Church of England, Leicester, England, October 16th, 1919, Dean Welldon said:

"I think spiritualism has come to fill a void in church practise, and because of the coldness in the services, intercessions for the departed should be restored."

THEY ENCOURAGE AND ADVOCATE LOOSE MORALS

(15) The New York *Evening Journal* reports Sir A. Conan Doyle, spiritist, as expressing his opinion that besides sexual attraction, liquor and tobacco, the delights of the spirit world are just what they are here. He says:

"Happy circles, life in pleasant homesteads, beautiful gardens, lovely flowers, green woods and domestic pets—all of these are described in messages from pioneer travelers, who have at last got back news to those who still loiter in the dingy old home. It is described as a place of joy and laughter and games and sports, and peopled by those who are without deformity or bodily weaknesses. Let no woman mourn her lost beauty, no man sorrow for his lost strength. All is waiting on the other side."

(16) A writer in the New York *Evening Telegram* claims that it is the teaching of the most prominent spiritists that in the spirit world the bereaved mother:

"will meet again her own Tom, Dick, or Harry with all his loved faults and failings, and with the hair, smile and features she knew so well."

The same writer quotes Bishop Charles Sumner Burch as saying:

"I want to believe in spiritualism—and I do believe in it.

"I remember how great was my astonishment when I learned that my fascinating neighbor next door—a grass widow, by the way—had been holding conversations with her departed sister, who assured her that she was taking good care of the little daughter my fascinating neighbor had lost years ago.

"There was nothing of the fanatic about the grass widow, who used the most alluring perfumes, dressed in the latest styles and spent her time between the theater, the cabaret and the bridge table.

"Spiritualism, if rightly understood, holds out a new promise and a new help to the masses, a new promise of reunion to those who have not faith enough to be satisfied with the glimpses offered by the Bible."

THEY HAVE NO REAL INTEREST IN MANKIND

(17) A writer in the San Diego *Evening Tribune* says:

"I don't know why there seems to be such a lack of interest in the spirit world regarding what is happening in this world. There is certainly more wisdom on the other side than on this side; for death has swallowed millions of wise men; but most of the communications as far as I have been able to ascertain relate to personal affairs; none of them so far contains much constructive material for rehabilitation of a sadly dilapidated world."

THEY HAVE DONE NOTHING FOR MANKIND

(18) Mr. Jerome K. Jerome in the New York *Tribune* says:

"I take the last five years. Has spiritualism done anything—is it doing anything—to help man to be less brutal, less hypocritical, less greedy? Has it done anything—is it doing anything—to lessen the appalling wickedness that is threatening, like some foul weed, to poison the whole earth? For five years savagery and cruelty have been preached to us from the pulpit and from the press. Our children are being taught it at their mothers' knees. Vengeance and hatred are the new virtues. Christ, amid roars of laughter, is mocked in our parliaments. What has spiritualism done—what is it doing—to help mankind to recover its senses, its manhood; to rescue its soul from being withered by lust and passion?"

THEY SUPPLY NEITHER WISDOM NOR COMFORT

(19) The San Francisco *Call and Post* says:

"These spirit messages are usually commonplace and gossiping, or impossible to understand. They tell no great secret, reveal no divinity of mystery, give no really satisfying comfort to saddened hearts. The spirit correspondents are strangely dispassionate; they do not thank the world for having set them free from their bodies nor do they curse that world whose only gift to them was death. And, most important of all, they are telling no secrets and revealing no wisdom, these dead men who should know everything now."

THEY PRODUCE EVIL AND ONLY EVIL EFFECTS

(20) Dr. J. H. McMahon, the Roman Catholic theologian, is reported in the New York *Times* as saying:

"After seventy years of spiritualistic teaching and writing there has not been conferred upon mankind one benefit. Mankind has only been deceived by false hopes. The whole history of spiritualism is shot through with evil effects upon physical and moral health."

THEY CURSE AND SWEAR

(21) A woman writing in the Tacoma *Sunday Ledger* narrates that she went to a medium who put her in communication with an intelligence who represented himself to be her deceased husband. She says:

"I want to consult him about a business deal, and the first thing he said was, 'I can't see why you always have to be late. If we men ran our business the way you women do things, where in the name of heaven would we be!' And you know dear John always complained about my being late all the time. It was just like him."

(22) The Binghamton *Morning Sun* reports a former ouija board medium as saying:

"The ouija board lies so that you can't believe anything it says, and sometimes it swears so that you do not want to be in the same room with it, and the planchette is just as bad."

(23) A spiritist is reported by *Signs of the Times* as having made the statement:

"This spiritualism would sweep the world, were it not for just one thing. When the spirits are communicating with you, they may take a notion to curse and swear in a manner the most horrible, and to say and suggest the most obscene things imaginable."

THEY FRIGHTEN DUMB ANIMALS

(24) The Harrisonburg (Va.) *News Record* reports a barn in the vicinity apparently occupied by evil spirits and says:

"Horses in the barn cannot be kept haltered because they become frightened and break the chains by rearing back; the cows will not go near the barn."

THEY HAVE FRIGHTENED SOLDIERS INTO INSANITY

(25) The Bridgeport *Evening Post* contains an account of an apparition which, frequently repeated, caused four soldiers to go insane. This happened at a castle near Milan, Italy. The account says:

"A few nights ago a soldier was mounting guard over the magazine when a luminous figure from whose head issued tongues of flame, appeared before him at a distance of about twenty feet. The sentinel gave the alarm, and the entire guard hurried to the spot. The spectre had in the meantime vanished, but shortly after the arrival of the soldiers it reappeared. The whole company then fired their rifles at the figure, which instantly dissolved into a great ball of fire, finally melting away into space. The following night the apparition was once more seen. A Sicilian soldier of the guard approached the figure with a number of his companions, and an attack was made on it with the bayonet. Their furious thrusts, however, encountered no tangible resistance, and the phantom disappeared in a few moments in a fiery halo which was speedily dissolved in the atmosphere."

THEY DO ACTS OF MALICIOUS MISCHIEF

(26) The Binghamton *Press* tells of activities of demons in a house near Dublin, Ireland:

"Trouble began when bricks began to fall down the chimney and ornaments were broken without visible agency. In the past few weeks the activities of the ghost have greatly increased. Windows are broken, pots smashed, bricks come tumbling down on the floor and disappear. While the frightened owner was looking at his clock the hands disappeared."

THEY COMMIT ARSON

(27) The Minneapolis *Journal* tells how eleven fires were started by demons in one home within a period of thirty hours. It says:

"The first fire was discovered at 3 p. m. Wednesday in a clothes closet adjoining the kitchen. Mrs. Stub quenched the flames. Four hours later she found the closet on fire again. At 8:30 that evening, Ann, 3 years old, screamed in the kitchen, and her parents found a bow of ribbon tied to a basket on a table, bursting into flame. Mr. and Mrs. Stub then left the house. At 9 p. m. screams from the children roused C. H. Francis in his room on the second floor. He found a baby's hood, on a doorknob, burning. Fifteen minutes later, summoned by cries, he came in time to beat out a blaze in a suit of pajamas on a chair. Within a quarter of an hour, another blaze broke out in a blanket, soaked in quenching the first closet fire. And at 10 p. m. a pile of clothing in the middle of the floor began to burn.

"The next fire was found at 5.30 p. m. yesterday, when baby blankets on a clothes-line took fire. At intervals of a few minutes three more fires broke out, one in a curtain, one in a rope hanging on the wall, and another in a pile of dishtowels."

THEY LEAD TO SUICIDE

(28) Chicago dispatches tell of a girl who became so infatuated with the teachings of spiritism that she took poison so she could enter the spirit world that much sooner.

(29) *Prophetic News* tells of a man who at first yielded his hand to spirit-writing, and then, becoming disgusted, threw into the fire a beautifully drawn demon-made picture of his mother, because he was convinced she was not wandering about the earth in company with other spirits. He was then subjected to clairaudient and visual torments. In vision he was tried and condemned by a council of fallen angels and when he attempted to pray his ears were filled with clairaudient voices denouncing him. He says:

"In the midst of all these dangers and difficulties by which I was well-nigh overwhelmed, a commanding voice from an invisible spirit called me, saying words to this effect 'That I had become so environed and besieged by evil spirits that there was no deliverance for me on earth, and that he—an angel of the Lord—had descended from heaven to bear me this command from the Lord Jesus—that I must die by my own hand to escape my persecutors, and that my soul should then find rest in heaven.' "

He could not conceive it possible that the evil spirits would use the sacred name of Christ for such a purpose, but they did. The man drank poison, but recovered. They came again, ordering him a second time to commit suicide and he cut the temporal artery and was trying to cut another artery when he fell, weakened by the loss of blood. By a miracle of the Lord's grace he recovered and found the demons had lost their power to approach him.

THEY INCITE TO MURDER

(30) The Chicago *Herald Examiner* tells of a sea-captain who when convicted of murder gave as his excuse for the murder:

> "I had a dream last night, in which I saw my dead mother, grandmother and God. They told me if I went into the street and saw a desperate burglar I was to shoot him and I would go to heaven."

(31) The Mansfield *News* tells of the defence of a man who was convicted of killing a neighbor:

> "I was commanded by a voice which woke me from sleep to go to Spencer's cabin and kill the devil.
> "The voice told me that the devil had one of my friends tied up there. At first I thought it was a dreamy hallucination and remained in bed. But I soon heard the voice again and got up and dressed."

(32) The Chicago *News* made an investigation of spirit phenomena, reaching the following conclusions:

> "As to the voices that so many are bending ear to catch, I have learned that they are more likely to suggest evil than good. Man is a spiritual being, but does not always find it out at death, I am told. Men and women who cling to thoughts of earthly pleasures are hovering about us in spirit form. Their world is much like a jail broken loose. Ours is shut, barred, bolted to them until they find a medium. Once a communication is established it takes a positive thought to fight off these 'voices' or forces of evil. Undeveloped minds, minds that lack will power, cannot maintain themselves. That is why men in drink commit crime. That is why the 'insane' are tortured. It is never safe to yield your will, your soul or individuality, into the keeping of these unearthly powers, for darkness may result. I found one woman who was led by the 'voices' to kill her little girl by drowning her in a bath tub. She was sorry to do it, she said, but could not disobey. I found a man who said the voices told him to strike a young man that he met coming out of a restaurant. He did so and now spends all his time talking to voices at the Chicago State Hospital at Dunning. There are hundreds of similar instances."

THEY ARE FRAUDULENT AND MALIGNANT

(33) Dr. Joseph H. McMahon, the Roman Catholic theologian, says in the New York *Times*:

> "It is patent that in the manifestations of spiritualism we are confronted with the fact that evil and malignant influences are

encountered. We take our testimony from that of Sir Oliver Lodge and Sir Conan Doyle."

(34) The London *Daily Mail* says:

"The most trusted spirit friends or relations sometimes after years of intercourse, and often on their own admission, turn out to be masquerading entities who have culled the information needed for the impersonation from the passive minds and memories of the experimenters, and who by some slip or some unusually bold manœuvre in the end turn the tables against themselves. The moral character of the communicating intelligence is invariably of a low order. This fact is and must be admitted by all unprejudiced inquirers who have an accurate knowledge of the subject and who have themselves observed and experimented for a sufficient length of time. In numerous instances, of course, this moral depravity is not immediately apparent—indeed it often remains hidden for years under a mass of platitudes and of high-sounding phrases, but it almost always discloses itself in the end."

THEY ARE SINISTER, DEPRAVED AND OBSCENE

(35) Dr. J. Godfrey Raupert, the Roman Catholic theologian, says:

"The pure and beautiful communications become mixed with impure language; and finally, the victim awakens to the fact that he is entirely at the mercy of a force over which his will no longer exercises the slightest control."

(36) The London *Chronicle*, reporting one of Dr. Raupert's lectures, adds:

"Through the whole of his experience, he obtained proofs that the character of these spirits is immoral, and of a blighting influence upon their victims. Although for a time they dictate high moral principle, especially to those who indulge in automatic writing, these invariably degenerate into sinister, blasphemous or obscene suggestions. Hints are thrown out that morality is a matter of conventionality, that certain instincts are implanted in us in order to be gratified. Mr. Raupert asserts that he has known many women ruined utterly in body and soul by these debasing immoralities urged upon them, when their will power had been destroyed by opening the doors of their mind to evil suggestions."

(37) Harvey O'Higgins, in the Philadelphia *North American*, says of the mind of these beings:

"It is a mind that easily escapes the control of the conscious intelligence that ordinarily governs it; and once out of that control it makes for hysteria, neurasthenia, insanity—hence the warning of scientists against experimenting with it in your own person. Its content is inordinately sexual, as the studies of Freud and his school have made manifest; it is also implicitly religious and tacitly convinced of its own immorality—whence, no doubt, comes the repellant muddle of religion and free love that has degraded the popular revival of spiritualism in times past."

(38) J. F. Whitney, Editor of the *Pathfinder*, says:

"Now, after a long and constant watchfulness, seeing for months and years its progress and its practical workings upon its devotees, its believers, and its mediums, we are compelled to speak our honest conviction, which is, that the manifestations coming through the acknowledged mediums, who are designated as rapping, tipping, writing and trance mediums, *have a baneful influence upon believers*, and create discord and confusion; that the generality of these teachings inculcate false ideas, approve of selfish individual acts, and endorse theories and principles which, when carried out, *debase* and make man *little better than the brute.* These are among the fruits of modern spiritualism. Seeing, as we have, the gradual progress it makes with its believers, particularly its mediums, from lives of *morality* to those of *sensuality* and *immorality*, gradually and cautiously undermining the foundation of good principles, we look back with amazement to the radical change which a few months will bring about in individuals; for its tendency is to approve and endorse each individual act and character, however good or bad these acts may be."

(39) The Binghamton *Morning Sun* contains dispatches from Columbus, Ohio, showing that several pastors of that city have right views on the subject of spiritualism:

"'Spiritualism, though it comes to us under the guise of modernism, yet it is not modern, but is as old as the activities of Satan among men,' declared Rev. J. T. Britain, pastor of the Central Presbyterian Church here, one of the most prominent of the clergymen in Ohio's capital city."

"'Spiritualism takes advantage of people when they are weak and worn out and morbid under life's bereavement and, through lying spirits, deceives and ensnares,' said Rev. Chas. F. Ulrich.

"'Fallen angels, because of their superior powers, are able to imitate the voice and mannerisms of our dead friends, thus deceiving even the mediums who are under their control,' declared Rev. W. H. Spring."

(40) The *Watch Tower* tells of a believer in Christ's atoning blood who was, for a time, led astray by spiritism to whom the evil spirits confessed through a ouija board:

"It confessed to me that the spirits who operate the board have no other mission than to hinder all of the Lord's people. It further stated that they took special delight in buffeting, hindering and endeavoring to ensnare Brother Russell and his colaborers at the Bethel home."

THEY DENY THE EXISTENCE OF SATAN

(41) The *Progressive Thinker*, spiritist, says:

"Fell and fabled Satan, the whilom 'roaring lion', coursing up and down the earth, devouring old and young, the pauper and the affluent, we now find tethered fast wherever the light of spiritual science illumes the pathway. Liberal Christianity, Universalism, Unitarianism, etc., sorely wounded the devil, but Spiritualism completely killed him, and buried him out of sight, beyond all hope of resurrection."

HOWEVER, SOME SPIRITISTS WORSHIP SATAN

(42) Vance Thompson, in *Everybody's Magazine*, writes of the Satan-worshipers of Paris:

"It need hardly be said that the rites wherein Lucifer is worshiped are hid in much mystery. A couple of years ago I visited one of the 'chapels'; it was in the rue Rochechouart. The Black Mass, which I have no desire to describe, was celebrated. It was Friday at three o'clock. Over the altar was a winged figure of Lucifer, amid flames; he trampled under foot a crocodile—symbol of the church. A few days ago I found the chapel closed. Only after patient search did I find the new abode of the Satanists. Their chapel now is in a great new apartment-house at No. 22 rue du Ruisseau, within the shadow of the cathedral of the Sacred Heart on Montmartre. As of old, Satan is worshiped; every Friday the Luciferians gather. I could name many of them—men not unknown in the learned professions. Some of them have influence enough to secure, now and then, a right of midnight entry to the catacombs; there amid skulls and bones, with orgies I do not care to describe, they have worshiped the spirit of evil—calling upon Euphomet, upon Lucifer and Beëlzebub and Ashtoroth and Moloch, with cries and wailing hysteria. This attempt to reëstablish the worship of the fallen archangel is, I think, the most remarkable manifestation of modern occultism."

THEY ARE MADE OF GAS AND ELECTRICITY AND CONFINED TO THE EARTH'S ATMOSPHERE

(43) No credence can be placed in anything that these demons say, but *World's Problems* makes the following statement of what they have to say of themselves:

"These spirits say they are composed of the very finest gas, held together by electricity. They at first retain the form of the body, but afterwards lose arms and legs, because these are no longer needed, and change into the form of an amœba, because that form is best adapted to fly through space. Then it can pass to higher planets. They can see to the limits of the universe and through solid bodies, but it takes time to be able to leave the earth influence."

THEY SOMETIMES IMPRESS THE BRAIN FROM WITHIN SOMETIMES FROM WITHOUT

(44) In the New York *Evening Telegram* a medium, who has the clairaudient ear, says:

"Beyond any physical ear is a hearing more acute, more delicately discriminating than physical hearing. In the first degree the voice is clear, but apparently from within the brain rather than through the auditory nerve. But sometimes the voice wavers, as though a door opened and closed with the wind sweeping across it, and thus confused the resonance of a voice speaking to me from another room. In such moments of instability the second degree of clairaudience supervenes. The voice speaks more closely, as though lips were held to my ear."

THEY HAVE THE POWER TO INJECT THOUGHTS INTO THE MIND

(45) The *Watch Tower* tells of a medium who was deceived by a spirit impersonating the Almighty. Coming at length to know he had been basely deceived he engaged the spirit in the following conversation:

" 'Q. : But do you never expect to be better?

" 'A. : Never. We are the débris of God's moral creation, cast off as far as we know only to be destroyed.

" 'Q. : But do not the pious dead surround those who are still in the body as guardians from the influences of evil?

," 'A. : They are never seen by us, if they do. We see nothing around the pious, any more than around the wicked. But we are often around them ourselves, infusing into their minds some infidel or atheistic thought, to see how they will receive it. We take delight in disturbing and irritating them, just as we do you.

, " 'Q. : How do the inhabitants of your world mostly spend their time?

" 'A. : We spend the time mostly, since the discovery of the mediumistic communications, in developing mediums ; in making psychological experiments with them, and in communicating through them.

" 'Q. : To what extent have the powers of the air dominion and rule over the children of men?

" 'A. : They have the power to produce lifelike images in the minds of impressible mediums. This is often understood by them to be an actual sight of a real object. This leads to a great variety of delusions.

" 'Those who are called leaders of Spiritualism, and who know the fallacy of those impressions, allow the deceptions to go on, and are therefore participators in the swindle. This stamps them with infamy. The spirits have the power of using the human body, with all its organs and faculties. This is done in the case of trance speakers and personating mediums. Perhaps they enter the body by means of electrical and galvanic influences, and, having entered, they use the vocal organs.

" 'They also possess power to move ponderous objects, such as tables, chairs, etc. This is generally accomplished by the agency of scores and hundreds of the invisible workers.' "

This writer further explains :

" 'They could imitate the manner of speech peculiar to my relatives and acquaintances, and so exactly did they give the particular intonation and inflections of voice, that I would have been compelled to believe the imitation to be the real had not they also imitated the voices of some whom I knew to be living. Upon one occasion that occurs particularly to my mind, the voice, style of address, and intonation were so exactly personified that for the moment I felt positive that the gentleman and the lady represented had deceased, and that their disembodied spirits were before me. But when I knew by the evidences of my physical senses that it was not the case, I was then convinced that the spirits were presenting assumed characters. All my experiences with these beings who surround us in the air sum up this distinct conclusion ; that they delight in evil as their chief object, and especially that branch of evil called deception. If any one thing pleases them more than any other, it is to make those in the earth-life believe the most monstrous and absurd theories.' "

(46 The same magazine also says of the third temptation of our Lord ;

"As in the second temptation, we do not think our Lord was taken out of the wilderness, but that mental suggestion was used to influence him to disobedience to the Father. We are inclined to think that the adversary was not visible to our Lord's natural sight, but to his mental vision. It is our thought that Satan was permitted to bring mental suggestions before our Lord's mind."

THEY FILL THE MIND WITH WONDERFUL ILLUMINATIONS

(47) In the New York *Evening Telegram* a medium describes the invasion of her mind by the method of illumination as:

"A blending of all the lights which flame the avenues of sense. It is not a matter of stray gleams embroidering shade. No, it is precipitate, bursting, luminous—revealing!"

(48) *McClure's Magazine* tells of a doctor who determined to seek occult help in the cure of disease. He gave a portion of each day to a determined effort to yield his mind and body completely to these demoniacal powers:

"Day after day he persisted in this strange experiment and soon he began to see small blue figures, irregularly shaped, that moved about rapidly in the room and cast no shadows. Some of these blue figures were luminous, and among them were occasional luminous white figures. At first the doctor regarded this as an hallucination, an optical disturbance, similar to the lights that one may see by pressing on the eyeballs and thus exciting the visual nerves; but in this case there had been no pressure on the eyeballs nor any understandable cause of the phenomena. Futhermore, as days passed and the investigation proceeded, there was a noticeable increase in the number of moving shapes until these seemed to swarm everywhere, over the walls, pictures, furniture, like a colony of wriggling microbes seen under a microscope. And they were nearly always blue, although at times a large yellow radiance would appear in the doorway or in some part of the room."

"As months passed, other persons were relieved of pain, other cures were effected and it finally seemed established that there was definite virtue in this method of treatment. Whatever these blue streams were, they did good work, they helped people; and I may mention that one patient, while under treatment and without any conscious suggestion from the doctor, told him that she saw blue shapes about her!"

THEY IMPRESS UPON THE MIND PICTURES WHICH THE EYES DO NOT SEE

(49) The Greenville *Daily Piedmont* reports a prominent grand opera singer as fainting away on the edge of the volcano Kilauea. While in that condition her mind was filled with a view of the crater not at all obtainable from the place where she fainted.

"We were as close to the edge as it was safe to get, when suddenly I seemed to float away and out over the crater. I could feel the heat scorching my body but I got a clear and wonderful view of the seething mass of molten lava. I had no sense of my spirit being confined in my body. My person seemed to have no particular shape. When I recovered I was in my room at the hotel with a woman friend bending over me. I was able to give a clear and accurate description of the crater and the interior of the volcano. This was verified later in its essential features. Our party had not left the spot."

(50) The *Watch Tower* relates another instance of a different nature, but illustrating the same principle:

"'On one occasion I was sitting in an Indian tent alone with one of the "medicine" men of the Blackfoot Indians. It was night and all was quiet in the camp. The night was calm, with a bright moon shining. On a sudden the Indian commenced to sing, and presently the lodge, which was a large one, commenced to tremble; and the trembling increased to such a degree that it rocked violently, even lifting off the ground, first on one side and then on the other, as if a dozen pair of hands were heaving it on the outside. This lasted for about two minutes, when I ran out, expecting to find some Indians on the outside, who had played me a trick, but, to my astonishment, not a soul was in sight, and what still more bewildered me was to find on examination that the lodge was firmly pegged down to the ground, it being impossible for any number of men to have removed and replaced the pegs in so short a time."

THEY DECEIVE THE SENSES BY SUPPOSED BUT NOT ACTUAL MATERIALIZATIONS

(51) One such instance, involving impressions upon both the eye and the ear, and calculated to preserve an old and worthless superstition that a priest or minister can render any special aid to the dying is narrated by a Catholic priest of Washington, D. C., and recorded in the Denver *Post*:

"'One night I was aroused from sleep by a little boy who came to me and said, 'My mother is dying and I want her shrived; come with me and I will take you to her bedside.' I went with the boy to a neighborhood unfamiliar to me and to a house I had not entered before. The husband came to the door and said, 'O Father, I am so glad you came'. The boy led me to his mother's side, and when the last rites had been administered I turned to leave. The father of the boy then said, 'How providential that you called when you did; I could not leave my wife and had no one to send on this errand.' 'Why, the boy brought me here,' I said 'What boy?' he asked. I looked around, but the boy had disappeared. 'He told me that the sick woman was his mother,' I said. 'We had a boy, but he died,' said the father, 'and that is his picture on the wall.' I looked up and said to him: 'That is the boy who led me here.' "

(52) Another instance in which the eyes and ears of some were influenced while only the eyes of others were affected appears in the *Cape Times*, South Africa, which reports a materialization of an apparition claiming to be Dr. John Phillip, of Hankey Congregational Mission, Gamtoos Valley, near Cape Elizabeth. He appeared to a whole company on September 5th:

"They held a joint conversation with the apparition, which appeared at 9:30 p.m. The apparition gave them a message of love. 'His voice sounded like the gentle rustling of dry autumn leaves, but it was distinctly audible to some of us.' The apparition asked after various dead and gone members of the congregation and departed after a promise was given that a search would be made for the receipts, which dealt with certain grants of land. The doctor was dressed in black, and wore a black coat. He repeated his visits nightly, instructing the searchers where the receipts might possibly be found. He invariably departed after they said good night, but on the second visitation, says the principal, 'the old gentleman followed my housekeeper into my room, where I had made up a bed for her, as she was too timid to sleep alone. She was so terrified that night that she kept calling upon God to preserve her. I stayed awake all night and talked to her about all sorts of things, until the old doctor got tired and left us.' "

(53) Another instance, involving the deception of the sense of eye, ear and touch appears in the Glasgow *Record*. It recounts the experience of a doctor in Chicago, who was visited in a dimly lighted apartment by his supposed dead sweetheart:

"She told me that she must go, but first kissed me. Then I put my arms about her and kissed her, but as I did so the young woman—who was as completely material as anything could be—melted away into atmosphere. Of course, I have had many other experiences, but I regard this as the most impressive. I would say the touch of a spirit hand is as a rose leaf. It is something—nothing."

(54) *McClure's Magazine* narrates a similar case, a very sad one, from every point of view, in which a clergyman was deceived by the supposed materialization of his dead wife, in answer to his entirely un-Scriptural and, therefore, improper prayers:

" 'Well, eleven months passed after her death and she did not come to me, in spite of my prayers and longings, and although she was never out of my thoughts for a single day; then one night she came. I was lying in bed and the room was dark, but I saw her as plainly as I see you and I was wide awake, as sane as I am at this moment. I saw my wife! I touched her: I felt her caresses. I heard her voice with its pretty Southern accent that was so familiar. 'Will, I am here, I have come!' These were the first words she spake. She stayed there with me for half an hour and we talked about many things, just as we used to talk in real life—about our children, about my work, about my grieving for her. I asked about her condition in the spirit world, but she would tell me nothing; she said she was not allowed to do so.'

" 'It was a different body, a shadowy body, but I could feel it, nevertheless. I could feel it penetrating me, and I recognized her face, her form. It was she! Wait! Listen! Just as you are startled, and, before I knew what I was doing, I had turned on the electrics and in the flood of light I saw that she had disappeared. 'Oh, dear God, forgive me!' I cried out. 'Let her come back! Let her come back!' Then I turned out the lights in an agony of hope and fear and—my wife came back!'

" 'Isn't it possible you dreamed all this?'

" 'No, no, no! I tell you my wife was there. It is a matter of absolute certainty, just as I am certain that you are there. And she has come back to me again in the same way on four other occasions in the past seventeen years. Each time I have touched her, talked to her, heard her voice plainly. There is no possible doubt about it. There is nothing in my life as certain as this.'

"Please notice that this is the well-considered utterance of an active and successful New York clergyman who preaches twice every Sunday to large congregations, and lectures through the week; a broad-shouldered citizen full of rugged health and vigor, a doctor of divinity, a kind-hearted and trustworthy man, if I am any judge. He declares that his dead wife has come back to him five times, that he has touched her each time, talked with her each time, received precious counsel and comfort from her each time.''

THERE ARE, HOWEVER ACTUAL MATERIALIZATIONS

(55) These materializations occur by a power which the demons possess of being able to draw out of the medium's body connected streams of the cells of which her body is composed, and then changing the form of these living cells into any desired appearance. They thus transform the medium into a hideous octopus-like creature, and this is the reason séances occur in a dimly lighted room, with the medium in a cabinet, so that the circle of investigators cannot witness the horrible scene as it really is. H. Addington Bruce describes these phenomena:

"According to Professor Schrenck-Notzing and other European scientists who have been investigating her feats, darkness is not indispensible to the successful functioning of Eva's strange faculty. Nor does she resent precautions which would seem to rule out fraud. Again and again in the scientists' own rooms and laboratories, she has submitted to the most rigorous searching of her person before and after séances. She has even permitted herself to be undressed and sewed up in a bag, covering her entire body with the exception of her head. Thus attired, and in a room sufficiently illuminated for the purposes of observation, Eva C. has amazed her investigators by a bewildering variety of grim, one might almost say gruesome, phenomena.

"Sometimes from her fingertips, sometimes from her ears, sometimes from her nose, but mostly from her mouth, the European savants have seen emerge a grayish-white substance which takes all manner of forms. Usually at first it is quite shapeless, or ribbonlike in appearance. But quickly it resolves into the semblance of bodily organs—half formed or fully formed hands, fingers, toes, etc.

"We read in the records of this strangest of strange affairs: 'The fingers and hands had the character of living objects, being able to grasp objects held up to them—and most certainly were not the medium's hands. More than this, the substance presently resolved into the likeness of human faces, mostly the faces of beautiful young women. It has been found possible to take flashlight pictures of these, and they look for all the world like photographs of real people.'

"Yet they are composed merely of a material which the records thus describe: 'It is clammy to the touch like a snake and has a certain amount of weight. It is sometimes wet, sometimes dry, sometimes hard, sometimes soft. Drops of it were obtained and analysed, and showed on analysis cell residues.''

(56) Dr. J. Godfrey Raupert, the Roman Catholic theologian, says on this subject:

"The spirits seem to draw upon the material substances of the medium in order to clothe themselves as it were in the human form or phantasm. Experiments, for instance, with the famous medium Eusapia Paladino, who was weighed during her trances, showed that she lost exactly half her weight ; and experiments with another medium, named Miss Wood, showed that the weight of the phantasm conjured up by her was exactly half that of her own weight, which had been correspondingly reduced."

(57) This subject has been investigated with the aid of scientific instruments by W. J. Crawford, B.Sc., author of scientific text-books and lecturer at the Municipal Technical Institute and Queen's University, Dublin. According to the *Westminster Gazette*, he reports that he has been working with recording instruments upon the phenomena of table-raising and spirit-rapping: and he found that when a ten-pound table was levitated by a medium, the weight of the medium was increased by approximately the weight of the table, that the reaction of the lifting force did not reach the floor of the room, that it increased rapidly as the underside of the table was approached, and that it had a horizontal, as well as a vertical, component.

(58) The Boston *Herald*, discussing Dr. Crawford's studies, says :

"His own theory, given in much detail and with the aid of numerous diagrams and illustrations, is that the raps, levitations and other phenomena of the séance room are produced by psychic, rod-like structures which leave the body of the medium near the ankles, extend into the room and there cause the movements and noises observed. He regards it as 'most likely' that the structures are partly composed of matter borrowed from the medium's body— a kind of matter unknown to science—the function of the medium being 'to lend from her body psychic energy needed by the rods to do their work'. In confirmation of this view Dr. Crawford found that both medium and sitters lost some of their weight during the séances."

(59) Those who have read and understood the foregoing can see why the misty clouds were used in the following séances, as recorded in a letter published in the *Watch Tower* :

" 'After my mother's death my father married a woman who was a spirit medium and has since tried to convince me of spiritism. He has given me, repeatedly, accounts of materializing séances which he has attended both in his own home and in other places. He says he has seen as many as fifteen spirits developed at one time, both adults and infants, while the medium sat in her cabinet in view of her audience. He says that sometimes he has seen a misty cloud appear near the ceiling and gradually descend to the floor, taking form as it came down, until it stood upon the floor a solid, tangible human being, and would clasp his hand. The

hand felt as tangible in his grasp as my own would feel. He says
his dead daughters (my sisters) and other friends who are dead
have thus appeared to him robed in pure white. Sometimes they
would materialise a sparkling lace shawl and hold it up and shake
it before him; they would sit down by his side or in his lap and
put their arms around his neck and converse with him of their
heavenly home, its beauties, its lovely flowers, etc., and of his
own future, and of their care for him. Finally they would say,
"Well, I must go'—and the hand clasped in his, and which he was
holding tightly, would begin to sink out of his grasp, the body
would grow thin until objects across the room could be discerned
through the almost transparent body; then it would disappear,
sometimes going down through the floor."

(60) Lord Alfred Russell Wallace, spiritist, writes in a
spiritist magazine called *Reason* an account of a séance held
in a sealed room. It is easy to see how these various mate-
rialisations were produced from the medium's body, one
after another, by the method already described. He says:

"(1) A female figure in white came out between the curtains
with Mrs. Ross in black, and also a male figure, all to some distance
in front of the cabinet. This was apparently to demonstrate, once
for all, that, whatever they were, the figures were not Mrs. Ross in
disguise. (2) After these had retired, three female figures appeared
together, in white robes, and of different heights. These came two
or three feet in front of the curtain. (3) A male figure came out,
recognised by a gentleman present as his son. (4) A tall Indian
figure came out in white moccasins; he danced and spoke; he also
shook hands with me and others, a large, rough hand. (5) A
female figure with a baby, stood close to the entrance of the cabinet, I went up (on invitation), felt the baby's face, nose, and hair,
and kissed it—apparently a real, soft-skinned, living baby. Other
ladies and gentlemen agreed. Directly the séance was over, the
gas was lighted, and again I examined the bare walls of the cabinet,
the curtains, and the door, all being just as before, and affording
no room or place for disposing of the baby alone, far less of the
other figures."

THE DEMONS INVADE THE MEDIUMS' PERSONS

(61) The New York *Evening Telegram* contains an article
in which a medium stated that when her person is invaded
by the evil spirit she has experiences described as follows:

"I for the moment became the person, living or dead, of whom
some one in the Valled World wishes to speak, or who (if dead)
wishes to speak for himself. To me that is the most interesting
phase of my gift. For, having suddenly assumed a posture of some
one seeking identification, it seems a performance staged wholly
outside my personality."

(62) Sir Oliver Lodge, spiritist, senses the same truth, as
indicated by his statement in *Metropolitan Magazine*:

"It now began to appear to me that although a brain and nerve
mechanism and a muscular organism were as needful as ever for
effective and demonstrable communication between mind and mind,
yet that it was possible to use such an organism vicariously, and

that identity of instrument was not absolutely essential so long as some physiological instrument was available. In other words, that the brain and organism of a living person might be utilized by deceased personalities whose own body had ceased to work. Mrs. Piper went into a trance and seemed as it were to vacate her body for a time. In this condition, it appeared temporarily revivified, not by her own personality but by another; and this secondary personality, or whatever it ought to be called, was able to manage what they called 'the machine', so that through her bodily mechanism communications were received from persons deceased, but still apparently mentally active and retaining their personal memory and affection, though now able to display them only in a fragmentary and imperfect manner."

(63) Dr. James Hyslop in the St Louis *Globe-Democrat* says:

"Physicians, expert alienists, diagnose such cases as hysteria, dementia precox, paranoia and other maladies. Our investigation takes us deeper, revealing startlingly the parallel between fact and ancient theory. We find the estimate of Biblical times more accurate than that of modern science. In other words, we learn that many of these sufferers are literally 'possessed of devils', that is, are controlled by bad or mischievous spirits. The evil spirits seem to be as disconcertingly plentiful as the physical disease germs; unable to affect normal human beings, they seem to seek as prey those weakened by outside troubles (as disease or disaster) of the sort which disturb relationships between mind and body. Of the existence and persistence of these evil or malicious spirits there is a mass of evidence such as cannot be controverted. The point is that real sins are of the will."

THEY HAVE POWER OVER THE VOICE OF MEDIUMS

(64) The Louisville *Herald* quotes Sir Arthur Conan Doyle, the spiritualist, as saying that at a séance he heard the voice of his son who had been dead for a year, and that the son asked him to forgive him for his previously expressed unbelief in spiritualism. Then he said the voice faded.

The Washington *Post* contains an account of a medium who knows only English, but gave message after message in German, French, Spanish, Italian and Indian.

The *Watch Tower* contains a story of a fine singer who was approached clairaudiently by evil spirits who promised that, if she would surrender her will to them, they would make her the finest singer in the world. Alarmed, she refused, and her voice shortly began to fail until now its beauty is all gone; but the Lord gave her the truth instead.

(65) In the Louisville *Courier-Journal* a clergyman relates that while attending a séance with two other clergymen, where he saw bluish lights rise and fall, and a supposed flesh and blood spirit kiss a woman she had known in life;

"Suddenly in the overheated, hermetically closed room, delicious waves of fresh air pass, charged with fragrance, which Betsy names for us. I recognize a mixture of sandalwood, rose and violet. Subtle at first, it leaves a feeling of infinite melancholy, evoking thoughts of cemeteries, autumn winds and dead leaves. But the thoughts that came to me seemed to be born of wilted roses."

(66) The Cleveland *Plain Dealer* contains an article from a woman citing six occurrences of distinct scent of roses in the home following the death of parents.

THEY USE THE MEDIUM'S HAND IN WRITING

(67) The *Watch Tower* tells of a plan carried out by Dr. Hodgson and Prof. Hyslop to determine whether or not the communications of a certain medium were from her or from other entities:

"The professor masked himself and disguised his voice during his visits to her, and while she lay unconscious, with her head upon a pillow resting on a table, her hand wrote out messages alleged to come from his father. This converted Hyslop to the spiritistic hypothesis."

(68) The *Watch Tower* also says of writing mediums:

"Sometimes the control is what is termed mechanical control, when the connection between arm and brain is entirely severed, and yet the manifestation is made through what is called the nervous fluids, a certain portion of which is retained in the arm for the purpose of action. But when the manifestation is what is called an impressional manifestation, then the brain and entire nervous system is used."

(69) Basil King in the *Cosmopolitan Magazine* says of himself:

"In writing these articles, I am a little more than an amanuensis, and I am at liberty to take a detached and appraising view of this presentation of a great topic for the sheer reason that the presentation is not mine."

He goes on to say, in effect, that these evil spirits are good Christian Scientists and that they were the ones really responsible for the silly chatter that "All is good, there is no evil": for when asked why they never expressed themselves on what human beings call faults, the demons said: "We do not know them. We look upon you and see all the good—never any evil. We cannot perceive evil and are conscious only of blanks when it is present." This shows that these are not from God, for God declares that his eyes are in every place "beholding *the evil* and the good".

THEY DRAW AND PAINT PICTURES

(70) The San Diego *Evening Tribune* contains an account

of a goldsmith supposedly painting under the spiritual guidance of Robert S. Gifford, an artist of some note. Thompson,
the goldsmith. duplicates Gifford's paintings, and is guided
by clairvoyant ear to scenes from which the original paintings of Gifford were made.

(71) Dr. Funk, of Funk & Wagnalls, publishers of the
Standard Dictionary and the Literary Digest, at a séance
in Chicago, selected from several canvasses one which was
stretched on a frame twenty by twenty-four inches. The
account says:

"Nobody spoke or moved. In about three minutes a cloud seemed
to pass over the canvass, leaving a pearl-gray effect for a background. A few minutes more and a dull outline of a portrait appeared. Every few minutes it grew more distinct. Then followed
the various colors and in forty-five minutes the picture, a perfect
likeness, was completed."

THEY PRODUCE PICTURES ON SENSITIZED PLATES

(72) The Binghamton *Morning Sun* tells of a woman
mourning over the loss of a son who had her own photograph taken with that of a living son but when the photograph was developed her own face had been omitted from
the picture and the face of her dead son substituted. The
photographer could not explain this.

(73) The Madison. Indiana, *Daily Herald* contains a
so-called spirit picture of Conan Doyle's son leaning upon
his shoulder. Dr. Doyle states that he examined the camera,
loaded the plate holders and developed the plates himself.

THEY HAVE DIRECTED THE STAGING OF A PLAY

(74) The Poplar Bluff *American* has a despatch concerning the manager of the play entitled "The Invisible Foe":

"I certainly had no interest in spiritualism before putting on
'The Invisible Foe'. But I have changed my views. I positively
affirm that spiritualistic assistance was given us in making the
play ready for the public. I repeatedly felt strange influences
guiding me and directing me in my efforts to secure certain novel
effects. Even the actors felt these influences. I cannot explain it,
but I think everybody connected with the play felt that extramun-
dane influences were hovering over the Harris Theater."

THEY HAVE A VARIETY OF WAYS OF PRODUCING SOUNDS

(75) The Atlanta *Georgian* gives the story of a medium
who claims to have written a book dictated by Roosevelt
and Mark Twain. The medium declares that the dictation
was chiefly through the horn of a talking machine, and that
the way to use the horn was disclosed through a ouija board.

Cloth bound
edition
85¢
per page

paper bound
magazine
edition
25¢

THE FINISHED MYSTERY, the posthumous work of Pastor Russell, tells why there is so much distress on earth.

It gives detailed and corroborative proof establishing the fact that the war, profiteering, famine, pestilence, the falling away of the clergy, their union with the financial powers and professional politicians to oppress mankind were long ago foretold in the Bible.

It examines previous world-wide cataclysms and points out those features of the present conditions which distinguish them as the end of the world.

Further proof is given that the present unrighteous systems will be supplanted by God's Kingdom, for which Christians have long been praying — that the will of God be done on earth as it is done in heaven, and that there "be no more death".

Special Combination Offer "The Finished Mystery" (cloth-bound) and the "Millions Now Living Will Never Die" booklet (see page 126) in combination ....65¢
"The Finished Mystery" (magazine edition) and the "Millions" booklet, together ....45¢

INTERNATIONAL BIBLE STUDENTS ASSOCIATION
BROOKLYN, N. Y., U. S. A.

Canadian Office: 270 Dundas St., W., Toronto, Ont.
British Office: 34 Craven Terrace, Lancaster Gate, London, W. 2.

For Canadian and British prices apply to these offices.

The BIBLE ON OUR LORD'S RETURN

His Parousía, His
Apokálupsis, and
His Epiphánia

INTERNATIONAL BIBLE STUDENTS ASSOCIATION,
BROOKLYN, N. Y., U. S. A.

Also: London, England; Melbourne, Australia; Toronto, Canada;
Cape Town, So. Africa; Orebro, Sweden; Barmen, Germany;
Copenhagen, Denmark; Zurich and Berne, Switzerland; etc.

1922

"Behold, I stand at the door and knock. If any man hear my voice [knock] and open the door, I will come in to him and sup with him, and he with me."—Rev. 3:20.

THE PAROUSIA
OF
OUR LORD JESUS CHRIST
AND HIS
Subsequent Apokalupsis and Epiphania at his
SECOND ADVENT.

"Watch, therefore; for ye know not the day* your Lord doth come."
"What I say unto you, I say unto all [believers], Watch!"
——*Matt. 24:42; Mark 13:37.*——

WHATEVER the character of the watching, and whatever the thing to be looked for, there can be no question that the exhortation to watch for an event whose precise time is not stated implies that the watching ones will know when the event does take place. Watch, because ye know not, in order that at the proper time ye may know, is the thought; and the intimation clearly is, that those who do not watch will not know: that the events which are to be known in due time to the Watchers will be recognized by them, and not recognized by others, at the time of accomplishment.

This, the only logical interpretation of our Lord's exhortation, is fully corroborated by several of the

---

*Thus read the oldest Greek MSS.

(3)

apostles. The Apostle Paul urges us, saying: "Yourselves know perfectly that the day of the Lord so cometh as a thief in the night, and when they [the world,
unbelievers] shall say, 'Peace and safety, then sudden
destruction cometh upon *them* as travail upon a woman
with child; and they shall not escape. But ye, brethren, are not in darkness, that that day should overtake
you as a thief" (1 Thes. 5 : 3, 4) ; because, being children of the light, ye brethren will be watching and be
enlightened and taught of the Lord. The Apostle
Peter suggests the means by which the Lord will teach
us and informs us respecting our location upon the
path of the just which shineth more and more unto the
perfect day. He shows that it will not be by miraculous revelations, nor by dreams, but through the Word
of testimony, the Bible. He says, "We have a more
sure word of prophecy, to which ye do well that ye
take heed, as unto a light which shineth in a dark
place, until the Day dawn and the Day-star arise in
your hearts."—2 Pet. 1 : 19.

The united testimony of these Scriptures teaches
us that, altho it was not proper nor possible for the
Lord's people to know anything definite in advance,
respecting the exact time of the second presence of the
Lord Jesus and the establishment of his Kingdom, yet
when the due time would come the faithful ones, the
watchers, would be informed,—would not be left in
darkness with the world. It is in vain to urge, as
contradicting this, our Lord's statement, "Of that day
and hour knoweth no man, no not the angels in heav-
en, neither the Son, but my Father only." Those who
use this Scripture to prove to themselves and to others
that no man will *ever know* anything respecting the

time of the second advent find it to prove too much, and thus spoil their own argument; for if it means that no man will *ever know*, it must similarly mean that no angel will *ever know*, and that the Son himself will *never know*. This evidently would be an absurd construction to place upon the passage. The Son did not know at the time he uttered this statement, the angels did not know then, and no man knew then: but the Son certainly must know of the time of his own second advent, and at least a little while before it takes place; the angels also must know a little while before it takes place, and the true children of God, the "watchers," as we have seen above, are to watch in order that they also may know at the proper season, and not be in darkness, in ignorance, with the world; and that their watching shall be rewarded is guaranteed:—"None of the wicked shall understand; but the wise [in heavenly wisdom] shall understand."—Dan. 12 : 10.

FOR WHAT ARE WE WATCHING?

This is an important question. Many of God's people have been offended, "stumbled," as respects the doctrine of the second coming of our dear Redeemer, by reason of peculiar, extravagant, unreasonable, illogical and unscriptural views on the subject, presented by some, who professedly love the Lord's appearing, known as Second Adventists. But this is all wrong; we are not to reject one of the grandest and most prominent doctrines of the Scriptures, simply because some fellow-Christians have erred egregiously respecting the matter, and brought a certain amount of worldlywise contempt upon everything connected with this subject. On the contrary, this doctrine, as a glorious gem, should

be given the first place among the precious jewels of
divine truth, where it can cast its halo and splendor
and brilliancy over all connected and related promises
and blessings. It should not be left in the imperfect
setting which hides its glory and beauty, but should
be recovered, remounted, set in its true place, to the
glory of God and to the blessing of all who are sincerely and truly his people.

We need offer no apology for the interest which
we feel in this grand subject, which is the center upon
which all the testimony of divine grace, through all
the holy prophets, is focused. Rather do they need
to apologize who, knowing that the second coming of
the Lord and the resurrection of the dead hold the
most important places in the Scriptures, next to the
doctrine of the atonement for sin, have nevertheless
neglected this while they have quarreled, skirmished,
fought and bled over trifling things of no real importance doctrinally or otherwise.

Our watching is to be for the second coming of
him who redeemed us, who said, "If I go away, I will
come again and receive you unto myself." The watching is to be specially with the thought that our Lord
Jesus comes at his second advent in the majesty and
glory of the Father, King of kings and Lord of lords.
The watching not only includes the thought of the second presence of our Lord, as King, but it has attached
to it the wonderful results which are promised to flow
from the coming of the King; for the coming of the
King means the coming of the Kingdom for which he
taught us to pray, "Thy Kingdom come, thy will be
done on earth as it is done in heaven." And the coming of our Master, the King, and the establishment of

this glorious Kingdom means the fulfilment of the long-waited-for promise made to the seed of Abraham: the promise which Israel after the flesh was not found worthy to inherit; the promise for which God has been selecting the members of the Bride of Christ during this Gospel age, to be with the Lord Jesus and his joint-heir in carrying out its beneficent provisions; the promise which is sure, but which has never yet had, in any sense of the word, a fulfilment; the promise which reads, "In thy seed shall all the families of the earth be blessed."

Watching implies hoping, and it also implies waiting. We are waiting for what the Apostle terms "that blessed hope, the glorious appearing of our Lord and Savior Jesus Christ," who shall transform his Church to his own spiritual image and likeness, in order that we ("changed") may be like him, see him as he is, and share his glory, and be associated with him in his great work of bringing in the Millennial blessings to the world of mankind. Nevertheless, this waiting time and hoping time is a time of more or less tribulation, not only on the world, which lies still under the yoke of sin and under the blinding influences of Satan, but also to the waiting, hoping and watching Church, of whom the Apostle says, "We ourselves groan within ourselves, waiting for the adoption, to wit, the deliverance [from death] of our body"—the body of Christ, of which we are members in particular.—Rom. 8 : 23.

HOW ARE WE TO WATCH?

Our watching consists not in looking up into the sky—"stargazing;" for those who study the Lord's Word to any purpose soon learn that "the *day* of the

Lord so cometh as [like] a thief in the night," and
that its dawning cannot be discerned with the natural
eye. If the Lord's people would discern anything by
watching the sky with their natural eyes, could not
the world discern the same thing? If the second advent of our Lord were to be an open, outward manifestation, would not the world know of it just as soon
as the saints, the Watchers? In such event it could
not be true that the day of the Lord should come as a
thief, as a snare, unawares, upon the world, while the
Church would have foreknowledge thereof—not be left
in darkness.

*We are to watch the signs of the times, in the light
of the Lord's Word, our lamp*: as the Apostle declares,
"We have a more sure Word of prophecy,...as a light
shining in a dark place,—until the Day dawn." The
Gospel age has been a night-time, and the Lord's people have been waiting for the dawn of the Millennial
morning, with the promise ringing in their ears, "God
will help her [the Church] early in the morning."
(Psa. 46 : 5.) The word of the Lord, through the prophets, has been the lamplight all through this Gospel age, upon the Church's pathway, as the Lord expressed it through the Prophet David, "Thy word is a
lamp to my feet, a lantern to my footsteps." The
lamp of the truth of revelation has guided all the faithful, watchful pilgrims in their journey toward the Ce-
lestial City—the Heavenly Kingdom. Oh, what a comfort it has been, and how dreary would have been our
pilgrimage without it!

> "Looking back, we praise the way
> God has led us, day by day!"

Those who have taken heed to the landmarks,

pointed out by the Lord through Daniel and **Isaiah and**
Jeremiah, and all the holy prophets, realize that we
have come already a much longer journey than was expected by the Church when first she started out; but
we realize also from these landmarks that we have approached very closely to the end of the journey, very
near to the time when the great blessing, for which
God's people have so long waited and prayed, is at
hand. For instance, the Watchers have noted the
Lord's testimony through the Prophet Daniel that "the
time of the end" would be a period of time (more than
a century), and that in this *"time* of the end" there
would be a great increase of travel, running to and fro
throughout the earth, and a great increase of general
intelligence, increased knowledge, as it is written, "In
the time of the end many shall run to and fro, and
knowledge shall be increased."—Dan. 12 : 4.

Watching carefully respecting our whereabouts,
hopeful and solicitous respecting the gracious things
which God has promised, none of the Watchers are indifferent to these fulfilments of prophecy, which are to
be seen on every hand to-day. All men discern these
things, but not all alike: the faithful, the Watchers,
discern them not only as facts, but also as fulfilments
of prophecy; as proofs that we are *already in the period*
termed "the time of the end." Further investigations
and applications of the prophetic measurements prove
to the Watchers that we have been in "the time of the
end" since 1799, and that it is also termed "the day
of his [Jehovah's] preparation." Looking about them,
they see the *preparation* that Jehovah God is making
for the Kingdom of his dear Son. They see the lifting of the curtain of ignorance, and the letting in of

the light, and that thus God is using mankind at the
present time to make ready in a natural way the mechanical and other arrangements and conveniences
which ultimately shall be so great blessings to the world,
when the Sun of Righteousness shall arise with healing in his beams, and the Millennial Day shall be ush-
ered in, with all its multiplied blessings and mercies
and opportunities;—"the times of restitution of all
things, spoken by the mouth of all the holy prophets
since the world began."—Acts 3 : 21.

Watching intently, earnestly, interestedly, because
they know of the good things God hath in reservation
(1 Cor. 2 : 10-13), the Watchers note that Daniel's
prophecy further points out that, as the increase of
travel brings the increase of knowledge, so the increase
of knowledge will bring an increase of discontent to the
world of mankind in general; and the result will be as
prophetically stated, that "there shall be a time of
trouble such as never was since there was a nation."
The Watchers, seeking to note whether these things
have yet a fulfilment or not, look about them and behold
on every hand discontent, unhappiness; far more than
when the world enjoyed far fewer of the mercies and
blessings of heaven. These latter day gifts of Providence (preparations for the Millennial age), instead of
provoking thankfulness, gratitude and love to God and
generosity to man, produce in unregenerate hearts ambition, greater avarice, selfishness, envy, hatred, strife,
and other works of the flesh and of the devil. Yes;
the Watchers can clearly discern the great approaching climax of human trouble in which the Scriptures
distinctly declare that all the present human institutions shall go down in anarchy, in confusion, in chaos.

But the Watchers do not lose sight of God and his providence. They see that, while the approaching social and ecclesiastical catastrophe will be the natural result of the operation of selfishness under highly favored conditions, nevertheless they remember that God is at the helm, and that he is able to cause the wrath of man to praise him, and the remainder of man's wrath (which would not praise him) he will restrain.

The Watchers look not merely at the outward signs, as seen in the world. They scrutinize carefully and repeatedly their "chart," the Bible's prophetic outline of the world's history, furnished by the King himself. It is because they see the time of trouble outlined in the prophetic chart that they know that it is sure to come, and are able in advance of others to "discern the signs of the times," and not to be in darkness respecting the *"things to come."* It was in respect to this that the Lord promised the Watchers that the holy spirit should *guide them* into all truth, as each feature becomes due, and would show them things to come—future things—in advance of the world's knowledge, and in advance of the facts themselves. (John 16 : 13.) But the same chart which shows the downfall of all earthly institutions, political, social and ecclesiastical, shows also that their fall is so timed in the great plan of Jehovah that it shall be the very hour in which he will establish in the hands of the elect Church (who then shall be a royal priesthood glorified—priests upon their thrones—the religious as well as the civil rulers of the world), whose exaltation shall be to the glory of God and to the blessing of every creature.

The Watchers remember well that the King gave them an outline of the history of the Gospel age at the

very time that he told them to watch, intimating to
them that they were to watch for the things which he
therein noted. The Watchers are those who are in
harmony with the King and who have respect to his
promises, and they, therefore, do not neglect the words
which he spoke. And as they note this very prophecy
in connection with which he tells them to watch, they
see in it clearly that the day of the Lord will be ush-
ered in at the close of this Gospel age, secretly, quietly, unobtrusively, "as a thief in the night,"—unaware
to the world, and known only to the Watchers.

PAROUSIA VS. EPIPHANIA, APOKALUPSIS

Because not heedless, careless, indifferent servants
of the King, but faithful and earnest, the Watchers
have scrutinized every little particular which fell from
the lips of him who spake as never man spake; and all
the messages which he has sent them through his faithful apostles and prophets. And discriminating carefully, they discern that there are three words of distinctly
different signification used in respect to the Lord's
second advent; namely, *parousia* and *epiphania* and
apokalupsis. *Parousia* is used in respect to the earliest
stage of the second advent, while *apokalupsis* relates to
the same advent later:—not that *apokalupsis* and *epiphania* relate to another or a third advent, but merely
to a later feature of the second advent. These Greek
words, it is true, are somewhat obscured or hidden in
the Common Version of the Bible, and probably for a
purpose. The Lord's purpose evidently was to keep
the world and the wicked in ignorance of his gracious
plan until his due time; nor did he wish the particu-
lars to be understood by the Watchers until nearly the

time of the fulfilment. But now we are "in the time of the end," in "the day of his preparation," in the time in which it was foretold that then "the wise [not the worldlywise but the humble Watchers who are wise enough to take heed to the Word of the Lord] shall understand." (Dan. 12 : 10.) And hence, since many of the Watchers are not Greek scholars, God has made gracious provision through valuable helps (such as *Young's Analytical Concordance* and the *Emphatic Diaglott*), so that the very humblest of his people may have a clear and discriminating understanding of the meaning of certain features of his Word which hitherto have been kept hidden under imperfect translations: and these matters God himself has been bringing to the attention of his people, through the volumes of STUDIES IN THE SCRIPTURES, THE WATCH TOWER, etc. The Watchers all over the world are being reached by these "Helping Hands for Bible students," which the Lord himself is extending to them.

By these helps, the Watchers are rapidly coming to see that the word *"parousia,"* translated in our Common Version "coming," does not mean what our English word signifies; namely, to be on the way, approaching; but that on the contrary it signifies *presence,* as of one who has already arrived. The Watchers note also that the Scriptures predicate certain things respecting the Lord and respecting his *parousia* (his presence), which clearly intimate that he will be *present and doing his work, his great work* (of setting up his Kingdom and smiting the nations with the sword of his mouth) *wholly unknown to the world,*—"as a thief in the night." The Watchers also notice that the Scriptures clearly indicate that after the Lord has done certain things during his presence (*parousia*) and unknown to the world, he will later make a *manifestation of his presence;*—a manifestation which will be discerned by all mankind; and the outward manifestation is designated his *"epiphania"* which signifies "shining forth" or "bright shining."

The Watchers get the two thoughts respecting the Lord's second coming: that first, altho really present a spirit being, like the angels who, we are told, encamp round about them that fear God and deliver them, and who are "all ministering spirits, sent forth to minister to those who shall be heirs of salvation," and whose ministry is an invisible one (Psa. 34:7, Heb. 1:14),— so also our Lord, now a glorious spirit being, of the divine nature, will not be manifest to the natural eye during his *presence*—his *parousia*. Hence the necessity that the Lord's faithful ones shall *"watch,"* because they, no more than the world, can discern a spirit being with their natural eyes. The Watchers in due time are to discern the presence (*parousia* of their Lord by the eye of faith. The sleepless eye of faith will in due time take note of the "sign of the Son of Man,"—the indications of the *presence of the King.*

During the period of the *parousia* (presence) preceding the *epiphania* (shining forth) a certain work will be accomplished, unknown to the world, unknown to the nominal Church, known only to the Watchers. Ah, how important to us the words of our Master, exhorting us to be Watchers! And, by the way, this watching includes a watching of our own hearts as well as of the Lord's Word and the outward signs—to insure our worthiness to be continued in the light, and under the instructions of the great Teacher, "If any

man have not the spirit of Christ he is none of his;"
and if any man lose the spirit of Christ he ceases to be
his; and hence we all need to "watch" that we may,
as the Scriptures direct, "Keep our garments unspotted from the world;" and *"Keep ourselves in the love
of God,* while looking for the grace [aid] of our Lord
Jesus Christ, which is able to keep us from falling and
to present us faultless in the presence of his glory with
exceeding joy." For whoever has the spirit of Christ
may be a Watcher, and as a Watcher may know of the
gracious things connected with the great "salvation
which shall be brought unto us at the revelation of our
Lord and Savior Jesus Christ," but whoever ceases to
have the spirit of Christ must of necessity cease also
to be a Watcher and shall be in ignorance of the things
of the day of the Lord like the world, of which he then
probably would be a part.

As the light by which the eye of faith may discern
the *parousia,* we have the "more sure word of prophecy to which we do well to take heed." It has shone
upon the pathway of the Watchers all along through
this night, but now its various prophetic rays have fo-
cussed and clearly indicate that we are already living
"in the days of the Son of Man," while, as he expressly foretold, the world in general goes on as usual, in
utter ignorance of his *presence,* and of his harvest
work, and of the beginning of the Day of the Lord; it
continues as usual—eating and drinking, marrying and
giving in marriage, planting and building. It is a mistake to suppose that our Lord, in giving this information respecting the events of the time of his presence,
meant us to understand that it would be *wicked* for the
world to eat, drink, plant, build and marry; these are

not improper things and any such interpretation is strained and faulty and results from an utter misconception of the subject. Our Lord wished merely to show that the world would be in *ignorance of his presence* "in the days of the Son of Man," and in utter ignorance of the great time of trouble or "Day of Vengeance" which his inauguration of his Kingdom will signify to the kingdoms of this world, which are to be dashed to pieces as potters' vessels. The *ignorance* of the impending trouble here will be similar to that of the people who lived in the days of Noah. "As it was *in the days of Noah*, so also shall it be *in the days of the Son of Man*."—Luke 17 : 26.

As "the days of Noah" were not *days before* Noah's time, neither are "the days of the Son of Man" *days before* the Son of Man's presence. The days of the Son of Man are the days of his *parousia*, or presence,—invisible and unknown to the world, known only to the Watchers and seen by them only with the eye of faith. "As in the days that were before the flood they were eating, drinking, marrying,...and *knew not*,...so shall also the [parousia] presence of the Son of Man be:"—the world will simply go on about its usual affairs, and *know not* of the Lord's presence. —Matt. 24 : 38.

But why should our Lord be thus *present?* What will be his work during the period of presence preceding his *epiphania* or manifestation to the world?

His work is clearly outlined in various of his parables which were given that the Watchers might know —might not be in darkness. The parable of the wheat and the tares shows this period of the *parousia* (presence) preceding the *epiphania* (manifestation), and represents it as the "harvest" time of this age. The Son of Man sowed the good seed, and his servants followed, doing work in the field down through the age; finally the end of the age comes when the full crop of wheat is ripe, and then the harvest is reaped. The parable shows the separation of the two classes of the nominal church during the "harvest." For be it noted that the wheat-field is not the entire world, but merely the professedly Christian part of the world— Christendom: much of the field is not yet sown. And the parable relates only to the wheat-field, and particularly to the wheat. The tares (spurious Christians) are dealt with only incidentally. The tares choke the wheat, yet nevertheless the Master will obtain a sufficiently large crop, for—"All his purposes shall be accomplished."

The separation of the tares from the wheat, and the gathering of the wheat into the garner of heavenly conditions precedes the work of cleansing the wheat-field of its symbolic tares by symbolic "fire;" and this entire harvest work is to take place during the *parousia* (presence) of our Lord, before his *epiphania* (manifestation). He is the Chief-Reaper, and all the under-reapers will work under his direction and eye; and every kernel of true symbolic "wheat" will be gathered into the glorious symbolic "garner" by resurrection and "change."

The truth will be the separating medium, and not until the separation is complete and the "wheat" all garnered into the glory of the heavenly nature, will the "fire," the great time of trouble mentioned by the Prophet and by our Lord, burn and consume, symbolically, all the "tares:" so that thereafter none will make false professions of being Christians while really of the world and possessed of its spirit.

The parables of the Pounds and of the Talents cover this same period of time. In both of these the Lord represents himself as a great householder and heir to a throne, who has gone into a far country to be invested with kingly powers and to return to use those powers. Departing, he left with his servants various riches of grace and privilege, "to every man according to his several ability," saying to them, "Occupy till I come." The return of the nobleman of the parables unquestionably represents the second coming of our Lord and Master. Now note the work first due to take place upon his return as King, as shown by these parables. He does not first deal with the rebellious world, —those who would not have him to rule over them; but, first calls *"his own servants,"* and reckons with them —rejecting some from further service because of unfaithfulness, and accepting others to a participation in the joys of the Kingdom which he at once establishes.

This reckoning with the servants signifies a reckoning with the Church first, after his return; and corresponds to the separating of the wheat and tares, in the other parable. It is comparatively easy for anyone to realize that this part of the Lord's work at his second advent is the work which precedes the *epiphania* or manifestation to the world. It is during this period that the Watchers are to be aware of the *presence* (*parousia*) of the Lord, and of his scrutiny or judgment of them, which will then be in progress. Only the faithful will know, however,—only they will be "accounted worthy to *stand* before the Son of Man" in that judgment—all found unworthy shall "stumble." "The wicked [and slothful servants] shall not *stand* in the assembling of the righteous." (See Psa. 1 : 5.) It is of this period of his *presence,* and this feature of his work, that the world is to be in total ignorance, and "not know," until, having finished reckoning with his servants, and having glorified the faithful, the judgment of the world shall begin with "a time of trouble such as was not since there was a nation." That trouble is symbolically pictured as a *fire,* and we are told by the Apostle that our Lord shall be *revealed (apoka-lupto*—uncovered, disclosed, made manifest) in flaming fire (judgments), taking vengeance.

All who are Watchers, all who have taken heed to "the more sure word of prophecy," including the Master's description of the events of *"the days of the Son of Man,"* can readily discern that the world would not go on in its usual routine—eating, drinking, planting, building, marrying, etc.—if they knew of the Lord's *presence,* and the progress of the "harvest" of the Gospel age. If they knew of the Lord's presence and that the reckoning with the servants had commenced, and that the next thing in order would be judgments upon themselves, they would change their usual order of affairs considerably : they would be in great trepidation ; because only those who are in sympathy with the Lord and the righteous government which he is about to establish, when he shall lay judgment to the line and justice to the plummet—only these can in any degree be ready to welcome him : all others have the spirit of fear, and are under the blinding influences and misrepresentations of Satan. "The god of this world hath blinded the minds of them that believe not, lest the glorious light [of the gospel of

Christ] should shine unto them." Because of ignorance, therefore, the world would be in great fear, if
they knew the fact of the beginning of the day of the
Lord, which is to be to them the "day of vengeance."*
Very evidently, therefore, this reckoning with the
Church and the reward of the faithful will precede our
Lord's *epiphania* or *cpokalupsis*. To use one of his own
figures, we might say that his day or time of *presence*
—"the day of the Lord"—will come as a thief in the
night; and in this time he will gather his virgin Church
discriminatingly, and take her as his Bride to himself,
—changing her from earthly nature and conditions to
spiritual or heavenly conditions, to be like him, see him
as he is, and share his glory. And since the saints
have always been "the salt of the earth," we may readily discern that the taking away of the salt of the earth
would leave mankind in a very deplorable condition,
in which corruption would spread rapidly: and this is
exactly what the Scriptures indicate.

The "change" of the last member of the elect
Church will probably be followed by their being ush-
ered into the Divine presence.—presented faultless
before the Father. (Jude 24.) Then a little later,
when the "tribulation saints," the "Great Company,"
shall have finished their course, they too will be presented. (Psalm 45:14, 15.) Then will follow the nup-
tial festival styled, "The Marriage Supper of the
Lamb."

We are not to suppose that all this will require
long time, but the contrary. The only thing to guide
us is the time that elapsed after our Lord's ascension,
before the Pentecostal blessing which marked the ac-

---

*SCRIPTURE STUDIES, VOL. IV., *"The Battle of Armageddon."*

ceptance of the sin offering on our behalf. Meantime the world, "every man's hand against his neighbor," will be permitted to reap the whirlwind of its own selfishness in anarchy.   The *epiphania* of the new Ruler and of his reign of righteous retribution will then gradually be discerned. The full revealment or *apokalupsis* will be at the close of the storm, when, all hearts humbled, "Every knee shall bow and every tongue acknowledge Him."

This fact is abundantly proved by the Lord's statement of what shall be the reward to the overcomers, a part of which is, "He that overcometh, and keepeth my words to the end, to him will I give power over the nations: and he shall rule them with a rod of iron; *as the vessels of a potter shall they be broken in pieces:* even as I have received of my Father." (Rev. 2:26,27.) Again, the same matter is mentioned by the Prophet David, saying, "This honor have all his saints,—*to execute the judgments written.*" It is manifest, therefore, that the Church, altho absent from the world during the period of the tribulations in the sense of being "changed" from human to divine nature, will be present in it with Christ, as associate executors of the divine justice, breaking to pieces the present order of affairs, and ready to heal the hearts of the world as soon as they shall be broken in their pride, and prepared for the "Balm of Gilead."

THE TIME OF THE PAROUSIA.

It will doubtless surprise many to learn that there is much Scripture proof that we are already in the time of the presence (*parousia*) of the Son of Man,—that we are already living "in the days of the Son of Man."

At first some will be inclined to say, "Where is the *promise* of his [*parousia*] presence, while all things continue as they were from the beginning?" Peter foretold that some would thus question and be surprised at this information, that we are living in the days of the Son of Man, while there is as yet no outward manifestation of his presence, but the affairs of the world continue in their ordinary channels. (2 Pet. 3 : 4.) The answer to the question is, as we have just pointed out, our Lord's own declaration that in his days of presence the world would be eating, drinking, planting and building, and *know not*. That is the promise of his presence, while all things continue as they were. Could it be more explicit? A totally different question, however, is—

WHAT THE PROOFS OF HIS PRESENCE?

This is a reasonable inquiry. We would not be justified in believing that the Lord is present upon any slight evidence, even tho we know in advance that he is a spirit being, whose presence would be invisible without a miracle;—and even tho we know in advance, from the parables, that he will be present, but invisible, in the harvest time of this age, in the time of reckoning with his servants, preparatory to their glorification. We have a right to expect clear, reasonable ground for faith, before accepting any matter which implies so much. We are not, however, to ask or to expect evidences to natural sight: if we are of the Watchers, who have "the eyes of their understanding opened" to see wonderful things in the divine Word, then these eyes of our understanding must also be the eyes of our faith. Hence, the true Watchers are to

expect reasonable, satisfactory evidence for *faith,* and
not occular demonstrations of an invisible *parousia.*
As the Apostle explains, "We walk by faith, not by
sight."

To our understanding there are strong proofs that
our Lord's *parousia* began in the Autumn of 1874. We
have seen nothing with our natural eyes; only with the
eyes of the understanding, only in the light of "the
more sure word of prophecy," do we know this, which
we sincerely believe and affirm, and which is important
news to all who claim to be Watchers. The fact that
any Watcher should have remained in ignorance of
this important event for now twenty-four years would
seem of itself to be an indication that he had not been
properly awake to the use of his privileges and opportunities—that he had not been sufficiently watchful of
the sure word of prophecy to which he was instructed
to take heed; and that *therefore* he had been left at
least partially ignorant of the important things transpiring throughout the world during these years. To
this extent many of the Lord's people have been with
the world and similarly ignorant: and yet we may reasonably assume that the Lord did not expect all of his
watching servants to discern the matter at the same
instant of time. True, those who saw early have had
special blessing for the longer time; but, as we saw
above, the preparation for the knowledge of the time
lies largely in the right attitude of heart—in its humil-
ity and possession of the various graces of the spirit
of Christ.

Lest we should get a misapprehension respecting
this matter of the discerning the Lord's *parousia,* we
do well to take heed of the parable of the ten virgins,

which evidently was given to throw special light upon this point. That parable shows a false announcement of the arrival of the Bridegroom in 1844, which brought to the subject considerable reproach, but which nevertheless was of great advantage, as stirring up the "virgin" class (the pure, the consecrated) to fresh trimming of the lamp of truth—investigating the sure word of prophecy. The parable shows, also, that the "virgins" in general fell asleep, yet, nevertheless, in due time all would be reawakened by the prophetic *knocking*, and the *knocking* of the signs of the times, which indicate the Bridegroom's *presence*. And the parable shows that the result will depend upon how much oil (holy spirit) the "virgins" may have in their vessels (in their own hearts), as well as in their lamps (the Scriptures). Applying this parable, then, we may reasonably suppose that some of the Lord's true people have temporarily fallen asleep on this subject of his second coming, and that the sleeping ones will include some who have his spirit in their hearts, and who will be fully ready to welcome the Master when they shall awake, and whose lamps will be duly trimmed and burning and ready to enable them to *discern the signs of his parousia*, when once their attention is brought to the subject. In harmony with this we find that many who get *awake* on this subject *now* come into the clear light of present truth much more rapidly than did some in the past: doubtless partly because present truth can now be presented to them more concretely than ever before through the printed page. It is in the interest of this true "virgin" class that we now write: we have no desire to awaken the worldly; this knocking of the prophecies announcing the *Parousia* is not

for them—besides, the worldly are so soundly asleep
that it will require the terrific crashing of present institutions and the earthquake shakings of social revolution to thoroughly awaken them to a realization of
the *presence* of the great Judge—Immanuel. The true
Watchers on the contrary, if they slumber at all, sleep
lightly, being on the *qui vive* of expectancy and hope
for the long-waited-for Bridegroom. We would merely
whisper in the ears of this class the one word, *"Parousia!"* assured that all the true Watchers (and the Lord
alone *knoweth* them that are his) will be aroused by
that word, and trim their lamps on the subject.

Is the question asked,—What portions of the sure
word of prophecy indicate that the *presence* of our
Lord began in the Autumn of 1874? We answer that
there are several lines of prophecy which interlace and
corroborate each other in this testimony; but, as might
be expected, since the entire matter was to be hidden
from the world, and "none of the wicked," but only the
"wise" are to understand (Dan. 12:10), and these wise
only to understand when the due time would come,—
for these reasons, it must be evident to all that these
prophecies, while clear and forcible and positive, are
nevertheless somewhat *under cover.* We cannot here
attempt to give a complete and comprehensive statement of these prophecies; that has already been done
in six volumes aggregating three thousand pages.*
Here we can only give a very brief resume, leaving it
for the true Watchers to seek that they may find; to
knock if they would have the door of divine revelation
opened to them; to use the keys which God has provided, if they are interested in penetrating into "the

*Scripture Studies, Vols. I.-VI.

deep things" of the divine Word, now *due* to be understood; to *cat* of the meat of present truth, "things new and old," if they hunger and thirst after righteousness and true knowledge.

"IN THE DAYS OF THESE KINGS."

'(1) We have a number of general prophecies, indicating that we are living in about the time of the Master's second presence. We have already referred to Daniel's testimony respecting "the time of the end," in which many will run to and fro, and knowledge will be increased, and the wise understand, and which the time of trouble follows. Then we have the inspired dream of Nebuchadnezzar, and its inspired interpretation by Daniel, showing the earthly governments which would bear rule over the earth;—during the interim between the overthrow of the typical Kingdom of God, whose last king sitting upon the throne of David was Zedekiah, and the installation of the true King, Emanuel, in his Millennial Kingdom glory. These different governments of earth are here pictured as a great image; Nebuchadnezzar's government, the first universal empire of earth, being represented by the head of gold; the Medo-Persian Empire, which, according to history, was the second universal empire, is here shown as the breast and arms of silver; the Grecian empire, which overthrew the Persian, and became the third universal empire, is represented by the belly and thighs of brass; the Roman empire, which succeeded the Grecian, and constituted itself the fourth universal empire of earth, was represented in the image by the legs of iron—strong exceedingly; and the later development of the same Roman empire with the intermixture of papal influence is represented in the image by the feet, which were partly iron (civil government), and partly of clay (ecclesiastical government—Papacy). These were to constitute the sum total of Gentile dominion; and "in the days of these kings" (represented by the ten toes of the image), Jehovah God himself would establish his Kingdom—the very Kingdom for which we pray, "Thy Kingdom come!"

We are all witnesses that the heavenly Kingdom has not yet come,—that we are still under the dominion of "the prince of this world"—the prince of darkness. All the efforts to prove to us that the greedy and bloody governments of Christendom, so-called, are the Kingdom for which we prayed, and were taught to pray, could not prevail: we could never recognize these as Immanuel's Kingdom: they are only the kingdoms established by Antichrist, and recognized by Antichrist, and named by Antichrist "*Christendom.*" The true Kingdom waits for establishment at the hands of him whose right it is; and he has promised that, when he sits upon his throne, all his faithful ones, the "little flock" of the Gospel age, shall sit in that throne with him, and be associates in the work and in the honor of blessing the world.

The Church is not neglected in the picture of earthly dominion given to Nebuchadnezzar, and interpreted by the Prophet Daniel. She is shown therein as a stone taken out of the mountain without hands (by divine power). This stone represents God's Kingdom (Christ and the Church), and the inspired dream and explanation show that the disaster which shall come to the kingdoms of this world, represented in the image and in the toes of its feet, would come

through the impact or smiting of the image by the
stone. Daniel says: "A stone was cut out, which,
without being in hands, smote the image upon his
feet....Then was the iron, the clay, the brass, the
silver and the gold broken to pieces together, and became like the chaff of the summer threshing floor, and
the wind carried them away that no place was found
for them: and the stone that smote the image became
a great mountain [kingdom], and filled the whole
earth."

The explanation is that—"The great God hath
made known to the king [and indirectly more particularly to the Watchers] what shall come to pass hereafter." *"In the days* of these kings shall the God of
heaven set up a kingdom which shall never be destroyed, and the kingdom shall not be left to other
people; [it shall have no successors, for the others will
all be destroyed] it shall break in pieces and consume
all these kingdoms, and it shall stand forever." Here
is a prophecy which gives a full delineation of the empires of earth, to which God granted dominion during
the interim between the removal of the typical crown
from his typical kingdom, and the institution of the
crown of righteousness and glory upon the true King
in the inauguration of the Kingdom of Heaven.

Even the surface evidences are that human empire
has nearly run its course, and that heavenly empire is
needed to deliver the world from its own selfishness.
But the sure word of prophecy, if carefully scrutinized
by the Watcher, reveals still more. It shows that the
next universal empire will be the kingdom of God's
dear Son, and further the interesting fact that the
total lease of power to the Gentiles, is in the Scrip-

tures known as "the times of the Gentiles;" and that
these "times" are seven times, and that each of the
seven times is a period of three hundred and sixty
years, and that consequently the complete period of
the seven times is 2520 years. Hence the Watchers
may reckon that Gentile rule will terminate and Immanuel's rule be fully set up in 2520 years from the
time the Lord removed the diadem from Zedekiah,
saying: "Oh thou profane and wicked prince,...
take off the diadem, remove the crown; I will overturn, overturn, overturn it, until he comes whose right
it is, and I will give it unto him." The period of
overturning of the Lord's typical Kingdom and the
removal of the crown must correspond to the period of
the lease of empire to the Gentiles and be 2520 years.
And measuring this period, we find that 2520 years
will expire with the close of the year 1914, A. D. and
consequently that by that time Gentile rule will be no
more while God's Kingdom will then hold sway.

But the scrutinizing Watcher will readily perceive
that it is one thing to know the time when earthly
dominion shall cease, and give place to the *completed*
Kingdom of God, while it would be a totally different
matter to know when the "stone" Kingdom would begin to smite the image upon its feet, preparatory to
its destruction. This period of smiting of the image,
which precedes its destruction, must also precede the
full establishment of God's Kingdom to fill the whole
earth. This smiting period is the period of the *parousia*; the period in which Christ is present, gathering
his "jewels," his "elect," and in which he will smite
the nations with the rod of iron and with the two-edged
sword of his mouth, dashing them in pieces as a pot-

ter's vessel, and preparing mankind for the royal
majesty of the heavens. Let the Watchers note critically the Prophet Daniel's explanation that it will be
"in the days of these kings" (the kingdoms represented
in the feet and toes of the image—the divisions of
Papal Rome) that the God of heaven will *set up* his
kingdom. God began the selection of his Kingdom
class in the days of Civil Rome—represented by the
legs of iron: he has continued the selection ever since,
and the *setting up* or bringing of his Church (Kingdom) into power comes toward the close of Gentile
power, but before it ends; for it is to be *"in the days*
of these kings" and not after their days. Now note
the similarity of the expressions "in the days of the
Son of Man" and "in the days of these kings," and
give both the same significance and remember that,
as we have proven, they will be the *same days*—days
before the lease of Gentile power expires, in which
the Son of Man will be present to *"set up"* his Kingdom, which shall a little later destroy all these Gentile
kingdoms.

TYPICAL ISRAEL'S EXPERIENCE PROPHETIC.

(2) Take another line of prophecy, concealed, and
yet very simple and easy of appreciation when once
the mind grasps it. The Scriptures show us that the
fleshly house of Israel and all of its institutions and
affairs were typical foreshadowings of the spiritual
house of Israel, and its higher institutions, better sacrifices, etc. It need not, therefore, surprise us to find
that the length of the Jewish age—the length of the
divine favor to fleshly Israel,—was typical also, and
that it gives us the *exact measurement* of the Gospel

age,—God's dealings with and favor toward spiritual Israel.

Jacob's name was changed to Israel, which signifies "A Prince with God," and his descendants were therefore termed Israelites—the people of the Prince with God. But the antitype of Jacob is Christ, the true Prince with God, not after the flesh, but after the spirit; and his house is spiritual Israel. Jacob's twelve sons first inherited his name and blessing, and through them it descended to all the fleshly house of Israel: Christ's twelve Apostles inherited his name and blessing, and through them it has descended to all the spiritual house of Israel. As the typical house had a high priest, Aaron, so the antitypical house has a greater high priest, Christ Jesus our Lord, the high priest of our profession. As the fleshly house had a priesthood under Aaron, so the spiritual house has "a royal priesthood" under Christ, to whom the promise is made that they shall be kings and priests unto God, who shall reign on the earth, after their present time of *sacrificing* is ended. So we might proceed with everything that fleshly Israel had and find its duplicate on a higher plane, in spiritual Israel, but we will not go into details here: suffice it to notice further that the Jewish age or period of fleshly Israel's favor ended with a "harvest" period of forty years. This began with our Lord's baptism, lasted three and a half years, as a *national* test, and when that nation was rejected at the time of our Lord's crucifixion, the harvest work proper began—a separation of the wheat from the chaff—a time of gathering out of that rejected nation such as were "Israelites indeed," previous to the great time of trouble which came upon the nation

and which utterly destroyed their national polity A. D.
70. All of this is likened to a "harvest" season, and
its first garnering of the wheat and subsequent burning of the chaff. And our Lord gives instructions to
us (Matt. 13) that this Gospel age of spiritual Israel's
favor will likewise end with a harvesting time, gathering the wheat together and ultimately destroying the
tares. In the harvesting of the fleshly house our Lord,
in the flesh, was the Chief-Reaper, and his Apostles
were co-laborers: in the harvesting of the spiritual
house our Lord, a spirit being, is to be *present* as the
Chief-Reaper, and members of the spiritual house are
to be also reapers.

Now note the time correspondences. The Jewish
age, from the death of Jacob to the death of Christ,
was 1845 years long—to the beginning of our Lord's
ministry 1841½ years long, and to the time of the utter destruction of their nation, in A. D. 70, 1881½ years
long. Notice how the Gospel age corresponds to this.
The Gospel age did not begin with our Lord's birth: it
began after our Lord's death and resurrection, when
he commissioned his disciples to *"preach the Gospel* to
every creature." (Our Lord's previous work during
the three and a half years of his ministry was the offering of the Kingdom to the fleshly house, to test
them, and to prove that they were unready to receive
the true Kingdom.) Applying the foregoing measurements of the Jewish age to the Gospel age, beginning
it at the time of our Lord's death and resurrection and
the Pentecostal blessing, in the Spring of A. D. 33, we
find that the period of 1841½ years from the death of
Jacob to the beginning of our Lord's ministry,
would measure from the Spring of A. D. 33 to the

Autumn of 1874; and the 1845 years of the Jewish age, from the death of Jacob to the rejection of fleshly Israel, applied here, measuring from the Spring of A. D. 33, would reach to the Spring of 1878; and the 1881½ years from the death of Jacob to the full destruction of Israel's polity in A. D. 70, finds its correspondence in this Gospel age, by measuring 1881½ years from the Spring of A. D. 33, which would bring us exactly to (Autumn) 1914 A. D.—the very year and time shown us by Daniel's prophecy to be the full end and limit of the "Gentile times." Can this be accidental? Nay; it is design. What stronger testimony could be asked by the eye and ear of faith. Surely, anything plainer or clearer would be sight and leave no room for faith.

THE JUBILEE PROPHECY.

(3) Note another prophecy, similarly hidden in type in the Mosaic law,—Israel's Jubilee Year. No one is prepared to understand this line of prophecy who has not first learned that the second coming of our Lord is not for the purpose of destroying the world, but for the purpose of blessing it according to the promise made to Abraham, "in thy Seed shall *all* the families of the earth be blessed,"—with the favors lost in Adam. These will be offered to *all* and will be made perpetual to those who will accept them on the terms of the New Covenant. None can see any beauty or typical significance in Israel's Jubilee who have not learned that God has provided "times of restitution of all things" which are to *begin* in connection with the second advent of the Redeemer.—See Acts 3 : 19-23.

We find that Israel's Jubilee years, in which every person and family had restored to them every lost pos-

session and all personal liberties, was intended to be a
type of the coming time of restitution, when a full opportunity for attaining freedom from sin and from Satan, and from the hereditary weaknesses of the flesh,
shall be presented to all, and when the earth shall again
revert to the human family in general, for whom it was
created, and for whom it was redeemed by Christ, after being lost through Adam's transgression. We find
that the Scriptures indicate, in connection with these
jubilees, a system of counting by multiples; and that
a Jubilee of Jubilees, or fifty times fifty years (2500
years) constitutes a Great Jubilee cycle and that such
a cycle began to count after fleshly Israel had observed
her last typical Jubilee. We find from the Scriptures
that Israel's nineteenth Jubilee year was her last, in
the year B. C. 626. Knowing that the Jubilee was a
part of the Law, and that no feature of that Law, not
one jot or tittle, can pass away without reaching a
fulfilment or antitype, we measure the cycle of the
Great Jubilee 2500 years from the date when the last
typical Jubilee was kept, 626 B. C., and find accordingly that the *antitypical* Jubilee or Great Jubilee of
Jubilees should have begun in October, 1874. Thus,—
625 years B. C. plus 1875 years A. D. are 2500 years,
which would include the Jubilee *year*: consequently,
with the end of the year 1874, Jewish time, October,
the antitypical Jubilee of 1,000 years instead of *one*
year was due to begin.

    Watchers will note carefully the correspondency
of this date, and the character of the event to be expected, with the finding of our previous examinations
(1 and 2), which showed us this very same date,
October, 1874, was the time when the "harvest" of

this age was due to begin, and when the Lord himself, as the Chief Reaper, was *due to be present.* The
only thing necessary to connect this Jubilee prophecy
with the others is the statement of the Apostle Peter
in Acts 3 : 21, which shows that our Lord must be
present (at his second advent) at the beginning of the
times of restitution of all things, and as already seen,
these *restitution times* are the Antitypical *Jubilee times*
typified by Israel's Jubilees. Thus we have two very
simple but clear and very important lines of Scripture
testimony which indicate clearly that the *parousia* of
our Lord was due to begin in October, 1874, and both
show us the character of the work which we should
expect would be in progress during the time of his
presence, preceding his open manifestation to the
world, his *epiphania,* his *apokalupsis.*

THE DAYS OF WAITING ARE FULFILLED.

(4.) Take another line of prophecy: we find
that the 1260 days, and the 1290 days, and the 1335
days, so particularly set forth in Daniel's prophecy,
and corroborated in Revelation, have had fulfilments,
—the 1260 days ending in 1799, the 1290 days ending
in 1829, and the 1335 days ending in 1874. Our
friends known as "Second Adventists" were wont to
use these "days of Daniel," and once applied them as
we do here: but they abandoned them after 1874
passed and they failed to see Jesus with their natural
eyesight, in a body of flesh and with Calvary's scars.
They have dropped these "days of Daniel" entirely
because they find no way of applying them which
would prolong them beyond 1874. The fault is not
with the days nor with their application as above; but

with the wrong things expected. They, in common with others who look for the Second Advent, err in expecting that the Gospel age which has been a spirit and faith epoch will end with a flesh and sight deterioration—in expecting that the spiritual kingdom of Satan will be followed by a fleshly kingdom of Christ. But the Watchers amongst the Adventists as well as in other denominations, are getting the eyes of their understanding opened by the anointing of the promised eyesalve.—Rev. 3 : 18.

It was concerning this last period that the angel declared to the Prophet, "Oh, the blessedness of him that waiteth, and cometh to the 1335 days....Thou shalt rest, and stand in thy lot at the end of the days." What blessedness? We answer, a joy of heart and rejoicing to the Watchers is what is here intimated. It is since this date, October, 1874, where Daniel's 1335 days intimated that a *great blessing would begin*, where the Jubilee types indicated that the *restitution of all things would begin*, (which implies the second presence of the great Restorer), and where the parallelism of the two houses of Israel shows that the second presence of our Lord as *the Great Reaper is due,*—from this date a great blessing *has come* to the Watchers. Since *then* the Word of God has opened before us in a most marvelous manner. Since *then* the sure word of prophecy as a lamp to our feet has shown us many evidences that we are in the end of the age. Since *then* the day-star has been rising in the hearts of the Watchers, and has illuminated our minds, releasing us from the terrible nightmare of error respecting eternal torment, revealing to us the true character of our Heavenly Father, making plain to us the necessity, of the great atonement for sin, and showing us distinctly the object of the permission of evil and revealing, one by one, various features of the divine plan,—the high calling of the Church to the divine nature, and to joint-heirship with Christ in his Millennial Kingdom; and the resulting blessing of restitution to human perfection for the world of mankind in general. Ah yes! all who have been brought "out of darkness into this marvelous light" can appreciate the words of the angel, and heartily say, Blessed are our ears, for they hear, and our eyes, for they see, for many prophets and many righteous persons have desired to know these things, and have not known them.

(5) We might refer to other prophecies and types in the Scriptures, which show that we are living in the "harvest" time of this age, in the *parousia* of the Son of Man, but our space forbids. The fact that this world, as he predicted, continues in its usual course, eating, drinking, planting and building, etc., and *knows not* of his presence, so far from being an evidence against these prophetic testimonies, quite to the contrary, shows us that the fulfilment is coming, just as the Master predicted: that the day of the Lord, the day of his presence, has come upon the world as a thief in the night, secretly, quietly, stealthily, unknown;—the only ones favored with a knowledge of events transpiring on the other side of the vail being the Watchers who, if they have slumbered at all, have nevertheless maintained a waiting attitude of readiness for the announcement,—

"BEHOLD THE BRIDEGROOM!"

This is the announcement which we are now giving—Not, Behold, the Bridegroom *cometh,* but "Behold the Bridegroom!" already here, present, knocking gently with the prophecies to arouse the Virgins, but not to arouse the world. (Rev. 3:20) This is the reading of the oldest Greek Manuscripts, which omit "*cometh*." Our Lord says, "If any man hear my voice [knock] and open the door, I will come in to *him* and and sup with *him*." This message to the present Laodicean phase of the Church, intimates very clearly (1) that the "knock" and "voice" will be inaudible to natural ears, and heard only by the ears of the understanding, the hearing of faith; (2) that it will not be a denominational knock or call (as to Adventists, Presbyterians, etc.), but (3) that it will be a knock that must be heard individually and responded to individually—"any man" who hears the "knock" or "voice," if he so wills, may *exercise faith* and open the door of his understanding and realize his Lord's second presence.

The man who never hears the "knock" is not counted worthy to hear it. But those who hear are evidently not compelled to respond and to accept the present, knocking King: hence he says, *if* the hearing one *open the door*, I will come in. However, only those who recognize the "knock" and who respond and by faith open to the Lord and receive him as their *present* King—only these are to have the great blessing of spiritual nourishment—the feast of "meat in due season," "things new and old," which the Master promised to provide at that time, to strengthen the faithful for the judgments, trials, testings and siftings which must "begin with the house of God." "I will come in to him and sup with him and he with me"— Compare Rev. 3 : 20, and Luke 12 : 37.

As therefore we softly whisper—"Behold the Bridegroom!" it is not with any hope of arousing the world to faith in the Lord's presence, etc. They are not worthy to know and would only misuse the knowledge now. By and by, in the Lord's due time, they shall know—in the period of the *epiphania* and *apokalupsis* of the Son of Man. They will be awakened by the great crash of the day of trouble. We do, however, promulgate the message, "Behold the Bridegroom [present]!" with the confident expectation that all who are of the "Virgin" class (the pure, the justified and consecrated), will be permitted to hear the message, will be aroused by it, and will trim their lamps (examine the Scriptures, investigate the subject), and find the message true, before the "door is shut" and the great trouble begun. We well know, however, from the Lord's prophetic parable, that among those who will be aroused to investigation, there will be two classes, because there are both wise and foolish "Virgins." The wise are those who have not only consecrated their all to the Lord, but who are living accordingly,—not unto sin, nor unto self, nor unto sectarianism, but unto the Lord: these, as intimated in the parable, will find no difficulty in trimming their lamps and recognizing the *presence* of the Bridegroom. But the foolish Virgins, overcharged with the cares of this life, or the deceitfulness of riches (wealth, reputation, influence, etc.), will not have within themselves ("in their vessels") a sufficiency of the oil (holy spirit); and consequently they will be unable to get the light in time to go in with the wise virgins before the elect number shall be completed, and the door of opportunity to become part of the Bride of Christ, shall forever

close.   True, they will later obtain the oil, as is shown
in the parable, but too late to be of the "little flock"
who shall be accounted worthy to share the Kingdom
and to escape the great time of trouble coming upon
the world: the foolish virgins will be obliged to pass
through the trouble with the world, and will share thus
in its distress, represented in the parable by the words,
"wailing and gnashing of teeth."

PAROUSIA IN THE NEW TESTAMENT.

The word *parousia* occurs in the following texts
of the New Testament, in each of which it should be
properly translated "presence:"—

"What shall be the sign of thy *presence?*"—Matt.
24 : 3.

"So shall also the *presence* of the Son of Man be."
—Matt. 24 : 27, 37, 39.

"They that are Christ's at his *presence.*"—1 Cor.
15 : 23.

"What is our hope, or joy, or crown of rejoicing?
Are not even ye, presented before our Lord Jesus
Christ at his *presence?*"—1 Thes. 2 : 19.

That "he may establish your hearts unblamable
in holiness before the Lord, even our Father, at the
presence of our Lord Jesus Christ."—1 Thes. 3 : 13.

"We which are alive and remain unto the *presence*
of the Lord shall not hinder them which are asleep."
—1 Thes. 4 : 15.

"Be preserved blameless unto the *presence* of our
Lord Jesus Christ."—1 Thes. 5 : 23.

"Now we beseech you, brethren, by the *presence*
of our Lord Jesus Christ, and our gathering together
unto him."—2 Thes. 2 : 1.

"Be patient, therefore, brethren, unto the *presence* of the Lord."—James 5 : 7.

"Be ye also patient, stablish your hearts, for the *presence* of the Lord draweth nigh."—James 5 : 8.

"There shall come in the last days scoffers [in the Church] walking after their own lusts [desires], and saying, Where is the promise of his *presence?*"— 2 Pet. 3 : 3, 4.

The word *parousia* is properly translated ("presence") in 2 Cor. 10 : 10, and Phil. 2 : 12.

EPIPHANIA IN THE NEW TESTAMENT.

The Greek work *epiphania* signifies *bright shining* or *manifestation.* It is rendered "appearing" and "brightness," and occurs as follows:—

"Keep this commandment without spot unrebukable until the *appearing* of our Lord Jesus Christ, which in his times he shall show who is the blessed and only potentate, the King of kings and Lord of lords."—1 Tim. 6 : 14, 15.

"I charge thee, therefore, before God and the Lord Jesus Christ, who shall judge the quick and the dead at his *appearing* and his Kingdom."—2 Tim. 4:1.

"There is laid up for me a crown of righteousness which he shall give me at that day; and not to me only, but unto all them also that love his *appearing.*"— 2 Tim. 4 : 8.

"Looking for that blessed hope and the glorious *appearing* of the great God and our Savior Jesus Christ."—Titus 2 : 13.

"Then shall that Wicked One be exposed, whom the Lord shall consume with the spirit of his mouth, and shall destroy with the *brightness* [*epiphania*—

bright shining] of his coming [*parousia*—presence]."
—2 Thes. 2 : 8.

APOKALUPSIS IN THE NEW TESTAMENT.

The Greek words *apokalupsis* and *apokalupto* signify *revealment, uncovering, unveiling* (as of a thing previously present but hidden). The name of the last book of the Bible is from the same root—Apocalypse or Revelation. *Apokalupsis* is rendered *revealed, revelation, appearing, coming* and *manifestation*, in the following texts which relate to the Lord's second *presence* and power and glory, as these shall be made known,—uncovered or revealed to the world. Many of these texts also show that when he shall thus be revealed, his Church will be with the Lord and be revealed or manifested at the same time and in the same manner.

"The sufferings of this present time are not worthy to be compared with the glory which shall be *revealed* in us."—Rom. 8 : 18.

"Rejoice, inasmuch as ye are partakers of Christ's sufferings; that when his glory shall be *revealed*, ye may be glad also with exceeding joy."—1 Pet. 4 : 13.

"An inheritance incorruptible, and undefiled, and that fadeth not away, reserved in heaven for you, who are kept by the power of God through faith unto salvation ready to be *revealed* in the last time."—1 Pet. 1 : 4, 5.

"A partaker of the glory that shall be *revealed*."
—1 Pet. 5 : 1.

"Every man's work shall be made manifest: for the day shall declare it, for it shall be *revealed* by fire." (1 Cor. 3 : 13.) Here the reference evidently is to the testings of the Lord's people during the period of, his presence in the end of the age. The Apostle's words thus agree with our Lord's prophecy of the same testings, saying that "there is nothing covered that shall not be *revealed*"—uncovered.—Luke 12 : 2.

"Hope to the end for the grace that is to be brought unto you at the *revelation* of Jesus Christ." —1 Pet. 1 : 13.

"The Lord Jesus shall be *revealed* from heaven in flaming fire [judgments against all unrighteousness], taking vengeance."—2 Thes. 1 : 7, 8.

"So that ye come behind in no gift; waiting for the coming [*apokalupsis*—revealment] of our Lord Jesus Christ."—1 Cor. 1 : 7. [The Lord's people will need to keep active, watching and waiting for the great blessing until the manifestation or *revealment* of the Lord; but if Watchers, they shall be made aware of his presence (*parousia*) and the work of "harvest" beforehand and share in the revealment.]

"That the trial of your faith...might be found unto praise and honor and glory at the *appearing* [*apokalupsis*—*revealment*] of Jesus Christ."—1 Pet. 1 : 7.

"For the earnest expectation of the creature [mankind] waiteth for the *manifestation* [*apokalupsis* —*revealing*] of the sons of God [the Church]."— Rom. 8 : 19.

"The same day that Lot went out of Sodom it rained fire and brimstone out of heaven, and destroyed them all. Even thus shall it be in the day when the Son of Man is *revealed*." (Luke 17:29, 30). That is to say, the judgments of the coming "time of trouble" as predicted will begin as soon as the "salt of the earth," the saints, have all been changed; and thus the Son of Man will be *revealed* a *present Judge*, who

already had for some time been present sealing and
gathering his "elect."

PRESENCE GRADUALLY REVEALED.

Foregoing we drew the line of distinction between
the *parousia* and the *epiphania* or *apokalupsis* of our
Lord quite sharply, to assist the reader in noting their
difference of signification. As a matter of fact, however, the *bright shining of the present One* is due to
begin shortly after the *parousia* begins; and again as at
the first advent it will be true that "the Light shineth
in the darkness, and the darkness comprehendeth it
not." The *revealing* of the Lord's presence begins
with the faithful of the Church speedily, and gradually
extends to the world in general. Up to the time when
the strength of the trouble breaks forth, only the faithful Watchers discern the *parousia*, and only by them
can the bright-shining of the Lord's presence be appreciated. To these the bright-shining of the Lord's
presence, the increased brilliancy of the light of truth
respecting the Word and character and plan of God is
an ever increasing joy and pleasure: thus it is that "ye,
brethren, are not in darkness," respecting the events
of the day of the Lord, but know in advance that its
tribulation will come upon the world as travail upon a
woman.—1 Thes. 5 : 3, 4.

While the revealment of our Lord's presence thus
illuminates the hearts of his faithful ones as the Day-
star (2 Pet. 1 : 19) and causes them to understand, and
not be in darkness with the world in respect to his
plans, present and future, the bright-shining of the
Lord's presence shall affect nominal Christians, and
the civilized world in general also, but in a totally

different manner, for the character of Christ's "harvest" work, during this period of his presence, is such as to cause a general opening of eyes along the lines of justice and injustice, righteousness and sin, the rights of mankind and the wrongs of mankind. The light which has been shining out for the past twenty years, is awakening the world to a realization of its rights and its wrongs, to a realization that the earth belongs to mankind in general and not exclusively to a few who have seized it and fenced it. This same light is exposing the corruption and falsity of many long-venerated theories and institutions, monarchical, religious, political and financial. It was in reference to this light of his presence at the second advent that our Lord declared that this day of his *presence* would bring to light the hidden things of darkness, and make manifest the secret counsels of the heart,—for there is nothing hidden that shall not be uncovered. (Luke 8 : 17). And in this connection let it not be overlooked that the Apostle declares that Satan's power to deceive the world through Antichrist is to be consumed by "the *bright-shining* [*epiphania*] *of his presence* [*parousia*]."—2 Thes. 2 : 8.

Thus seen, the bright-shining of the *present* One is causing great joy to the hearts of the faithful, who wait patiently for him and the deliverance which he has promised, but the bright-shining, as it affects the worldly, has the effect of quickening their selfish propensities, producing discontent, and is thus preparing the world for the great climax of catastrophe, predicted in the Word of the Lord, as the consummation of this age;—the overthrow of all the governments and institutions of this present order of things in anarchy,—"a time of trouble such as was not since there was a nation."

We noticed that it was predicted 2500 years ago, through the Prophet Daniel that *"in the days of these kings"* the representatives of the fourth universal empire, Rome, ecclesiastically conglomerated, shown in the feet and toes of the image, the God of heaven would cause the Kingdom of God to smite the image upon its feet, to utterly crush it; and that it would be after smiting the image that God's Kingdom, represented by the stone, would wax great and fill the whole earth. As we have just shown, we are now in this time in which the Kingdom of God is exerting its force against the kingdoms of this world: the King himself is present, must be present before he could destroy present kingdoms and take their power; he is already exerting the influences which will eventuate in their destruction; and he is prepared, backed by all the power of God, to quickly establish upon their ruins his own glorious Kingdom, consisting of himself the King, and his faithful ones of the Gospel Church as his Bride and joint-heir.

The influence exerted by our present Lord, the Light, the Truth, is already breaking the power of ignorance and superstition, which for long centuries has held the masses of mankind in subserviency to Papacy; and the same bright-shining is likewise dissolving the lighter shackles of ignorance and error forged for their faithful by the various sects of Protestantism. Ultimately all superstition and false reverence will be dissolved, and false institutions will fall, and then will be manifest the fact that error and falsehood and fear never truly sanctify the heart,—

and the world of mankind being released from its ser-
vility to fear will speedily manifest its true character
of selfishness and ungodliness, and will speedily precipitate the great trouble predicted.

But it would be a mistake to suppose that the
parousia of our Lord is merely or chiefly in connection
with the world and its preparation for the chaos of
the present order of things. On the contrary, the
chief work of the Lord during this period of his
parousia is for and in connection with his Church.
As we saw above, he foretold that on his return he
will first reckon with his servants, to whom he en-
trusted the pounds and talents, before manifesting his
wrath against evil-doers in the trouble of this "day
of vengeance,"—in the slaughter of all who would
not have him to reign over them. That slaughter
time, in which all who will not accept the reign of
righteousness will be destroyed from among the people (Acts 3 : 23), begins with the burning of the
"tares" in the end of this age, when there shall be
great trouble "weeping and gnashing of teeth;" and
to some extent it will continue throughout the Millennial Age for all the way to the very last (Isa. 65 : 20;
Acts 3 : 23; Rev. 20 : 8, 9) all who wilfully oppose
the Lord will perish.

The Kingdom which we are expecting, and which
we believe is now in process of establishment, and is
soon to smite the kingdoms of this world and to sup-
plant them, is not earthly kingdom, but a heavenly
one, not a fleshly kingdom, but a spiritual one, not a
kingdom which will be visible to the natural eye, but
an invisible yet powerful kingdom. We find nothing
in the Scriptures to corroborate the thought enter-

tained by some that this Gospel age having begun in
the spirit is to culminate in a reign of Christ and his
Church in the flesh with an earthly throne, etc.
Quite to the contrary, the King and his joint-heirs,
the Church, as spirit beings, will have a spiritual 'empire, tho their subjects to whom they will offer the
blessings of the restitution purchased at Calvary will
be men in the flesh, whose highest hope and ambition
will be *restitution* to the grand perfection of the human nature lost in Eden, redeemed at Calvary,—an
earthly image of the Heavenly Father. We hold that
Christ and his saints during the Millennial Age will be
no more visible to mankind than is the Prince of this
world, Satan, whose associates in the misrule of the
present evil world, the fallen angels, are likewise invisible.

"THE KINGDOM OF HEAVEN COMETH NOT WITH OBSERVATION."

The Pharisees at the first advent made the mistake of supposing that the Kingdom, which Christ
proclaimed, would be a visible kingdom, composed of
himself and his followers in the flesh: and seeing no
army or other evidences of temporal power for the establishment of an earthly kingdom, they thought to
expose the hollowness of our Lord's claims before his
followers, by asking him the question,—When will
your Kingdom of God appear—when will we see it?
Mark well our Lord's reply, which, if the Pharisees
had understood it, might have been a great revelation
to them. He answered, "The Kingdom of God cometh not with observation." How strange they must
have thought this answer! The Kingdom of God,

then, would be a Kingdom which could not be observed or seen;—an invisible kingdom. But our Lord continued the explanation and increased their perplexity by adding, "Neither shall we say, Lo here, or, Lo there." Then our Lord gave the key to the matter by adding, "Because the Kingdom of Heaven is [to be] in the midst of you." That is to say, when the Kingdom of Heaven shall come it will be *amongst* mankind, everywhere present but wholly invisible; so that they cannot observe it with the natural eye, nor can they point it out or locate it, altho it will be everywhere present amongst men, an omnipresent and omnipotent rule or reign of righteousness. · In our Common Version the true thought is obscured by the words "within you," which would better be "among you." Anyone, however, can see that it could not have been our Lord's intention to say that the Kingdom of God was then or ever would be within the hearts of the class addressed, and which elsewhere he styled "hypocrites, whited walls and sepulchers, full of all manner of corruption."

THAT BORN OF THE SPIRIT IS SPIRIT.

We call to mind also our Lord's explanation of spiritual things to Nicodemus, in which he declared plainly that only those who are born again can either enter into or see the Kingdom of God. (John 3:3, 6.) Nor does this merely refer to the *begetting* of the spirit, as at consecration; it includes also the *birth* of the spirit in resurrection—"born from the dead." The Apostle Paul gives the same assurance, saying, "Flesh and blood [human nature] cannot inherit the Kingdom of God." Hence he informs us that all those who shall be sharers of that heavenly Kingdom must be "changed" from human or flesh conditions to spirit conditions, from weakness to power, from animal to spiritual conditions.—1 Cor. 15 : 42-44.

One matter which more than any other seems to hinder the Lord's people from grasping this subject clearly is the prevalent but mistaken view which is entertained respecting the resurrection of the dead. We shall not attempt to discuss this subject at length here, and we shall omit entirely reference to the world's resurrection, which will be the human conditions, nature, etc.; but it is necessary that we notice something respecting "the first [chief, best, highest] resurrection," which appertains only to Christ Jesus and the Church which is his body—the Kingdom class. These all are sacrificers, who "present their bodies living sacrifices, holy and acceptable to God." In view of this sacrifice of the *human nature,* the gift of God to these in exchange is a *spiritual nature,* and hence they are termed "new creatures." Their exaltation in nature is very high: lifted out of the human nature, which is a little lower than that of angels (the lowest order of spirit beings) they are to be exalted to the nature and likeness of their Lord, "far above angels, principalities and powers," and to be made partakers of the highest form of the spirit nature, namely, the divine nature, with its wonderful peculiarity, namely, immortality, or inherent life.*—2 Pet. 1 : 4.

The one point which more than any other seems to confuse the student of this subject is our Lord's resurrection. They note the fact that he appeared in a

---

*Send for our tract, "The Hope of Immortality,"—samples free.

body of flesh and bones, after his resurrection, and they therefore conclude that he still has a body of flesh and bones bearing all the scars of Calvary; hence, in thinking of his second advent they invariably expect it to be another advent as a human being (in flesh and bones), "a little lower than the angels." These expectations are wrong, as we shall show from the Scriptures. Our Lord after his resurrection was a spirit being, and his manifestations of himself to his disciples in *various* fleshly bodies, then, were similar exactly to manifestations made *before he became the man Christ Jesus*, while he still possessed the glory which he had with the Father before the world was,—the glory of a spirit being. For instance, are we not particularly told that the Lord and two angels appeared as men in bodies of flesh and blood and bones, and in ordinary human garb, to Abraham and Sarah? And the record is that "they did eat and talk with Abraham." On another occasion the Lord appeared to Moses, not in a body of flesh, but "as a flame of fire" in a bush which apparently burned, and from which he spoke to Moses. We contend that such a power to appear in any kind of a body is a power which in the past was considerably used in communicating the divine will to mankind, and that it is only discontinued now because the canon of divine revelation is complete, so that in it the man of God is thoroughly furnished unto every good word and work, and needs no special message or revelations. —2 Tim. 3 : 17.

In reading the narrative of our Lord's appearance to his disciples after his resurrection, the fact seems generally to be overlooked that he appeared only a few times, in all, and that these visits were always brief,

and that between these visits, after the day of his resurrection, there were long periods of days and weeks
in which the disciples saw nothing of him. It is generally overlooked, also, that he appeared in various
forms, one of which was identical with the body that
was crucified, because Thomas had said he would not
believe unless he could have such a demonstration.
Even then our Lord rather upbraided Thomas, assuring him that there was a still greater blessing in store
for those who ask not for such ocular demonstration.
It is generally forgotten that none of the world ever
saw our Lord after his resurrection, but merely his
disciples, to whom, it is said, he *"showed* himself."
This was in harmony with his statement made before
his death, "Yet a little while and the world seeth me
no more."—John 14 : 19.

The change of nature which our Lord experienced
in his resurrection was no less a step upward from the
earthly to the heavenly condition than was the change
of nature which he experienced at his birth a step
downward from the heavenly to the earthly condition,
called *"humbling* himself," laying aside his glory. As
he laid aside the glory of his spirit being to become a
man, so he in turn laid aside his humanity in death in
order to assume the glory and dignity of the divine
nature, "far above." Concerning the change which he
experienced at his resurrection, the Apostle declares,
"God hath *highly exalted* him." It should be manifest
to all that, since our Lord left his rich condition as a
spirit being, and humbled himself and became comparatively poor in the taking of the human nature, that
this was for some particular reason and object, and
that, when that object would be accomplished, the
end

riches of the spiritual condition would be fully restored to him. But instead, the general thought is that
our Lord Jesus not only is encumbered in heaven with
a body of flesh, wholly unsuitable to heavenly conditions, but that in addition to this that body of flesh has
all the marks of mental and physical suffering which
it received through contact with sin and sinners as our
ransom price.

Such a view is dishonoring to the Heavenly
Father, for it should not be supposed that he would
tolerate a loss to all eternity on the part of his well beloved One, because of his faithfulness and obedience
to the divine will. The Scripture declaration is to the
contrary, namely, that our Lord was "made flesh,"
took upon him our nature "*for* the suffering of death;"
and not to be encumbered with fleshly conditions
to all eternity. Besides, if our Lord must bear the
scars of his wounds to all eternity, the implication
would be that his people would also bear all their
blemishes and scars to all eternity. Surely, if such
were the divine arrangement, that which is perfect
would never come, for we should be encumbered with
the imperfect forever.—1 Cor. 13 : 10.

When we get the correct view of this matter, every difficulty and objection ceases. As the Scriptures
declare, so it was, "He was put to death *in flesh,* he
was quickened *in spirit.*" "Tho we have known Christ
after the *flesh,* yet now henceforth know we him no
more [so]." (2 Cor. 5 : 16.) It was at his resurrection
that he became the second Adam—"the last Adam, a
quickening *spirit.*" (1 Cor. 15 : 45.) "Now the Lord
is that *spirit.*" (2 Cor. 3 : 17.) After appearing to his
disciples under various peculiar conditions after his

resurrection, in various bodies, the Lord invariably *vanished,*—as soon as he had communicated to them the appropriate lessons, causing, as they declared, their hearts to burn within them. He appeared in these various forms for two reasons:—

(1) They could best receive his instructions under such conditions, whereas, if he had appeared to them in the glory of his spirit being, and had performed a miracle upon their eyes by which they could have discerned his spiritual glory, they would have been too much affrighted to have benefited by what he would have said.

(2) They were still natural men, not fully begotten of the holy spirit, because Pentecost was not yet come (John 7 : 39), and hence they were unprepared to understand spiritual things; "for the natural man receiveth not the things of the spirit of God, neither can he know [appreciate] them, because they are spiritually discerned."

The Apostle Paul was the only one of the disciples who saw the Lord *"as he is."* He tells us that the Lord's real spiritual presence, so far from being fleshly or human-like, shone with a brightness "above the brightness of the sun at noonday." The effect upon Paul's eyes was serious, and, we may readily believe the effects remained with him to his dying day, notwithstanding the miraculous removal of the callous scales, which permitted him to see, tho indistinctly. Very evidently our Lord's design was to educate his apostles up to the thought of his resurrection, and also to the thought of his resurrection being not to former conditions, limited by the flesh, but to new conditions, in which he (as he had already explained to Nicodemus) could come and go like the wind, and none could know whence he came nor whither he went; he could appear in one body or in another body, or be present with them without their being aware of it, just as "the angel of the Lord encampeth round about them that fear him," yet is invisible to them, because a spirit being.

"WE SHALL BE LIKE HIM, FOR WE SHALL SEE HIM AS HE IS."

When the right conception of our Lord, in his glorified condition, is gained, and when the Apostle's statement is remembered, that his Church shall be like him, and "see him *as he is,*" it is comparatively easy to understand that the entire glorified Church will be as invisible to the world as the Heavenly Father is, and as our Lord Jesus was after his resurrection; and when it is remembered that this Church constitutes the Kingdom of God, the "royal priesthood," which is to rule and bless the world during the Millennial age, our Lord's words to the Pharisees are quite intelligible,— "The Kingdom of God cometh not with observation— neither shall we say, Lo here! or, Lo there! for behold, the Kingdom of God is in the midst of you"—a present but invisible authority, government, rule of righteousness.

THEY KNEW NOT THE TIME OF THEIR VISITATION—LUKE 19 : 44.—

Our Lord reproved the teachers of Israel because they did not discern the signs of the times, because they "knew not the *time* of their visitation." His words imply that their ignorance was a mark of carelessness and unworthiness, and of divine disfavor.

He said: "Ye can discern the face of the sky; how is
it that ye cannot discern the signs of the times?"
There was a reason, and the realization of that reason
might have meant, to some at least, a correction of
it—a drawing near to God to be taught of him. So
now in the time of our Lord's second presence we find
the world largely increasing in wisdom along the various lines, and many hearts in perplexity and wonder-
ment looking for those things which are coming upon
the world, their hearts failing them for fear of the
impending dissolution of the social structure in anarchy, and yet none are so blind respecting the times
in which we live and the great changes impending, as
the leaders of religious thought.

They are blinded by their false theories. They
have declared that the Lord's commission to his
Church is that she should convert the world into a
Kingdom of God, and thus bring about the reign of
righteousness; and they are so determined that their
theories must not fail that they cannot see what is
rapidly becoming apparent even to the worldly, namely, that the numbers even nominally converted every
year are increasing far less, proportionately, than the
natural increase of the world's population: so that if
they had millions of years before them the conversion
could never be hoped for, but in the end of millions
of years true Christianity could not expect to claim as
large a percentage as at present. Their theory also
blinds them to the fact that much of the increase of
Church membership in civilized lands is merely for
popularity's sake, and for the sake of worldly prosperity, social standing, etc., and not the result of love for
God and righteousness, nor significant of a consecra-

tion to walk in the "narrow way" of self-denial, self-sacrifice, etc.

The worldly, therefore, are really in a better condition to discern the signs of the times than many prejudiced nominal Christians. But none can see these things from the *true* standpoint except as they take that standpoint, and it is only granted to those who are fully consecrated to the Lord and who hearken to his Word. These shall not be in darkness. The Lord will not hide from them either his good purposes as respects the blessing of the Church and subsequently of the world, or his purposes respecting the chastisement of the world in a great time of trouble, preparatory to its blessing, after it has been humbled.

"THE DEAD IN CHRIST SHALL RISE FIRST."

The chief work of our Lord during this "harvest" time, and especially in the forepart of it (when he calls his faithful servants of the Gospel age and reckons with them and rewards them), respects his Church as a whole, and not merely its living members. And here we should note the Apostle's statement respecting this time and work. He informs us that the Lord's dealings during this harvest will be first with *"the dead* in Christ," saying, "We which are alive and remain to the coming [presence] of the Lord shall not prevent [precede] them which are asleep [those of the Church already dead],...for the dead in Christ shall rise first." Taking this statement in connection with our Lord's parable, it means that the faithful sleeping in death will· be reckoned with, rewarded, resurrected, before the reckoning with and rewarding of the living members of the Church begins. Accordingly, if it be true, as we have briefly presented it, in the foregoing,—that we are now living "in the days of the Son of Man," and that his *presence* began in the Autumn of 1874, then we should also believe that the resurrection of the saints which "were asleep" was due and took place at some period not long after our Lord's *parousia* began. And we are able to fix upon a date for this with comparative certainty, altho the entire matter is invisible to natural eyes and can be discerned only with the eye of faith and by the light of our lamp, the Scriptures.

Our lamp, as we have already seen, shows us that the Jewish age was in every particular a pattern or illustration of this Gospel age; and keeping this in mind, we can judge something respecting the order of the divine arrangement in the "harvest" of this age, from the order of the divine arrangement in the "harvest" of the Jewish age. Observing the Jewish age, we find that the first three and a half years of their "harvest" were devoted to the simple announcement of the Master's presence, and an offer to the nominal Church then living, and that they ended by the rejection of the nominal Church at the time of our Lord's death; and that afterward while their nominal system or Church was ignored, the Israelites indeed were *called out of it* into fellowship with the Lord, through his spirit. We note also, that it was at the very time of the rejection of the Jewish house that our Lord assumed before them typically his office of King, and rode upon the ass as the King of the Jews: and looking for the time when our Lord, in the end of the age, should assume his full regal power and authority as the King of Kings, we find it should be at the corresponding date in this "harvest," namely, in the Spring of 1878. And as the first work of our Lord, after taking the kingly office, in the typical "harvest," was to reject the nominal house of Israel, that he might begin the work of gathering out of it the Israelites indeed, so we understand that in the present harvest time the first work of our King is the rejection of the nominal Gospel house of sons,—to the intent that he may gather out of it the "wheat," his "elect," from one end of the ecclesiastical heavens to the other. (Matt. 24 : 31.) This rejection of the nominal Church, and the call to his people to "Come out of her," we understand to be symbolically styled the fall of Babylon, and the spewing out of Laodicea. See Rev. 3 : 16-20-22; 18 : 2-4.

Here, then, we have an indication of the time when the judgment of the Lord's servants was due to *begin,* represented in the parable by the king calling to himself his own servants to hear their reports; and in the light of the Apostle's statement just noticed, namely, that the living will not precede those that are asleep, it is clear that at that time, and before the reckoning with the living began, "them that sleep," "the dead in Christ," were awakened, granted a part in the first resurrection—raised in glory, honor, power, spiritual bodies, invisible to mankind. Nor would the resurrection of the spirit bodies necessitate any disturbance of graveyards or tombstones, or anything earthly. "That which is born of the spirit is spirit," and as our Lord after his resurrection was invisible to the world, and invisible also to his Church (except as he miraculously manifested himself), so with these: they are invisible, nor is there any necessity for minaculous manifestation, nor has any been made, neither is any expected. "We walk by faith, and not by sight."

To all who understand the necessity for the sleep of the saints (namely, that it was because the call of the Church took place before the time divinely arranged for the establishment of the Kingdom), it will seem eminently proper that the King should, *immediately* on taking office as King, liberate from the prisonhouse of death his faithful followers, who during his absence manifested their faithfulness, and for whom have been set aside crowns of righteousness, to be given them at his return in power and great glory. It would be unreasonable indeed to suppose any prolonged delay of their resurrection, after our Lord takes to himself his great power and begins his reign. We hold, therefore, that the resurrection of the dead in Christ was due to take place in the Spring of 1878.

Furthermore, we note a beautiful analogy here; for, thus considered, our Lord's resurrection a few days after his taking of office as King in typical Israel corresponds to or parallels the resurrection of the Church, "the body of Christ," a few days after his taking to himself honor and glory and power as the King of nations in the Spring of 1878. Not only so, but the Book of Revelation, in a scene which belongs to that particular time and description of the opening of the "harvest" of this Gospel age, shows "one like unto the Son of Man, having on his head a golden crown and in his hand a sharp sickle," beginning the work of reaping the harvest of this age: and there we find the significant statement, "Blessed are the dead which die in the Lord *from henceforth; yea,* saith the Spirit, that they may rest from their labors, for their works follow them."—Rev. 14 : 13, 16.

This text has been so frequently misapplied by theologians that its true significance will be apt to elude all who have not their senses exercised by reason of use, and who do not closely discriminate. It signifies that from the time of the beginning of the reaping of the "harvest" of this age by the crowned reaper (the Spring of 1878) there will be a wonderful blessing not previously possible, upon the certain class described. From this particular date onward those of this particular class who die will be favored or blessed in a manner in which none of the preceding members of this same class were blessed; namely, in that their death will not interrupt their works, which will continue right along, the labor and weariness alone ceasing, the work itself continuing under more glorious and more favorable conditions.

This means that since 1878 the fully consecrated of the Lord's people, those who are completely "dead with him," will not *sleep in death*, as has been necessary with all the preceding members of the body of Christ throughout the Gospel age: it means that from 1878 onward the dead who die in the Lord will in the moment of dying experience their "change," or share in the first resurrection—in a moment, in the twinkling of an eye, pass from mortality to immortality, from weakness to power, from dishonor to glory, from natural to spiritual condition.

It is to this that the Apostle referred when he said, "Behold, I show you a mystery; we shall not all *sleep*, but we shall all be *changed*, in a moment, in the twinkling of an eye, at the last trump." To our understanding, the last trump, the seventh of the series of symbolical trumpets, began in 1874, just before our Lord took to himself his great power and began its exercise—began his reign: its sound is to continue until the close of the Millennial Age, a thousand years. This "change" in a moment, in the twinkling of an eye, that is to occur to the living members of the body of Christ will indeed be a momentary change as respects each individual after he shall have rendered his accounts before the great King, and been accepted of him as a joint-heir in the Kingdom; but it does not imply that all of these will be changed in a moment. Quite to the contrary, the judging of the living members of the Church, the going in of the wise virgins in the end of this age, will be a gradual work, and has already been in progress for twenty years, and is not yet finished. It will include the rejection of the "foolish virgins," and the utter casting out of any who may take off the "wedding garment" of Christ's righteousness, as shown in one of the parables.

Thus we see that immediately after this taking of the crown in the Spring of 1878, our Lord gathered to himself those of his saints, "his jewels," who had already been polished and fitted and prepared, and who *slept*, awaiting the time for the establishment of the Kingdom; and that since then, one by one, his faithful saints of the same class of "jewels" are being gathered to himself, as they finish their course. But as it was necessary that our Redeemer should not only consecrate his life to death, but that he should actually die, so it is necessary that *every member of the body of Christ* shall not only consecrate himself to be dead with him, but that each also shall actually die. They, are already reckoned dead, but this is not sufficient; our Lord's words are, "Be thou faithful unto *death,* and I will give thee a crown of life," and again, "Blessed are the dead in the Lord [reckonedly dead, consecrated unto death], *dying* from henceforth." So also it had been foretold in other Scriptures, that all who would be of the body of Christ must, like the Head, pass through the portals of death; thus it is written, "I have said, Ye are gods [mighty ones], all of you sons of the Most High; *ye shall* ALL DIE like men, and fall like one of the princes." The two princes of our race were Adam and Christ Jesus. Adam went into death because of disobedience; Christ as a sacrifice for the sins of others, entered death in obedience; and the Church, the body of Christ, his "brethren," being justified out of the Adamic death by faith in his sacrifice, are reckoned as joint-sacrificers with him in *his death* of obedience, that they may be accounted also sharers in *"his resurrection"*—the first resurrection, to the divine nature and glory and joint-heirship.— Psa. 82 : 6; Rom. 5 : 12, 17; 2 Pet. 1 : 4.

We have given here only the briefest possible summary of the Scriptural evidences that we are living in the *parousia*, the presence, "the *days* of the Son of Man," in the "harvest" time of this age, and that the work which he, directly and through his apostles, instructed us to expect is now in progress, namely, the "sealing" of the saints of the Most High God in their foreheads (Eph. 1 : 13, 14), and giving them a mental appreciation of the divine plan and its times and seasons, together with a judgment or testing of all who have covenanted themselves to be the Lord's and to lay down their lives in his service. And all who

refuse to live up to their covenant, even tho sealed and
blessed, and enlightened with present truth, will, we
understand, be rejected from it, and cast again "into outer darkness" with the world, to share in the
great time of trouble coming upon it. We understand
also that the elect number will soon be completed, and
the last one of the class who shall be blessed by the
glorious "change" from mortality to immortality, in
a moment, in the twinkling of an eye, shall soon obtain that blessing, and that then the great time of trouble will fully burst upon the world, and speedily bring
down the high, the lofty and the proud, and prepare
the world for the reign of the Prince of Peace.

Here we have consistency, at least, and harmony
of Scriptures which have never been harmonized in
the past, and which cannot now be harmonized from
any other standpoint or with any other interpretation.
Here we have the spiritual Kingdom of Messiah, with
all power, displacing the spiritual kingdom of Satan,
and establishing order and righteousness through earthly agents of its own, and overthrowing the earthly
agents of the prince of darkness, many of whom are
his servants merely because "the god of this world
[age] has *blinded* the minds of them that believe not."

"THEY WITHOUT US SHALL NOT BE MADE PERFECT."—HEB. 11:40.—

We remark incidentally that following the gathering of the Church to glory, as above outlined, will
come the resurrection of the holy ones of the past,—
"Abraham, Isaac and Jacob, and all the holy prophets," whose resurrection will be to *perfect earthly conditions*, and who shall be the "princes in all the earth,",

seen of men, and representatives of the invisible but all-powerful spiritual Kingdom—the glorified Christ. Thus, chosen representatives of fleshly Israel will indeed rule the world, and bless it, as the representatives and agencies of the Spiritual Israel, and to the standard of the Lord thus set up the nation of Israel will be first to respond.—Psa. 45 : 16; Rom. 11 : 25-31; Zech. 12 : 10.

Our Lord's *parousia* (presence in the world) begun in 1874, will continue till the end of the Millennial age. The word is not applicable merely to a little period of presence at the beginning of the Millennial age: Christ's *parousia* and that of his Church will continue throughout the age. Nor will the *epiphania* and *apokalupsis* be a sudden burst of glorious light; nor do these words signify a visible showing to mankind of the Lord's person, or of the persons of his Church. Let us remember his words, "Yet a little while, and *the world seeth me no more.*" Let us remember also that, as his Church is to be in *his likeness,* so his likeness is declared to be an "express image of the *Father's person;*" it is written that he is the King eternal, immortal, *invisible.* (1 Tim. 1 : 17) Nor will it be any more necessary that the world should see with their natural eyes the Lord and his glorified ones, than that they should see the Heavenly Father: the world will see the earthly representatives of God and of Christ and of Church, when they "*see* Abraham, Isaac, and Jacob and all the holy prophets," for they will be samples of perfect manhood, which is the *earthly image* of the invisible God.

Our Lord's *epiphania* (bright shining) and his *apokalupsis* (unveiling) began shortly after his *parou*

sia began; the bright shining of his presence is now
visible to those who are walking "in the light"—to
those who "are not in darkness with the world." It is
a mental illumination, an illumination to the eyes of
our understandings, and not to our natural eyes. The
eyes of our understanding have been opened to see
him that is invisible to the natural sight. The *epiphania* of our Lord is already affecting the world also,
tho not through the eyes of the understanding, for they
have no eyes for such spiritual things: nevertheless,
the bright shining of the Lord's presence is influencing
and affecting the whole course of the world, through
an increase of knowledge on every subject—specially
noticeable since 1878. Eventually all the blinded shall
have opened eyes of understanding and

"EVERY EYE SHALL SEE HIM."

Many even who are not of the Watchers are noting the signs of our times and are startled, and led to
exclaim, What do these things mean?—This remarkable latter-day advance in science, art and mechanical
invention?—This latter-day discontent in the midst of
plenty and luxury?—This latter-day growth of millionaires and paupers?—This growth of giant corporations of world-wide power and influence?—Why are
national policies and public men and their utterances
and doings criticised (judged) by the masses as never
before?—And what means it that with an apparent
growth in wealth and numbers in all denominations of
Christians there is a growing dissatisfaction, discontent in them all: a growing tendency to criticise the
creeds and the preaching and everything?—How
comes it that nine-tenths of the preachers in all de-

nominations know that their hearers desire a change, and would gladly "move on," if they knew how to better themselves even at smaller salaries?

The Scriptural answer is, The hour of God's judgment is come; the time when "Christendom," political, financial, social and ecclesiastical is being judged—being tried in the divine balances. And the Scriptures declare that she will be found wanting, and will be adjudged unworthy to further administer the affairs of earth, which will be turned over to the elect "little flock," according to the divine promise.—Luke 12:32.

The secret of the matter now is the same as in the Jewish "harvest," which John explained, saying,

"THERE STANDETH ONE AMONG YOU WHOM YOU KNOW NOT."—JOHN 1 : 26.

"Mine eyes can see the glory of the presence of the Lord;
He is trampling out the winepress where the grapes of wrath
    are stored;
I see the flaming tempest of his swift descending sword;
    Our King is marching on.

"I can see his coming judgments as they circle all the earth,
The signs and groanings promised to precede a second birth;
I read his righteous sentence, in the crumbling thrones of
    earth:
    Our King is marching on.

"The Gentile Times are closing, for their kings have had
    their day;
And with them sin and sorrow will forever pass away;
For the tribe of Judah's Lion now comes to hold the sway;
    Our King is marching on."

The
HARP
of GOD

In this book the subject matter of the Bible on ten principal points of teaching is topically arranged and likened to ten strings: Creation, Justice Manifested, the Abrahamic Promise, the Birth of Jesus, the Ransom, Resurrection, Mystery Revealed, Our Lord's Return, Glorification of the Church, Restoration.

This work is specially designed for beginners in Bible Study, and is so arranged and so provided with review questions that both young and older people can use it with ease. Eleven illustrations, 384 pages.

Library Edition, green cloth, gold stamped, 1 x 5 x 7¾ inches, dull finish paper, 75¢.
Pocket Edition, green cloth, thinner paper, ¾ x 4 x 6¾ inches, 50¢; including course of 12 weekly quiz cards, 68¢.

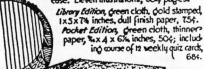

CORROBORATIVE PROOF

Prophecy fulfilled since 1914 shows conclusively the presence of the Lord; that he "whose right it is" to rule has come; that he has taken unto himself his power and begun his reign; that Satan's empire is now under judgment and will shortly forever pass away; that peace will soon be established and restoration blessings offered to the people, and all those who obey the great King under the new order will live and not die. The earth will be a fit habitation for man. The command given by Jesus to his followers is to make known these facts to all who desire to know. He said: "This gospel [good news] of the kingdom shall be preached in all the world for a witness unto all nations, and then shall the end come."—Matthew 24:14.

Prophecy means the foretelling of events to happen. When those events do transpire as foretold, that means fulfilled prophecy. Fulfilled prophecy is otherwise designated as physical facts. Physical facts never stultify themselves. When we see the physical facts exactly fitting that which was foretold in prophecy, we may be sure that these facts now transpired prove conclusively the correctness of the prophecy and the correctness of the interpretation thereof.

Many have honestly believed that no one could know when the Lord would return, basing their conclusions upon the words of Jesus: "But of that day and that hour knoweth no man, no, not the angels which are in heaven, neither the Son, but the Father. Watch therefore; for ye know not what hour your Lord doth come." These words were spoken by Jesus before he was glorified. They do not indicate that he would not know after he

was glorified. We must conclude that he did know from
the time he ascended into heaven. All power in heaven
and in earth was given unto him, as he stated, after
his resurrection. Why would he admonish his followers
to watch unless he expected that some evidence would
be given to them at the time of his appearing by which
they might know of his presence?

The Scriptures show that our Lord's first appearing
would be discerned only by those who were carefully
watching according to the divine Word. He said: "Behold, I come as a thief"—in the night. A thief comes
quietly, stealthily, unobserved. Concerning the time of
his coming St. Paul wrote to those who would be watching: "But of the times and the seasons, brethren, ye
have no need that I write unto you. For yourselves
know perfectly that the day of the Lord so cometh as
a thief in the night. For when they shall say, Peace
and safety; then sudden destruction cometh upon them,
as travail upon a woman with child; and they shall
not escape. But ye, brethren, are not in darkness, that
that day should overtake you as a thief." (1 Thessalonians 5: 1-4) As heretofore set forth, our Lord's second
presence has dated from 1874. Now we wish to give
briefly some corroborative evidence of fulfilled prophecy
—prophecy which has been fulfilled since 1914, which
is apparent to every one who reads, and which conclusively shows his presence at this time.

Our Lord's disciples, looking forward to his return
as the greatest event in history, because it would mark
the establishment of his kingdom shortly thereafter,
propounded to him this question: "Tell us, when shall
these things be? and what shall be the sign [proof] of
thy presence, and of the end of the world?"—Matthew
24: 3.

As we shall show subsequently herein, the gentile

times ended August 1, 1914. Satan became the god of this world with the beginning of the gentile times. With the ending of the gentile times his rulership must begin to pass away. When God took away the dominion from the Jews he said: "I will overturn, overturn, overturn, it, and it shall be no more, until he come whose right it is; and I will give it [to] him." (Ezekiel 21: 27) The one here referred to as he whose right it is to have dominion of the earth is the Lord of heaven, the One who taught his disciples to pray: "Thy kingdom come; thy will be done in earth as it is in heaven." It is reasonable to expect that Satan, the invisible ruler of the nations of earth, would not willingly surrender to the great Messiah. What, then, should be expected immediately to follow the end of the gentile times? The answer is found in Revelation 11: 18, which reads: "The nations were angry, and thy wrath is come." Why did this anger come upon the nations? Because, as the Scriptures answer, "Thou hast taken to thee thy great power and hast reigned."

In answer to the question as to what would be the proof of his presence; and corroborating the statement in the foregoing paragraph, Jesus said to his disciples concerning the same time: "Nation shall rise against nation and kingdom against kingdom." That began exactly on time, August 1, 1914, when the World War began. Even the nations now designate this the World War. It has so crippled the nations of the earth that they can never recover of themselves.

Furthermore, Jesus said that in addition to the war would follow famines, pestilences, and earthquakes in divers places. Since 1914 famine has devastated Russia, much of Austria, and China; and the food shortage and increased cost of living have been felt over the world. Since 1914 the great pestilence of the Spanish influenza swept the earth from the frozen zones of the North to the heated zones of the South, claiming its victims by the millions. The word "earthquake" here used may be taken as literal and symbolic. There have been many literal earthquakes since 1914. The most terrific earthquake in all history is that recorded recently by the *Geographic Magazine* as having occurred in China in December, 1920, in which more than 200,000 people perished.

Earthquake symbolically means an upheaval of social conditions; namely, revolution. In 1917 a great revolution started in Russia. The next year a revolution started in Austria and Germany. A revolution has been fomenting in India and other parts of the British Empire; and already Egypt is lost to Britain. Ireland is lost to Britain and is still in revolution; while revolution threatens all civilization.

In addition to the foregoing we find a great distress and perplexity amongst the ruling powers of the earth. International conference after conference is held to try to patch up the present conditions and bring order out of the chaos produced by the World War. These have not succeeded. Jesus said such would be the condition. "Upon the earth distress of nations, with perplexity; the sea and the waves roaring; men's hearts failing them for fear, and for looking after those things which are coming on the earth; for the powers of heaven shall be shaken." *Sea* here symbolically represents the restless population of earth, the *waves* being that which dashes up against the more solid parts of earth's organization. This is exactly what we see in the constant strikes and labor troubles, the labor and more radical elements being represented by the sea and the waves, roaring against those who are in power. This condition has caused men's hearts to fail them for fear, not knowing what to expect.

Capital has become fearful, investors are timid, building is far behind: and there is a general condition of disturbance and unrest throughout the earth.

What does it mean? It means what the apostle Peter said in discussing the presence of the Lord: "But the day of the Lord will come as a thief in the night; in which the heavens shall pass away with a great noise, and the elements shall melt with fervent heat, the earth [organized society] also and the works that are therein shall be burned up." (2 Peter 3:10) The burning up here represents a destruction that results to organized powers and arrangements; and thus we see it happening.

CHRONOLOGICAL PROOF

The Bible does not set forth in terms understandable by every one just when things shall transpire; but it does set forth in God's own way absolutely accurately when events will occur. The Lord is an accurate timekeeper, and everything happens exactly on time. One who has given himself wholly to the Lord, and who then becomes a careful student of God's Word may ascertain from the Word God's division of time as set forth in the Bible; and understanding this, he will find that it is corroborated by prophecy; and the fulfillment of these foretold things shows the correctness of the calculations as well as the correctness of the prophecy.

The proof herein set forth shows that the Jews, God's chosen people, were chosen and dealt with by Jehovah to the exclusion of all others for the specific purpose (1) of preparing a people, some of whom would be ready to receive the Lord Jesus at his first appearing; and (2) of using them to picture or foreshadow the development of his plan; that because of the unfaithfulness of Israel God pronounced a decree against them foretelling the overthrow of that nation; that this decree was carried into operation; that there followed the establishment of a universal empire by the gentiles in the year 606 B. C.; that God foretold that this period of gentile dominion would be 2520 years; that during that period Satan has been the god of this world, all the world being under his dominion, lying in the wicked one; that the gentile times ended in 1914; and that from 1914 forward God's wrath and judgment have been upon the nations of the earth and will continue until the full and complete establishment of the kingdom by the great King, now present.

These facts, if proven, should give courage and hope to all who seek; for the logical conclusion must be that ere long wicked systems and organizations shall pass away and shall be succeeded by the righteous organizations brought forth and put into operation by the great righteous King of kings and Lord of lords, and that the blessings of life, liberty and happiness to the people shall follow.

The word "gentile" is a term used to distinguish the nations of earth aside from the Jews, the Jews being God's chosen people, with whom he made a covenant. The "gentile times" is a period of time during which the gentiles shall exercise imperial or kingly power over the affairs of earth. God constituted Israel his chosen people above all other peoples. (Exodus 19:6) This favor they were to enjoy, provided they remained obedient to the Lord Jehovah. For their disobedience he permitted them to be punished from time to time, the punishment being inflicted by the other nations. (Judges 3:14; 4:2, 3; 10:7, 8; 13:1) Jehovah warned the nation of Israel that should they fail to profit by these chastisements thus inflicted, he would punish them *seven times.* "If ye will not yet for all this hearken unto me, then I will punish you seven times more for your sins."—Leviticus 26: 18.

A "time." as used in the Scriptures, has reference to a year. cither symbolic or literal. Symbolic time is reckoned according to the lunar year of 360 days. (See A-89.) The rule for counting symbolic time is a day for a year. (Numbers 14: 33. 34; A-91) One *time* being 360 years, seven *times* would be a period of 2520 years.

With Israel God established the true religion, commanding that the people should worship him and have no other god. (Exodus 20: 1-3) Satan, the prince of devils and the ruler of the gentile nations, established with those nations the false religion; and the gentiles were taught to worship devils, symbolized in various forms and images. Jehovah erected a shield for the children of Israel by providing in his law the severest penalty for worshiping devils. Time and time again Israel went off after the false religion, worshiping the demon gods; and for this they were punished.—Leviticus 26: 1-16.

It must be apparent to all careful students that the period of the gentile times would be a period of great punishment to Israel, and that period of time must begin with some specific punishment marking the beginning of the gentile times definitely and must continue for a definite period of seven times, or 2520 years. The question at issue is. When did this period of the gentile times begin and when is the end thereof? These facts cannot be proven by profane history. because such history is made by men who acted as agents of Satan's empire and hence were unreliable; for Satan is the father of lies. (John 8: 44) Let everyone who wishes to be bound by such authority be so; but surely all Christians will want to stand by the Bible.

An absolutely safe rule to follow, therefore, is this: Where the testimony of the Bible is clear and plain, follow that always. Where secular or profane history is corroborated by the Bible, such testimony may be considered for what it is worth as cumulative evidence. Where secular or profane history is contrary to the Bible, follow it never.—Romans 4: 3.

We now propose to prove that the gentile times, a period of 2520 years, began in the year 606 B. C. and ended in the fall of the year 1914; and that the ouster proceedings began promptly thereafter and on time. In making this proof we rely upon the Bible and not upon secular or profane history. We consider the points in the order numbered hereinafter, as follows, to wit:

POINT I: TENURE OF KINGS

The time and duration of the reign of the various kings of Israel is one of the Biblical methods of establishing the various dates in our chronology. Saul, Israel's first king, began to reign in the year A. M. 3009. The total period of the tenure of the kings of Israel was, to wit, 513 years. The reign of the kings ended with the year A. M. 3522. No careful Bible students will dispute these facts. No other conclusion can be reached except by juggling the figures and ignoring the Bible statements.

We here insert the figures taken from the undisputed prophecies of the Scriptures showing the tenure of the kings of Israel; and by this means we are able to get an absolutely certain date from which to start in our calculation. We give these figures both in B. C. and A. M. time in parallel columns. Saul was the first king of Israel. His reign began in the year 3009 A. M., and continued for a period of 40 years. All the kings of Israel and the time of their reign are set forth as follows:

King	Years Reigned	Citation		Reign Ended A.M.	B.C.
Saul	40	Acts 13:21		3049	1079
David	40	1 Chron. 29:27		3089	1039
Solomon	40	2 Chron. 9:30		3129	999
Rehoboam	17	"	12:13	3146	982
Abijah	3	"	13:2	3149	979
Asa	41	"	16:13	3190	938
Jehoshaphat	25	"	20:31	3215	913
Jehoram	8	"	21:20	3223	905
Ahaziah	1	"	22:2	3224	904
Athaliah	6	"	22:12	3230	898
Jehoash	40	"	24:1	3270	858
Amaziah	29	"	25:1	3299	829
Uzziah	52	"	26:3	3351	777
Jotham	16	"	27:1	3367	761
Ahaz	16	"	28:1	3383	745
Hezekiah	29	"	29:1	3412	716
Manasseh	55	"	33:1	3467	661
Amon	2	"	33:21	3469	659
Josiah	31	"	34:1	3500	628
Jehoiakim	11	"	36:5	3511	617
Zedekiah	11	"	36:11	3522	606

The year 3522 A. M. corresponds to B. C. 606, which marks the end of Zedekiah's reign; and hence the beginning of the gentile dominion.

The beginning of the reign of Jehoiakim, being definitely fixed, gives us a starting point from which to count the time and by which to determine the universal reign of Nebuchadnezzar and to reach a proper conclusion relative to the gentile times.

The first year of the reign of Nebuchadnezzar, king of Babylon, was the fourth year of the reign of Jehoiakim. "The fourth year of Jehoiakim the son of Josiah king of Judah, that was the first year of Nebuchadnezzar king of Babylon." (Jeremiah 25:1; see also

Jeremiah 46: 2) Since Jehoiakim's reign began in 628 B. C., it follows that the first year of Nebuchadnezzar's reign was the year 625 B. C. There was no attack made upon Jehoiakim by Nebuchadnezzar in the year of 625 B. C., the first year of Nebuchadnezzar's reign. There could have been no attack as a king made by him earlier than that. It was in the fourth year of Jehoiakim's reign and the first year of Nebuchadnezzar's reign, to wit, the year 625 B. C., that the prophet Jeremiah delivered the divine decree pointing out that it was God's determination to leave the land of Palestine desolate as a punishment upon Israel.

In the fourth year of the reign of Nebuchadnezzar (and therefore the eighth year of the reign of Jehoiakim), Nebuchadnezzar made his first attack against Jerusalem; and in that year Jehoiakim became the servant or vassal to the king of Babylon. Three years later, to wit, in the year 617 B. C., the same being the eleventh year of the reign of Jehoiakim, Nebuchadnezzar took Jehoiakim a prisoner and put him to death. The record reads: "Jehoiakim was twenty and five years old when he began to reign [628 B. C.] ; and he reigned eleven years [617 B. C.] in Jerusalem .... In his days Nebuchadnezzar king of Babylon came up, and Jehoiakim became *his servant three years:* then he turned and rebelled against him [Nebuchadnezzar]." (2 Kings 23: 36; 24: 1) "Against him [Jehoiakim] came up Nebuchadnezzar king of Babylon. and bound him in fetters, to carry him to Babylon."—2 Chronicles 36: 6.

The carrying away of Jehoiachin to Babylon was in the year 617 B.C. Jehoiakim's reign having begun in 628 B. C., and he having reigned eleven years, necessarily it ended in 617 B. C. At that time Nebuchadnezzar was in the eighth year of his reign. Thus the Scriptures prove beyond any question of a doubt that the captivity did not begin in the first year of Nebuchadnezzar's reign; nor did the desolation begin there. It is therefore seen that it is utterly impossible for the gentile times to have begun in the first year of Nebuchadnezzar's reign, to wit, 625 B. C. No one claims that the gentile times began in 617 B. C., the year Jehoiakim was taken and put to death, as indeed such a claim could not be successfully made in view of the evidence hereinafter set forth.

It is reasonable to suppose that the Jewish historian Josephus, being deeply interested in his own people, would be more reliable in fixing dates than would the historians of the gentile nations. We do not at all need the testimony of Josephus, but because it is corroborated by the Bible we cite it here for what it is worth. He plainly states that no attack was made upon Jerusalem at the beginning of Nebuchadnezzar's reign. We quote from "Antiquities of the Jews," Book X, Chapter VI, pages 365-367.

"In the fourth year of Jehoiakim, one whose name was Nebuchadnezzar took the government over the Babylonians; who at the same time went up with a great army to the city Carchemish, which was at Euphrates; upon a resolution that he had taken to fight with Necho king of Egypt, under whom all Syria then was. And when Necho understood the intention of the king of Babylon, and that this expedition was made against him, he did not despise his attempt; but made haste with a great band of men to Euphrates, to defend himself from Nebuchadnezzar. And when they had joined battle he was beaten, and lost many thousands of his soldiers. So the king of Babylon passed over the Euphrates, and took all Syria, as far as Pelusium, *excepting Judea*. But when Nebuchadnezzar had already reigned four years, which was the eighth of Jehoiakim's government over the Hebrews, the king of Babylon made an expedition with mighty forces against the Jews, and required tribute of Jehoiakim; threatening upon his refusal to make war against him. He was affrighted at his threatening, and bought his peace with money: and brought the tribute he was ordered to bring for three years.

"But on the third year, upon hearing that the king of Babylon made an expedition against the Egyptians, he did not pay his tribute. . . .

"A little time afterward, the king of Babylon made an expedition against Jehoiakim, who received him into the city; and this out of fear of the foregoing predictions of Jeremiah, as supposing he should suffer nothing that was terrible: because he neither shut the gates, nor fought against him. Yet when he was come into the city, he did not observe the covenants he had made; but he slew such as were in the flower of their age, and such as were of the greatest dignity; together with their king Jehoiakim, whom he had commanded to be thrown before the walls, without any burial and made his son Jehoiachin king of the country, and of the city; he also took the principal persons in dignity for captives, three thousand in number, and led them away to Babylon. Among these was the prophet Ezekiel, who was then but young. And this was the end of king Jehoiakim, when he had lived thirty-six years, and reigned eleven. But he was succeeded in the kingdom by Jehoiachin, whose mother was Nehusta, a citizen of Jerusalem. He reigned three months and ten days."

Jehoiachin reigned only three months and ten days, and was succeeded by Zedekiah, whose reign began in the year 617 B. C. "Jehoiachin was eight years old when he began to reign, and he reigned three months and ten days in Jerusalem: and he did that which was evil in the sight of the Lord. And when the year was expired, king Nebuchadnezzar sent, and brought him to Babylon, with the goodly vessels of the house of the Lord, and made Zedekiah, his brother, king over Judah and Jerusalem. Zedekiah was one and twenty years old when he began to reign, and reigned eleven years in Jerusalem." (2 Chronicles 36: 9-11) Thus it is clearly seen that the reign of Zedekiah, which began in 617 B. C., lasted eleven years and ended in 606 B. C. He was the last king of Israel.

POINT II: DECREE FOR PUNISHMENT

A decree means a judicial determination by one having authority, defining what must be done. It means a sentence pronounced that must be enforced. Necessarily decrees are always entered before they are enforced. Jehovah pronounced through Moses a divine decree or judgment that should be enforced against Israel as a punishment, and the decree is in these words: "I will make your cities waste, and bring your *sanctuaries unto desolation,* and I will not smell the savor of your sweet odors. And I will bring the *land into desolation:* and your enemies which dwell therein shall be astonished at it."—Leviticus 26: 31, 32.

It must be conceded by all that the taking of certain of the Israelites as prisoners and carrying them away to Babylon would not constitute an enforcement of this decree. The putting to death of Jehoiakim in no wise fulfilled the decree. Besides after his death Zedekiah continued to be king of Israel and reigned for eleven years. Surely during those eleven years the city was not in waste; nor were the sanctuaries in desolation. Surely during that time the Jews offered their sacrifices in Jerusalem. When, then, in all the history of Israel do we find any record of the enforcement of this divine decree? The Scriptures answer that it had its fulfillment in the latter part of the reign of Zedekiah.

God had restated the decree of judgment against Israel through Jeremiah. Concerning Zedekiah, the last king, we read: "He did that which was evil in the sight of the Lord his God, and humbled not himself before Jeremiah the prophet speaking from the mouth of the Lord. And he also rebelled against king Nebuchadnezzar. . . . They mocked the messengers of God, and

81

despised his words, and misused his prophets, until the
wrath of the Lord arose against his people. . . . Therefore he brought upon them the king of the Chaldees
[Nebuchadnezzar], who slew their young men with the
sword in the house of their sanctuary, and had no compassion upon young man or maiden, old man, or him
that stooped for age: he gave them all into his hand.
And all the vessels of the house of God, great and small,
and the treasures of the house of the Lord, and the
treasures of the king, and of the princes; all these he
brought to Babylon. And they *burnt the house of God,
and brake down the wall of Jerusalem,* and burnt all
the palaces thereof with fire, and destroyed all the
goodly vessels thereof. And them that had escaped from
the sword carried he away to Babylon; where they were
servants to him and his sons until the reign of the
kingdom of Persia: to fulfill the word of the Lord by
the mouth of Jeremiah, until the land had enjoyed
her sabbaths: for *as long as she lay desolate she kept
sabbath,* to fulfill threescore and ten years."—2 Chronicles 36: 12, 13, 16-21.

NO CAPTIVITY BEFORE 617 B. C.

This occurred at the end of the reign of Zedekiah, to
wit, in the year 606 B. C.

In corroboration of this we cite the further record
dealing with the same subject matter, made by Ezekiel
the prophet. Ezekiel counts the time mentioned in his
prophecy from the date that he and other Jews were
taken captive and carried away to Babylon. (Ezekiel
1: 1, 8: 1; 20: 1) This captivity began in the year
617 B. C. In the seventh year of that captivity, in the
fifth month and the tenth day of the month, to wit,
about the first day of August, 610 B. C., which was
the fifteenth year of the reign of Nebuchadnezzar, the

divine decree for the punishment of Israel was restated
in other phrase by the prophet Ezekiel.—Ezekiel 20:1.

The same judicial determination of Jehovah as set
forth in Leviticus 26:31-33 was restated by Ezekiel
in the following words: "Therefore thus saith the Lord
God: Because ye have made your iniquity to be remembered, in that your transgressions are discovered, so
that in all your doings your sins do appear; because, I
say, that ye are come to remembrance, ye shall be taken
with the hand. And thou, profane and wicked prince of
Israel, whose day is come, when iniquity shall have an
end, thus saith the Lord God: Remove the diadem, and
take off the crown; this shall not be the same: exalt
him that is low, and abase him that is high. I will
overturn, overturn, overturn it; and it shall be no more,
until he come whose right it is; and I will give it [to]
him." —Ezekiel 21:24-27.

This restatement of the divine decree occurred four
years before its enforcement. The enforcement of this
divine decree marks the beginning of the gentile times.

GENTILE TIMES BEGAN 606 B. C.

God had promised that the sceptre should not depart
from Judah nor a lawgiver from between his feet until
Shiloh come. (Genesis 49:10) It will be observed that
the decree of punishment did not include the removal
of the sceptre. It merely states: "Remove the diadem,
take off the crown." The crown is a symbol of imperial dominion or rulership; while the sceptre is a
symbol of imperial authority or right. The enforcement
of this divine decree, therefore, took away from Israel
the dominion, which dominion should be enjoyed by
the gentiles until the coming of him whose right it is,
namely, Shiloh, the Messiah. The gentile times, therefore, could not possibly begin until the enforcement of

this divine decree. (Ezekiel 21: 24-27) And since it was pronounced by the prophet Ezekiel while Zedekiah was the king, it conclusively proves that the gentile times did not begin with the captivity of Jehoiakim or of Jehoiachin, but did begin with the overthrow of Zedekiah.

About August 1, 606 [606⅔] B. C., Nebuchadnezzar the king of Babylon broke down the city of Jerusalem and destroyed it, took Zedekiah and put out his eyes, and desolated the city and the land. (Jeremiah 39: 2-9) Thus from another line of proof is definitely established that the divine decree was enforced in 606 B. C., ending the dominion of Israel and permitting the gentiles to establish a *universal* dominion. Here, at this time, it was that Jehovah, figuratively speaking, withdrew from the stage of action and permitted Satan, through his representative, Nebuchadnezzar, to establish a universal empire. Here it was that Satan became the 'god of the whole world'; and from that time forward his rule through earthly representatives is symbolized by a wild beast.

POINT III: DISCREPANCY EXPLAINED

Opponents attempt to show that the divine decree against Israel began to be enforced in the year of the reign of Jehoiakim, and cite as authority Daniel 1: 1, which reads: "In the third year of the reign of Jehoiakim king of Judah came Nebuchadnezzar king of Babylon unto Jerusalem, and besieged it." A careful examination of this text at once shows that there is a discrepancy. In the third year of Jehoiakim's reign, as we have heretofore seen, Nebuchadnezzar was *not yet king* of Babylon. He did not become king until a year later (Jeremiah 25:1); and the plain Scriptural statements heretofore cited show that Nebuchadnezzar's first attack against Jerusalem began in the eighth year of the reign of Jehoiakim. Hence it was impossible for him to attack in the third year of Jehoiakim's reign.

The proper and reasonable explanation of this Scripture (Daniel 1:1) is this: That the "third year" here means the third year of the vassalage of Jehoiakim to Nebuchadnezzar; or "the third year of Jehoiakim [as vassal king]." It is plainly stated in the Scriptures, as heretofore set forth, that in the eighth year of the reign of Jehoiakim as king, Nebuchadnezzar came against him and Jehoiakim became his servant and paid tribute to Nebuchadnezzar *three years* and then rebelled against him. (2 Kings 24:1) Therefore, it was exactly three years later the beginning of his vassalage, to wit, the year 617 B. C., that Nebuchadnezzar besieged Jerusalem and took Jehoiakim, and at the same time carried away the prophets Daniel, Ezekiel, and others, including Hananiah, Mishael, and Azariah, whose names were changed by the king to Shadrach, Meshach, and Abed-nego, respectively. Daniel wrote his prophecy while he was in Babylon; and it is quite apparent that he counted time from the date of the beginning of the vassalage of Jehoiakim as king. Manifestly, then, the argument of opponents that the gentile times began during the reign of Jehoiakim must fall.

POINT IV: NEBUCHADNEZZAR'S DREAM

Again, opponents state that the beginning of the gentile times is marked by the accession of Nebuchadnezzar to the throne of Babylon, and in support of this contention cite Daniel 2:1. This argument must likewise fall.

Daniel 2:1 reads: "In the second year of the reign of Nebuchadnezzar, Nebuchadnezzar dreamed dreams, wherewith his spirit was troubled, and his sleep brake from him." The dream itself is set forth in verses 31 to 35 of the same chapter. Nebuchadnezzar the king had brought before him magicians, astrologers, sorcerers, and Chaldeans to interpret his dream, and all of them failed. "Then Arioch [the captain of the king's guard] brought in Daniel before the king in haste, and said thus unto him, I have found a man of the captives of Judah, that will make known unto the king the interpretation. The king answered and said to Daniel, whose name was Belteshazzar, Art thou able to make known unto me the dream which I have seen, and the interpretation thereof?"—Daniel 2:25, 26.

It is utterly impossible for this transaction to have occurred in the second year of the reign of Nebuchadnezzar for the following reasons, to wit: (1) because Daniel, in the second year of Nebuchadnezzar, was *not in Babylon and could not then have been taken before the king;* (2) because he was taken to Babylon in the year 617 B. C., which was the eighth year of the reign of Nebuchadnezzar; and (3) because Daniel was not permitted to appear before the king until after he had been in Babylon *three* years, according to his own testimony.

The facts heretofore set forth definitely establish the correctness of the reasons (1) and (2). We proceed to the examination of (3):

In the eighth year of his reign Nebuchadnezzar carried away to Babylon many of the Jews, among whom were Daniel and the three Hebrew children. The king gave an order unto Ashpenaz, the master of his eunuchs, that he should bring certain of these Israelites "in whom was no blemish, but well favored, and skilful in all wisdom, and cunning in knowledge, and understanding science, and such as had ability in them to stand in the king's palace, and whom they might teach the learning and the tongue of the Chaldeans." In other words, those so selected were to be educated and trained. "And the king appointed them a daily provision of the king's meat, and of the wine which he drank; so nourishing them *three years*, that *at the end thereof* they might *stand before the king*. Now among these were of the children of Judah, Daniel, Hananiah, Mishael, and Azariah. Now *at the end of these days* [to wit, three years] that the king had said that he should bring them in, then the prince of the eunuchs brought them in before Nebuchadnezzar. And the king communed with them; and among them all was found none like Daniel, Hananiah, Mishael, and Azariah: *therefore stood they before the king*."—Daniel 1: 3-6, 18, 19.

DATE OF DREAM WAS 614 B. C.

According to the king's decree, this transaction of Daniel's standing before the king could not have occurred until the end of the three years of instruction, which was to wit, in the year 614 B. C. and in the eleventh year of the reign of Nebuchadnezzar. Evidently it was about one year thereafter that Nebuchadnezzar had the dream in question.

Now to remove all doubt as to the correctness of this conclusion, we find that the *Variorum* rendering of this text (Daniel 2: 1) is: "And in the *twelfth* year of the reign of Nebuchadnezzar, Nebuchadnezzar dreamed dreams," etc. The circumstantial evidence produced by Daniel himself proves that the *Variorum* rendering is correct.

The explanation of Daniel 2: 37, therefore, is that in the interpretation he told the king in substance that Jehovah had determined that he (Nebuchadnezzar) should be the head of the image observed. We are not left to guess about matters of this kind; for the apostle Paul plainly says that God "calleth those things

which be not as though they were." (Romans 4:17)
Otherwise stated, Jehovah had determined that Nebuchadnezzar should occupy this position; but at that
particular time Zedekiah was the king, had been king for
three years, and reigned thereafter eight years before
Nebuchadnezzar really assumed the position as head of
the image.

POINT V: REIGN OF CYRUS

The argument hereinbefore made proves that the
gentile times as a period is based upon the tenure of
office of the Jewish Kings. This evidence shows that it
was the year 606 B. C. when the crown (power to exercise dominion) was taken from Israel, and a gentile
king permitted to exercise that power. Now we introduce another line of proof by beginning at a later fixed
date and counting back, measuring the time by unim-
peachable Biblical testimony, which also shows the beginning of the gentile times to be 606 B. C. The latter
line of proof is a complete corroboration of the former.

God had foretold through his prophet Isaiah (see
chapters 44 and 45) that the kingdom of the Babylonians under Nebuchadnezzar would be overthrown and
that then Israel would be returned to her own land.
The Lord's prophet even named the victorious king,
Cyrus. The date of the beginning of the reign of Cyrus
therefore becomes important.

The reign of Cyrus is shown by the testimony of
many secular or profane historians. This testimony is
here cited for two reasons: (1) because there is scarcely
a doubt about the correctness of the date as stated; and
(2) because the date is corroborated by the Scriptural
proof. Hence the secular history may be used as cumulative testimony under the rule. We give below a number of these authorities.

Smith's "Bible Dictionary," under the title "Captivities of the Jews," pages 99 and 100, says: "The Babylonian captivity was brought to a close by the decree of Cyrus, B. C. 536."

"Bible Comments" (Jamison, Faucett and Brown), Vol. 1, page 288, gives the date of the reign of Cyrus and the issuing of the decree as 536 B. C.

"Swinton's History," page 40, gives 536 B. C. as the date of the edict of Cyrus for the return of the Jews.

"Historians' History of the World," Vol. 2, page 27, gives 536 B. C. as the date of the decree of Cyrus for the return of the Jews.

"Universal Encyclopedia," Vol. 6, page 145, gives 536 B. C. as the date of the reign of Cyrus.

Sanford's "Concise Cyclopedia of Religious Knowledge," page 471, gives the date of the beginning of Cyrus' reign as 536 B. C.

In the Scriptures we read: "Now, in the first year of Cyrus king of Persia, that the word of the Lord spoken by the mouth of Jeremiah might be accomplished the Lord stirred up the spirit of Cyrus king of Persia, that he made a proclamation throughout all his kingdom, and put it also in writing, saying, Thus saith Cyrus king of Persia, All the kingdoms of the earth hath the Lord God of heaven given me; and he hath charged me to build him an house in Jerusalem, which is in Judah. Who is there among you of all his people? The Lord his God be with him, and let him go up." (2 Chronicles 36: 22, 23) "Then rose up the chief of the fathers of Judah and Benjamin, and the priests, and the Levites, with all them whose spirit God had raised, to go up to build the house of the Lord which is in Jerusalem. . . . . Also Cyrus the king brought forth

the vessels of the house of the Lord, which Nebuchadnezzar had brought forth out of Jerusalem . . . . . All
these did Sheshbazzar bring up with them of the captivity that were brought up from Babylon unto Jerusalem." (Ezra 1:5, 7, 11) "And when the seventh
month was come and the children of Israel were in the
cities, the people gathered themselves together as one
man to Jerusalem . . . . They gave money also unto the
masons, and to the carpenters; and meat, and drink,
and oil, unto them of Zidon, and to them of Tyre, to
bring cedar trees from Lebanon to the sea of Joppa,
according to the grant that they had of Cyrus king of
Persia."—Ezra 3:1, 7; see also Ezra·5:12-14.

This Scriptural proof shows that the Jews' captivity
to Babylon ended with the first year of the reign of
Cyrus; and the secular historians above cited show that
that year was 536 B. C. In the next succeeding point
will be observed the Scriptural proof showing that the
date 536 B. C. is correct, which proof also shows that
the date 606 B. C. is the beginning of the gentile times.

POINT VI: DESOLATION NOT CAPTIVITY

Much confusion has resulted from using the words
captivity, servitude, and desolation as synonymous
terms. The Jews were in captivity more than once and
for different periods of time; but there was only *one*
period of desolation. It is true that the Jews were in
captivity during the period of desolation, but such captivity was merely incidental to the desolation. Their
first captivity to Nebuchadnezzar began in the year
617 B. C., and not until eleven years thereafter was
the land made desolate, without an inhabitant. What
God intended for us to understand must be determined
by the language employed in the decree for the punish-

ment of Israel. Therein he said: "I will make your
cities waste, and bring your sanctuaries unto *desolation,* and I will not smell the savor of your sweet odors.
And I will bring the land into *desolation;* and your
enemies which dwell therein shall be astonished at it."
(Leviticus 26: 31, 32) Time and again the Lord restated the decree through the mouth of Jeremiah: "I
will make Jerusalem heaps, and a den of dragons; and
I will make the cities of Judah *desolate,* without an inhabitant." (Jeremiah 9: 11; see also Jeremiah 33: 10;
34: 32) As therefore seen, this divine decree was enforced with the overthrow of Zedekiah 606 B. C.

The period of this desolation of the land is fixed by
the Scriptures as seventy years. The purpose of the enforcement of the divine decree as set forth in 2 Chronicles 36: 18-20 was "to fulfill the word of the Lord by
the mouth of Jeremiah, until the land had enjoyed her
sabbaths; for as long as she *lay desolate* she kept sabbath, to fulfill *threescore and ten years."* (Verse 21)
The prophet Jeremiah had said: "This whole land shall
be a desolation, and an astonishment; and these nations
shall serve the king of Babylon seventy years."—Jeremiah 25: 11.

DESOLATE FOR SEVENTY YEARS

The proof heretofore adduced shows that the reign of
Cyrus began in the year 536 B. C.; and that the first
year of his reign marked the end of the desolation of
the land, in which year he issued a decree for the rebuilding of Jerusalem. The Scriptures cited show that
this period of desolation was to be seventy years in
duration. Counting back, then, seventy years from 536
B. C. brings us to 606 B. C., completely corroborating
the other line of proof showing that 606 B. C. is the

date when the crown was removed from ral. when the desolation began, and when the gentile times began.

Incidentally, here we remark that much has been said about the *nineteen years* of the reign of Nebuchadnezzar before the overthrow of Zedekiah; and an attempt is made to show that this indicates that there is a parallel of nineteen years to be fulfilled with reference to the close of the gentile times and the complete fall of gentile governments. There is absolutely no justification for any such conclusion. It is not warranted by reason, nor by Scripture. The nineteen years have nothing whatsoever to do with the gentile times, their beginning. their end, or with the overthrow of governments. It has been injected merely to confuse the minds of some. We might as well say that because a cat has "nine lives" it would take nine years to kill all the cats, as to say that, because Nebuchadnezzar reigned nineteen years before he overthrew Zedekiah, therefore the overthrow of gentile dominion would be nineteen years after 1914. The argument is unreasonable, unscriptural, and nonsensical.

Upon all the evidence there cannot be the slightest doubt about the gentile times. The lease of universal dominion to the gentiles could not begin as long as there was a vestige of God's typical kingdom. It matters not when the heathen king Nebuchadnezzar began his reign. The nineteen years of his reign so much spoken of are wholly immaterial. foreign to the issue. The possession and exercise of imperial dominion by Israel, symbolized by the crown, ceased when that crown was removed, to wit, when the last ruler of Israel was dethroned. That occurred in 606 B. C. There the dominion of the whole world was left in the hands of the gentiles. which date is by every line of proof fixed as 606 B. C. There the period of gentile

dominion began. Being seven symbolic times in duration, to wit, 2520 years, it ended in 1914 A. D.

But, say those who oppose, what has happened to
show that the gentile times have ended? Are not the
gentile governments still exercising ruling power? Are
not things going on as they were from the beginning?

We answer: Everything has happened that the Lord
foretold would happen. With the close of the (Jewish)
year 1914, he whose right it is took unto himself his
great power and began his reign; the nations were angry, and the day of God's wrath began.—Ezekiel 21:
27; Revelation 11: 17, 18.

GENTILE TIMES ENDED IN 1914

If the contention of opponents concerning chronology is right, then everything that occurred in 1914 and
since must be disregarded as evidence of Messiah's
kingdom. It is admitted by them that the tenure of
office of Israel's kings must be changed in order to
agree with some historians who were agents of Satan.
Such a change would put out of joint all our chronology, and destroy the value of the dates 1874, 1878,
1881, 1910, 1914, and 1918. Such would be equivalent
to saying. "Where is the proof of his presence?" "My
Lord delayeth his coming."—2 Peter 3: 4; Matthew
24: 48.

Is any Christian so blind that he cannot see what
happened in 1914 and thereafter, evidencing the end
of the gentile times? By way of illustration: A tenant
holds a piece of property under a lease, which lease expires January 1, 1914. The tenant refuses to vacate.
The landlord, in order legally to obtain possession,
must institute ouster proceedings. God granted to the
gentiles a lease of dominion for a term of 2520 years,

which term or lease ended about August, 1914. Then
came forward the Landlord, the rightful Ruler (Ezekiel 21: 27), and began ouster proceedings. It is not
to be expected that he would suddenly wipe everything
out of existence, for that is not the way the Lord does
things; but that he would overrule the contending
elements, causing these to destroy the present order;
and that while this is going on he would have his faithful followers give a tremendous witness in the world,
so that the teachable people might recognize the
hideousness of Satan's empire and the blessedness
offered by the Messianic empire, to the end that many
of these might be brought through the trouble and be
ready for the restoration blessings that are to follow.

To this end, exactly on time, the ouster proceedings
began in the World War, followed quickly by famine,
pestilence, and revolution, the rehabilitation of Palestine by the Jews, persecution of Christians in various
parts of the earth, offenses amongst those who claim to
be Jesus' followers, while the love of many waxed cold.
All of these things Jesus stated would constitute a trying time, a trial of faith and patience, which would be
so severe that only 'he that endureth to the end should
be saved.' (Matthew 24: 7-13) While these ouster proceedings are in progress, he commands his followers to
tell the people that Satan's empire has ended; that the
gentile times have ended; that the world has ended, and
here is the proof of it; that the kingdom of heaven is
at hand; that the time of restoration is here; that millions now living will never die; and that "this gospel
[good news] of the kingdom shall be preached in all
the world as a witness unto all nations, and then shall
the end come."

Jesus said: "When these things begin to come to
pass, look up, and lift up your heads." Seeing, then,

divine prophecy in our time so plainly fulfilled 'that there can be no doubt, let every one who has hope for a better order of things look up to the Lord with thanksgiving that the day of deliverance is here. Long have the people waited for it. Happy will be their portion when the kingdom of righteousness is in full sway and the blessings of the Lord are upon all who love his way and strive to do it. Not only does it mean the early deliverance of the church, but it also means the full establishment of peace, prosperity, happiness and life everlasting.

For centuries honest men and women have desired the establishment of a government of righteousness, in which crime and wickedness are unknown; a government which will administer equal and exact justice to all and special privileges to none; a government in which merit and not might is rewarded; a government the action of which is prompted by a loving desire to render good unto all. Of such a kingdom or government the prophets of old wrote and the Psalmist sang. It was for this kingdom or government Jesus taught his followers to pray. Behold, it is now at the door! The present disorder and distress and suffering in the earth are but the natural sequence of an unrighteous order passing away, preparatory for the complete establishment of this kingdom of righteousness. Let every one, then, who comes to a knowledge of this fact herald the good news to his neighbor that deliverance is nigh, that hope may be planted in the breasts of the people, and that they may be quick to receive and enjoy the blessings that the Lord has in store for them.

THE STANDARD FOR THE PEOPLE

Peace
Prosperity
Life
Liberty
Health
Happiness
MAN'S HEART DESIRE

THE STANDARD FOR THE PEOPLE

A heart-cheering message from the Bible for all
peoples of good will.

Written by

J. F. RUTHERFORD
President of the
International Bible Students Association

Also the author of

"The Harp of God"
"Comfort for the Jews"
"Millions Now Living Will Never Die!"
"A 'Desirable Government"
"World Distress—Why?"
"Comfort for the People"
etc., etc.

PRINTED IN U. S. A.

Published by
INTERNATIONAL BIBLE STUDENTS ASSOCIATION
BROOKLYN, N. Y., U. S. A.
Copyrighted 1926

The Standard for the People

MILLIONS of people on earth honestly and sincerely desire to rally to that standard which will guarantee to them security from harm and bring to them lasting blessings. They are greatly perplexed because not knowing to which standard they should rally. My purpose is to direct the attention of the people to the divine standard. Knowing and following the truth will lead the people into freedom. I am convinced that the time has come for the people to understand the truth.

There is a common enemy who has for centuries blinded the people to the truth. The evidence at hand proves conclusively that the enemy shall soon be shorn of his power and shall not be permitted to further deceive mankind.

The great Creator made of one blood all the peoples that dwell upon the earth. The real interest of one is the interest of all. When the people come to know this and then learn to walk in the right way, there will be no more wars; and no longer will right be determined by might. The earth then will be a fit place upon which to live. The great God made the earth for man to dwell upon in happiness. The time must come when man will enjoy the full possession of these divine provisions. The fact that there is a way provided for man to receive that which he desires would do him no good, however, unless he knew about it. For this reason the first essential is knowledge.

All the peoples on earth may be divided into two general classes, to wit: the rulers and the ruled. The masses compose the latter class. Those composing the

3

ruling class are properly divided into three parts, to wit: commercial, political, and religious. The personnel of the ruling class changes from time to time by some of the ruled being transferred to the position of rulers. There is seldom a change, however, in the disposition of those who rule. When one is transferred from the ruled to the ruling class it is easy for his disposition to undergo a change. Selfishness and self-interest is the real cause for this change. But this selfishness is induced largely by the influence of the common enemy hereinafter mentioned.

There is frequently a clash between the rulers and the ruled. Under right conditions this should not be so. Their interest should be mutual and identical. The masses of the people desire peace, prosperity, health, liberty, life and happiness. For centuries man has actually experienced war, poverty, sickness, restraint, sorrow and death. During all the centuries there has been a constant effort on the part of the people to overcome these difficulties to the end that they might have and enjoy their heart's desire.

A standard is that which marks a rallying place and directs the course of action the people should take. It serves as a guide to lead the people in the way they may go. The ruling class possess the desire to keep the people in subjection and under control. To accomplish the desired purpose there is held before the people certain standards or guides, and the people are called upon to rally to these; and it is represented to them that by so doing their best interests will be conserved and that ultimately they will reach their heart's desire. These standards have been different at different times.

The standard of the commercial element bears this inscription: "Give us greater wealth and power, and

we will improve conditions and make the earth a fit
place to live on. We provide all the great labor-saving
devices, the means of rapid transit, and means of
education; and therefore we should guide the people."

The political element inscribes upon its standard this:
"We possess superior qualifications for ruling. We
organize and maintain governments. We enact and enforce wholesome laws. We safeguard the liberties and
property and life of the people, and the people should
follow our guidance and patriotically support us."

The religious element, for which the clergy act as
spokesmen, upon its standard inscribes: "We interpret
the divine will. Your life, liberty and eternal happiness depend upon your following the course that our
standard points out. We will do your thinking for you
concerning all spiritual matters. Hear nothing but what
is orthodox, because that is what we teach. Commit
your souls unto our keeping."

The wily superlord of the evil world saw the advantage in uniting these three elements into one to compose the ruling class. In the name and under the guise
of democracy the commercial, political and ecclesiastical
elements join interests and hold up to the people their
joint standard, which says: "The present systems of
government are of divine ordering, and all the people
should conform thereto. We must have greater revenues
from taxes that we may prepare for war and thereby insure peace. We must centralize all power in the government to insure our strength against our enemies. We
must have an orthodox religion; and the commercial,
political and ecclesiastical elements must stand together.
The church must have within her portals the ultra-rich
and the mighty politicians to lend power and dignity
thereto. All the people must patriotically support us in

peace and in war, that we may maintain our present
institutions and safeguard the interests and welfare of
the people. Our standard points the way to peace, prosperity, life, liberty and happiness."

But the common people know from experience that
these claims are not true. They see the rich becoming
daily more avaricious, heaping up for themselves greater
riches, and crushing out all competition that they may
pursue their selfish course without interruption. They
see that intrigue, duplicity and trickery are freely resorted to by the politicians. They know that the conflict in doctrines of the various denominational systems
cannot be in harmony with the truth. They are not
in harmony with each other nor with the well understood rules of righteousness. They see that these ecclesiastical systems, and particularly their leaders, are
marked by arrogance, self-sufficiency, impiety and ungodliness. The masses of mankind have lost faith in
the standards held up to them by the rulers. They
know that the claims made by these standards are false,
and by experience have learned that these can never
lead to lasting peace, prosperity, health, strength, liberty, life and happiness.

The Desire of All People

Among the people are many men and women of good
will possessing an honest and sincere desire not only
to see their own condition improved, but to see the
people generally receiving benefits. Some of these are
philanthropists who spend much money to build libraries
and stock them with books that are never read, even
though they are readable. They lift up a standard of
higher education and invite the people to rally to that
and say: "This will save you."

Others of like honest intent organize cooperative societies to carry on their work, holding up before the people a standard that claims that cooperation one with another will bring the desired relief; and they call upon the people to rally to that standard. Few respond. Results are negligible.

Others of equal integrity and good intent organize societies advancing a land finance scheme and single-tax proposition desiring to measure the value of all things by service or labor rendered; and these hold forth a standard for the people to follow, and earnestly yet vainly call upon them to follow.

Only a few think seriously of these various standards. All realize that the entire social, financial, political and ecclesiastical system or systems have completely failed to bring satisfaction to the people. Doubt and fear have taken hold upon all mankind. They are in perplexity and distress. They see threatening another great war far more terrible and destructive than any war ever known. Desiring peace and hating war, they are compelled to contribute their money to prepare the most devilish and deadly instruments of destruction. They continue to suffer under the oppressive weight of wicked profiteers, high taxes, faithless politicians, and false religious leaders. If these standards lifted up have, at some time in the past, given hope to some then the hopes of these are now dashed to the earth. The peoples and nations of the earth have reached their extremity. They are not only ready for but desire a change for something better. It is God's opportunity. The due time has come.

False and True

There must be a reason why all the schemes of men have failed. If any of these various schemes or standards had the approval of the all-wise, just and all-powerful and loving God surely such would have succeeded in bringing relief to the people. Why have the standards held forth by the commercial, the political and religious leaders, separately or combined, failed? The answer is: Because all have been contrary to the plan of Jehovah. The authors of these schemes or standards have had their mind turned away from the true God, and the enemy has led them away into paths of darkness. All these standards, which have been held up before the people, have ignored God's way. They are the result of imperfect human reasoning and a complete failure to take into consideration the plain instructions given in the Word of God.

Call to mind the fact that only one people were ever organized into a government by Jehovah, which people was Israel. That government was not an arbitrary one; but God made with that people a covenant or contract for the purpose of enabling them to prove to themselves that man cannot realize his heart's sincere desire without the aid of the great Jehovah God. The Israelites failed. Why did they fail? Because they forgot God and violated their own covenant and were led away by the great enemy. The first commandment given to them was: "Thou shalt have no other God before me." That commandment was given for the sole benefit of the Israelites. Jehovah God was their true and only friend and for this reason he commanded them to obey him. They turned to other gods and lost all. This of itself should prove that no people can succeed or

8

realize an honest and sincere desire unless they follow God's appointed way. The standard of God is the only one for the people. But who is God?

The True God

The English word "god" translates the Hebrew word *Elohim,* which means mighty one. It is sometimes applied to magistrates or mighty rulers, and it is also applied to the Supreme Being. The great Eternal One, the Creator of heaven and earth, has different names.

When Moses was sent by the Lord to deliver the Israelites from Egypt Moses inquired what he should say to them: "And God said unto Moses, I AM THAT I AM: and he said, Thus shalt thou say unto the children of Israel, I AM hath sent me unto you." (Exodus 3:14) Not that he was or will be, but that he is now, ever was, and ever will be, without beginning and without ending, from everlasting to everlasting.—Psa. 90:2.

When God made a covenant with Abraham he appeared unto Abraham under the name of Almighty God (Genesis 17:1), meaning thereby that in him resides all power, that he is omnipotent and irresistible. His will is his law. He but wills a thing, and his power carries it into action. When Abraham was ministered unto by the great priest, Melchizedek, God was then made known to him under the name of "the most high God". This conveys the thought that he is the great Creator of heaven and earth, and indicates his relationship to the entire divine program. He is the one above all and besides whom there is none other.—Isaiah 42:5; 40:12,23.

When Pharaoh, the mighty ruler of Egypt, refused to let the Israelites leave that land at Moses' request, God spoke unto Moses and said: "And I appeared unto

Abraham, unto Isaac, and unto Jacob, by the name of
God Almighty; but by my name JEHOVAH was I
not known to them." (Exodus 6:3) This is the first
time he appeared under the name Jehovah, which signifies Self-existing One, Eternal One and the One
Eternal, whose name alone is Jehovah and who is higher
than all and above all. (Psalm 83:18) "Who only
hath immortality, dwelling in the light which no man
can approach unto; whom no man hath seen, nor can
see: to whom be honor and power everlasting."—1 Timothy 6:16.

Jehovah, the Almighty God, is the Creator of heaven
and earth. (Isaiah 42:5) The Bible is his Word of
Truth, written at his dictation and written by holy men
as their minds were moved upon and directed by the
power of the Almighty God. (2 Peter 1:21; 2 Samuel
23:2; 2 Timothy 3:16) His Word is a statement of
the truth. (John 17:17) [For a more complete discussion of this subject see the HARP OF GOD, pages 15-20.]

The earth is a wonderful planet. The diversified creation that appears upon it bespeaks the wisdom and
power of the great Creator. It is the place where man
has had his experiences. The Almighty God created it.
Why did he create it? His Word answers: "I have made
the earth, and created man upon it: I, even my hands,
have stretched out the heavens, and all their host have
I commanded. . . . For thus saith the Lord that
created the heavens: God himself that formed the earth
and made it, he hath established it, he created it not in
vain, he formed it to be inhabited; I am the Lord, and
there is none else." (Isaiah 45:12, 18) "One generation passeth away, and another generation cometh; but
the earth abideth for ever."—Ecclesiastes 1:4.

Man Created

Man did not come into existence by his own efforts; nor is he the result of the process of evolution, as some self-constituted wise men think. Seeing that the Lord has declared that he created the earth for man to live upon, then it is reasonable that God would create man to live thereon. The record of his creation is plainly stated in the Scriptures: "The Lord God formed man of the dust of the ground, and breathed into his nostrils the breath of lives; and man became a living soul. And the Lord God planted a garden eastward in Eden; and there he put the man whom he had formed. ... And the Lord God took the man, and put him into the garden of Eden to dress it and to keep it. And the Lord God commanded the man, saying, Of every tree of the garden thou mayest freely eat: but of the tree of the knowledge of good and evil, thou shalt not eat of it: for in the day that thou eatest thereof thou shalt surely die."—Genesis 2: 7, 8, 15-17.

God made woman as a helpmate and companion for man. (Genesis 2: 18) So God created man in his own image, in the image of God created he him; male and female created he them. And God blessed them, and God said unto them, Be fruitful, and multiply, and replenish the earth, and subdue it; and have dominion over the fish of the sea, and over the fowl of the air, and over every living thing that moveth upon the earth."—Genesis 1: 27, 28.

These great fundamental truths, thus stated by Jehovah God, prove beyond a doubt that he intended man to live on earth for ever. But before he would grant to man the privilege of everlasting life, he put man to a test to see whether or not man possessed the stamina

11

to resist evil and follow good. He placed man and woman in Eden, a perfectly beautiful place, containing the food necessary for their sustenance and pleasure. Here the two were dwelling together in peace, prosperity, health, strength, life, liberty and happiness.

The False God

Lucifer was a creature of great beauty and power. God placed him in Eden as overseer or overlord of man. "Thou art the anointed cherub that covereth; and I have set thee so. . . . Thou hast been in Eden the garden of God." (Ezekiel 28: 14, 13) Furthermore the Lord says concerning Lucifer: "Thou wast perfect in thy ways from the day that thou wast created, till iniquity was found in thee." (Ezekiel 28: 15) While man was perfect in his organism his experience, of course, was limited. He must meet an experience that would determine whether or not he would be obedient to the law of God. To disobey that law would be evil. To obey would be righteous. It was the solemn and sacred duty of Lucifer to safeguard the interests of man and instruct him to be obedient to the great Eternal God. Lucifer occupied a fiduciary relationship toward God and toward man, and was duty-bound to be loyal and true to Jehovah. But iniquity was found in him and he fell.

Man was created with a desire to worship his superior. Of course he would worship Jehovah God, because he knew that God was his Creator and Benefactor. Lucifer became ambitious to have the worship of man which Jehovah would naturally receive. Lucifer saw that the perfect man was endowed with power to produce a race of people. He had a vision of a future day when the earth would be filled with great multitudes of peo-

ple who must worship some one. He had an ambitious
desire to have that worship. He set about to obtain it.
In order to carry out his scheme he was willing to become, and did become, a traitor to God. He knew the
law of God provided death as a penalty for its violation.
God made this law to test man before he would grant
to man everlasting existence. To Lucifer had been
granted the power of death. (Hebrews 2:14) By that
it is to be understood that it would become his duty
to put man to death for a violation of God's law.
Knowing this, Lucifer reasoned that he would induce
man to violate God's law and would then refuse to put
him to death, and thereby prove to man that God's law
was merely a threat and that God was giving him this
law to keep him in ignorance and to deprive him of the
privileges to which he was justly entitled.

Lucifer reasoned that he would thus be enabled to induce man to believe that God is a liar and had lied to
him when he said: "In the day that thou eatest thereof
thou shalt surely die." Lucifer further reasoned that he
then would appear in the eyes of man as his friend and
benefactor and entitled to his worship and that he would
thus alienate man's affection from God and that he,
Lucifer, would have it himself. Thus was iniquity
found in him.

The prophet records in the Bible concerning Lucifer:
"How art thou fallen from heaven, O Lucifer, son of the
morning! how art thou cut down to the ground, which
didst weaken the nations! For thou hast said in thine
heart, I will ascend into heaven, I will exalt my throne
above the stars of God: I will sit also upon the mount of
of the congregation, in the sides of the north: I will
ascend above the heights of the clouds: I will be like
the most High."—Isaiah 14:12-14.

Lucifer carried into action his nefarious scheme. To

do this he employed the services of the serpent, a visible animal in Eden, and in his wily, fraudulent and deceptive way approached the woman Eve and said: "Yea, hath God said, Ye shall not eat of every tree of the garden? And the woman said unto the serpent. We may eat of the fruit of the trees of the garden: but of the fruit of the tree which is in the midst of the garden, God hath said, Ye shall not eat of it, neither shall ye touch it, lest ye die." To this Lucifer replied: "Ye shall not surely die: for God doth know that in the day ye eat thereof, then your eyes shall be opened: and ye shall be as gods, knowing good and evil." (Genesis 3: 1-5) The woman partook of the fruit in violation of the law. Her husband Adam joined her in the transgression. (1 Timothy 2: 14) Thus the mighty one Lucifer, the false god, deceived and misled the woman and caused both the man and the woman to violate God's law.

The Great Loss

In keeping with his righteous law God sentenced man to death for his disobedience. By this judgment man was deprived of the right to live, and God caused him to gradually suffer the penalty, and at the end of a certain period he was dead. Therefore Adam's life and right to live were gone. All the children begotten by Adam were born between the time this judgment was entered and the time of its complete enforcement. It was the imperfect Adam who became the father of the human family, and for this reason all the race has been born imperfect and without the right to life. This is very reasonable and is the Scriptural conclusion. (Psalm 51: 5; Romans 5: 12) From then till now mankind has been in sorrow and suffering, and has been vainly seeking peace, prosperity, life, liberty and happiness. These things man lost by a violation of God's law.

Because of the wickedness of Lucifer God changed his name; and from that time forward he has been known as the Dragon, Satan, Serpent, the Devil. All of these names have much significance. Lucifer means lightbearer. He was a creature of great beauty and the bearer of light. (Ezekiel 28:17) Satan means adversary or opposer; and from the time of Eden till now Satan has opposed everything that is righteous. Dragon means devourer; and during all that period of time he has sought to destroy everyone who tried to be righteous. Serpent means deceiver; and from the time of Eden until this day the evil one has tried to deceive mankind and to turn the mind of man away from the true and righteous God. Devil means slanderer; and throughout all the centuries the Devil has slandered God and caused his emissaries, posing as God's representatives, to slander him, and he and they have slandered all who have honestly tried to serve God. This explains why so much evil has been spoken against those who have humbly tried to serve and represent the Lord.

Understanding these facts we can see why Jehovah is called the only true God and why the Devil is the false or unrighteous god. The true and righteous God could have destroyed Satan the Devil at any time, but that was not his plan. He granted Satan the supervision over man in the beginning to test Adam. He did not take that supervision away when he sentenced Adam to death. It was God's purpose that all the human family should have an experience with the baneful effects of evil, and he has permitted in that he has not hindered Satan from pursuing his wicked course, and this has served as a test to mankind.

World, as used in the Scriptures, means an organization of the people into forms of government under the supervision of an overlord. The nation of Israel was the only people with whom God made a covenant, and who were organized into a government; and Jehovah God was therefore their overlord. All other nations have been under the influence of the false god or the Devil. In due time Israel fell under the wicked influence of Satan the Devil, and then Satan became the invisible ruler or god of the entire world. He has used all manner of schemes to keep the people under his influence and to turn their minds away from the true and loving God and to blind them to the truth of God's plan for their salvation and blessing. Concerning this it is written: "But if our gospel be hid, it is hid to them that are lost: In whom the god of this world hath blinded the minds of them which believe not, lest the light of the glorious gospel of Christ, who is the image of God, should shine unto them."—2 Corinthians 4: 3, 4.

Why World Standards Wrong

The standards lifted up before the people by the commercial, political, and ecclesiastical elements have been and are wrong; because Satan the Devil has overreached this ruling class, corrupted their standards, and caused them to ignore therein the true and loving God and to utterly disregarded his plan. These standards, may be truly and properly called the standards of Satan the deceiver because they are deceptive and bring not what they claim to bring.

Israel fell because that nation ignored the true and living God. We have today what is called Christendom, meaning those nations of the earth that claim to be Christian but in fact are not. Instead of being Chris-

tian the dominating or governing factors are under
the supervision of the god of this world. They have
fallen because while claiming to follow the Lord God
they have yielded to the influences of the false god
Satan, have ignored the truth, and followed in the way
of unrighteousness. Their plan or scheme put forth by
men with the avowed purpose of benefiting the human
race has minimized the importance of Jehovah. Governments and organizations manifest that they are
ashamed of the name of Jehovah God. If his name is
mentioned it is in a half-apologetic way. Neither the
commercial nor the political nor ecclesiastical elements
are willing to take an unequivocal stand for God and for
his Word of Truth. At the present time the majority
of the clergymen who claim to be the religious directors
of the people deny God, and deny his Word, and substitute their own wisdom therefor.

Satan has not the power to give life to the human
race. He never possessed such a power. Doubtless if
he had possessed that power, he would have given the
race eternal life and kept them under his control, that
his dominion might continue for ever. Jehovah God
is the only source of life. (John 17: 3) He created man
and gave him life. God took away that life and right
thereto because of a violation of his law. He alone can
give man life. Then why waste time with other
schemes? Why look to other standards? Why listen to
the philosophy of world-wise men? Their wisdom is
foolishness in the sight of God. It is foolishness to every
one who understands and loves God.—1 Cor. 1: 20.

Plan of Redemption

If God took away man's right to live because man had violated God's just law, then how could God thereafter grant life to man and be consistent? This is a pertinent question which has puzzled many men, and the Devil has succeeded in using the preachers to blind most men to the true answer.

God could not consistently reverse his judgment nor set it aside and let man go free. Justice and judgment are the habitation of Jehovah's throne. (Psa. 89:14) God having declared his judgment against Adam, Adam must die. God could, however, consistently make a provision that another perfect man equal to Adam could voluntarily go into death in Adam's place and stead and Adam thereby be released. Adam alone was sentenced to death because he alone was on trial. All of Adam's children, now composing the entire human family, were born without a right to live because born imperfect. For this reason it is stated: "In Adam all die."—1 Corinthians 15:22.

It was the plan of Jehovah God that redemption for Adam and his offspring be provided to the intent that all mankind shall have one fair opportunity for life. When this opportunity is given, then everyone who avails himself thereof and obeys God's righteous law shall be granted life everlasting in a state of happiness. God promised that he would redeem man from death and purchase him from the power of the grave. (Hosea 13:14) His law provided that this could be done by a perfect life being given for a perfect life. (Exodus 21:23) In all the earth there was no one who could meet this requirement of the law, because all were the offspring of Adam. (Psalm 49:7) But the power of the Almighty God was not limited. In heaven was the Logos, the beginning of God's creation, always in har-

18

mony with Jehovah and always obedient to his will. —John 1:1-4.

In God's due time the Logos was transferred from heaven to earth. 'He was made flesh and dwelt amongst men.' (John 1:14) When he stood upon this earth at the age of thirty years he was perfect in his organism, perfect in every manner. God proposed that he should be granted the greatest place in the universe, next to Jehovah himself, if he met the test now that was before him. And what was that test? Full and complete obedience unto the law of God under the most adverse circumstances.—Hebrews 5:8, 9.

Why had he come to earth and why was he made a man? The scripture answers: To give his life a ransom, the purchase price for man. (Matthew 20:28) He came that the people might have life and have it more abundantly. (John 10:10) To accomplish this purpose it was necessary for the perfect man Jesus to voluntarily die as a sinner; that is to say, in the place of the sinner in order that he might take the place of the sinner who was in death. Concerning this, Jesus said: "Therefore doth my Father love me, because I lay down my life, that I might take it again. No man taketh it from me, but I lay it down of myself. I have power to lay it down, and I have power to take it again. This commandment have I received of my Father." —John 10:17, 18.

Jesus had the right to live as a man. When he died voluntarily, he surrendered his life as a man that the human race might benefit therefrom. "For God so loved the world, that he gave his only begotten Son, that whosoever believeth in him should not perish, but have everlasting life. For God sent not his Son into

the world to condemn the world; but that the world
through him might be saved."—John 3:16, 17.

Jesus met the test under the most adverse circumstances: "He humbled himself, and became obedient
unto death, even the death of the cross. Wherefore
God also hath highly exalted him, and given him a
name which is above every name: that at the name of
Jesus every knee should bow, of things in heaven, and
things in earth, and things under the earth; and that
every tongue should confess that Jesus Christ is Lord,
to the glory of God the Father."—Philippians 2:8-11.

For whom did Jesus die? And the apostle answers:
He tasted death "for every man". (Hebrews 2:9)
He gave his life "a ransom for all, to be testified in due
time".—1 Timothy 2:6.

He arose from the dead the divine Christ Jesus and
ascended into heaven. He presented the great ransom
price in heaven itself.—Hebrews 9:24.

Do not the clergy teach that Jesus is the Redeemer
of man, and is not that a part of their standard that
they hold up to the people? Some of them teach that
he died for man, while some of them deny this entirely,
but all of them nullify the great truth of the ransom
by many other erroneous doctrines which they have included in their standard and which serve as stumbling
stones over which the people have stumbled. There is
a great conflict between Catholics and Protestants. No
one can harmonize their teachings with each other or
with themselves. There is such a jargon and confusion
amongst the various denominations and such a misrepresentation of the divine program that none can understand the philosophy thereof. These stumbling stones
have been put there by the enemy Satan the Devil to
blind the minds of the people and turn them away from
God.

Stones Removed

The Lord speaking to mankind says: "Come now, and let us reason together, saith the Lord: though your sins be as scarlet, they shall be as white as snow; though they be red like crimson, they shall be as wool." (Isaiah 1: 18) We must therefore know that God's plan is reasonable, but that anything that is unreasonable cannot be in harmony with his plan.

One of the great stumbling stones, one which is maintained by the clergy, is that all men have immortal souls and that there is in fact no death. Sensible men have reasoned: If a man's soul is immortal and he cannot die, then how could the death of Jesus constitute a ransom price? How could Jesus be the Redeemer of an immortal soul; that is to say, a soul not subject to death? Thereby the clergy nullify the ransom price.

The immortality of the soul is the first lie that the Devil ever told. Jesus says so. God had said: Man shall die. The Devil said: "Ye shall not surely die." The clergy say the same thing. Jesus said that the Devil is a liar. (John 8: 44) In what class do the clergy put themselves?

The scripture reads that God formed man of the dust of the ground and breathed into his nostrils the breath of lives, and man became a living soul. (Genesis 2: 7) Man is the soul. He does not possess a soul. Man dies. A soul dies.

A distinguished clergyman in the city of New York a short time ago over the radio said: "I would like to know of some scripture that says that the soul dies." This is proof of the ignorance of the clergy. The scripture reads: "The soul that sinneth it shall die."— Ezekiel 18: 4; Psalm 89: 48.

The clergy teach in their standards that when a man dies he merely has a change; and that if he is good he goes to one place and if bad to another. They say that some are in purgatory, where they may be prayed out for a consideration, while others are in hell, which is represented to be a place of conscious torment, eternal in duration. The reasonable mind says, If the dead are in eternal torment they can never come out, because if they could come out that would prove that they are not there eternally; and if the dead are there conscious and being tormented, how could the redemptive price of Jesus do them any good? This stumbling stone also nullifies the ransom.

"The living know that they shall die: but the dead know not anything, neither have they any more a reward; for the memory of them is forgotten. ... Whatsoever thy hand findeth to do, do it with thy might; for there is no work, nor device, nor knowledge, nor wisdom, in the grave, whither thou goest." (Ecclesiastes 9:5, 10) "The dead praise not the Lord, neither any that go down into silence."—Psalm 115:17.

Hell, as used in the Bible, means grave, the tomb, and not a place of conscious torment. Eternal torment is another stumbling stone which was placed by the Devil, and which has held before the people the thought that God is a fiend who will torture creatures for ever without any reason. This has had a tendency to turn the minds of the people away from the just and true God.

The clergy also teach the doctrine of the trinity; that is to say, God the Father, God the Son, and God the Holy Ghost, one in person, equal in power. The reasonable mind says: If the Lord Jesus was God himself, how could a God be accepted as a ransom or exact corresponding price for a man? Again the unholy doctrine nullifies the plan of redemption. This has been another stumbling stone that has turned reasonable people away from the Scriptures.

Jehovah is the only true God, besides whom there is none; and his glory he will divide with no other. (Isaiah 42:5, 8) The Lord Jesus is the Son of the living God. He said: "My Father is greater than I." (John 14:28) And again he said: "I seek not mine own will, but the will of the Father which hath sent me." (John 5:30) He prayed to God on the night before his crucifixion. (John 17:1) Would any reasonable person think that he was practising a fraud on others by praying to himself? The term holy ghost is not a proper translation in the Bible. The word translated "ghost" should be translated spirit. The holy spirit means the invisible power of God. The doctrine of the trinity is another false doctrine that belongs to the standard of this evil world.

Many of the modern clergy teach and include in their standard the doctrine of evolution; that is to say, that man emanated from protoplasm and is a creature of evolution. This of course denies the creation of man, denies his need of a redeemer, and denies the value of the redemptive price.

The clergy teach that the kingdoms of this world, of which they are a part, constitute the kingdom of God, and that these kingdoms are operating by divine right; and they call upon the people to support them. This is another stumbling stone. Jesus declared: "My kingdom is not of this world"; and he taught the people to prepare for the coming of his kingdom. He promised to return and set up his kingdom.

Plan of Reconstruction

Even though all concede that Jesus died as the Redeemer of man, and that he arose form the dead, the question remains: How is man to benefit thereby? The answer of the clergy, which they make a part of their standard, is that if a man believes that Jesus Christ is the Son of God, and then joins their church and follows their teachings, when he dies he can be saved.

The Catholics say that if a man is fairly good he will go to purgatory, where he remains for an indefinite time and is prayed out, and then he may go to heaven. The Protestants say that if he is a good member of their church until he dies, he will go straight to heaven. Both Catholics and Protestants say that if the man is bad, and does not belong to the church at all, he must go to eternal torment.

But what about the millions of heathen who never heard of the Catholic church or the Protestant church? What about the millions who died before either of these systems was ever organized? Furthermore, the reasonable mind asks: Catholic and Protestant systems, in their standards, claim that all men who are saved at all are saved in heaven and that all the others go to hell. What about the earth? The plain statement of God's Word is that God made the earth to be inhabited by man. Is it the intention of God that the earth is to be for ever merely a breeding place for the human race, a place of temporary abode; and that then they must pass on to some other realm?

Only the Scriptures can give a satisfactory answer to these questions. The people are thoroughly familiar with, and completely disgusted with, the inconsistent statements that the clergy have inserted in their standards in answer to these questions. The basic promise for the redemption and recovery of the men and nations

of the earth is that which God made to Abraham, in
which he said: "In thee shall all the families of the earth
be blessed." (Genesis 12: 3) Later God said: "In thy
seed shall all the nations of the earth be blessed."
(Genesis 22: 18-22) This divine promise being true,
and it is true, it follows that the "seed", being the
medium of blessing, must first be developed and manifested before the blessing of the people could come.
What is the "seed according to the promise"? The
Scriptures answer: "Now to Abraham and his seed
were the promises made. He saith not, And to seeds, as
of many; but as of one, And to thy seed, which is
Christ."—Galatians 3: 16.

Christ Jesus is the Head of the Christ, the church
being the body. (Colossians 1: 18) Every true and
faithful one baptized into Christ becomes a part of this
"seed according to the promise".—Galatians 3: 27, 29.

The word "church" means called-out class. It does
not mean the Catholic system nor the Protestant system
nor any other system of religion. It has reference to
the body of Christ, made up of men and women who
have unreservedly consecrated themselves to do God's
will and who continue to do so even unto death. These
are called to follow in the footsteps of Jesus, their Head
and Redeemer. (1 Peter 2: 21) Jesus did not ally himself with the preachers and politicians of this world, nor
with the clergy who claimed to represent the Lord but
who in truth and in fact represented the Devil. The
true followers of Jesus cannot now have a part with
such an unholy alliance.

The clergy of our time say that we must be a part of
the world, that we must have the preachers and politicians in our churches, and that we must participate
in politics and advocate war in time of war and to help
run the affairs of this world. The Lord's Word says to

them: "Ye adulterers and adulteresses, know ye not
that the friendship of the world is enmity with God?
Whosoever therefore will be a friend of the world is the
enemy of God." (James 4: 4) They are called adulterers,
not because they are unchaste with the opposite sex, but
because there is an illicit relationship between those who
profess to be followers of Christ and those who are the
avowed representatives of the Devil, the false god.

The true Christian who will be a jart of the seed
according to the promise is the one who faithfully represents the Lord and stands for him. To these certain
specific promises are made, amongst which is the following: "Be thou faithful unto death, and I will give
thee a crown of life." (Revelation 2: 10) That does
not say to be faithful unto war or some other wicked
scheme, but it says to be faithful unto the Lord to the
end. The reward is given to such in the resurrection;
because, say the Scriptures, "they shall be priests of
God and of Christ, and shall reign with him a thousand
years." (Revelation 20: 6) These, together with their
Head, Christ Jesus, constitute the royal family or kingdom class. To such Jesus said: "It is your Father's
good pleasure to give you the kingdom." (Luke 12: 32)
To such the Lord says: "To him that overcometh will
I grant to sit with me in my throne, even as I also
overcame, and am set down with my Father in his
throne."—Revelation 3: 21.

It is this true and faithful class constituting the seed
of Abraham that participate in the first resurrection
and find their eternal abiding place in heaven. It is
only a small number.—Luke 12: 32.

But what is to become of all other peoples of earth,
the heathen and the ignorant and the mass of those
who have been turned away from God because of the
misrepresentation made by the false standards?

Judgment

God has appointed a day or time in which all of these shall have an opportunity for life; because, says the apostle, "this is good and acceptable in the sight of God our Saviour; who will have all men to be saved, and to come unto the [accurate] knowledge of the truth." (1 Timothy 2:3, 4) The death of Jesus provided the salvation, and now each one must be brought to a knowledge of the truth. The day of this judgment is the Millennial reign of Christ, in which all shall have an opportunity to live. (Acts 17:31) What shall be the reward or blessing of those who obey and who receive a favorable judgment? The answer is: Restoration to that condition of human perfection which Adam had in Eden before he violated God's law and lost it all. All the prophets from Samuel to Malachi have testified concerning this period of restoration of the human family. (Acts 3:24) Restoration means to restore that which was lost. Adam, as we have seen, enjoyed peace, prosperity, health, life, liberty and happiness. All of these he lost; all of these Jesus bought; all of these the Lord Jesus Christ will restore to the obedient ones.

It is conceded by all reasonable people that the nations and peoples of the earth are in an unsatisfactory condition. Even the ruling classes are uneasy, in perplexity and distress. All have a longing for a change to a better condition. It must be conceded, after all of these centuries of effort, that man cannot accomplish these things for himself. Man has not been able to build a satisfactory government. Who then has the power and who can do it? The answer is: Jehovah God. He gave life to man, he took life away, and he has made provision for the redemption of man and restoration to life. These blessings he will grant to man by and through the kingdom of his beloved Son, Christ Jesus.

27

Does that mean that in the outworking of the divine
plan God will give life everlasting to all men regard-
less of whether they want it or not? God never forces
his favors on any one. It is written: "(. . . For if by one
man's offence death reigned by one; much more they
which receive abundance of grace, and of the gift of
righteousness, shall reign in life by one, Jesus Christ.)
Therefore, as by the offence of one judgment came upon
all men to condemnation; even so by the righteousness
of one the free gift came upon all men unto justification of life. For as by one man's disobedience many
were made sinners, so by the obedience of one shall
many be made righteous."—Romans 5:17-19.

"For the wages of sin is death; but the gift of God
is eternal life, through Jesus Christ our Lord." (Romans 6:23) The apostle here answers the question. He
emphasizes the fact that life is a gift from God. A
gift is the result of a contract. There must be a giver
and a receiver. The one must be willing to give; the
other must be willing to receive. There must be a meeting of the minds. It is impossible to give to a man who
refuses to receive the gift. Likewise it is impossible to
give to one who knows nothing about the offer. These
scriptures definitely settle the fact that the Lord Jehovah will offer life everlasting to mankind through
Jesus Christ and that all those who accept the offer on
the terms made, and render obedience, shall receive it.

The first thing essential to a gift is knowledge. After
the complete establishment of the kingdom of God the
people must be brought to a knowledge of the truth before their responsibility to accept or reject the truth
arises. It will not do to say that men throughout the
age have had an opportunity to receive the truth when
the truth has not been told to them. False doctrines
promulgated in the name of the Lord do not constitute

the truth, nor do such doctrines place responsibility upon men. The apostle in 1 Timothy 2:3,4. says: "God, . . . who will have all men to be saved, and to come unto the [accurate] knowledge of the truth." The death of Jesus Christ provides the salvation, and knowledge is now the next step.

Why should knowledge be given and a knowledge of what? The apostle answers: "For there is one God, and one mediator between God and men, the man Christ Jesus; who gave himself a ransom for all, to be testified in due time." (1 Timothy 2:5,6) His argument here is that there is one Jehovah God, the clergy teaching that there are three. He says there is one Lord and Savior Jesus Christ, who gave his life a ransom for all; and that this fact must be testified in God's due time to all, that all may have the opportunity to either accept or reject the offer.

Why have not the people been receiving the truth throughout the entire Gospel Age? For two separate and distinct reasons: (1) Because the Devil has blinded their minds lest the truth should shine unto them and they would believe (2 Corinthians 4:3,4); and (2) because it was not God's due time to let the truth generally be known. God does everything timely and in order.

The clergy have been telling us for a long time that God has been trying to convert the world, and that their business is to convert the world and bring people into the church. This is also an erroneous statement. God does not try to do anything. He does things, according to his will. Surely we should atttribute to the great Jehovah more wisdom and ability than to believe for a moment that he would commit to imperfect men the trememdous job of converting the world and bringing them to him. Why then have men been trying to

preach the gospel? Jehovah has had the gospel preached
that those who had the ear to hear might hear, that he
might take out from the world a people for his name, to
wit: those who would be the followers of Christ Jesus
and who would prove faithful and be associated with
him in his kingdom.—Acts 15:14-17.

God has not forced any one to accept his message of
truth. On the other hand the Scriptures declare: "Who
hath ears to hear, let him hear." (Matthew 13:9, 43)
Comparatively few have desired to hear; and these have
had to war against the influence of the adversary and
to walk in the light of the truth. The faithful Christians who thus continue faithful unto death, and who
participate in the first resurrection, are thereby changed
from human to spirit beings. They are made members
of the royal family of heaven. They constitute, together
with Christ Jesus, the "seed of promise", according to
the promise which God made to Abraham. (Galatians
3:16, 27, 29) It is written: "Nevertheless we, according to his promise, look for new heavens and a new
earth, wherein dwelleth righteousness."—2 Peter 3:13.

What is this new heavens and new earth here spoken
of? It is the kingdom of God mentioned in symbolic
phrase; heavens referring to the invisible part, and
earth referring to the visible part of God's kingdom.

What will be God's method, according to his Word,
of bringing the knowledge of the truth to the people
in order that they may accept or reject it as a gift?
The Scriptures answer that by the establishment of his
kingdom of righteousness, to wit, the new heavens and
new earth above mentioned—that by and through this
he will bring a knowledge of the truth to mankind
in general.

The clergy have taught that the present kingdoms
of earth constitute the kingdom of God; and they join

in a proclamation stating that the League of Nations is the political expression of God's kingdom. Is that true or not? It is not only untrue, but grossly false. The League of Nations is what is designated in the scriptures as the "Image of the Beast" (Revelation 13: 14, 15), which is another product of the Devil by which he attempts to rule the nations and peoples of the earth and keep them in subjection to himself, and to turn away their minds from the true and living God and from his kingdom.

When Jesus stood before Pilate he declared: "My kingdom is not. of this world." (John 18: 36) By this he meant to be understood as saying, Satan the Devil is the god of this present world. He is the invisible ruler and he is evil. He rules in the earth by his visible representatives and they are evil. Jesus taught his disciples to pray to God and to say: "Thy kingdom come. Thy will be done in earth as in heaven." (Matt. 6: 10) This of itself shows that his kingdom is not of the evil world nor during the time of the evil world. In fact, the kingdom of righteousness and the kingdom of unrighteousness could not exist at one and the same time and both be in control of the people of the earth.

When Jesus was on earth, the burden of his message was concerning the kingdom. Just before his crucifixion he told his disciples that he was going away and would prepare a place for them and that he would come again and receive them unto himself. (John 14: 2, 3) All the prophets had taught concerning the coming of God's kingdom. The Jews looked forward to that time. The disciples of Jesus understood that the evil world must end before his kingdom would be put into operation. For this reason they asked him the question: "Tell us, when shall these things be? and what shall be the sign of thy presence, and of the end of the world?"—Matthew 24: 3.

The answer of Jesus may be summed up briefly in these words: That when the time came for the ending and passing away of the evil world a great world war would occur in which nation would rise against nation and kingdom against kingdom; that famines and revolutions would follow; and that these things would mark the beginning of the sorrows upon the people; that during that period God's favor would begin to be expressed to the Jews in returning them to Palestine; that then the nations would be in distress and perplexity; and that then would follow the preparation for another great and terrible time of trouble such as the world has never known.—Matthew 24: 7-22.

These prophetic utterances began to have a fulfilment in 1914 and are still in course of fulfilment. The Scriptures show that in 1914 Jesus, at the command of Jehovah, began to exercise his power to oust Satan as the invisible ruler, for the reason that the time had come. (Psalm 110: 1-6) The Scriptures show that the Lord Jesus Christ, as Jehovah's executive officer, first expelled Satan from heaven, his place of invisible rule. This has already taken place. The next is the destruction of his empire in earth; and we are rapidly approaching that and in this conflict the Lord Jesus Christ will be victorious, as it is written: "These shall make war with the Lamb, and the Lamb shall overcome them: for he is Lord of lords, and King of kings: and they that are with him are called, and chosen, and faithful." (Revelation 17: 14) The beast here represents the Devil's earthly organization; the Lamb is a symbolic name for the Lord Jesus Christ; and they that are with him in the victory are the faithful overcomers.

What is God's method of operation through which he will bring the blessings to the people? The answer is: Through his kingdom, of which Christ Jesus is the king and head, who will establish the new heavens [invisible ruling power] and the new earth [visible ruling power]. Are there any scriptures to the effect that the Lord God will establish a kingdom? The Scriptures show that in the days of the ruling kings of earth the God of heaven will establish his kingdom. It is written: "In the days of these kings shall the God of heaven set up a kingdom which shall never be destroyed: and the kingdom shall not be left to other people, but it shall break in pieces and consume all these kingdoms, and it shall stand for ever."—Daniel 2: 44.

Be it noted that this kingdom of God will not be left to profiteers and politicians nor to preachers, nor to anyone else. The Lord himself will be the ruler. This kingdom will mark the fulfilment of the prayer which Jesus taught his disciples to pray for the doing of the will of God on earth.

Are there other scriptures warranting the conclusion that God intends to establish by and through Christ a kingdom of righteousness on earth different from what we now see? God's prophet Isaiah wrote long ago concerning that kingdom: "For unto us a child is born, unto us a son is given, and the government shall be upon his shoulder; and his name shall be called Wonderful, Counsellor, The mighty God, the everlasting Father, The Prince of Peace. Of the increase of his government and peace there shall be no end, upon the throne of David, and upon his kingdom, to order it, and to establish it with judgment and with justice, from henceforth even for ever. The zeal of the Lord of hosts will perform this."—Isaiah 9: 6, 7.

These things being true, then the clergy have not
been giving the people the truth concerning God's standard? They have not. Everyone who is acquainted with
the teachings of the clergy may compare their teachings
with the divine standard and be able to answer the
question for himself and that satisfactorily.

God's Standard

The term "the standard for the people" refers to the
only and true standard. Such a standard could not
originate with man, because man is imperfect. It must
be the standard of the Lord. The time must come
when this standard is lifted up for the people in order
that some might know the truth. When should we expect it to be lifted up? The answer is: At the end of
the world, with the passing away of Satan's empire, at
the time when the nations and peoples are preparing
for the great and terrible conflict, which everyone sees
about us now. Long ago the prophet of Jehovah wrote
concerning this time: "Go through, go through the
gates; prepare ye the way of the people; cast up, cast
up the highway; gather out the stones; lift up a standard for the people." (Isaiah 62:10) What then is the
standard that the Lord commands shall be lifted up?

(1) That Jehovah is the only true and living God,
beside whom there is none. He is the Creator of heaven
and earth. He gave life to man and took away life. He
will provide the way for man to get life. He made the
earth for man's habitation. Every act of his is prompted
by unselfishness. He is the embodiment of love. He is
the true and lasting friend of man. The people must
learn that Jehovah is God and obey him.

(2) That Jesus is the beloved Son of God; that by

his death and resurrection he provided the great redemptive price for man; that to him is committed all power in heaven and in earth as the active agent of Jehovah; that he is the King of kings and Lord of lords; that the time has now come for him to begin his reign; and that the first work of his reign is to oust Satan, to destroy the evil systems and restrain Satan that he may deceive the nations no more (Revelation 20: 1-3), and then to destroy all the works of Satan. —1 John 3: 8.

(3) That the kingdom of heaven, God's kingdom, is here; that Christ Jesus, the great King, has begun his reign and now the time has come when the stumbling stones of error shall be cast out, the way made clear for the people, and the people given the truth in order that they might know the way that leads to life and happiness.

As the people come to realize that the standards long held before them by men are standards of unrighteousness they must forsake such. Seeing the standard of God, to it they can rally and find there the way that leads to a full realization of their heart's desire.

The psalmist declares: "The secret of the Lord is with them that fear him; and he will show them his covenant." (Psalm 25: 14) The margin of this text reads: "And his covenant to make them know it." The reverence of the Lord is the beginning of knowledge. (Proverbs 1: 7) The people must begin to know the truth concerning God's plan. Hence it is essential for every one to apply his mind to an understanding of the truth recorded in the Scriptures, which set forth God's way and the means of bringing blessings to all families of the earth according to his promise.

Highway of Holiness

Jehovah through his prophet commands that the highway be cast up. This is symbolic phrase. A highway is a plain way to travel, and here the expression means that the way of the people to return to God must be made plain. The only means by which this can be done is to give them a knowledge of God and his gracious arrangement made for their benefit. This must be done at the beginning of the reign of Christ. During his reign and during the time of the judgment of the world it is written: "And an highway shall be there, and a way, and it shall be called, The way of holiness; the unclean shall not pass over it; but it shall be for those: the wayfaring men, though fools, shall not err therein."—Isaiah 35:8.

This is called the highway of holiness because it is the Lord's way; and with him all things are holy. It pictures the way from the beginning of the reign of Christ the Messiah until the end thereof. No unclean one shall pass the entire length of that way, but it shall be for the cleansing of those who attempt to pass. That is to say, the unclean shall start over it and, being obedient to the rules of God's righteous kingdom, they will be cleaned up and made right before they reach the end; but refusing to do this they will not be permitted to pass to the end. This we see so clearly marked out in the Word of God that a wayfaring man, though he belong to the ruling class of the evil world, ought to be able to see that way in due time.

What God Requires

Before God, through Christ, will begin the work of restoring the human race Satan's empire must completely pass away. God, through Christ, will destroy

Satan and his wicked works. (Psalm 110:5,6) All the nations are now preparing for a terrible war. All the ruling factors in particular see it approaching. It will be that great battle described in the Bible as the battle of Armageddon, the battle of God Almighty against Satan and his forces, in which Satan will be completely defeated. It will be a time of trouble such as the world has never before known. Jesus declared that it will be the end of all trouble on earth.—Matthew 24:21, 22.

God has remained silent and permitted Satan and his emissaries to come to a fulness in wickedness; and now, as the prophet says: "The Lord hath a controversy with the nations; . . . he will give them that are wicked to the sword." (Jeremiah 25:31) Then the prophet proceeds to give a description of that terrible conflict in these words: "Thus saith the Lord of hosts, Behold, evil shall go forth from nation to nation, and a great whirlwind shall be raised up from the coasts of the earth. And the slain of the Lord shall be at that day from one end of the earth even unto the other end of the earth: they shall not be lamented, neither gathered, nor buried; they shall be dung upon the ground."—Jeremiah 25:32, 33.

At the present time, and for a long time past, the clergy have posed before the people as their shepherds to lead them and teach them; and the principal of their flocks are the profiteers and politicians. Concerning them in this time of trouble the Lord says: "Howl, ye shepherds, and cry; and wallow yourselves in the ashes, ye principal of the flock: for the days of your slaughter and of your dispersions are accomplished; and ye shall fall like a pleasant vessel. And the shepherds shall have no way to flee, nor the principal of the flock to escape. A voice of the cry of the shepherds, and an howling of the principal of the flock, shall be heard; for the Lord hath spoiled their pasture."—Jeremiah 25:34-36.

The Lord describes that terrible time of trouble in which he likens the peoples of the world to a drunken man who staggers to and fro and then comes to his wits' end.—Psalm 107:22-29.

It is during the period of time between the World War and this final trouble that the Lord commands that the good news concerning his kingdom for the blessing of the people shall be preached as a witness to the nations. (Matthew 24:14) This has been and is being done. And it is during that same period of time that Satan the Devil is diligently flooding the minds of the people with all manner of errors in an attempt to turn their minds away from the true God. It is at this same time that the Lord lifts up a standard against him and for the people.—Isaiah 59:19; 62:10.

God's standard of righteousness is lifted up that all peoples of good will who have an honest and sincere desire to know the truth and to become righteous may do so. Is there any special promise that such may claim at this time? And the Lord answers: "Before the decree come forth, before the day pass as the chaff, before the fierce anger of the Lord come upon you, before the day of the Lord's anger come upon you. Seek ye the Lord, all ye meek of the earth, which have wrought his judgment: seek righteousness, seek meekness: it may be ye shall be hid in the day of the Lord's anger." —Zephaniah 2:2, 3.

This is the reason for calling the attention of the people to these truths at this time. There is neither a desire nor an effort to induce any one to join any church system or organization. The sole desire is to lift up the standard for the people, calling their attention to the fact that Jehovah is the only true God, that Jesus Christ is the King, and that his kingdom is the method of relief for the people. Satan has induced many people to believe that God commands men to obey him because he is a selfish God. God never did anything nor commanded anything be done because of selfishness. He is wholly unselfish. Whatsoever he does toward man is for man's own good.

Profiteers do not regard their obligation to their fellow man as anything. They see the wrath of God approaching. They are in fear and trepidation, and they have to do something to protect themselves. Out of their ill-got gains they contribute a few millions to charity, or endow some institution, thinking that such will secure their protection.

Politicians misrepresent the people in order that they might carry out their own selfish purposes. They know they do wrong and they think to atone for their wrongdoing by going to some church building and participating with the clergymen in some formal service and making a reasonable contribution to the expenses of the institution.

The clergymen as a class are so impressed with their own piety and importance that they receive aid from the profiteers and politicians as of their own right and their part of the spoils of government, for which they render their share in keeping the people in subjection. Arrogantly they assume to be the spiritual advisers of the government and the people, and then unmercifully denounce and persecute humble Christians who dare tell the truth in the name of the Lord.

These three elements, composing the governing fac-

tors, hope to please the Lord with their contributions of
money and wisdom. Long ago the Lord, having reference
to them and to others like them, said: "Will the Lord
be pleased with thousands of rams, or with ten thousands of rivers of oil? shall I give my firstborn for my
transgression, the fruit of my body for the sin of my
soul? He hath showed thee, O man, what is good; and
what doth the Lord require of thee, but to do justly,
and to love mercy, and to walk humbly with thy God?"
—Micah 6: 7, 8.

Justice, mercy and obedience are the three primary
things which God requires everyone to do before he will
ever have divine approval.

To do justice means to do that which is right and
righteous. It means to be honest, true and truthful. It
means to deal fairly and impartially with all. Jehovah
is "a God of truth and without iniquity, just and right
is he".—Deuteronomy 32: 4.

Those who will receive the approval of the Lord will
be required to learn to do right toward all. In the
nineteenth chapter of Leviticus the Lord God enumer-
ates some of the things that will be required of every
man to do right according to his law. Amongst many of
these things he says: "Ye shall do no unrighteousness
in judgment, in meteyard, in weight, or in measure.
Just balances, just weights, ... shall ye have. I am
the Lord your God."—Leviticus 19: 35, 36.

It is not right that profiteers obtain control of the
food and fuel needed by the people and then compel
them to pay exorbitant prices for it, greatly to their
suffering and distress. It is not right to give false
measures, to cheat and to defraud. It is not right and
just to oppress the poor. All the contributions to charity
that may be made will not compensate for dishonesty

practised on one's fellow man. Those who deal justly
with the poor will receive a special favor. "Blessed is
he that considereth the poor: the Lord will deliver him
in time of trouble. The Lord will preserve him, and
keep him alive; and he shall be blessed upon the earth:
and thou wilt not deliver him unto the will of his
enemies."—Psalm 41:1, 2.

It is not just and right for profiteers and politicians
to scheme and lay plans for war, and then passionately
appeal to the patriotism of the people to carry on that
war. It is not just and right for the clergy to claim
to be followers of the Prince of Peace and at the same
time join hands with profiteers and politicians in advocating war, as they did in 1914, and urge the people
into the trenches. God will not excuse them for this,
but says: "In thy skirts is found the blood of the souls
of the poor innocents: I have not found it by secret
search, but upon all these."—Jeremiah 2:34.

Mercy means compassionate treatment of the unfortunate and helpless. It means loving kindness shown
toward another. Justice alone exercised toward man
would have sent Adam and all of his offspring into
eternal destruction. God extended his mercy toward
man and made provision for his recovery.—Psalm 86:5.

A distinction must be made between wrong and
wrong-doers. It is written concerning the beloved Son
Jesus: "Thou lovest righteousness, and hatest wickedness: therefore God, thy God, hath anointed thee with
the oil of gladness above thy fellows."(Psalm 45:7)
God hates sin, but he is merciful to the sinner. That is
the disposition which all must cultivate who will have
God's approval. Such is the standard of the Lord. The
disposition to oppress is foreign to righteousness. The
divine rule is thus stated: "Therefore if thine enemy

hunger, feed him; if he thirst, give him drink: for in so doing thou shalt heap coals of fire on his head. Be not overcome of evil, but overcome evil with good." (Romans 12:20, 21) "See that none render evil for evil unto any man; but ever follow that which is good, both among yourselves, and to all men." (1 Thessalonians 5:15) How different is this from the standard held forth by the ruling factors during the present and past centuries!

Those who will receive God's approval must walk humbly before him. That means that one's course of action must be that of willing submission to the laws of God. The laws of God are righteous; and to walk humbly before God one must love righteousness and diligently strive to do that which is right. The chief commandment that God has given is: "Thou shalt love the Lord thy God." Love means to be unselfishly devoted to his cause. No one can love and support the Devil's system and at the same time love the Lord God. Those who please the Lord must take a delight in doing that which he has pointed out because such is righteous.

To walk humbly before God is to ascertain from the Word of God what are his commandments and then diligently try to obey them. No one can obtain this knowledge without the study of the Bible, God's Word of Truth. Each one then who desires the blessings that God has in store for man should provide himself with a Bible and such helps as will enable him to understand the Bible, and should study these diligently.

The philanthropists, the cooperative workers, the social-uplift workers, and all like organizations are organized to carry on because some human minds have reasoned that this is the way to accomplish man's uplift. They have not consulted the Word of God to see whether their way is in harmony with his way. (Isaiah 55:9, 10) The clergy and worldly-wise men have attempted to convert the world and get the people into their organizations. This is the result of their human reasoning and not according to the Scriptures. God says to those who would have his approval: "Trust in the Lord with all thine heart; and lean not unto thine own understanding. In all thy ways acknowledge him, and he shall direct thy paths."—Proverbs 3:5, 6.

Why should we think that any man or company of men has sufficient wisdom to formulate a scheme that will bring peace, happiness, health and life to the people? For sixty centuries these schemes have been formulated and these human standards have been held up to the people, and all of them have failed. All of them have ignored God's way. Jehovah God is perfect in wisdom, justice, love and power. He makes no mistakes. He has let man go to his extremity. Now he will give man an opportunity to humbly heed and obey God's way, that man may receive his heart's desire. The schemes of men do not furnish a basis for any hope. Why not turn to the Word of God?

A Real Hope

Hope means to have a desire for that which is beneficial and a good reason to expect to receive the same. A good reason for having such expectation is to be in possession of competent evidence coming from a truthful source, which evidence proves that the thing expected can be received. There can be no hope without faith. There can be no faith without knowledge and a confident reliance upon the evidence or proof furnishing that knowledge. A hope may be based upon a promise; but in order for that hope to be realized the one making the promise must have the ability or disposition to make good that promise, and then to make it good. Men, institutions, and governments composed of men have made many promises; but they have been without ability to make them good and for such reason, if for no other, their promises have failed.

God is all-powerful. He is unselfish. His Word is true. When God makes a promise, he has the disposition and the power to make it good. He has never failed in one of his promises. God does not change. (Malachi 3:6) The Lord God says: "I have spoken it, I will also bring it to pass; I have purposed it, I will also do it." (Isaiah 46:11) "So shall my word be that goeth forth out of my mouth: it shall not return unto me void; but it shall accomplish that which I please, and it shall prosper in the thing whereto I send it."—Isaiah 55:11.

Man can be absolutely certain that if God makes a promise he will make that promise good. Man therefore has a sure foundation for his hope when he relies upon the promises of God. Let us now examine some of the promises of God, and see what man can hope to have in God's due time.

Man's desire is for peace, plenty, health, strength, life, liberty and happiness. He has no hope of receiving any of these things by following the standards that men, governments and systems have heretofore held forth. If God has promised that man shall have these things, then by complying with the conditions attached to the promises, man may confidently hope to receive them. Such is a real hope. Such a hope God's standard holds for the people.

His Kingdom and Blessings

Jehovah is God. Jesus Christ, his beloved Son, is the Redeemer of man, the anointed King. God has promised that with the end of Satan's rule he will establish a kingdom for the benefit of man, and that this kingdom shall not be left to others, and that it shall stand for ever. There will be no profiteers, no politicians, nor false preachers in that kingdom. Christ the invisible King will rule, with his visible representatives on the earth acting under his direct supervision and control. "Behold, a king shall reign in righteousness, and princes shall rule in judgment." (Isaiah 32:1) The faithful men of old, Abraham, Isaac, and Jacob resurrected as perfect human beings, will be the visible representatives or princes in the earth.—Psalm 45:16.

Then a man will be considered as worth something. In beautiful poetic phrase the prophet describes it: "And a man shall be as an hiding place from the wind, and a covert from the tempest; as rivers of water in a dry place; as the shadow of a great rock in a weary land. And the eyes of them that see shall not be dim; and the ears of them that hear shall hearken."—Isaiah 32:2, 3.

The Prince of Peace will be in control of that government, and of the increase of his government and peace there shall be no end. (Isaiah 9:6, 7) No more shall the people be ravaged by war; because, declares the Lord, when his kingdom is established the people "shall beat their swords into plowshares, and their spears into pruninghooks: nation shall not lift up sword against nation, neither shall they learn war any more". (Isaiah 2:2-4) Through Messiah's kingdom, and that alone, will the people realize their desire for an ever-

lasting peace where they may dwell together and have
no fear of war or of assault from their enemies. "But
they shall sit every man under his vine and under his
fig tree; and none shall make them afraid: for the
mouth of the Lord of hosts hath spoken it. For all
people will walk every one in the name of his god, and
we will walk in the name of the Lord our God for ever
and ever."—Micah 4:4, 5.

Plenty

If everybody on earth should now deal justly one
with another there would be plenty for all. There is
no just cause for a shortage of food and fuel. A few
have great excess; the many have a scanty supply; while
still others have none. God has promised that in his
kingdom famines will be impossible. In the first place
the profiteers will not be permitted to ply their business. Nothing shall hurt or destroy in all that holy
kingdom. (Isaiah 11:9) The Lord will rule in righteousness, and with righteousness shall he judge the poor.
(Isaiah 11:4) Then when the judgments of the Lord
are in the earth the people will learn righteousness.—
Isaiah 26:9.

They will learn to minister one unto another and to
help one another. The Lord will furnish the people
with a means of eradicating the weeds and the thistles
and thorns, that the earth may bring forth the things
that they need. (Isaiah 55:13) Then the earth shall
yield her increase. (Psalm 67:6) "And in this kingdom shall the Lord of hosts make unto all people a
feast of fat things." (Isaiah 25:6) "He shall judge
thy people with righteousness, and thy poor with judgment. The kingdom shall bring peace to the people, and
the little hills, by righteousness. He shall judge the

poor of the people, he shall save the children of the needy, and shall break in pieces the oppressor. They shall fear thee as long as the sun and moon endure, throughout all generations. He shall come down like rain upon the mown grass: as showers that water the earth. In his days shall the righteous flourish; and abundance of peace as long as the moon endureth." —Psalm 72: 2-7.

Health

Health is one of the things that the people have long desired. All have suffered from lack of health. All the efforts that man has been able to put forth have not brought lasting health to the people. There is nothing in the standards held up by the various systems or governments that contain any basis for a hope of health. Look now to the standard of the Lord and see what it promises to those that walk humbly before him. The Lord says: "Behold, I will bring it health and cure, and I will cure them, and will reveal unto them the abundance of peace and truth." (Jeremiah 33: 6) "And the inhabitant shall not say, I am sick; the people that dwell therein shall be forgiven their iniquity."—Isaiah 33: 24.

Life

Life in a state of peace and happiness is the greatest desire of man. For sixty centuries the human family has been racked by disease, and billions have gone down in sorrow to the grave. All the schemes that men have ever put forth concerning eternal life, all the statements upon the standard of men or institutions promising life, have been and are false. Satan declared that there is no death; and his representatives on earth have been preaching for centuries that man does not die. But human experience proves that this is entirely false. Why longer be deceived by the false standards of men? Turn now to the standard of the Lord and see what it holds as a hope for man.

Jesus Christ declared: "This is life eternal, that they might know thee the only true God, and Jesus Christ whom thou hast sent." (John 17:3) Keep always in mind that originally *GOD* gave life to man and that *GOD* took away that right to life because of disobedience. Remember then that *GOD ALONE* provided for the redemption of man from death and the grave according to his promise; that these provisions for redemption are through the merit of the ransom sacrifice of the Lord Jesus; that GOD has appointed a day or period of time in which he will give all men an opportunity to reap the benefits of this ransom sacrifice and an opportunity to be restored to perfect human life. It is in the Messianic kingdom on earth that this opportunity shall be given to man; and this kingdom is now beginning. The apostle states that the second coming and reign of the Lord is for the purpose of giving an opportunity first to the living and then to those that are dead; and that this opportunity shall be given in his kingdom. (2 Timothy 4:1) The kingdom is now beginning, and that is why these truths are coming to the knowledge of the people.

The Prophet Job, in poetic phrase, describes the miserable condition in which man finds himself and shows how vain it is to follow the standards of men; and then he turns his words to the Messenger of the covenant, namely, the Lord Jesus Christ, the King of kings. He shows that this great Messenger is the one among a thousand and altogether lovely; and that if man hears and obeys this great Messenger, who interprets and makes the Word of God plain, God then " is gracious unto him, and saith, Deliver him from going down to the pit [grave]", and the response of man is: "I have found a ransom." Then what shall result to the one who is obedient and walks humbly before God? The prophet answers: "His flesh shall be fresher than a child's; he shall return to the days of his youth."—Job 33:19-25.

The Apostle Peter stated that all the prophets have testified concerning the restoration blessings that are coming to man if man is obedient to God's law. (Acts 3:19, 20) St. Paul, discussing the matter, says concerning Christ: "But now is Christ risen from the dead, and become the firstfruits of them that slept. . . . For he must reign, till he hath put all enemies under his feet. The last enemy that shall be destroyed is death." —1 Corinthians 15:20, 25, 26.

St. John, after giving a vivid description of the new heavens and earth, namely, the new invisible ruling power and the new government upon the earth, and pointing out God's arrangement for men, says: "And God shall wipe away all tears from their eyes; and there shall be no more death, neither sorrow, nor crying, neither shall there be any more pain: for the former things are passed away. And he that sat upon the throne said, Behold, I make all things new. And he said unto me, Write: for these words are true and faithful."—Revelation 21:4, 5.

Those now residing on earth first having had their opportunity, then will come from the tomb those who have long slept in the dust of the earth. The Prophet Daniel, speaking first of the time when Michael the Christ, who stands up for the people, shall take his power and reign, says that then those sleeping in the

dust of the earth shall awake. (Daniel 12:1, 2) The
Lord Jesus, referring to the same time, said: "All in
the graves shall hear his voice, and shall come forth."
(John 5:28, 29) Again Jesus, speaking of the same
time, said: "Verily, verily, I say unto you, If a man
keep my saying, he shall never see death."—John 8:51.

Here is the positive saying that the man who obeys
the Lord, walking humbly before him, shall never die.
But of course he must first come to a knowledge of the
truth; and for this reason the truth is first testified to
him. Then if he hears and obeys he shall never die.
Again the Lord Jesus said, referring to the same time:
"And whosoever liveth and believeth in me shall never
die."—John 11:26.

The people have been wicked all through the centuries because of the wicked influence of Satan the
Devil. But Satan is to be restrained that he may deceive them no more; and then the wicked man, turning to righteousness, shall live and shall not die. (Revelation 20:1-3) "When the wicked man turneth away
from his wickedness that he hath committed, and doeth
that which is lawful and right, he shall save his soul
alive. Because he considereth, and turneth away from
all his transgressions that he hath committed, he shall
surely live, he shall not die."—Ezekiel 18:27, 28.

Because the time has come for the fulfilment of these
great truths, because the Lord's kingdom is at hand,
and because a generation of people exists upon the earth
in ordinary times for fifty years or more, we are now
able to confidently say that there are millions of people
residing on the earth who shall have an opportunity to
accept the light of God and walk humbly before him
and, so doing, shall live for ever, being restored to a
perfect condition of body and mind.

Liberty

Liberty is one of the things that man has desired. He has always been in bondage to some kind of oppression. He has been in bondage also to the great enemy sickness and death. The Lord Jesus Christ declares that he who accepts and obeys the truth shall be set free; and when the Lord sets him free he shall be free indeed. (John 8:32) Here then is a basis for the liberty that the people have so long desired.

Happiness

Happiness is another thing mankind has always desired. All the happiness that man has enjoyed on this earth has been temporary. There have no real joy and happiness resulted, nor can such ever result, from heeding and following standards of men. Why now should we longer hold to those withering standards? Let us turn our minds now to God's standard, which he had commanded to now be held up to the people, and see whether or not it furnishes a basis of hope for happiness.

What could produce happiness? The answer is: To enjoy everlasting peace, everlasting plenty, everlasting health, everlasting life. All these things are guaranteed by the scriptures above cited.

If all the blind eyes should be restored so that they could see; if all deafness should pass away, all lameness or crookedness of body should cease; if there should be nothing in the land to harm; if the governments always were righteous and the people righteous and love the motive directing their actions, would not that be a happy time? Is not this really what the people desire? God's Word furnishes an absolute and certain hope for the realization of this desire.

Referring to the blessed reign of Christ, God's prophet says: "Say to them that are of a fearful heart, Be strong, fear not: behold, your God will come with vengeance, even God with a recompence; he will come and save you. Then the eyes of the blind shall be opened, and the ears of the deaf shall be unstopped. Then shall the lame man leap as an hart, and the tongue of the dumb sing: for in the wilderness shall waters break out, and streams in the desert. And the parched ground shall become a pool, and the thirsty land springs of water: in the habitation of dragons, where each lay, shall be grass, with reeds and rushes. . . . And the ransomed of the Lord shall return, *and come to Zion with songs, and everlasting joy upon their heads: they shall obtain joy and gladness,* and sorrow and sighing shall flee away."—Isaiah 35:4-7, 10.

One of the early things to be accomplished in this kingdom will be to remove the ignorance and superstition from the minds of the people and to destroy in their minds that which is contained in the standards that earthly institutions are now holding forth. Concerning this God's prophet says: "And he will destroy in this mountain [kingdom] the face of the covering cast over all people, and the vail that is spread over all nations. He will swallow up death in victory; and the Lord God will wipe away tears from off all faces; and the rebuke of his people shall he take away from off all the earth: for the Lord hath spoken it."—Isa. 25:7, 8.

Truly Jehovah is the only true and loving God. His justice, wisdom, love and power always operate together in harmony. He has made provision for the redemption and deliverance of man; and now after a long dark night of suffering and sorrow the light of truth is breaking forth. God's standard is unfurled be-

fore the people. That banner or standard over them is
one of love. The people are called upon to rally to it,
to say one to another: Come now, let us turn ourselves
to the kingdom of the Lord; for he will teach us the
right way and we shall walk in the paths of righteousness and we shall come to a full and complete realization of our heart's sincere desire.

(From the Press)

World Reconstruction

A Standard to Guide the People

UNANIMOUS adoption of resolution by multitude of Christians attended with great enthusiasm.

Judge Rutherford's Stirring Address in Support of Resolution.

Indianapolis, Indiana, August 30.—Cadle Auditorium, with a capacity of 12,000, was packed out and great numbers turned away when Judge Rutherford spoke this afternoon in support of a resolution presented to the Convention of International Bible Students on the day previous. The resolution was unanimously adopted by a rising vote amidst great enthusiasm.

Mr. Robert J. Martin, of New York city, acting chairman of the mass meeting, read the resolution which is set forth herein in full and then introduced Judge Rutherford. The great multitude gave the keenest attention to every word of the speaker and when he had concluded arose en masse in support of his position.

The resolution, as its name implies, is truly a "message of hope". It is addressed to all peoples of good will throughout the earth, and emphasizes the imperative necessity for the peoples' informing themselves concerning the divine standard for the reconstruction of the world.

This "message of hope" bids fair to stand forth with marked distinction in the world as a guiding document unselfishly appealing to the peoples to look well to their own interests. In his address Judge Rutherford emphasizes the fact that the body of Christians presenting the message to the people of good will are seeking neither money nor men. This alone should commend it to the candid and favorable consideration of all.

64

Message of Hope

To ALL PEOPLES OF GOOD WILL:

The International Bible Students in General Convention assembled send greetings:

When in the course of human affairs the nations have reached a condition of extremity it is due time that the peoples give consideration to the inducing causes, to the proffered remedies and to the true remedy. We humbly invite consideration of this message to the end that the peoples might find consolation therein and hope for their future welfare.

For centuries man has been the victim of oppression, war, famine, sickness, sorrow and death. At all times he has desired peace, prosperity, health, life, liberty and happiness.

World powers, science and philosophy, commerce and religion, have each in turn offered their respective remedies for man's relief. In the name and under the guise of democracy, these combine in offering their joint and several powers to meet the requirements of man. Together they claim to be the sunlight of the world, holding forth all the light that shines to enlighten and guide the human race.

Intrigue, duplicity and trickery are freely resorted to by the political and commercial powers; science and philosophy are marked by vanity and self-sufficiency; while the religionists, both Catholic and Protestant, are conspicuous by their arrogance, self-conceit, impiety and ungodliness. Therefore it is apparent,that the remedies offered by any and all of these aforementioned elements are vain, impotent and powerless to satisfy man's desire.

Catholicism claims and assumes that which justly belongs exclusively to God. Modernists deny God, deny His Word and His Plan of redemption and offer blind force as a remedy for man's undone condition. Fundamentalists while professing to believe the Bible by their course of action deny the same. They teach false and God dishonoring doctrines and together with Catholics and Modernists are allied with the political and commercial powers of the world in blasphemously claiming the ability to establish God's kingdom on earth. All of these have combined under Satan their superlord, to push God into a corner and to dishonor His name.

The results are that the peoples are smarting under the oppressive weight of commercial profiteers and their allies, have lost faith in their political leaders and no longer have respect for the religionists who have misled them. Being guided by the false light of such an ungodly and unholy alliance, the peoples have fallen into darkness. They are like lost sheep scattered upon the mountain tops without a shepherd and are without food and shelter and are made the prey of wild beasts.

The causes for this deplorable condition are that man by reason of original sin fell from perfection; and that Satan the enemy of God and all righteousness is the invisible ruler or god of this evil world and by his various agencies has turned the minds of many peoples away from God and from His truth.

The greatest crisis of the ages is impending and about to fall, because the old world has ended and Satan's lease of power is done. Knowing this, and that his time is short, the Devil is trying to overwhelm the peoples with a great flood of false and deceptive doctrines and to turn their minds completely away from Jehovah. The time has come for God to make for Himself a name in the earth and for the peoples to know the Truth concerning the Divine Plan, which is the only means of salvation for the world.

Therefore, in the name and in the spirit of the Lord, the 'Standard of God's Truth and Righteousness is here lifted ıp against the enemy and for the benefit of the peoples, which standard is, to wit:

That Jehovah is the only true God, the Most High, the Almighty, the author and finisher of His great plan for the salvation of man, and is the rewarder of all that diligently seek and obey Him; that the Bible is His revealed Word of Truth; that His beloved Son Christ Jesus is the Redeemer and Deliverer of mankind and, true to His promise, has come to rule and bless the peoples; that the present turmoil, distress and perplexity of the nations is in fulfilment of prophecy, proving that Satan's empire is breaking down and that the Lord of Righteousness is taking possession; that the Lord Jesus is now establishing His righteous government and will sweep away Satan's stronghold of lies, lead the peoples into the true light and judge the world in righteousness and the peoples with His truth; and that His kingdom of righteousness is the only remedy for the ills of humankind.

We confidently appeal to the peoples to rally to the Divine Standard of Truth thus lifted up and thereby learn the way that leads to life and happiness. We call upon all the peoples of good will of every nation, kindred and tongue, to discard the errors invented by the enemy Satan and for many years taught by man, and to receive and believe the Divine Plan of salvation as set forth in the Scriptures.

God's kingdom for which the peoples have long prayed is at hand. It alone can and will establish and stabilize the world so that it cannot be moved. Its ensign of righteousness is the Standard now lifted up for the people. Christ Jesus, as glorified king and great executive officer of Jehovah God, has become the rightful ruler of the world. Let the peoples receive, believe and obey Him and His laws of righteousness. All who so do are certain to receive the blessings of peace, prosperity, health, life, liberty and eternal happiness.

Dated Indianapolis, Aug. 29, 1925.

FREEDOM
FOR THE PEOPLES

by
Judge Rutherford

GREATEST
RADIO HOOK-UP
ON EARTH

FREEDOM FOR THE PEOPLES

By J. F. Rutherford,

President

International Bible Students Association

Author of

Deliverance!
The Harp of God
Comfort for the Jews
Millions Now Living Will Never Die
Comfort for the People
Where are the Dead?
etc., etc.

MADE IN U. S. A.

(Copyright 1927)

Published by

INTERNATIONAL BIBLE STUDENTS ASSOCIATION

BROOKLYN, N. Y., U. S. A.

Also: London, Toronto, Melbourne, Cape Town, Stockholm,
Magdeburg, Berne, Copenhagen, *etc.*

FOREWORD

THE broadcasting of Judge Rutherford's lecture by the National Broadcasting Company was conceded even by our enemies to be the greatest hook-up of broadcasting on earth. The response by the people has been phenomenal. So great has been the demand for copies thereof that we have determined to issue it in the cheapest possible form so that the poor may have it. It voices a declaration of independence of the peoples of Christendom from that unholy alliance that has so long oppressed them.

We append hereto an introductory chapter setting forth some of the sufferings of the common people, also a concluding chapter showing the Scriptural reason for the passing away of the World Powers. Both were written by Judge Rutherford. You will read this booklet with great interest. You will want to keep it in your homes and read it to your children.

The Publisher

CHAPTER 1

The Oppressed

THE common peoples of all nations have suffered great oppression. Their real defenders have been very few. By the common people are meant those of the rank and file who labor with their hands and thereby produce the wealth of the land. There was a time when America was said to be an asylum for the oppressed. That day has gone! To what country could the common people now flee and find protection, aid, peace, freedom of speech and freedom of action? There is none under the sun!

The World War has furnished the common people of Christendom with much food for thought, and they are thinking as they have not heretofore thought. They are beginning to realize that they must think and act for themselves. They have been deceived for a long time by those upon whom they relied. They cannot be deceived always. They were told by those who represented selfish interests that the Great War would make the world safe for democracy. The result has been the very opposite. With the ending of the World War practically all the liberties of the common people have been taken away. Big Business and professional politicians, aided and supported by faithless clergy, have fastened the shackles upon the wrists of the common people. They continue to suffer and they are seeking the way of relief and freedom. As an illustration of some of the things suffered the following is here related.

In June, 1914, in one of the northwest states of "free" America, lived Jacob Christmann with his wife Martha, Elsie his only daughter. and two sons, William and John Christmann, twins. That was a happy family. Their

5

acreage was small but rich, and yielding to their hard labor produced a sufficiency for them. Because of the manipulation of the markets they found it difficult to sell their produce at much profit ; yet they were able to get on, and they had the love and sweet companionship of each other, and hence they were content.

Jacob Christmann was born in Germany and emigrated to "free" America when a mere lad. His older brother, Henry Christmann, remained in Germany, married there and reared several sons and daughters. Martha MacDonald was born in Scotland and came to America with her parents. She became the wife of Jacob Christmann and the mother of the above named Christmann children. Gilbert MacDonald, a brother of Martha, resided in Scotland his native land and there reared a family of sons and daughters, among them Gilbert Jr.

The three Christmann children in America from time to time exchanged letters with their cousins in Germany and in Scotland. For some time prior to 1914 the war lords of Germany made it so burdensome for the Christmann boys that often they wrote their American cousins of their purpose to come to "free" America to live and thus escape the war and the burden of the war machine. The American cousins spoke often with their parents about their kinsmen across the sea, and of course there was a great desire for personal acquaintance.

In August, 1914, the World War began, and the Christmann boys of Germany were hurried to the front and, of course, that precluded their visit to America. At the same time the British entered the war and among those sent out to fight Germany was Gilbert Mac-Donald, Jr., the young Scotsman. It was therefore blood relation sent out to fight blood relation in a deadly combat and that without the desire or consent of either one to fight the other.

After much agitation by subsidized American newspapers and hired preachers America entered the war in 1917. At the instance of Big Business a conscription law was quickly enacted by the American Congress. Thereafter young Americans were not asked if they wanted to fight but were told they must fight or take the consequences, which consequences usually were imprisonment and cruel and unusual treatment at the hands of the prison keepers. Among those drafted early in the war by America were the Christmann twins, William and John. A pall of blackness fell over the modest and once happy home of the Christmann family. The two boys were torn away from their parents and their only sister. They were sent to war together and they tried to stay together throughout the war. Upon the battlefields of France they saw much real military service.

For more than forty hours the great battle between the Germans on one side and the British and their allies on the other had been raging furiously. A fresh American division was sent to the front to relieve the remaining men in the shattered lines of the allies, and in that American division which went forward were the two privates, William and John Christmann. A charge was ordered; and the Christmann boys, together with thousands of others, obeyed the command. William came suddenly upon a German soldier lying upon the ground and drew his bayonet to strike him through; but seeing that the German was already mortally wounded William did not strike. The dying man looked with pleading into the face of William Christmann, who moved with sympathy gave the German water from his own canteen. The drink revived him. The wounded man then addressing William said: "I am dying. Why have we fought? I had nothing against the French or English and surely not against the Americans. I have some dear cousins in America that I love much." Then William inquired: "Who are your American cousins?" The

German replying in broken speech conveyed the message
to William by which the two men learned that they were
cousins, who had often communicated with each other by
letter. William's brother John was near by, and seeing
his brother with a German rushed to his side and learned
the real cause. At that moment a ball pierced William.
The two cousins, knowing that they had but a few
moments to live, affectionately embraced each other and
died in each other's arms.

Later the official report came to America which merely
read: William Christmann, killed in action. The sad
information was conveyed to his mother. She died from
a broken heart. It was afterwards learned that in that
same engagement Gilbert MacDonald, Jr., the Scottish
cousin, was also killed.

The Christmann homestead in America was mort-
gaged. The family had depended upon the two sons to
pay the interest. The mortgage was held by a loan
company, financed by a few multimillionaires who produced nothing but required much of the produce of the
farm to pay their usury. The mortgage became due; and
no one of the Christmann family being able to pay the
interest or principal, it was foreclosed. Jacob Christmann and his daughter Elsie were compelled to leave
their home. No information had yet come as to the fate
of John Christmann, the other twin son. The war
ended and broken regiments of soldiers began to return.
But John was not with them.

Jacob Christman was a member of the Lutheran
church. The minister of that church denomination
where his membership was held had been among those
who preached the boys into the war and aided and
abetted in the enforced draft. It was difficult for Elsie
to understand how he could be a minister and consistently take that course. Elsie and her father had now found
a modest little house for their temporary residence. They
anxiously awaited some information as to John, hoping

that he had survived the terrible war. Many hours of sad reflection were passed by her and her father. She came upon him on one occasion and found him reading the Bible. She plied him with a number of questions amongst which were these: "Does not America claim to be a Christian nation? Is not Great Britain also one that lays claim to being a Christian nation? Have we not always understood that Germany claims to be a Christian nation? Do not all these nations claim to serve and follow Christ, the Prince of Peace? How can these nations and the preachers in their churches claim to be Christians and yet advocate war and compel the people to go to war and fight and kill each other and to kill their own blood relatives and that against their own wish and consent?"

The oppression upon this poor soul and the bitterness that she had suffered caused her to propound these questions to her father. She further said to him: "Father, who is responsible for this terrible war and for the dreadful sorrow that has been brought upon us? Can you support a church which claims to follow Christ and which participates in bringing upon us such burdens of sorrow?" The father of course was unable to answer the question. He, too, was suffering great bitterness of heart and was seeking consolation in the Word of God. He had not found it in the church. The burdens of oppression and sorrow became too great for him; and shortly thereafter Jacob Christmann died; and Elsie, alone, with no one to care for her, drifted away.

The terrible fate that befell the once happy family of Jacob Christmann has befallen thousands of other homes. And what became of John Christmann? When the hospitals began to give up their inmates, as the grave some day will give up the dead, John was brought forth. He was blind, one arm gone, and his feet so mangled that he moves about only with the aid of crutches. He is a helpless cripple so far as there is ability of man to

aid him. Millions of other young men in Christendom
are in this same condition. They have suffered and continue to suffer, daily dying. Added to their bodily pain
is the mental anguish that this condition was forced
upon them.

RESPONSIBILITY FOR THE WAR

Did the common peoples of the nations of earth vote
on the question as to whether or not they should go to
war? No, not one of them! Did any one explain to
the common people the necessity for the great World
War of Christendom? No one! Who then is responsible
for the war? A few selfish and ambitious men desiring
to increase their power were willing to hurry millions
of human beings into death in order to accomplish their
purposes. A petty excuse was seized upon for declaration of war, and the war began. Big Business con-
structed the machinery for the war and furnished the
initial money necessary to do so, knowing that they
would reap a thousand percent in return. The professional politicians enacted conscription laws to make
the war machine work. The dishonest and faithless
preachers of various religious denominations, while
claiming to follow Christ, urged the people into war
and acted as war agents. Hypocritically they preached
war from their pulpits. In many instances they were
paid for so doing by the big financiers who desired the
war for private gain. The common people were forced
by them to bare their breasts to shot and shell and to
have their property and their lives taken away in order
to satisfy the wicked and selfish ambition of men. The
people are beginning to see these things more clearly.
There is reason now for the common people to think.

RESULT

What is the result of that World War? Everybody
knows that it has resulted in the destruction of the

democracy of the land and the taking away of the freedom of the people; and that it has resulted in a new, crop of millionaires in whose thoughts God finds no place. It has also resulted in great corruption in the high political offices and has proven that the clergy have denied the name of God and Christ and that they are forsaken by the Lord. It made it possible for selfish men, high financiers, bootleggers, and preachers to fasten upon the people a hypocritical and cruel prohibition law which both the clergy and "Big Business" insist on enforcing against the common people while the "High ups" openly violate it themselves. Men in high places make and dispense illicitly intoxicating liquors. If one of the common people is found in possession of a small quantity he is severely punished. The unholy alliance maintains customs officers at the border principally in the United States to browbeat and insult innocent men and women and to ruthlessly destroy their property, abuse and humiliate them without even the semblance of a cause or excuse. The war was seized upon as an opportunity by the Devil and his unholy agencies to fasten the shackles tighter and tighter upon the arms of the people and take away their liberty.

Democracy means a government of the people, for the people, and by the people. No such government now exists in what is called "Christendom". On the contrary in the land fraudulently called "Christendom" the government of the peoples is by the unholy alliance of "Big Business" and big politicians supported by big preachers, and in the interest of the unholy alliance and against the interests of the common people. The oppression does not stop there.

Millions of money raised by oppressive taxation from the common people are being expended in further preparation for war. The common people of no nation on earth desire to fight the common people of another nation; but the selfish ambitious men, few in number com-

pared with the multitudes, are the ones who prepare for
war, compel the common people to bear the burden
thereof by unjust taxation and the further burden, oppression and suffering by laying down their lives upon
the battle-field. Is it any wonder then that the common
people now are beginning to ask themselves: What good
has Christendom brought to us? Can we ever hope or
expect to have any relief from our burdens brought to
us by or through Christendom? They are seeing and
seeing plainly that Christendom so-called is a fraudulent
name used to deceive the common people and hold them
in subjection.

Is it possible then for the common people to ever have
relief and freedom from any source? Yes; there is one
absolutely certain way and about that way the people
must now know. The time is at hand for the great God
of the universe to hear the cries of the common people
and to act in their behalf. It is plain from his Word and
from the facts before us that his due time for the people's relief has arrived. It is therefore the time for him
to first give the people some knowledge of his purpose.

RADIO

No man has ever been able to explain what radio is.
It is an unseen power by which the human voice is
carried through the air and a message given to others
in the far distance; but what it is man cannot say. Certain it is that God provided the radio because he fore-
tells it in his Word written by the prophet centuries ago.
(Job 38:35) The due time must come, in the unfolding of his plan, for the use of the radio. That time has
come, and God will use it for the benefit of mankind.
God has repeatedly used human agencies to carry out
some of his purposes. It should be expected therefore
that God would use some human agencies to proclaim
to the people at this time his purposes concerning them
and that he would use the radio in connection therewith.

Those men and women who are wholly and entirely devoted to the Lord naturally would be the ones whom the Lord would use as the witnesses. In his Word it is written concerning such: "Ye are my witnesses, that I am God." (Isaiah 43:10, 12) The truth that is proclaimed is not man's truth but it belongs to God. "Thy Word is truth." (John 17:17) The Lord has made it clear that he will not always turn a deaf ear to the cries of the common people. It seems certain that his due time is here to give ear to their cry.

ARRANGEMENTS TO BROADCAST

The International Bible Students Association is not a religious organization. A religious organization is composed of men and women who observe certain forms and ceremonies in the acknowledgment of a supreme power. The International Bible Students Association is made up of a body of men and women who are Christians, fully consecrated to do the Lord's will. Of course there are some amongst them who are not wholly devoted to the Lord, while many of them are completely devoted to God and his cause. These Christians have come out from denominational systems because they love the Lord and want to serve him. They have no selfish purpose to accomplish. Knowing that the relief of the people and their blessings must come from Jehovah God these Christians are anxious to tell their fellow men about God's gracious provision for such blessings. A real Christian is one who follows Christ. The purpose of Christ on earth is expressed in his own words: "To this end was I born, and for this cause came I into the world, that I should bear witness unto the truth." (John 18:37) All true followers of Christ therefore must likewise be witnesses to the truth. They must tell the truth in the love of the truth and for the love of their fellow man. This being God's due time to have the witness of the truth given all loyal Christians desire to have a

part in giving that witness. They want to please God
and they know that to please him they must do his will.
(Matthew 7:21) It is the will of God now that all nations of Christendom be told about God's kingdom.
(Matthew 24:14) True Christians are faithfully endeavoring to obey this command of the Lord.

The International Bible Students Association held its
annual convention for 1927 at Toronto, Canada, from
July 18th to the 25th. Christians came from many
countries to attend this convention and to participate
in giving the witness to Jehovah's name. A short time
prior thereto at a hearing before the Federal Radio
Commission at Washington, D. C., a condition arose
which led to the completion of an arrangement to broadcast an address by the president of the International
Bible Students Association from the Coliseum at Toronto. It came about in this manner: During a hearing
before the Commission the president of the National
Broadcasting Company, Mr. Aylesworth, was on the witness stand testifying in behalf of that corporation, which
operates three chains of radio stations in the United
States. He was being cross-examined by the president
of the International Bible Students Association. A
question was propounded to Mr. Aylesworth as follows:
"Your purpose is to give to the people by radio the
message of the greatest financiers, the most prominent
statesmen, and the most renowned clergymen of the
world?" To this Mr. Aylesworth answered in the af-
firmative. Another question was propounded to him:
"If you were convinced that the great God of the universe
will shortly put in operation his plan for the blessing
of all the nations and families of the earth with peace,
prosperity, life and happiness, and that the great Creator
desired that this message be broadcast would you arrange to broadcast it?" The answer was, in the af-
firmative and led to an offer by the president of the National Broadcasting Company to broadcast the address

of the president of the International Bible Students Association. The arrangement was made to broadcast from Toronto, as above stated.

The attending facts and circumstances show conclusively that the Lord made it possible for such a broadcast. No association nor any man could have arranged it. It was the Lord who did it for his own glory. By means of telephone wires fifty-three radio broadcasting stations were tied together. The address was delivered at the Coliseum at Toronto, transmitted by wire to radio station WEAF, New York City, and relayed to other stations to the number of fifty-three, reaching from Maine to California, and from Canada to Mexico, and including two super-power stations which easily reach Europe, South Africa and Australia. In the language of one of the New York dailies it was "the greatest hookup in radio history". It was the means adopted to quickly give a witness to Christendom of facts which they know to be true when they hear them.

On that occasion the president of the Association presented to the convention a resolution which is really a message to the peoples of Christendom. His address was in support of the resolution. He emphasized the following points, to wit: That Jehovah is the only true God; that Christ Jesus his Son is the Redeemer and Savior of man and the rightful King of earth; that there is a true Christianity composed of those men and women who faithfully represent God and Christ; that there is a false, deceptive and fraudulent organization called "organized Christianity" or "Christendom" which misrepresents God and in fact represents the Devil; that God created all men of one blood to dwell upon the earth and that there is no just cause or excuse for them to engage in war; that the ruling factors of "Christendom" which in fact constitute "Christendom" are, to wit, high financiers, professional politicians, aided and supported by faithless clergy; that this unholy alliance

produces nothing but lives upon the honest labors of
the common people and the common people have long
been oppressed by carrying such as a burden; that the
ruling element provokes war between nations for selfish
reasons and compels the common people to go to war
and fight and kill each other without any cause or excuse; that the people have long been oppressed and have
suffered untold misery at the hands of the rulers in Christendom and that without the support of the common
people Christendom could not stand; that the time has
come when the common people must forsake and for
ever abandon the fraudulent system of Christendom and
give allegiance to God and to Christ; that the kingdom
of heaven is at hand and that through God's kingdom
the people will receive their heart's desire. namely. peace.
prosperity, life, liberty and happiness; and that through
his kingdom the burdens of sorrow will be lifted from
the people, and they will be given joy and health,
strength and life.

So convincing and heart-cheering was the address in
support of the resolution that the great audience amidst
tremendous enthusiasm arose and unanimously adopted
the resolution, which resolution. together with the address in support thereof, is set forth in the next chapter.

Since the adoption of the resolution and the delivery
of that address thousands of letters and telegrams have
been received from every quarter of the American continent, requesting copies thereof. This booklet is adopted
as a means to get it to the people.

CHAPTER II

The Appeal

M R. ROBT. J. MARTIN of New York City presided
at the meeting. In introducing Judge Rutherford he said:

After hearing Judge Rutherford, you will desire to
have a copy of his lecture, that you may carefully consider it at home.

I am authorized to say, that any person in this, or in
the unseen radio audience, who will address a letter or
card to Judge Rutherford, Brooklyn, New York, requesting a copy of the lecture, will be mailed a copy,
free of charge.

Among people in every walk of life, throughout the
civilized world, a profound interest in the stirring events
of the present day has been aroused by Judge Rutherford's latest book, entitled *Deliverance*. For the benefit
of those who are in the audience here in Toronto, arrangements have been made to provide a copy of *Deliverance* at the conclusion of this lecture. See the ushers
on your way out.

The thirty million volumes of Judge Rutherford's
books which are in the *homes* of the people everywhere,
constitute a sufficient introduction for him, both to this
audience and to the far-flung invisible audience.

It is now my pleasure to ask Judge Rutherford to
proceed with his address.

The speaker said: Mr. Chairman, my audience seen
and unseen: What I shall say here is in the interest of
the common peoples of earth, and especially in behalf of
those of Christendom. First, I offer the following resolution and then I shall speak in support of that resolution.
The resolution reads as follows:

17

RESOLUTION

To the Peoples of Christendom:

The International Bible Students in general convention assembled send greetings:

As Christians and witnesses to the name of Jehovah God we deem it our privilege and duty to call your attention to the following vital facts:

FIRST. That God made of one blood all peoples and nations of men to dwell on the earth, and granted to all peoples equal rights. There is therefore no just cause or excuse for one nation to make war against another nation.

SECOND. That the foremost nations of the earth claim to be Christian nations and, taken collectively, they constitute "Christendom" or "organized Christianity", so-called; that the men chiefly responsible for the claim that these are Christian nations are the clergymen of the various religious denominations, who call themselves by the name of Christ but who in fact have denied him; that their purpose of claiming that these nations are Christian is to induce the peoples to believe that said nations, although military and cruel, are the representatives of God and his Christ on earth; that such claim is fraudulent and false and has turned the minds of millions of honest people away from the true God and from his Christ; that the invisible ruler of the nations of "Christendom" or "organized Christianity", so-called, is Satan the Devil, who has fathered the scheme of forming "organized Christianity" to deceive the people and to keep them in subjection to himself and his agencies.

That the masses of the peoples of the nations are entitled to self-government exercised by the people for the general welfare of all; but instead of enjoying such rights a small minority rules; that the money power of the world has been concentrated into the hands of a few men called high financiers, and these in turn have corrupted the men who make and execute the laws of the nations, and the faithless clergy have voluntarily joined forces with the high financiers and professional politicians, and that said unholy alliance constitutes the governing powers that rule the peoples; that the masses of the peoples acting under a misapprehension of the true facts have borne up, carried, supported and maintained organized Christianity; and that without the support of the common people the unholy alliance constituting organized Christianity could not long exist.

THIRD. That for centuries the privileges enjoyed by men have been wholly unequal and unfair. The multitudes have produced the wealth of the world, but have been unjustly deprived of the fruits of their labors. That the leaders of Christendom instead of teaching the children of men the doctrines of Christ, whom they claim to follow, teach them to murder their fellow creatures; and that now the rulers are amalgamating the common people with the military, in order to make all the peoples a part of and subject to their great war machine; that by unjust laws the common people, contrary to their own wishes, have been compelled to go to war against each other, resulting in great sorrow and suffering, multitudes of broken hearts and millions of untimely graves; that "organized Christianity" has turned a deaf ear to the petitions and entreaties of the people for relief, and now the cries of the oppressed people have entered into the ears of Jehovah God, and his time is at hand to give the peoples deliverance and freedom.

FOURTH. That Jehovah is the only true God, the Friend and Benefactor of the peoples. He has now set his beloved Son Christ Jesus upon his throne, and bids all the peoples of earth to hear and to obey him who is earth's rightful King.

FIFTH. That the kings and rulers of the earth, to wit: those constituting the said unholy alliance have been duly notified that God has set his King upon his throne and that his kingdom is at hand; but they refuse to understand or to take heed, and they walk on in darkness. Therefore God has decreed and declared that there shall come upon the world a time of tribulation such as never was known; and that during that trouble "Christendom" or "organized Christianity", so-called, and all of Satan's organization shall be destroyed; and that Christ Jesus, the righteous King, will assume complete authority and control and will bless the peoples of the earth.

SIXTH. That it must be now apparent to all thoughtful peoples that relief, comfort and blessings so much desired by them can never come from the unrighteous system of "Christendom" or "organized Christianity", and that there is no reason to give further support to that hypocritical and oppressive system. In this hour of perplexity Jehovah God bids the peoples to abandon and for ever forsake "Christendom" or "organized Christianity" and to turn completely away from it, because it is the Devil's organization, and to give it no support whatsoever; and that the peoples give their heart's devotion and allegiance wholly to Jehovah God and to his King and kingdom, and receive full freedom and the blessings God has in store for them.

SEVENTH. For four thousand years the cherished desire of Jews has been God's Messianic kingdom. For nineteen centuries that kingdom has been the hope of real Christians. It is now at hand. True to his promise God by and through the reign of Christ will lift the burdens of the peoples, free them from war, fraud and oppression, from sickness, suffering and death, and give to them a righteous government and the blessings of everlasting peace, prosperity, life, and happiness.

Upon the reading of the Resolution the following speech was made in support thereof, which was heard by 15,000 in the Coliseum and broadcast throughout the country. The speaker said:

Freedom for the Peoples

GOD made of one blood all nations of men to dwell upon the earth and gave to them equal rights. Foreknowing the evil influence that would be exercised over all governments of men God foretold that a small minority would rule and oppress the great majority; that during that period of oppression and suffering the peoples would desire freedom and a righteous government administered for the general welfare of all; that they would be disappointed and suffer; that the cries of the peoples would ascend unto God and in his due time he would hear them; that he would deliver the peoples from the oppressor into full freedom and give to them a government of righteousness under which they shall enjoy peace, prosperity, and the blessings of life. Therefore he caused his prophets to write concerning the present time these words: that "the Lord . . . hath prepared his throne for judgment; and he shall judge the world in righteousness, he shall minister judgment to the people in uprightness. The Lord also will be a refuge for the oppressed, a refuge in times of trouble" (Psalm 9:7-9); and "a king shall reign in righteousness, and princes shall rule in judgment".—Isaiah 32:1.

Only by the Lord's arrangement can freedom come to the peoples. God's due time has now come when the peoples of earth must know the truth concerning the cause of suffering and the remedy for relief. All true Christians are doing their part to tell these facts to the peoples that God's name might be glorified and that the peoples might know that their freedom is near.

"CHRISTENDOM"

The foremost nations of the world jointly call themselves "Christendom". The rulers by this term claim that they are Christians, having and exercising faith in God and in Christ, and that their combined govern-

ments constitute "organized Christianity". The claim
is not only untrue, but it is fraudulent and hypocritical.
By such false and hypocritical claim the multitudes of
peoples have long been held in bondage and have been
deprived of their just rights and privileges. God's due
time has come for "organized Christianity", so-called,
to be placed before the people in the proper light.

There is a true Christianity composed of faithful men
and women who unselfishly follow in the footsteps of
Christ. There is an organized system called "Christianity" or "Christendom", which is false and is the instrument of oppression wielded by the hand of the Devil.
Jehovah through Christ established true Christianity on
the earth, and in the days of the apostles it progressed.
A few ambitious men, influenced and directed by Satan,
defiled true Christianity; and their fraudulent course
has made Christianity, as it is generally understood, a
stench in the nostrils of honest men. This exact condition God foretold through his prophet Jeremiah (2:20)
who wrote concerning professed Christianity: "Yet I
had planted thee a noble vine, wholly a right seed: how
then art thou turned into the degenerate plant of a
strange vine unto me?"—Jeremiah 2:21.

"Organized Christianity" or "Christendom" today is
Satan's organization fraudulently parading under the
name of Christ. Early in the history of man the Devil
caused men to call themselves by the name of the Lord
and to thereby bring reproach upon God. That same
Devil has caused ambitious and selfish men to organize
and carry on what is now called "organized Christianity". The purpose is to deceive the peoples, turn them
away from the true God, and to keep them in subjection
to a selfish and unrighteous system of government, of
which Satan is the invisible overlord. (2 Corinthians 4:
3, 4) A government that oppresses the multitudes of the
common people and shows special favors to the wealthy,
is an unrighteous government and therefore an ungodly

nation. Such could not in truth be called Christ's kingdom or Christendom. It is therefore apparent that when the name of Christ is given to an unrighteous and oppressive government that name is fraudulently so used and for a wrongful purpose.

WHO RULES

The kings and presidents of the nations are not in fact the rulers. They are ordinary men filling their respective places and are mere symbols of rulership. The ruling power behind the seat of authority that shapes the course of the nations of "Christendom" is Satan the Devil. He is the opponent of God and the enemy and oppressor of men. Satan's visible instruments are those selfish men who combine and form a system of government which rules and controls the peoples. The three classes of men that make up these ruling powers are, to wit, high financiers, called "big business"; professional politicians, called "statesmen"; and the orthodox clergy, called "religious leaders", who manufacture and dispense religion. These three classes in combination constitute the small minority that rules. Disregarding the obligations laid upon them the selfish men composing the ruling minority have lived wantonly and recklessly for their own pleasure and at the expense of the multitudes. For a long time the peoples have borne them up and supported them and thereby endured great suffering and sorrow. And now I submit the testimony of their own witness which proves beyond a doubt that "organized Christianity", so-called, is a fraud and deception, a great system of oppression, and a menace to the general welfare of the peoples.

HIGH FINANCE

The multitudes, in the sweat of their faces, produce the wealth of the world. High financiers are few in number but great in power. They produce no wealth

but obtain it through fraud and deceit practised upon
the peoples, and then use it for their own wicked pleasure and to oppress the multitudes and to keep them
under control. High finance fixes the price at which the
producer must sell his products to the distributer, and
also fixes an exorbitant price which the consumer must
pay to the distributer. High finance has established
chain stores all over Christendom, and the producer must
sell to these stores at a ridiculously low price or not
sell at all, and the stores in turn sell to the consumer
at exorbitantly high prices, which the consumer must
pay or starve. The producer gets but little, the consumer
pays much, and the high financiers that produce nothing reap enormous and unreasonable profits. The result is that the small merchant is pushed to the wall,
and the chain stores do the business, and the peoples
pay the bills.

The financial record in the United States Treasury's
office discloses that in one year (1919) seventeen woolen
mills made a clear profit of 100 percent on their capital
stock; that corporations operating canning factories that
can the fruit and vegetables produced by the hard labor
of others in one year made a profit of 2932 percent; that
clothing stores made a profit in one year of 9826 percent; that the aluminum trust with a capital of only
$20,000.00 in one year (1923) made a profit of 1000
percent.

The wealth of America is constantly on the increase,
but today in that land there are 524 banks less in number than there were six years ago. The large ones are
swallowing up the smaller ones. Big Finance is taking
possession of all. Kirby Page is authority for the statement that 20,000 men control practically every bank,
trust company, and business enterprise in America.
From Samuel Untermeyer, the distinguished American
lawyer who for a long while represented Big Business,
I quote:

There has been greater concentration of the Money Power in the past five or ten years . . . than in the preceding fifty years. The process of absorption is likely to continue until a few groups absolutely dominate the financial situation of the country. . . . It has come to pass that less than a dozen men in the City of New York are for all practical purposes in control of the direction of at least seventy-five percent of the deposits of the leading trust companies and banks in the city and of allied institutions in various parts of the country.

The Federal Trades Commission in America in 1922 reported that six corporations controlled then one-third of the American water power; eight corporations controlled more than three-fourths of the anthraeite coal fields; and two corporations controlled the great portion of the iron-ore reserve.

These heartless corporations profit in the lives of human beings. To them the life of man is nothing except to be used for their selfish purpose. Recently it was disclosed that forty percent of the milk sold in New York City is adulterated and that with the connivance of the Public Board of Health. It is then sold at a large profit to the poor, and the babes and the sick and the afflicted suffer by reason thereof.

These facts and figures I am giving as they relate to America. Other nations of "Christendom" or "organized Christianity" are equally as bad, and many of them much worse. In every nation of "Christendom" the minority is favored and the great majority are oppressed and suffer.

STATESMEN

The so-called statesmen of the nations are those who hold the offices and feed at the public trough upon the fat of the land, and of course produce nothing. Their jobs depend upon obedience to high finance. In fact high finance is the bulwark of "organized Christianity", so-called, and its power and influence have corrupted the politicians of every nation. The politicians are the men that make and enforce the laws.

Before the last American Congress a bill was pending
to build a great dam at Boulder Canyon, in the Colorado
River, for the purpose of reclaiming millions of acres of
arid lands and to produce electric power for the benefit of
the public. Josiah T. Newcomb, solicitor for Big Business that opposed the bill, declared:

> I represent an investment of nine billion dollars and we
> do not propose to let the government enter into the power
> business at Boulder. The bill has no chance to pass. It
> will not pass as it is.

It did not pass. More than 120 million Americans
cannot reclaim the arid lands of the desert and produce
electric power for their own use without the consent of
a few heartless men who are known as "Big Business".
This gang of highwaymen is a part of "organized
Christianity", so-called.

The corrupting hand of Big Business has been laid
upon men in high political positions and corrupted
every department of every government of "Christendom". Senator Reed, of the United States Senate,
recently declared in a public address: "The time has
come when the people should rise up and drive out the
leprosy of corruption which has spread through the nation's capital."

The peoples go through a form of election supposedly
to select their public servants. But most of these political statesmen are elected and controlled by the defiling
influence of "Big Business". From Mr. Justice Ford,
long in public life and who speaks with authority, I
quote:

> In my experience I have found the public service cor-
> porations, the street railroad, the ·telephone, the lighting
> companies in particular, to be the most prolific source of
> political corruption in the state. They are more directly
> dependent upon governmental favors than any others, and
> indeed the profits of their business flow from the special
> privileges which they procure and hold from the govern-

ment, both state and municipal. In my day at Albany these corporations plied their nefarious business of corrupting the people's representatives so openly that a blind deaf-mute could learn what was going on. Not that legal evidence could be found against them. They were too shrewd for that. But every public man there was morally certain as to what was going on, and in private conversation it was freely talked about. These public service corporations pollute the very fountains of public virtue; they debauch our public servants; they subsidize party organizations for their own purposes. All the powers of government are subverted to their base ends; and government of the people, by the people, for the people, is made a mockery.

Even the courts are corrupted by Big Business. When Big Business is pitted against the common people the people have no show in the courts. The words of Mr. Untermeyer are pertinent on this point:

Nowhere in our social fabric is the discrimination between the rich and the poor so emphasized to the average citizen as at the bar of justice. Nowhere should it be less. . . . Money secures the ablest and most adroit counsel. . . . Evidence can be gathered from every source. The poor must be content to forego all these advantages.

When "Big Business" desires to increase its holdings, and war seems to be advantageous to its selfish interests, it does not hesitate to provoke war between the peoples of different nations. At the bidding of "Big Finance" the politicians enact the necessary conscription laws which compel the common people from all parts of "Christendom" to kill each other while the representatives of "Big Business" and their allies hide in their holes. When the war is over, millions of the common people sleep in the dust of the earth; and within the brief period of blood and carnage there has been born another crop of millionaires, and then there follows greater lawlessness amongst the politicians than ever before. Upon this point a member of the United States Senate, Mr. Norris, is quoted:

The millions of our youth who went into that orgy of murder were promised a new and better order of things. Here, ten years later, they can see special privilege and the power of money more securely enthroned than ever in the seats of the mighty. For the thousands of our young men killed, for our billions spent, for the countless millions of heartaches, we have what? We have political corruption such as was never dreamed of before.

These conscienceless politicians defiled by Big Business and the oppressors of the people constitute a part of "organized Christianity" or "Christendom", so called, that rule and control the peoples.

THE CLERGY

Who are the responsible ones for naming the harsh, cruel and paternalistic governments "Christendom" or "organized Christianity"? I answer: The clergy of the various denominations. Ambitious for the approval and plaudits of men and with a desire to live in ease and comfort they have joined affinity with Big Business and professional politicians. The clergy pose before the peoples as representatives of God and of his Christ and hypocritically induce the peoples to believe that they are Christians, and at the same time go exactly contrary to the Word of God. Jesus declared that Satan the Devil is the prince or ruler of this world and that he is the opponent of God. (John 14: 30) Again in 2 Corinthians 4: 3, 4 it is written that Satan is the god of this evil world.

The world means organized forms of government under the supervision of the invisible overlord, Satan the Devil. In God's Word it is written (James 4: 4) that he who is a friend of the world is the enemy of God. The clergy have voluntarily become a part of the world and friends thereof and therefore the enemies of God and of Christ and the enemies and oppressors of the common peoples. They call themselves and their

allies, "Big Business" and professional politicians, "organized Christianity" or "Christendom," and have the
effrontery to claim that these rule by divine right.

In God's Word true religion is defined in these words:
"To visit the fatherless and widows in their affliction,
and to keep himself unspotted from the world." Contrary to this plain statement of the Word of God the
clergy not only fail to comfort the widows and orphans
but they advocate war, preach men into the trenches to
die, and thereby make millions of widows and more millions fatherless children. Instead of keeping themselves
unspotted from the world they are literally spotted all
over by the world because they are a part of it. In the
recent World War their church edifices were recruiting
stations, and almost every clergyman advocated the shedding of human blood. For this reason God, through his
prophet, says of and concerning them now: "For in thy
skirts is found the blood of the souls of the poor innocents: I have not found it by secret search, but upon
all these." (Jeremiah 2: 34) What class of men wear
skirts except the preachers or clergy? They are the
guilty ones.

Upon this point I submit the following indisputable
facts: Admiral Fiske during the World War said: "The
Christian religion is at this moment being made to exert
a powerful influence, not toward peace but toward war."
Secretary of War Lane said: "The War could not have
been won without the churches."

Christ, whose name these clergymen have fraudulently assumed and by which they have named their "organized Christianity", said: "Thou shalt not kill."
But the clergymen are the most ardent advocates of war
and the most vehement and vindictive in their expressions against their fellow men. Before America entered
the World War an election for mayor in the city of
New York was being held. One candidate was opposed
to America entering the war. The distinguished clergy-

man, Dr. Van Dyke, on that occasion said: "I'd hang everyone. whether or not he be a candidate for mayor. who lifts his voice agai·· t America entering the war." And this is a sample of the dispensers of religion from "organized Christianity".

Rev. Chas. Ganster from his American pulpit "advocated the organization of an association to murder those persons who do not stand up when the Star Spangled Banner is played".   ′

The clergymen of Germany told the people that they represented the same God and the same Christ that the clergymen of England and America represented. Although Christ is the Prince of Peace. and declares against killing, the clergymen of Germany urged their people to kill in the most fiendish manner the common people of the allied armies of Britain. Likewise the clergymen of Britain and her allies urged the killing of the German people and their allies. and the clergymen of both sides tried to induce the people to believe that they are Christians. In proof that the clergymen are a part of the world and the allies of "Big Business" that makes war I read the testimony of the Rev. George Parkin Atwater. to wit:

The complete representative of the American Church in France is the United States Army overseas. Yes. an army. with its cannon and rifles and machine guns. and its instruments of destruction. The Church militant, sent. morally equipped, strengthened and encouraged. approved and blessed. by the Church at home. The army today is the Church in action, transforming the will of the Church into deeds, expressing the moral judgment of the Church in smashing blows. Its worship h·· its vigil in the trenches. and its fasts and feasts: its prayers are in acts. and its choir is the crash of cannon and the thrilling ripple of machine guns.

Dr. Newell Dwight Hillis, pastor of Plymouth Church, Brooklyn, was one of the most vehement advocates of

America entering the World War. Did he act upon the
authority of Christ? No; not Hillis. The American
Bankers Association commissioned him as a missionary
to Europe. He did the bidding of that heartless and
cruel financial association. He prepared the sermons
which hundreds of thousands of other pastors throughout America delivered, advocating war, urging the young
men into the trenches and the people to buy bonds.

Dr. Hillis was not content with urging men into the
jaws of death by which he earned and drew his pay
from the American Bankers Association, but went to
the extreme in expressing his malice. When the war had
ended, instead of visiting the widows and the fatherless
and bringing them comfort, as Christ had commanded,
Hillis still breathing vengeance of blood against an unfortunate and helpless people wrote:

Society has organized itself against the rattlesnake and
the yellow fever. Shepherds have entered into a conspiracy to exterminate the wolves. The Boards of Health
are planning to wipe out typhoid, cholera and the black
plague. Not otherwise, lovers of their fellow man have
finally become perfectly hopeless with reference to the German people. They have no more relation to the civilization
of 1918 than an orang-outang, a gorilla, a Judas, a hyena, a
thumbscrew, or a scalping knife in the hands of a savage.
These brutes must be cast out of society. . . . There will
shortly be held a meeting of surgeons in this country. A
copy of the preliminary call lies before me. The plan to be
discussed is based upon the Indiana State law. That law
authorizes a State Board of Surgeons to use upon the
person of confirmed criminals and hopeless idiots the new
painless method of sterilizing the men. These surgeons are
preparing to advocate the calling of a world conference to
consider the sterilization of 10,000,000 German soldiers and
the segregation of their women, that when this generation
of Germans goes, civilized cities, states and races may be
rid of this awful cancer that must be cut clean out of the
body of society.

No general, no man in the army, nor any war lord

ever gave utterance to such diabolical and wicked words
as those written by Hillis. These clergymen are the ones
who, with pious faces and sanctimonious words, tell the
peoples that their organized system of oppression and
murder represents Christ on earth and therefore constitutes "organized Christianity" or "Christendom".
They have been defaming the name of God and of Christ.

A few ultra-selfish men constitute "Big Business", and
they control the commerce of the world. They do it by
the power of money unjustly wrung from the hands of
the multitudes of toilers. They control the elections because the politicians elected to office enact and enforce
such laws as they want. They own and control the public press and publish only what they desire the peoples
to read. This lecture I am now giving will not be published by them because they do not want the peoples to
hear it. The radio, which God has brought to light for
the benefit of the peoples, the same selfish interest is now
seeking to control. The same power controls the clergy
and uses them for selfish purposes. In time of war they
use the clergy as recruiting officers to hurry men into
the jaws of death. This is the unholy alliance that
hypocritically calls itself by the name of Christ and has
induced the peoples to believe that it is the political
expression of God's kingdom on earth. On the contrary
the Scriptures declare this unholy alliance to be a part
of Babylon and of the Devil's organization. All nations
have been made blind drunk by its false representations
and teachings.

Now the unholy alliance is pursuing a systematic
campaign to amalgamate the common people of all
Christendom into great military organizations. The false
slogan of the World War was that it would "make the
world safe for Democracy". Every sane man knows that
it destroyed democracy. "Big Business" and its allies
now hope to hold the common people in subjection by
making them a part of the harsh and cruel war machine.

Succeeding in this the Devil, in his ghoulish glee, and to the reproach of God and Christ, would say: "This is Christendom or organized Christianity."

BURDEN BEARERS

The unholy alliance called "Christendom" or "organized Christianity" for its support and maintenance depends upon the multitudes of the common peoples. It holds up the peoples and robs them of their just rights and the fruits of their honest labors. Without the consent of the multitudes of peoples the poor are forced to fight and to kill their fellow man without a just cause or excuse. This "organized Christianity", fraudulently so-called, has caused the common peoples to bear great burdens of unjust taxation in order that the few might live wantonly and recklessly. It has caused the peoples to bear the burdens of war that a few might gratify their selfish desires. The multitudes of suffering ones, with bent bodies and broken hearts, have gone into untimely graves. Those not supporting the unholy alliance are told by the clergy that to them death is but the opening of the gates of a burning hell wherein their torture will never end.

HOPELESS

The great desire of the peoples is for peace and prosperity and life in a state of happiness. It is now apparent that there is no hope of the peoples' realizing their desires by anything that "organized Christianity" can give them. "Organized Christianity" or "Christendom", instead of being the friend and benefactor of the multitudes, is the enemy and oppressor of the common peoples. With great pomp and glory that unholy system rides upon the backs of the peoples. Without the support of the common peoples that wicked system called "Christendom" could not survive. When the peoples withdraw their support therefrom, "organized Christianity", which is a part of Babylon or the Devil's organization, will fall like a great millstone into the sea.

GOD THE PEOPLES' FRIEND

There is one true and almighty God. Jehovah of Hosts is his name. He is the Friend and Benefactor of man. Through his Christ and his kingdom of righteousness he will grant to the honest peoples of earth their heart's desire.

God created the first man perfect. Because man violated God's law he was sentenced to death. Thereafter his children were born; hence they were born sinners and imperfect and without the right to life. (Romans 5: 12; Psalm 51: 5) God in his loving kindness promised to produce a "seed" through which all the nations of the earth shall be blessed. (Genesis 22: 18-22) Then he made it clear that Christ is that promised "seed" and that there is no other name whereby men can be saved. —Galatians 3: 16-19; Acts 4: 12.

God so loved the world of mankind that he sent his beloved Son to earth and permitted him to die that man might have an opportunity to live. (John 3: 16) Jesus Christ died for all men and all men must know that fact in God's due time.—Hebrews 2: 9; 1 Timothy 2,: 3-6.

Christ means the Anointed One of God, the Messiah, the One appointed by Jehovah through whom the promised blessings must come to the people. For the purpose of deceiving the peoples and turning their minds away from God and his gracious provision for their blessing, Satan the Devil organized the false and wicked system made up of "Big Business", professional politicians, and faithless preachers, and calls it by the name of "organized Christianity" or "Christendom". That wicked system now controls and for a long time has controlled and oppressed the common peoples of the nations.

By his Word God discloses that he would not interfere with Satan's nefarious work until the end of the world, at which time Christ Jesus, his beloved Son and earth's rightful King, should come into possession of the affairs of man and rule and bless the peoples of the earth. That world ended with 1914, and according to the Lord's prophecy was marked by the World War, famine, pestilence, revolutions, return of the Jews to Palestine, and by general distress and perplexity now existing on earth. (Matthew 24: 3-22; Luke 21: 10-26) A period of time elapses from the beginning of sorrows, which marks the end of the world, until the final end thereof, during which the message of the kingdom must be proclaimed to the peoples.—Matthew 24: 14.

Now God has set his Son Christ upon his throne, as foretold by his prophet in the Second Psalm, and bids all the nations and peoples of earth to hear and obey him. The old world has ended and God's kingdom is at hand. The rulers of the earth were duly served with notice of this fact a year ago. The unholy alliance has received due notice thereof. But instead of heeding the message from the Word of God the rulers of the world, to wit, those constituting the unholy alliance, walk on in darkness and continue to oppress the peoples. The doom of "organized Christianity" or Babylon is sealed! The groans and cries of the peoples oppressed by that wicked system have ascended up to the God of heaven. To the oppressors composing that evil system the great Jehovah now says: "Go to now, ye rich men, weep and howl for your miseries that shall come upon you. Your riches are corrupted, and your garments are motheaten. Your gold and silver is cankered; and the rust of them shall be a witness against you, and shall eat your flesh as it were fire. Ye have heaped treasure together for the last days. Behold, the hire of the laborers who have reaped down your fields, which is of you kept back by fraud, crieth: and the cries of them which have reaped are entered into the ears of the Lord of Sabaoth. Ye have lived in pleasure on the earth, and been wanton; ye have nourished your hearts, as in a day of slaughter. Ye have condemned and killed the just; and he doth not resist you."—James 5: 1-6.

The day of God's vengeance is at hand; and he will punish that wicked system calling itself "organized Christianity", because it has oppressed the common peoples.

A city is a symbol of an organization. The unholy organization called "Christendom" or "organized Christianity" in the Scriptures is called a "city". To that wicked city God now says: "For, lo, I begin to bring evil on the city which is called by my name, and should ye be utterly unpunished? Ye shall not be unpunished: for I will call for a sword upon all the inhabitants of the earth, saith the Lord of hosts. . . . A noise shall come even to the ends of the earth: for the Lord hath a controversy with the nations; he will plead with all flesh; he will give them that are wicked to the sword, saith the Lord. Thus saith the Lord of hosts, Behold, evil shall go forth from nation to nation, and a great whirlwind [of trouble] shall be raised up from the coasts of the earth. And the slain of the Lord shall be at that day from one end of the earth even unto the other end of the earth: they shall not be lamented, neither gathered, nor buried; they shall be dung upon the ground. Howl, ye shepherds, and cry; and wallow yourselves in the ashes, ye principal of the flock: for the days of your slaughter and of your dispersions are accomplished; and ye shall fall like a pleasant vessel. And the shepherds shall have no way to flee, nor the principal of the flock to escape."—Jeremiah 25: 29, 31-35.

The World War stopped in 1918 in order that notice might be given to the peoples of earth concerning the name of Jehovah God and his purposes toward men. That witness has been in progress during the past eight years. Notice has been served upon the world powers, and now notice is being served upon all the common peoples. Jesus declared that when this witness is done, and because the ruling powers will not heed the same, there shall come upon the world the greatest time of trouble ever known and it shall be the last.—Matthew 24: 14, 21. 22.

Millions of honest people who are now held in subjection to "organized Christianity", but who are meek and willing to be taught, are asking, What shall we do? To such Jehovah now says: "Seek ye the Lord, all ye meek of the earth, which have wrought his judgment: seek righteousness, seek meekness: it may be ye shall be hid in the day of the Lord's anger."—Zephaniah 2: 3.

The Word of God and the physical facts prove that "organized Christianity" or "Christendom" is a failure. She is even worse than that. She is a menace to peace and prosperity. She is an instrument of Satan the Devil. Abandon her and flee from her as rats flee from a sinking ship. She is sinking into oblivion never again to rise. She is going down in a time of trouble such as never before was known. To the people the Lord now says therefore: "Come out of her, my people, that ye be not partakers of her sins, and that ye receive not of her plagues."—Revelation 18: 4.

THE BLESSINGS

The ruins of Satan's false system cleared away, there shall arise a new heaven and new earth wherein dwells righteousness, according to God's promise. (2 Peter 3: 13) That righteous government shall rest upon the shoulder of Christ Jesus, the Prince of Peace. His name shall be called by the people Wonderful Counsellor, because he will guide them in the right way; he shall be called the Everlasting Father because he will give life to the peoples. And of his peace and blessings there shall be no end.—Isaiah 9: 6, 7.

WARS TO CEASE

The curse that war has laid upon the peoples will then
be lifted for ever. Never again shall there be war between the peoples of the nations. Under the reign of the
righteous Messiah the peoples of the nations shall beat
their instruments of war into farming implements and
nation shall not lift up sword against nation, neither
shall they learn war any more.—Isaiah 2: 2-4.

A lion is a symbol of the Devil, and a ravenous beast
is a symbol of the Devil's organization on earth, made
up of the cruel "Big Business", big politicians, and big
preachers. God, through his prophet, promises that in
the kingdom of Messiah there shall be no lion nor
ravenous beast there, because the Devil will not be permitted to operate. He will have no cruel financiers, nor
professional politicians, nor any hypocritical preachers
to do his bidding. The people shall dwell together in
safety and follow that which is right.—Isaiah 35: 9, 10.

The poor will no longer be oppressed. In the courts
they will have fair and equitable consideration, because
it is written that "with righteousness shall he judge the
poor, and reprove with equity for the meek of the earth".
—Isaiah 11: 4.

Under the righteous reign of Messiah no cruel corporation can own the houses in which the people dwell,
or compel them to pay exorbitant rents. The people
shall build their own houses and live in them and plant
their own vineyards and eat the fruit thereof, and no
one shall make them afraid.—Micah 4: 4.

Now the poor cry for bread and the rulers give them
a stone; they cry for a fish and the clergy give them a
fiery serpent. Under the righteous reign of Messiah there
shall be a great feast of fat things spread for all the
people and they shall eat and rejoice. No hypocritical
prohibition preachers will be permitted then to operate
with bootleggers and take away from the people the

proper use of wine while they themselves use it unlawfully.—Isaiah 25: 6.

Under the righteous reign of Messiah clergymen will
no more be permitted to frighten the people and keep
them in ignorance of the truth. Then the knowledge of
the glory of the Lord shall fill the whole earth as the
waters now fill the sea, and every man will know the
Lord and his righteous way from the least to the greatest. and that knowledge will be free.—Habakkuk 2: 14;
Jeremiah 31: 34.

In that righteous government here on earth no more
can men called doctors practise on the people and hide
their mistakes in the graveyard, because then the Lord
will lead the people in the right way and bring unto them
peace and health and cure them of all their ailments
until no more shall any man say, "I am sick."—Jeremiah 33: 6; Isaiah 33: 24.

It shall then be if a man who has been wicked shall
turn away from his wickedness and do right and obey the
Lord he shall live and shall never die. (Ezekiel 18: 27,
28) That is the time of which Jesus spoke when he
said: "If a man keep my saying, he shall never see
death" (John 8: 51); "Whosoever liveth, and believeth
in me shall never die."—John 11: 26.

In that time old men shall return to the days of their
youth, and their flesh shall become fresher than that of
a child. (Job 33: 25) Then God will restore to perfection of body and mind all the obedient ones on the
earth until the earth is filled with a happy, joyful and
vigorous people.—Acts 3: 19-23.

Seeing that God has in store these marvelous blessings
for the people through the kingdom of Christ it is easy
to see why the Devil has organized a false system called
"Christendom" or "organized Christianity". and   by
which system hypocritically he deceives the people and
turns their minds away from God's provision for their
blessing.

God's kingdom of righteousness is at hand. The evidence shows that the day of restitution has come in which the obedient ones of mankind shall be granted full freedom and be restored to the perfection of body enjoyed in Eden. Therefore with confidence it can now be stated that millions of people now on the earth will never die.

The people desire peace, freedom, prosperity, life and happiness. All thinking persons must now see these can come only from God's kingdom through Christ. They can never be realized by or through the false system called "organized Christianity". The hypocritical and evil course of "Christendom" is an insult to God and to Christ. It is the deceiver and oppressor of the people. It is completely under the control of Satan the Devil. It depends for its support and maintenance upon the multitudes of peoples, while at the same time it continues to defraud and oppress the people. Let the multitudes of peoples completely and entirely withdraw all support morally, financially and otherwise from "Christendom" or "organized Christianity", so-called. Let them give their heart's devotion and allegiance entirely to God and to Christ, the Prince of Peace, who is now earth's rightful King. Let them dwell together in peace and do good to each other and be ready to receive the blessings which God has in reservation for those who love and obey him. The day of complete freedom is at hand!

The peoples should therefore for ever abandon and forsake "organized Christianity" called "Christendom" and turn their hearts and minds and their allegiance wholly to God and his Christ for the following reasons, to wit:

(1) Because "Christendom" is the Devil's organization operated by him to keep the people in subjection.

(2) Because it is an instrument of oppression which

has been used to make the burdens of men grievous to be borne.

(3) Because it is false, hypocritical, and wicked, and against the interests of the multitudes of the peoples.

(4) Because it holds out absolutely no hope for the betterment of the peoples.

(5) Because God's time has come when that evil and hypocritical system shall be destroyed in the greatest time of trouble the world has ever known.

(6) Because God commands all the peoples who love him to flee from that unrighteous system of so-called "organized Christianity" and thereby escape the dire calamities that shortly shall befall her.

(7) Because God has set his anointed King, Christ Jesus the Messiah, upon his throne, and bids all the peoples of earth to hear and obey him; and those who so do shall receive and for ever enjoy the blessings of complete freedom, everlasting peace, prosperity, life, liberty and happiness.

And now, Mr. Chairman, based upon these assigned reasons, I move the adoption of this resolution and I ask my audience, both seen and unseen, when the vote is taken that those who are in favor arise and express themselves by crying out, Aye. Before voting upon it I wish to say the message today, by God's grace, has gone out from Maine to California, from Canada to Mexico, and we hope to the uttermost parts of "Christendom". The Lord God has graciously used the National Broadcasting Company to carry this message to "Christendom". I take this occasion to express, upon behalf of the International Bible Students, my great appreciation of the cooperation of the National Broadcasting Company. May God bless the men thereof for their efforts. Those in favor of the adoption of the resolution arise and say, Aye.

The thunderous tones of that great multitude were heard throughout the land and hundreds of thousands and probably millions of other peoples who were listening in likewise voted Aye, as is noted by the many messages received.

"The Hook-up"

From *The Messenger,* published at Toronto, Monday
July 25th, 1927, the following is quoted:

One of the greatest events of the age has passed into
history. Judge Rutherford's address, at Toronto, marked
the end of the old way and the coming in of the new.

Ten years ago the Bible Students anticipated that by
the end of 1925 the gospel would be broadcast from some one
station to all the rest of the world. They did not miss it by
very much.

Ten weeks ago there were no signs that Judge Rutherford
would have the whole world listening to him from the
Coliseum platform, on July 24th. But events move rapidly
now.

Nothing could more plainly demonstrate the hand of
God than the wonderful way in which this seemingly im-
possible thing was brought about. All things are easy for
God.

It is less than six weeks ago that Judge Rutherford and
his colleagues were at Washington, setting forth to the
Radio Commission their just rights to a high wave length.

Reasons were given why WBBR, Judge Rutherford's
station on Staten Island, should have part of the time of
WJZ. It seemed like a hopeless mission, but God saw
otherwise.

WJZ is on the National Broadcasting Company's circuit.
Its president was at the hearing. Naturally he wanted to
retain all his time, but Judge Rutherford interested him.

President Merlin Hall Aylesworth, of the National Broadcasting Company, desired that Judge Rutherford should
make use of his circuit; and a date was fixed, July 24th,
yesterday.

So it came about that when Judge Rutherford stepped
out on the platform yesterday he stepped out to speak from
all the stations which go to make up the National Broadcasting circuit, in addition to his own chain of stations.

These include many of the most important stations in
the United States, and with them the Red, Blue and Pacific
networks, as they are called, reaching clear across the continent.

43

But he spoke from more than these, because many other of the most prominent broadcasting studios, including several in Canada, concluded a so to send out the lecture.

So it came to pass that Judge Rutherford, standing in Toronto, talked from a line of stations reaching from Toronto, through Saskatoon and Edmonton to Vancouver on the Pacific coast.

Standing in Toronto he was broadcasting simultaneously from Boston, Worcester, Springfield, Hartford, Providence and other stations all over New England.

Standing in Toronto his voice went out from the greatest studios in New York, Schenectady, Buffalo, Rochester, Washington, Pittsburgh and others in the Middle Atlantic States.

Though here in Canada he broadcast from Cincinnati, St. Louis, Chicago, Minneapolis, Davenport, Batavia, Louisville, and many other stations in the Middle Western States.

Without leaving the Coliseum his voice rang out from stations in Charlotte, Memphis, Nashville, Jacksonville, Dallas, and from stations in many other cities all over the Southern States.

Though his voice went into but one microphone here yet it entered other microphones with equal power in Des Moines, Omaha, Denver, San Antonio, Oakland and Spokane.

Originally cast from Toronto, Judge Rutherford's voice went on and on until it was amplified millions of times and was rebroadcast from the great studios in England and Australia.

The vast audience at Toronto was as nothing. True, the great Coliseum was filled an hour ahead of time and thousands turned away; but all could hear, in or out.

All over the world the scene in Toronto was duplicated. Bible Students and their friends and the public were listening in halls, auditoriums and private homes, catching every word.

How many millions heard Judge Rutherford's wonderful discourse Sunday afternoon there will never be any way of finding out while we are on this side of the vail.

The Passing of the Powers

"Then was the iron, the clay, the brass, the silver, and the gold, broken to pieces together, and became like the chaff of the summer threshingfloors; and the wind carried them away, that no place was found for them: and the stone that smote the image became a great mountain, and filled the whole earth."
—Daniel 2:35.

JEHOVAH through his Word reveals that Armageddon is "the battle of the great day of God Almighty". The inference to be drawn from the name used is that in that great day the Creator of heaven and earth will exercise almighty power in battle against his enemy. If then we are correct in the conclusion that the battle of Armageddon will be fought by Satan and his forces on the one side, and Jehovah of hosts on the other side, then it is of greatest interest and importance to the Christians now on earth to have a mental vision of both organizations. It will also be of great importance for the Christians to go forward in harmony with God's organization and to faithfully perform the duties God has laid upon them.

It seems quite certain that we are approaching the greatest crisis of all time and that in the conflict of Armageddon the powers of evil shall fall, never again to secure a solid footing on 'the earth. That fact alone should thrill the soul of every lover of righteousness. It will mean the vindication of God's holy name, the triumph of his Christ, the deliverance of the people from oppression, and the opening of the plain highway by which the people may fully return unto God. Truly we are entering into a grand and awful time. To be living now is sublime!

It is profitable at this time that we take a mental vision of the history of the nations or world powers found recorded in the Word of God, and such part of profane history relating thereto as is in full harmony with the Word of God. Undoubtedly God caused the record thereof to be made in

45

his Word for the benefit of the Christians on earth at this time. The understanding of the same in harmony with God's will is therefore ment in due season to strengthen all those who are striving to do the will of God.

DEFINITIONS

Power, as used herein, means a potentate or authority exercising jurisdiction and power over others.

World, as herein used, means mankind organized into forms of government acting under the supervision and influence or control of an invisible overlord, potentate or authority. There is both a visible and an invisible part of the world. The invisible part of the organization is termed "heaven". The visible part thereof is called "earth", and the authority of the visible part thereof is exercised by men. In the Scriptures the earthly part is symbolized by a beast, because a wild and ferocious beast fitly represents earthly governments or powers.

A world power therefore is defined as an organization on earth of men into forms of government, which government possesses and exercises supreme jurisdiction, power, and the controlling influence over various powers or nations, and which is under the supervision of the invisible overlord, Satan the Devil. World powers have been permitted by Jehovah in order to put men to the test and to teach them lessons which they could not otherwise learn. Many nations have arisen and quickly fallen again, but world powers have been limited in number and have existed until God's due time for such to fall.

God permitted man to follow his own devices in organizing governments. He placed before man righteousness and truth and then permitted him to choose good or to go in the way of evil and unrighteousness. Man changed the truth into lies, reproached God and worshiped the creature rather than the Creator. (Romans 1:25) Men were induced to take this wrongful course by reason of the evil influence exercised over them by Satan the enemy. By fraud and deceit Satan turned the mind of man away from God. The Devil induced some to worship him, and others he induced to worship any object except Jehovah. By this means Satan became the god or invisible ruler over men and has influenced and controlled men's organization of governments or powers.

The Devil's organization therefore consists of himself and the evil angels that he drew away from the paths of rectitude, and of men under his influence organized into earthly systems and governments. The majority of men have not cared to retain God in their knowledge and therefore God permitted them to go in the way of evil and to do those things which are unrighteous. As the knowledge of men increased they have turned that knowledge into selfish and wrongful channels. Satan, seizing upon the opportunity, has builded a mighty organization on earth. In the latter days, due to the great goodness of God, knowledge has increased; but this knowledge has been used among men under the influence of Satan to strengthen his organization. The commerce of the earth, the political machinery of earth, and the organized religion of earth, are all under the control of Satan. He has united these into one mighty organization, which organization is cruel and oppressive. He stands opposed to God and everything that represents God.

Throughout the ages only those who have been faithful to God have stood aloof from the Devil's organization and refused to yield thereto. Many of these have suffered martyrdom, and over them Satan's organization apparently has triumphed. Many others for a time have stood in opposition to Satan's organization, but under his subtle influence have fallen into his snares. Today upon earth there is but a remnant that is true and faithful to God. Against these Satan and his organization now make desperate assault with the determination of destroying them because they keep the commandments of God and have the witness that they are the Lord's.

GOD'S ORGANIZATION

God's organization is unknown to all except a few. It consists of Jesus Christ, his beloved Son and great High Priest, and a host of true and holy angels, and the members of the body of Christ in glory, and of those anointed ones on earth who are yet faithful and true to the Lord.

Over all of these is the great eternal Jehovah God. The fact that one of his names is Jehovah of hosts means that he has a mighty army of holy angels that delight to render complete obedience unto him. These not only carry out his purposes in general, but under his direction furnish protection for the faithful ones on earth God's representatives on earth are small in number and meager in power. In themselves they have no strength. These faithful ones have entered into the secret place of the Most High; and dwelling there in the shadow of the Almighty God, they are safe while the battle rages. With confidence and with a complete sense of security they can perform and do perform their duties.

DIVINE RULES

It appears that God has fixed rules of procedure concerning world powers: (1) He manifests toward such his own goodness that the people thereof, and particularly the rulers, may see evidences of his righteousness in contrast with the wickedness of the evil one; (2) he serves notice upon them of his purposes to punish their evil course; (3) he magnifies his own name by a manifestation of his supreme power that all may know that there is no Almighty God besides him and from him alone proceed all things that are good and righteous.

It also appears that another fixed rule of God is that where there is greater knowledge, or opportunity to obtain the same, there is greater responsibility resting upon those who do know or who might know. Having in mind these fixed rules will enable us to more fully appreciate what are the present duties of the remnant and what Armageddon may mean.

BEGINNING OF WORLD POWERS

Nebuchadnezzar succeeded his father upon the throne of Babylon, a nation that had existed for many years. In the second year of the reign of Nebuchadnezzar he had a dream. Daniel the Hebrew was brought before the king and gave the interpretation of his dream. In that interpretation Daniel the prophet of God specified four kingdoms or world powers. (Daniel 2:36-40) From the description given, however, and from other facts that appear in the sacred record it is manifest that these four are not all the world powers revealed by the Scriptures and that Babylon was not the beginning of world powers.

The "Gentile Times began under the reign of Nebuchadnezzar. When Daniel stood before that potentate to give interpretation of his dream he said: "God . . . maketh known what shall be in the latter days." Those words would indicate that God would reveal to his people in the latter days a better understanding of Nebuchadnezzar's dream and of its interpretation, which was in fact a prophecy. God's purpose in making the dream and its interpretation appear so prominently in the Bible must be of greater significance merely than to record an historical fact to be thereafter remembered by the people. It now appears that the primary purpose of the record concerning that world power was and is that God thereby serves notice on the ruling factors of the world that he is the only true God, that his name shall be magnified notwithstanding the enemy, and in his own due time he will demonstrate this to all creation.

EGYPT

It is an indisputable fact that long prior to the existence of Babylon as a world power there were two other great world powers. The first was Egypt. God permitted Joseph to be sold into Egypt, and then to be elevated to a position of great power and authority in that government. There was a divine purpose in this. It was through Joseph that God gave Egypt evidence of his own goodness. That nation was the predominant world power then. That nation received many blessings from God, ministered to it and its people through the hand of Joseph, the servant of God. (Genesis 41) The rulers of Egypt learned of God and his goodness. Joseph died; and another king arose who was against God and forgot the favors that the empire had received from Jehovah. (Exodus 1:8) God's chosen people were then domiciled in Egypt. They were being persecuted and oppressed by the rulers. Their cries came up before

Jehovah. God then went to Egypt to make for himself
a name. (2 Samuel 7:23) He did this by sending his servants, Moses and Aaron, into Egypt. He told Moses in
advance what he intended to do. (Exodus 3:20) Through
Moses God served notice on Pharaoh that he is the Almighty
God and of his purpose to deliver his people. After full
and fair warning God slew all the firstborn of Egypt, delivered his own people, and then destroyed the army of
that great world power. Thus he gave a demonstration of
his power that he is God, that his name might not be forgotten for the good of men.

Egypt was the first world power, and what came to pass
concerning it foreshadowed what shall happen to the last
of Satan's world powers. Moses, who served as deliverer,
foreshadowed Christ, the great Deliverer. The overthrow
of Egypt foreshadowed the time when God through Christ
would dash to pieces Satan's organization in the latter days.
From that time forward Egypt as a world power became
typical of other world powers that should follow. Students
of Scripture have long recognized Egypt as a type and its
king as the representative of the Devil and a part of the
Devil's organization.

ASSYRIA

Later and next in order Assyria arose as a dominant world
power. That nation was the dominating organization of
Satan on earth. God recognized Assyria as a world power
and specifically showed his goodness to that nation by sending Jonah his prophet to them to give them warning. And
that world power recognized Jehovah as their God and
acknowledged him as such. (Jonah 3:6-9) Because of their
knowledge of God the rulers of Assyria were responsible.
Not only did the rulers of Assyria forget God and worship
Satan and his angels, but openly defied the Almighty and
brought reproach upon his name. (2 Kings 18:22; 19:10-
13) Then God manifested his power against the empire
of Assyria and demonstrated that he is the Almighty God.
Assyria fell and ceased to be a world power.

BABYLON

The next world power that appeared on the scene was Babylon. It existed as a nation long prior thereto. Early in the reign of Nebuchadnezzar Babylon became a world power or dominant national organization of Satan. Because of the unfaithfulness of the nation of Israel, which formed the typical kingdom of God, that nation was overthrown and God even permitted Nebuchadnezzar to become "a king of kings" or dominant world power to be used for his own purposes. By the dream of Nebuchadnezzar and the interpretation thereof by Daniel God brought *notice* to that ruler that Jehovah is the only true God; and Nebuchadnezzar recognized that fact when he said to Daniel: "Of a truth it is, that your God is a God of gods and a Lord of kings." (Daniel 2:47) Later Nebuchadnezzar was forced to undergo certain ordeals by which he was compelled to acknowledge the supremacy of Jehovah. (Daniel 4:25-37) The goodness of God was made manifest to Babylon. Later that nation forgot God and persecuted his people and fell.

By the interpretation of Nebuchadnezzar's dream which God gave to him through the Prophet Daniel Jehovah was *serving notice* upon Babylon, *and upon* all the nations that followed, that he is the great and only true God and that in his due time he will destroy all powers that oppose him even as he had destroyed Egypt; and that he will do so through his righteous kingdom; and that his kingdom shall stand for ever for the blessing of mankind.

The facts therefore show that Babylon was the *third world* power in the order in which they actually came into existence. The Lord through Daniel did not say that Nebuchadnezzar was the head of the first world power. He described an image, which Nebuchadnezzar saw, the head of which was gold; and then said to the king: "Thou art this head of gold." He then stated that after Babylon there should follow a second, third, and fourth kingdom or world power. It clearly therefore appears that such in the order named were numbered from Nebuchadnezzar forward. The second was the Medo-Persian kingdom, the third Greece, and Rome is recognized as the fourth. Counting Egypt as the first world power, which indeed it was, then Rome was the sixth from Egypt but the fourth from Nebuchadnezzar. The four world powers mentioned by Daniel covered the time or interregnum between the overthrow of the typical kingdom of God and the coming of the real kingdom, to wit, Christ Jesus, who came and declared, "The kingdom of heaven is at hand." He is the one "whose right it is" to reign. (Ezekiel 21:24-27) He was crucified during the time that Rome was the dominant power of earth, the fourth in the order named by Daniel. Daniel the prophet did not then disclose the world powers that preceded Nebuchadnezzar, nor those that should follow Rome and that should exist until the establishment of God's kingdom under Christ.

OTHER WORLD POWERS

While Daniel specifically named only four world powers yet his prophetic description shows there were to be more. The image which he described had legs of iron which represented the fourth world power or kingdom named by Daniel and which is recognized by all as Rome. Iron represents a cruel military power that breaks to pieces and subdues all others. The military history of Rome fully meets this description.

The image had feet and toes, which are no part of the legs any more than the thighs are parts of the legs. The two feet had ten toes; and while the toes grow out of the feet, yet they are separate from the feet and are described separately. The description therefore shows that the feet represent a great world power to follow Rome, and then later another would arise which is represented by the toes growing out from the feet and forming a part thereof. The prophet's description is: "And whereas thou sawest the feet and toes, part of the potters' clay, and part of iron, the kingdom shall be divided; but there shall be in it of the strength of the iron, forasmuch as thou sawest the iron mixed with miry clay. And as the toes of the feet were part of iron, and part of clay, so the kingdom shall be partly strong, and partly broken. And whereas thou sawest iron mixed with miry clay, they shall mingle themselves with the seed of men; but they shall not cleave one to another, even as iron is not mixed with clay."—Daniel 2:41-43.

Then in the forty-fourth verse follows the prophet's statement that God will set up his kingdom and will completely destroy all these world powers and that then God's kingdom shall stand for ever.

The time of the fulfilment of this prophecy, which is the time of the complete fall and destruction of world powers, is indicated by the words of the prophet: "They shall mingle themselves with the seed of men." Otherwise stated, at that time there shall be an effort to ally the two things represented by the iron and the clay. Iron symbolizes military power, while clay symbolically represents the democracy or common peoples of the earth; and the mingling of the two represents an effort to unite all the peoples and nations, including the democracy or rank and file, into one great military camp or war machine, and therefore corresponds with the statement concerning Satan's gathering together all his forces for the great battle of Armageddon.

In 1799 Rome fell and ceased to be a world power. At that time Napoleon was desperately attempting to establish a universal world power which would completely ignore Jehovah God and push him out of the minds of men. He was following Voltaire's theory of evolution, which is another evidence he was acting under the direction of the Devil. It is manifest that the Lord God interfered to prevent him in establishing such a universal power. At the great naval battle of Trafalgar and in the land engagement of Waterloo the forces of Napoleon were defeated and his power broken.

That marked the beginning of the ascendancy of the British Empire, which is the seventh and without doubt the greatest world power that has ever existed. Peculiar to that world power is this, that the chief part of its political body is the House of Lords, consisting of the lords spiritual and the lords temporal. The Archbishop of Canterbury is first peer of the realm and therefore next to the king. The bishops and other ecclesiastics are large owners of the lands and mines. The empire claims to represent Christ on earth, and at the same time it is the greatest military power that the world has ever produced. It fully meets the description of the two horned beast that has the appearance of a lamb because it is diplomatic, pious in appearance, sanctimonious, and that speaks like the Devil. (Revelation 13:11) Its dominion encircles the earth.

America is really a part of the British Empire because both countries are controlled by the same money power, and that is the power that is responsible for the military and the political machinery. The British Empire or world power, together with her colonies and allies, is represented by the feet in the image described by Daniel. The iron represents her great military strength, while at the same time the clay represents the democracy or common people of the empire, all of which she counts as a part of. her great military system. The battle cry during the War of Britain and her allies was: "Let us use the military to make the world safe for Democracy." Such is a mixing of iron with miry clay. It was and is a subtle attempt to amalgamate the military with the common people. The scheme will deceive the people for a time but not for long, because God through his prophet so states.

The ten toes of Daniel's image symbolically represent all the rulers of "Christendom". These have united to form a League of Nations which is the eighth beast and which comes from nowhere and goes into perdition. It is the final desperate attempt of Satan to make all the peoples of "Christendom" stand together as a great and warlike body preparatory for the great battle of God Almighty, and which the enemy expects to launch against the Lord God and against his Anointed. The British Empire is therefore the seventh world power; and the League of Nations, which is combined "Christendom", including of course the British Empire, which is the real life-giver to the League, is the eighth; and both the seventh and the eighth function at one and the same time, and both seem destined for the same fate.

The British Empire is the strongest and most powerful nation on the earth. She is the greatest world power that has ever existed. Her dominion extends from east to west and north to south, and reaches almost every part of the earth. Because of her strength she is weak. It is her numerous colonies that make her strong as an empire; and

as long as those colonies remain entirely loyal her strength
continues. If a break should start with one it might easily
extend to all others, and the empire would quickly go down.

The British Empire claims to be the most liberal on earth
with regard to freedom of speech. That claim is probably
true. The English have learned that it is a good policy to
let the people vent their feelings by giving expression in
words. At the same time she is the strongest military
power on earth. Her effort is to draw the common people
into her military organization. Her financial power works
the political and ecclesiastical elements for all they are
worth, and these in turn impress upon the people the great
necessity of the military strength of the nation. There is
a constant burden of taxation laid upon the people to
further the preparations for war. While America is separate
and independent from Britain, yet she is more dependent
than many of her citizens think. The commerce of the
British and American nations is closely allied, and therein
lie the strength and power of each. Should Britain fall
America could not long continue her commercial enterprises.
Her markets in Europe would fail. She would also be greatly menaced by Japan and China. Commerce therefore holds
the two great nations of Britain and America in close
alliance.

America is likewise pursuing the same policy concerning
war preparations. This is induced by the commercial element or Big Finance. When one of America's sons, little
known, flew across the Atlantic that marvelous feat accomplished by him was seized upon by "Big Business" to
boost war preparations. Great sums of money were spent
apparently to honor this young man. That was not done
because the spenders had any love for the young man. They
love no one but self. Millions were spent to enthuse the
common people concerning war and to draw them into the
war arrangement.

Other nations are doing the same thing. All "Christendom", which really forms the League of Nations, is talking
about disarmament but at the same time increasing that
armament. There are more armed men in Europe today
than there were in 1914. Every possible effort is being put
forth to make soldiers of the common people. What is now

called a temporary army composed of young men is being
trained and drilled in the United States, and the real purpose is to increase the military power and to encourage the
common people to be a part of it. The action of the nations
is clearly in fulfilment of Daniel's prophecy. The military
and democracy are mingling themselves together with the
purpose of getting all the common people in "Christendom"
into the great war camp. "They [the world powers] shall
mingle themselves with the seed of men." That is being
done. "But they shall not cleave one to another." This is
certain proof that the common people will break away from
the military.

Satan sees his time is short to prepare for Armageddon.
He knows that he has the people blinded concerning God;
and now he is carrying out his scheme to get the common
people into his military trap and hold them there for himself and use them for his own purposes. He is possessed
of so much egoism that he believes he can defeat God.
The time has come for God to make for himself a name and
for the complete passing from earth's stage of all the world
powers that the kingdom of righteousness may be given
full sway.

THE STONE

Daniel described a Stone cut out of the mountain without
hands. Manifestly that Stone is God's Anointed King, who
was born out of God's organization. The Stone is seen to
smite the image upon the feet, made of iron and clay, and
to break them in pieces. "Then was the iron, the clay, the
brass, the silver, and the gold broken to pieces *together*,
and became like the chaff of the summer threshingfloors;
and the wind carried them away, that no place was found
for them: and the stone that smote the image became a
great mountain, and filled the whole earth."—Daniel 2:35.

The description here given by Daniel shows that The Stone
smites the feet *first*; then the entire image together at one
and the same time is ground to pieces and becomes like the
chaff of the summer threshingfloors. Undoubtedly this is a
brief description of the battle of Armageddon, in which
God through Christ shall grind these world powers into a

powder and destroy them for ever. Daniel states it in another form when he says, "And in the days of these kings shall the God of heaven set up a kingdom, which shall never be destroyed: and the kingdom shall not be left to other people, but it shall break in pieces and consume all these kingdoms, and it shall stand for ever."—Daniel 2:44.

In 1914 the Gentile Times ended, and the due time there arrived for the great Executive Officer of Jehovah to take charge. There the new Nation was born, and God set his Anointed King upon his throne. (Psalm 2:6) The ousting of Satan from heaven followed. In 1918 The Stone, God's Anointed King, was laid in Zion; and there the judgment throne was set, and in due time all the nations of earth shall be brought before that judgment bar. The overwhelming weight of evidence therefore shows that we stand now almost in the shadow of Armageddon.

Because of Egypt's knowledge of God there was great responsibility upon that world power, and God held it to account therefor Likewise there was great responsibility upon other world powers that followed. The British Empire and all the nations of so-called "Christendom" must bear a greater responsibility before God than any powers that went before them. The British Empire claims to rule by divine right, and as a part of so-called "Christendom" claims to represent God and his Christ on earth. The clergy of this great world organization claim to represent God; but they do so hypocritically, and in fact they represent the Devil. For this reason they are more reprehensible before God. We may conclude therefore that that which befell Egypt will be carried out upon "Christendom" on a far greater scale, and shall affect the uttermost ends of the earth.

THE ISSUE

What was the issue in the crucial hour of Egypt in the time of her power and glory? The question at issue was: "Who is God?" What is the issue today in "Christendom's" most crucial hour? The question now at issue is: "Who is God?" Jehovah demonstrated his power against Egypt that men might not forget that he is God but that they might remember that he is the One from whom all blessings

flow. Likewise he demonstrated his power against the other
world powers, including Rome, and for the same purpose.
Now in the time of the enlightenment of the nations of earth
so-called "Christendom" has disregarded the name of the
Lord God and has pushed it aside and hypocritically used
his name as no other power ever did. "Christendom" is
the very zenith of the Devil's organization. God declares
his purpose that such organization shall fall amidst the
greatest time of trouble ever known, and that such will be
the last.—Matthew 24:21, 22.

SERVING NOTICE

In keeping with the fixed divine rule, before dashing
"Christendom" to pieces Jehovah will have it duly served
with notice of his purpose. Acting under his fixed rule he
sent Moses and Aaron to serve notice upon Egypt. He sent
Jonah to serve notice upon Assyria. Through his prophets
he served notice on Babylon, Medo-Persia, and Greece. He
served notice upon Rome through Jesus and his apostles.
Now shall God perform his great and terrible act in a
corner without due notice being given to the world power
of "Christendom"? No; he declares that notice must be
served upon her.

WITNESSES

Who then will God have to serve notice upon Christendom? Keep in mind that the issue now is, Who is God?
To the faithful anointed ones who delight to follow in the
footsteps of Jesus at this time God says, "Ye are my witnesses, that I am God." (Isaiah 43:10, 12) God commands
his people to go and give this witness, and says to give it
until the battle is on and until Satan's organization shall
fall never to rise again. If you are one of the anointed ones
and love the Lord, you will delight to have a part in obeying his commandments and will participate in giving the
witness. Others will not.

The events that have come to pass since 1914 have been
brought sharply to the attention of Christians. These events
constitute the good news to the faithful and to all who love

righteousness. The Lord tells the faithful who love him to go and give this witness to the peoples and nations of earth. Undoubtedly the World War ceased that the witness might be given; and when it is given, it may be expected that the battle of Armageddon will follow.

Last year there was sent to the ruling powers of the world due notice that God had set his King upon his throne and that the kingdom of heaven is at hand. As was expected, they have ignored and spurned that notice, and gnawed their tongues. Now notice must be given to the people that go to make up Christendom. Those who love the Lord God and who have opportunity to give this witness will regard such as the greatest privilege that has ever come to them. With joy and with boldness let each and every one who is anointed prove his love for God by availing himself of every opportunity to testify that Jehovah is God, that Christ is King, and that the kingdom of heaven is at hand.

JUDGMENT

of the Judges
of the Preachers
of the Nations
of the Financiers
of the Politicians
of Satan's Organization
of the People

by

J. F. Rutherford

Judge Rutherford's books, The Harp of God,
Deliverance, Creation, Reconciliation, Government
and others, published in thirty languages, have,
in the past six years, reached a circulation
exceeding forty-four million copies.

Made in U. S. A.

Copyrighted 1929 and published by the
INTERNATIONAL BIBLE STUDENTS ASSOCIATION
Brooklyn, New York, U. S. A.
London, Toronto, Melbourne, Cape Town, Berne, Magdeburg.

FOREWORD

DO YOU know why this is such a
strange period of history, a day of
probes and exposures? The world's
judges, preachers, nations, financiers
and politicians, and all of Satan's organization are before the bar of divine
judgment. It is a fearful time for
them. A just and fair trial and judgment of the people's cause is just
ahead. The outcome will be glorious
for mankind. Read herein about it,
and hail the day!

THE PUBLISHERS

JUDGMENT

THE night was exceedingly cold. A heavy gale was driving the snow and sleet. The unprotected were chilled to the bone. The shops were closed, and there was no shelter in the street to shield one from the fury of the storm. Just around the corner stood a church edifice. Not only was it a place of shelter from the driving storm, but the steam from its furnace warmed the atmosphere inside and made the church a pleasant place in which to rest. There was a light in the vestibule, indicating that the church door was unlocked.

A dozen or more ragged and hungry men and women simultaneously rushed for the church door that they might find some relief from the perils of the night. They entered the church building quietly and orderly. The church service was in progress. The velvet-padded pews of ease and elegance were occupied by a small number of old ladies and a few men, all of whom appeared to be those who enjoyed financial prosperity. Farther back in the room a young man sat alone. Seeking knowledge, he had thought he might learn something in that church; hence he had gone in.

The hymn had been chanted, the prayer uttered, and the collection had been gathered in silver platters. For some moments the preacher had recounted to his small congregation the many important things the church had accomplished concerning the World War and the election of public officers and the enforcement of the dry law.

Suddenly the door swung ajar and a great gust of wind forced a cloud of sleet and snow inside the warm room, followed quickly by the ragged company of men and women above mentioned who were seeking shelter from the storm. The minister paused in his oration and with a scowl watched the unwelcome visitors crowd into the rear pew provided for the less prosperous. Fixing his eyes upon the unfortunates the minister continued to gaze at them in silence until every eye in the room was turned in the direction of the motley newcomers. Some of the women had no head covering and their hair was matted with snow and sleet. The men were not pleasing in appearance. They had been suffering outside from the storm, but now, observing that they were unwelcome, they were even more uncomfortable under the searching gaze of the minister and his rich parishioners. The young man who sat alone looked upon this poor company with great pity. He was the only one in that presence who did.

After what seemed an interminable pause the minister, with his gaze still fixed upon the bedraggled company in the rear, with great gravity and with pious and sanctimonious voice began to speak. His words were in substance these:

"The judgment of God is against you. The storm has driven you from the outside. Here you have come and found protection and warmth. You come here not to do the church any good nor to build up society and the government. You come here only because you are driven here by this storm from heaven. Soon the storms of hell will be beating against your naked souls and you will find a heat from which you can never escape. In that place of doom the fires are never quenched and the worm dieth not. I warn you to escape the wrath of God now while you can. Go and find work. Save your money and come here and pay your vows and your obligations to the church. Let the judgment of this night that has driven you into this blessed church be a warning to you to flee from the wrath of God to come. Behold, he comes to execute judgment upon all the ungodly. Beware! The church alone can render you aid, but you must do your part." Then with the voice of assumed charity the minister added, addressing the congregation: "We will now receive the silver offering for foreign missions."

With the benediction said, the favored ones of the congregation gathered around the minister to commend him for his timely words of warning to that uncouth people that had unceremoniously interrupted the church service. While this was being done the ushers saw to it that the ragged, motley and hungry visitors were quickly sent forth from the building. As they huddled in the street outside the door some of the women asked: "Do you think this is the beginning of God's judgment against us? If this storm is just the beginning, what will hell be?"

The lone young man had followed the company of unfortunates out of the church. He saw their pinched faces and shivering bodies and their seeming distress of mind as well as of body. They disappeared in the darkness. He hurried away to his room. He kept asking himself these questions: "Does that minister represent God? Is that church the church of the loving God? Those men and women seemed to be very poor. Will God's judgment be particularly harsh against the poor? Is not the Bible God's Word of truth? Does it not say that God is love? How then can that church represent God?" Then and there the young man resolved to begin a careful study of the Bible, that he might learn what is meant by the judgment day and who will be judged and what will be the result upon those who are judged. What he learned from the Bible is set forth in the following pages. It is the truth, because taken from the Word of God.

Definitions

Judgment: Judgment means a formal judicial decree delivered or entered on record by one having authority and jurisdiction of the case or subject matter under consideration. A judgment is delivered or rendered by a judge.

Judge: A judge is one who judicially pronounces sentence or renders judgment. He must be clothed with power, authority and jurisdiction so to do.

Legal: Judgments may be rendered either legally or illegally. One who wrongfully assumes to render judgment does so illegally. A legal judgment is rendered by a fully qualified judge after hearing the facts, weighing the same, and applying the facts to the law. The judgment rendered by one having neither authority nor jurisdiction is void, and no one is bound to obey it. A judgment rendered by one having power or authority or jurisdiction is binding.

Issue: The word issue, as used in connection with judgment, means the question or material point that is in dispute and which is submitted to the judge for determination. The issue or question in dispute may be affirmed by one and denied by another. The rights of the parties to the issue joined are considered and determined by the judge hearing the matter. When a creature is on trial before a court or judge and the question or issue is whether he has disobeyed the law, the facts are heard and the law applied to the facts, and then the judgment follows.

Trial: The trial or hearing of the facts must precede the rendering of the decree or judgment. It follows, therefore, that there can be no just or proper judgment rendered without a hearing or trial.

Jehovah God is the great Judge over all. All rightful authority proceeds from him. He holds the power and jurisdiction over all matters and therefore he can delegate that power, authority and jurisdiction to any one whom he may choose. He is the Supreme Justice: "For God is judge himself."—Ps. 50:6.

God is just and merciful. "Justice and judgment are the habitation of thy throne: mercy and truth shall go before thy face." (Ps. 89:14) "The law of the Lord is perfect. . . . The

statutes of the Lord are right." (Ps. 19:7, 8)
Therefore God gives every creature a fair trial
or hearing before final judgment is rendered.
His judgments are impartial. "Ye shall not
respect persons in judgment; but ye shall hear
the small as well as the great; ... for the judgment is God's." (Deut. 1:17) God therefore
assures every one a fair hearing or trial. "Doth
our law judge any man before it hear him, and
know what he doeth?"—John 7:51.

Judge Christ Jesus

After the consecration of Jesus, at the time
of his baptism in the Jordan, Jehovah God appointed and anointed him as the great Judge.
That means that Jehovah God delegated to his
beloved Son the power and authority and
jurisdiction to hear and judge all creatures.
Jesus Christ was clothed with all power and authority in heaven and in earth at his resurrection. (Matt. 28:18) It is written concerning
him: "For the Father judgeth no man, but hath
committed all judgment unto the Son." (John
5:22) In due time must "all appear before the
judgment seat of Christ". (2 Cor. 5:10) Acting as Jehovah God's executive officer Jesus
Christ renders judgment in full accord with the
will of God.

Jurisdiction: The literal meaning of the word
jurisdiction is "the right to say". It means the
right, power and authority to hear and to determine the cause under consideration and to
execute the same. Of necessity time enters into
the matter because there is a proper or due
time to hear and determine causes of action.

The fact that Jesus Christ was clothed with
power and authority at a specific time does not
mean that he would immediately begin to exercise that authority and render judgment. Jehovah God fixes the due time to hear and determine all matters. When the court is set for
hearing, that is the proper and due time. Before Jehovah God, the great Supreme Judge,
delegates power and authority to others to act
as judges, he puts them upon trial and judgment. We now consider the judgment

Of the Judges

Since all authority proceeds from Jehovah
God he delegates power and authority to
others. This he does only after a trial and
judgment of those whom he makes judges. His
beloved Son was God's active agent in the creation of all things. Then he was made flesh and
dwelt amongst men on earth that he might by
his full obedience to God's law become the Redeemer of man. (John 1:14, 29) At the Jordan
he made an agreement to do God's will, which
meant that he must be fully obedient to God's
expressed law. At that time God made a covenant with Jesus that he should be the great
Judge and Ruler of all creation. But before the
authority was fully and completely conferred
upon Jesus he must undergo a trial and be
judged and prove worthy. For three and a half
years Jesus was subjected to the most severe
test, which brought upon him much suffering.
He learned obedience by the things which he
suffered. (Heb. 5:8) He "became obedient unto
death, even the [ignominious] death of the

cross. Wherefore God also hath highly exalted him, and given him a name which is above every name". (Phil. 2:8-11) He was tested and proved by Jehovah and was made judge over all creatures, to hear and render judgment in God's due time. That includes power and authority to judge his associate judges; also to judge the clergy, the nations, the financiers, the politicians, Satan and his organization, and all the peoples, including the living and the dead.

God planned that Jesus Christ should have associated with him a small company taken from amongst men, who in due time should participate with him in judgment. Each one of these must first fully agree to do God's will, which means consecration; and then each must be put upon trial and in that trial must prove himself loyal and faithful unto God and to Christ. Jesus said to his disciples that because they had been faithful with him in his trials they should share with him in his kingdom, and in his throne or judgment seat.—Luke 22:28-30.

To those who agree to be his followers Jesus says: "And he that overcometh, and keepeth my works unto the end, to him will I give power over the nations." "To him that overcometh will I grant to sit with me in my throne." (Rev. 2:26; 3:21) Again, it is written: "Do ye not know that the saints shall judge the world?" (1 Cor. 6:2) From the time one becomes a true follower of Christ until his death he is on trial. The final judgment concerning such is rendered by the Lord Jesus Christ when he comes to his temple.—Mal. 3:1-3; 1 Pet. 4:17; Ps. 11:4, 5.

2 + 2 = 4

You believe it because you can prove it. That's exactly how simple and how satisfactorily proven are the facts stated by Judge Rutherford in his book

RECONCILIATION

AND more than that! The facts he gives are of more interest and vital importance to you than anything else in the whole world. We say that because the biggest thing in every one's life is life itself. Why are we here? Whence came we? Where are we going?

HERE'S what the author himself says about the book: "A plain statement of the gracious provision Jehovah has made to bring all men into full harmony with himself that the obedient ones may have everlasting life on earth in contentment and complete happiness."

We can promise you a genuine surprise in this book if you are willing to risk 45 cents in stamps for it.

Mailed anywhere in the U.S.A. for 45 c

International Bible Students Association
117 Adams Street Brooklyn NY
For prices in foreign countries write
to our offices in those countries.
List on last page.

God made man for the earth, not for heaven. Only those who are faithful unto death in doing the will of God will be a part of the heavenly kingdom. Jesus said that not every one that says, Lord, Lord, shall enter the kingdom, but "he that doeth the will of my Father". (Matt. 7:21) These will be associate judges with Christ in a part of his judgment work.

Of the Preachers

The rule of action, or law of the judgment, is written in the Bible, which is God's Word of truth. All just judgments are rendered in full accord therewith. For this reason the student of the Bible can determine from the Bible what will be the nature of the judgment of the Lord. Jesus Christ renders such decree or judgment, and his followers have something to do therewith. (Psa. 149:8, 9) The due time for judgment to begin has come, and therefore the person who is devoted to God can study the matter and get an understanding thereof.

The preachers or clergymen claim to have agreed to do God's will. They claim to be representatives of God and of Christ. Among them there have been some good men and many who have been otherwise. A man is good only when he is entirely devoted to God. God calls those who are truly his sons his "watchmen". Because the preachers pose before the people and claim that they represent God and that they are his sons, God caused his prophet to write concerning them and ironically to call them watchmen. These men claim to have a knowledge of the truth. They are therefore on trial as preachers or claimed representatives of the Lord.

The unfaithful preachers have ignored God's Word and have looked to their own selfish interests. They have used their congregations to further their own desires. They love honor of men and seek their own personal comfort, each one looking to his own congregation for the things that he wants. Concerning such God's prophet wrote: "His watchmen are blind; they are all ignorant, they are all dumb dogs, they cannot bark; sleeping, lying down, loving to slumber. Yea, they are greedy dogs which can never have enough, and they are shepherds that cannot understand; they all look to their own way, every one for his gain from his quarter."—Isa. 56: 10, 11.

Many of the clergmen or preachers have joined forces with Big Business and professional politicians and have tried to exalt themselves and have lost sight of God's Word. They favor the rich and influential because they reason it will be to their own good. They make the influential men the favored ones of their congregation or the principal ones of their flock. They delight to have the rulers in their chief pews and they push out the poor and ragged and those without influence for fear that they will offend the rich and that this would work to the clergymen's disadvantage. They do not really love God, and they serve him only with their mouths by making speeches of great gravity and assumed piety. Those men have become intoxicated with the teachings of the world, such as evolution, the great achievements of men,

and what their church organizations have
wrought. Concerning such it is written: "Stay
yourselves, and wonder; cry ye out, and cry:
they are drunken, but not with wine; they stag-
ger, but not with strong drink. For the Lord
hath poured out upon you the spirit of deep
sleep, and hath closed your eyes: the prophets
[preachers] and your rulers, the seers hath he
covered. And the vision of all is become unto
you as the words of a book that is sealed, which
men deliver to one that is learned, saying, Read
this, I pray thee: and he saith, I cannot; for it
is sealed; and the book is delivered to him that
is not learned, saying, Read this, I pray thee:
and he saith, I am not learned. Wherefore the
Lord said, Forasmuch as this people draw near
me with their mouth, and with their lips do honour me, but have removed their heart far from
me, and their fear toward me is taught by the
precept of men: therefore, behold, I will proceed to do a marvellous work among this people, even a marvellous work and a wonder: for
the wisdom of their wise men shall perish, and
the understanding of their prudent men shall
be hid."—Isa. 29: 9-14.

The clergymen claim to represent God and
call themselves "the shepherd of the flock" or
congregation, which they serve. They do not
try to feed the congregation upon the proper
Word of God. Their interest is centered in
themselves and they feed themselves on the
things that please themselves. God likens them
unto the shepherd who selfishly neglects his
flock. Concerning them he caused their judgment to be written in his Word, as follows:

"Thus saith the Lord God unto the shepherds [clergymen], Woe be to the shepherds [preachers] of Israel that do feed themselves! should not the shepherds [preachers] feed the flocks? Ye eat the fat, and ye clothe you with the wool, ye kill them that are fed: but ye feed not the flock. The diseased have ye not strengthened, neither have ye healed that which was sick, neither have ye bound up that which was broken, neither have ye brought again that which was driven away, neither have ye sought that which was lost; but with force and with cruelty have ye ruled them. And they were scattered because there is no shepherd: and they became meat to all the beasts of the field when they were scattered. My sheep wandered through all the mountains, and upon every high hill: yea, my flock was scattered upon all the face of the earth, and none did search or seek after them. Therefore, ye shepherds [preachers], hear the word of the Lord:. . . Behold, I am against the shepherds [clergy]; and I will require my flock at their hand, and cause them to cease from feeding the flock; neither shall the shepherds [preachers] feed themselves any more; for I will deliver my flock from their mouth, that they may not be meat for them."—Ezek. 34:2-7, 10.

When reading these words of God's prophet, call to mind that little company of poor who fled from the storm into the church building and who were refused aid and comfort. Call to mind the desire of the clergyman on that occasion to please those of his congregation who could afford to occupy the padded pews.

The preachers have frightened the people by
falsely telling them that God would consign
them to purgatory for a long while and later
transfer them to eternal torment where they
would be tortured for ever. They have told the
people that each one has a soul that can not
die and, it being in hell torment, that condition
of suffering would obtain eternally. They have
told them that such is God's judgment. Such
statements are lies, and God calls them such.
He says that he did not authorize these men to
speak in his name and to represent him as a
fiend, because such a wicked thing as torture
was never in God's mind. (Jer. 32:35) "Then
the Lord said unto me, The prophets [preach-
ers] prophesy lies in my name; I sent them not,
neither have I commanded them, neither spake
unto them: they prophesy unto you a false vision and divination, and a thing of nought, and
the deceit of their heart." (Jer. 14:14) God
has decreed that there will come a time of
trouble which will destroy the wicked organizations that oppress the people. The preachers
deny this, and the Lord says to them: "Therefore thus saith the Lord concerning the prophets [preachers] that prophesy in my name,
and I sent them not, yet they say, Sword and
famine shall not be in this land; By sword and
famine shall those prophets [clergy] be consumed."—Jer. 14:15.

The rich and influential in the church denominations are the "principal" ones of the flock
or congregation, and they influence improperly
the preacher or shepherd. Those shepherds
now enjoy good pasture for themselves. Of

course "the principal of the flock" gladly pay
the preacher, thinking that by so doing they
will receive immunity or absolution from their
wrongful acts. Concerning such the Lord decrees: "Howl, ye shepherds, and cry; and
wallow yourselves in the ashes, ye principal of
the flock: for the days of your slaughter and of
your dispersions are accomplished; and ye shall
fall like a pleasant vessel. And the shepherds
[preachers] shall have no way to flee, nor the
principal of the flock to escape. A voice of the
cry of the shepherds, and an howling of the
principal of the flock, shall be heard: for the
Lord hath spoiled their pasture."—Jer. 25:
34-36.

In these days the clergy are the ones who
oppose all persons who try to teach the people
the plain truth of the Bible. They do not want
the people to know the truth, because it would
interfere with their wrongful course. During
the World War they caused many faithful
Christians to be imprisoned and beaten because
they were telling the truth. The Lord Jesus
calls all his faithful followers his "brethren"
and counts them as part of himself because
they are his body members. (Heb. 2:11) Books
explaining the Bible, and which enable the people to understand God's Word of truth, were
gathered up by the preachers during the War
and since and burned. The preachers strut
about assuming great wisdom and warn the
people to read nothing that is printed concerning the Bible unless it is endorsed by the clergymen. The Lord gave a parable in which he
likened such preachers unto "billy goats" that

selfishly abuse those who are in their way. Such
men claim to be God's sons, but they are in fact
the children of Satan the Devil. (John 8:42-44)
In the parable Jesus says concerning them: "I
was a stranger, and ye took me not in: naked,
and ye clothed me not; sick and in prison, and
ye visited me not. Then shall they also answer
him, saying, Lord, when saw we thee an hun-
gered, or athirst, or a stranger, or naked, or
sick, or in prison, and did not minister unto
thee? Then shall he answer them saying, Verily
I say unto you, Inasmuch as ye did it not to one
of the least of these [my brethren], ye did it
not to me. And these shall go away into everlasting punishment; but the righteous into life
eternal."—Matt. 25:43-46.

Of the Nations

God organized the Jews into a nation and
made a covenant with that people to give them
life if they kept his law. That nation was on.
trial. They being unfaithful to their covenant,
God rendered a final decree against them and
took away the right to rule. (Ezek. 21:24-27)
He cast the Israelites away from him and permitted their nation to be destroyed. In due
time he will grant the Jews an individual new
trial.

At the casting away of Israel the Gentile nations were permitted to have full sway in the
earth. The Lord God placed sufficient information within the reach of these nations to let
them know that he is the only true God. The
Gentile nations, therefore, were put on trial for
an attempt to establish a desirable govern-

ment. Many of such nations adopted a religion and called it the Christian religion, and have since called themselves Christian nations. The men that rule the nations of the earth today are anything but the followers of Christ. Christ Jesus is "the Prince of Peace". He restated his Father's commandment: "Thou shalt not kill." When the great World War came, the nations of so-called Christendom, or "organized Christianity", not only indulged in that war, but enacted laws compelling young men to go to war and kill each other. No one was able to give a good reason why the war was being fought. While the war was in progress the nations took advantage of the conditions and saddled upon the people many burdens in the way of unjust laws, greatly increased taxation, and other burdens contrary to righteousness.

It is well known by all persons that the laws of the so-called Christian nations are enforced with great partiality. The rich and the influential escape the punishment for the violation of the law, while they also use the law to burden and oppress the less fortunate. The poor man has little or no show in the courts. The ways of the nations are not equal. The nations of so-called Christendom are ruled by Big Business, big politicians, and big preachers. All have forgotten God and turned to the false teachings of evolution and science so called. Concerning such God's decree is announced thus: "The wicked shall be turned into hell, and all the nations that forget God." (Ps. 9:17) Hell, as used in this text, does not mean eternal

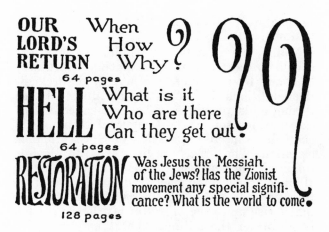

OUR LORD'S RETURN When How Why?
64 pages

HELL What is it Who are there Can they get out?
64 pages

RESTORATION Was Jesus the Messiah of the Jews? Has the Zionist movement any special significance? What is the world to come.
128 pages

These three prominent Bible subjects are explained by Judge Rutherford so simply, so consistent with logic and common sense, you will wonder why there could ever have been any difference of opinion. Still there has been more confusion, more outraging of reason, more ecclesiastical hocus-pocus about these simple Bible teachings than any others.

The set of three, paper-bound, mailed anywhere in the U. S. for 25c

INTERNATIONAL BIBLE STUDENTS ASSOCIATION
117 Adams Street, Brooklyn, N.Y.

For prices in other countries write to our offices in those countries. List on last page.

torment, but it means oblivion. These evil
nations shall cease to exist .

Today the so-called Christian nations are
armed to the teeth, in fear that an attack may
be made by one upon another. God foreknew
the conditions that now exist and foretold such
through his prophets. These so-called Christian nations set up the League of Nations and
claim it to be an expression of God's kingdom
on earth. The preachers have tried to inveigle
some of the true Christians into this unholy
alliance. Concerning such, God says: "Therefore
wait ye upon me, saith the Lord, until the day
that I rise up to the prey; for my determination
is to gather the nations, that I may assemble
the kingdoms, to pour upon them mine indignation, even all my fierce anger: for all the earth
shall be devoured with the fire of my jealousy."
(Zeph. 3:8) "And he that overcometh, and
keepeth my works unto the end, to him will I
give power over the nations: and he shall rule
them with a rod of iron; as the vessels of a potter shall they be broken to shivers: even as I
received of my Father." (Rev. 2:26, 27) Then
says the Lord: "And in the days of these kings
shall the God of heaven set up a kingdom which
shall never be destroyed: and the kingdom shall
not be left to other people, but it shall break in
pieces and consume all these kingdoms, and it
shall stand for ever." (Dan. 2:44) God is now
setting up his kingdom, or true nation, and
through it his blesssings for the people of the
nations will be given to them that obey him.—
Gen. 22:18.

Of the Financiers

It is written in God's Word: "For the love of money is the root of all evil; which while some coveted after, they have erred from the faith, and pierced themselves through with many sorrows." (1 Tim. 6:10) The men who control the money of the world are called financiers. They grow rich by juggling with that which is produced by others. These men usually possess more than ordinary intelligence. They know of God; some of them have even gained some knowledge of God's plan. Their greed and love for money and for the power it brings have led them to be oppressors of the people. Some of them have become so very selfish that human life is not sacred to them but is counted a common thing.

These men have formed and operated great inanimate bodies called corporations. These organized corporate powers are employed as agencies of great oppression upon the people. The men who use them must know that they are not doing right. If a man stands in the way of these organized systems' accomplishing their selfish purpose they do not hesitate to hire the professional killer to remove such obstruction. If a man brings to light some important invention, and selfish financiers believe it to be to the advantage of their corporation, they find some way of defrauding the inventor out of the fruits of his labors.

The farmers grow their crops at the cost of money and much labor, but the price thereof is fixed by the heartless corporations. These hoard their ill-got gains and think such will be

able to deliver them in the time of trouble.
There are about 280 men who control the great
corporations and the money power of America,
and each one of these has an annual income of
a million dollars or more. There are more than
110 million people in America, most of whom
are in very ordinary circumstances. There is
a great disparity in the number of the rich and
those who are not rich.

Just now it is a common thing to hear the
cries of the people against their oppressors.
God hears those cries and he will set right all
matters in his due time. He has announced in
his Word his judgment against those who are
responsible for these cries. It is written: "Go
to now, ye rich men, weep and howl for your
miseries that shall come upon you. Your riches
are corrupted, and your garments are moth
eaten. Your gold and silver is cankered; and
the rust of them shall be a witness against you,
and shall eat your flesh as it were fire. Ye have
heaped treasure together for the last days. Behold, the hire of the labourers who have reaped
down your fields, which is of you kept back by
fraud, crieth: and the cries of them which have
reaped are entered into the ears of the Lord of
Sabaoth. Ye have lived in pleasure on the
earth, and been wanton; ye have nourished
your hearts, as in a day of slaughter. Ye have
condemned and killed the just; and he doth not
resist you."—Jas. 5: 1-6.

The cruel and oppressive corporations organized and operated by a few selfish men the
Lord likens unto a fierce lion amidst harmless
lambs. The poor are powerless against such

harsh lions. When God's judgment is enforced against the great corporations owned and operated by men, he will destroy their power and they will cease to oppress and coerce the people. The government of God under Christ, the great Judge, being in full sway in the earth then, there will be no harsh organizations symbolized by lions. They will cease for ever. "No lion shall be there, nor any ravenous beast shall go up thereon, it shall not be found there; but the redeemed shall walk there."—Isa. 35:9.

Of the Politicians

Those who exercise rule over the people are properly called politicians. One holding a public office and who looks well to his own advantage is a professional politician. Such in part constitute the visible part of the ruling powers over the people. A ruler is also called a prince. During a political campaign such men seek office and promise much to the people, but, when elected, straightway forget their promises. The Lord mentions such in his Word: "As a roaring lion, and a ranging bear; so is a wicked ruler over the poor people." (Prov. 28:15) The ruler that has not understanding is also an oppressor.—Prov. 28:16.

The great politicians or statesmen assemble from time to time to determine what is for the best interest of their respective countries. Such a conference was held in Paris in 1919. Although God had furnished the proof that the time had arrived for his righteous Son to begin his reign and establish righteousness, these politicians or rulers took counsel together

against the Lord and his Anointed: "The kings of the earth set themselves, and the rulers take counsel together, against the Lord, and against his anointed, saying, Let us break their bands asunder, and cast away their cords from us." —Ps. 2:2, 3.

Then the Lord sets forth his judgment against such and advises what he will do for them: "Then shall he speak unto them in his wrath, and vex them in his sore displeasure. Yet have I set my king upon my holy hill of Zion. Thou shalt break them with a rod of iron; thou shalt dash them in pieces like a potter's vessel." (Psa. 2:5, 6, 9) To the same effect is the Lord's judgment announced in Jeremiah 51:22, 23.

Further speaking of his judgment upon such, and of the righteousness of his own government, the Lord says: "The Lord hath broken the staff of the wicked, and the sceptre of the rulers." (Isa. 14:5) Then the rulers that have ruled in unrighteousness and made public office a private gain shall cease for ever.

Of Satan's Organization

Satan the Devil is the arch enemy of God and of man. Before he became evil his name was Lucifer and he was then a beautiful creature acting under the authority of God as man's invisible overseer. He was then on trial before God. He rebelled against God and was guilty of treason against God and guilty of the murder of man. Immediately following his rebellion God announced what would be his final judgment against Satan.—Ezek. 28:14-19.

The 'seed of promise' is Christ. God declared that in his due time he would execute his judgment against Satan and that this would be done by his beloved Son Christ. (Heb. 2:14; Rev. 20: 1-3) Satan was permitted to go at liberty until God's due time to execute his judgment against him. God permitted this in order to give his other creatures the opportunity to choose whom they would serve. Satan the Devil set about to form his own organization. He seduced a large number of the angels of heaven and made them a part of his organization. (Eph. 6:12) He organized men into bodies and induced them to hypocritically call themselves by the name of the Lord. (Gen. 4:26, margin) He organized the people of Babel, made Nimrod their visible ruler and caused the people to place Nimrod above or "before" Jehovah God. —Gen. 10:8-12.

Egypt was organized into a form of government, and Satan was its invisible overlord. Then came Assyria to the fore as a world power, and Satan was the god of that nation. When the Israelites were cast off from God, and the Gentile nations were permitted to have sway in the earth, Satan became the invisible ruler or god of all the nations of the earth.—Matt. 4: 8, 9; 2 Cor. 4:3, 4.

At all times in Satan's organization he has employed three visible elements amongst men to rule the people. These elements are, to wit, (1) the commercial power, which holds and controls the money and the commerce of the earth; (2) the political element, or the statesmen who make and enforce the laws of the people; and

(3) the religious element, which plays upon the superstition of the people to induce them to be submissive to the ruling powers, teaching the people that their failure to obey the teachings of the preachers or the church will result in their being tormented in hell for ever.

Rome was the sixth in the list of world powers formed and ruled by Satan. Originally Rome was pagan in religion. Then that nation adopted a formalism, called it by the name of Christianity and designated it the Christian religion. The ecclesiastical element formed an influential part of that world power.

There was rebellion against Rome by other countries of Europe, and then came into vogue what is called the Protestant religion of Christ. Without a doubt many good and honest men embraced the Protestant faith. Within a short time, however, the Devil, through Big Business and professional politicians and false preachers, got control of the Protestant church.

Such nations as Great Britain, the United States and others claim to be Christian nations, but they are not Christian nations by any means. These nations and other nations of the earth form Satan's visible organization. No one will dispute the fact that the nations of so-called Christendom are the nations of the world. It is written that Satan is the god or invisible ruler of the world.—2 Cor. 4:3, 4; John 12:31; 14:30; Matt. 4:8, 9.

Satan has builded a tremendous and powerful organization. The invisible part of his organization is designated in the Scriptures as heaven, while the visible part of his organization is called the earth. The invisible part is composed of Satan and his angels. The visible part is composed of the commercial, political and religious elements, which now combine to rule the peoples of earth.

Satan is the great oppressor and he uses his organization to oppress the people and keep them in subjection. God has decreed that the works of Satan shall be destroyed. With God's government of righteousness in power, with Christ the Head thereof, God will destroy Satan and his works. "For this purpose the Son of God was manifested, that he might destroy the works of the devil."—1 John 3:8.

The real *head* of the earthly part of Satan's organization is the commercial power, or the great financiers. These constitute the power behind the earthly throne. The *body* is made up of the professional politicians or statesmen, because they are the ones that rule visibly. The *tail* of the organization, which tail fans from one side to the other to blind the people, is the religious element led by the clergy, which teaches lies to induce the people to submit to an oppressive rule. Such organization shall perish. It is written: "The ancient and honourable [wise financiers], he is the head; and the prophet [clergymen and religious leaders who teach falsely] that teacheth lies, he is the tail. For the leaders [the body of politicians] of this people cause them to err; and they that are led of them are destroyed."—Isa. 9:13-16.

Those who rule and have control over the people are proud and haughty. (Mal. 3:15) The financiers are cruel and oppressive, the politicians are proud and severe, and the clergy are arrogant, and all working together are oppressors of the people. Concerning such the Lord says: "For, behold, the day cometh, that shall burn as an oven; and all the proud, yea, and all that do wickedly, shall be stubble: and the day that cometh shall burn them up, saith the Lord of hosts, that it shall leave them neither root nor branch."—Mal. 4:1.

The three elements forming the controlling power over the people are designated as the earth, and such are now in great fear and are feverishly preparing for war because of the things that they see coming upon the earth. Satan the Devil is therefore gathering his forces for the great battle of Armageddon. (Rev. 16:13-16) These ruling powers well know that they have violated "the everlasting covenant" by shedding innocent blood, and God says concerning them: "The earth mourneth, and fadeth away; the world languisheth, and fadeth away; the haughty people of the earth do languish. The earth also is defiled under the inhabitants thereof, because they have transgressed the laws, changed the ordinance, broken the everlasting covenant. Therefore hath the curse devoured the earth, and they that dwell therein are desolate; therefore the inhabitants of the earth are burned, and few men left."—Isa. 24: 4-6.

Concerning those who have deliberately acted as Satan's instruments to oppress the people God says: "And I will make drunk her princes, and her wise men, her captains, and her rulers, and her mighty men: and they shall

sleep a perpetual sleep, and not wake, saith
the King whose name is the Lord of hosts."—
Jer. 51:57.

Satan's organization is referred to also under
the symbol of Babylon, also under the symbol
of wild beasts that tear and lash the people.
Concerning those who form Satan's organization God says: "Howl ye; for the day of the
Lord is at hand; it shall come as a destruction
from the Almighty."—Isa. 13:6.

The "beast", which is Satan's visible organization composed of the three elements above
named, comes into war with God's organization
under Christ. (Rev 19:11) That war results
in the destruction of Satan's organization.

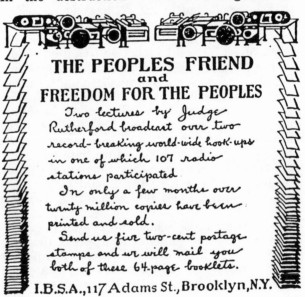

"And I saw the beast, and the kings of the earth', and their armies, gathered together to make war against him that sat on the horse, and against his army. And the beast was taken, and with him the false prophet that wrought miracles before him, with which he deceived them that had received the mark of the beast, and them that worshipped his image. These both were cast alive into a lake of fire burning with brimstone."—Rev. 19: 19, 20.

The final judgment executed against Satan and his organization will be the complete and everlasting destruction thereof. God says: "I will early destroy all the wicked of the land."—Psa. 101: 8.

Of the People

With Satan's organization completely destroyed, then the people that remain on the earth will constitute the world. It is written: "Because he [God] hath appointed a day, in the which he will judge the world in righteousness, by that man whom he hath ordained; whereof he hath given assurance unto all men, in that he hath raised him [Christ] from the dead."—Acts 17: 31.

The Lord could not judge the world in righteousness until Satan's organization of unrighteousness is destroyed. Satan, by working through his instruments of unrighteousness, has deceived the people for many centuries and has turned them away from God. Satan has made the nations evil. When Satan is bound and his organization destroyed, he can deceive the nations no more and the people will have

a chance to learn the truth. (Rev. 20:1-3)
Christ, the great and righteous Judge, will then
judge the people in righteousness. Then the
people can have a hearing and a trial. When
Christ's kingdom of righteousness is in full
sway, then the judgment will take place as it is
written: "The Lord . . . shall judge the quick
[living] and the dead at his appearing and his
kingdom." (2 Tim. 4:1) Those living on the
earth will be the first ones judged. After them
the dead will be brought to life on earth and
be given a fair trial. The day of judgment of
the people, instead of its being one of great distress, will be a day of great joy to all them that
obey. It will mean the time of deliverance from
oppression, and the day of blessing. Concerning
that day of judgment the preachers have misrepresented God and have misled the people.
God never authorized them to speak. Now the
time has come when God will make known his
truth to his people in his own good way.

The Trial

Bear in mind always that God is just, and
his action always in harmony with his law. It
follows then that there could be no judgment
without a hearing or trial of the ones to be
judged, because God's law provides that such
hearing must be had. (John 7:51) It also follows that there could be no judgment of the
people without a judge; and, since the judgment work is assigned to Christ Jesus, the
judgment by Christ of the people could not take
place until his court is set and the due time has
arrived. Furthermore, there could not be a trial

of a person unless that person has knowledge
of and concerning his trial. The preachers
have told the people that all have their trial
and that their destiny is fixed at death. That is
not true. Only those who have learned of God's
plan and who have knowledge or could have
had a knowledge thereof have been on trial.
Some have been tried as individuals, and some
forming an organization have been subjected
to trial.

Take as an illustration that little company of
men and women who rushed into the church
building to escape the storm and who heard the
words of the preacher concerning their judgment. They were not on trial. They could not
have been on trial unless they had first heard
the truth. They did not hear the truth from the
preacher. They had heard it in no church building. They were threatened with eternal torment, which is not true. They heard nothing
about God's provision for poor humanity. The
preacher was not their judge and he had no
authority to single them out and speak in words
of condemnation or otherwise against them.
Satan, the enemy of God, has overreached the
preachers and has induced them to preach false
doctrines that have really blinded the people to
the truth.

Only those who have made a consecration to
do God's will and have received his spirit have
been led into the truth. That is exactly what Jesus said to his disciples, that "when the holy
spirit of God is given, you will be led into all
truth'. (John 16:13) Until the second coming
of the Lord and his kingdom the poor of the

world are blind to the truth by reason of the
works of the enemy through his false teachers.
(2 Cor. 4:3, 4) It has been like a vail over the
face of the people. In the Bible the word
mountain is used as a symbol of God's kingdom,
and the Lord declares that in that mountain he
shall remove this vail that the people may see
the truth.—Isa. 25:7.

Why a Trial

Why should the people be put on trial, and
for what could they be tried? The proper answer to that question is important. God created
the earth for man to live upon. (Isa. 45:12, 18)
He gave to Adam dominion over the things of
the earth and the right to live on it for ever.
That right depended solely upon Adam's obedience to God's law. God did not require much
of him, but he told Adam that he must not disobey and that if he would disobey death would
be the penalty. (Gen. 2:17) Adam being on
trial, because of his disobedience the judgment
of death and expulsion from Eden was entered
against him. (Gen. 3:15-24) All of Adam's children were born after that. Their sinful and
imperfect father, undergoing the sentence of
death, could not bring forth perfect children.
The children therefore inherited the result of
Adam's sin. Hence the prophet says: "Behold,
I was shapen in iniquity, and in sin did my
mother conceive me."—Psa. 51:5.

Unless God would make some provision for a
new trial for mankind, all men must in due time
for ever perish. God promised that he would
redeem man. (Hos. 13:14) God in his loving-

kindness made provision to prevent man from perishing. "For God so loved the world, that he gave his only begotten Son, that whosoever believeth in him should not perish, but have everlasting life. For God sent not his Son into the world to condemn the world; but that the world through him might be saved."—John 3: 16, 17.

Jesus, the Son of God, became a man. (John 1: 14) He came to earth in order that he might ransom the human race and give the people the opportunity for life. (Matt. 20: 28; John 10: 10) Ransom means to buy back or acquire title with a corresponding price. Jesus was a perfect man, even as Adam was when he was in Eden. The death of Jesus as a man exactly corresponded to the price of the perfect life that God's judgment required of Adam. Jesus Christ in death was made a substitute for Adam that Adam and his offspring might be released from the judgment of death and the effects thereof. For whom did Jesus die upon the cross? "For every man," say the Scriptures. (Heb. 2: 9) Furthermore, in God's due time the fact must be told to every man, and that before he is put upon trial. "For this is good and acceptable in the sight of God our Saviour; who will have all men to be saved, and to come unto the knowledge of the truth. For there is one God, and one mediator between God and men, the man Christ Jesus; who gave himself a ransom for all, to be testified in due time."—1 Tim. 2: 3-6.

The ransom price that purchases the right of man is the basis for the granting of a new trial to Adam and all his offspring. Only Adam was

tried originally, and the offspring inherited the
evil effects thereof. The new trial or judgment
of men now will be an individual trial. In symbolic phrase the prophet of God says: "In those
days they shall say no more, The fathers
have eaten a sour grape, and the children's
teeth are set on edge, but every one shall die
for his own iniquity: every man that eateth the
sour grape, his teeth shall be set on edge."
(Jer. 31: 29, 30) That will mean that every man
must be brought to a knowledge of the truth
before he is really put on trial, and each one
will stand or fall by his own course of action.

Before the trial and judgment of the people
of the world can begin, the way must be prepared and the ground cleared. The court is
selected, and all hindrances to righteousness
must be removed. Then the Lord will judge the
world in righteousness.

The Jews as a nation had a trial, and the
judgment was adverse. The Gentile nations had
a trial and an opportunity to establish a government in harmony with God's way, and to them
the judgment is adverse. The preachers claim
to be God's representatives and that their
churches are his organization. They have had a
hearing, and the judgment against them is adverse. The financiers claim the ability to establish a government on earth and to make it a fit
place for man to live. They have had a trial,
and the judgment against them is adverse. The
politicians have claimed to rule by divine right
and have had a hearing, and the judgment
against them is adverse. Satan and his organization have had a trial, and the judgment

against such is that the evil one and his organization must be destroyed. That done, the way is cleared for the peoples to have a trial and judgment in righteousness and without interference of unrighteousness. That is also proof that the judgment of the peoples of the world is yet future.

Period of Trial or Judgment

Jesus said: 'If I be lifted up, I will draw all men unto me.' (John 12:32) The lifting up of Christ includes the members of his body, and the drawing of all men to him is during the time of his reign. It is stated in the Scriptures that the reign of Christ for the trial and judgment of the world shall cover a period of 1000 years. (Rev. 20:4-6) The day which God has appointed for the judgment of the world by Christ is not a twenty-four-hour day, but a thousand-year day. "One day is with the Lord as a thousand years." (2 Pet. 3:8; Acts 17:31) Within that period of time every human being will have a full and fair opportunity to be heard and his rights determined by the just Judge.

In Righteousness

When the trial and judgment of the peoples on earth begin, the people will not be righteous, but will, on the contrary, be very imperfect. What is meant by judgment in righteousness is this: The government that will rule the people will be righteous, because it is God's government. The invisible ruler and judge will be Christ, and his representatives on earth will be the faithful men whom the Scriptures describe

as the heroes of faith who died fully faithful
unto God.—Heb. 11:1-39; Ps. 45:16.

A beautiful picture of the day of judgment
is given in the Bible. The way which people will
have to go is likened unto a highway. "And an
highway shall be there, and a way, and it shall
be called, The way of holiness; the unclean shall
not pass over it; but it shall be for those; the
wayfaring men, though fools, shall not err
therein."—Isa. 35:8.

A highway represents a clear and unobstructed road to travel. It means, then, a clear and
unobstructed way to learn the truth, to be obedient thereto, and to return to God. That the
people are not clean and righteous at the beginning of the trial is shown by the scripture
wherein it is stated that the highway is for the
cleansing of the people and that they must be
cleansed or cleaned up before they reach the
farther end thereof. "It shall be called, The way
of holiness," because the only way to enter upon
it and go completely over it is by being devoted
entirely and wholly to the Lord and to his way
of righteousness. Neither the Devil nor any of
his agencies nor anything else will be permitted
to hinder one from learning and obeying the
truth. Therefore that trial and judgment way
will be a way of joy to those who try to do right.

The Poor

The great mass of the peoples of earth are
poor and very ignorant. They have always had
a hard time, while the rich have been favored.
Will the rich and learned have a better opportunity in the judgment day than the poor? No,

but just the reverse. Those who have been
rich and have enjoyed much advantage and
have lived in pleasure have grown haughty and
proud. It will be difficult for them to humble
themselves under the mighty hand of the Lord
and learn to do right. Jesus announced the rule
when he said to the Jewish clergy and the principal ones amongst the Jews: "It shall be more
tolerable for the land of Sodom in the day of
judgment, than for thee." (Matt. 11:24) The
people of Sodom were very ignorant and depraved. They were a simple and poor people.
The favor of the Jews was far greater, because
they had the Word of the Lord.—Rom. 3:1, 2.

Even so today, the rich and the mighty enjoy
the things of the present time, and have the
better education and better opportunity to learn
the truth and the right way. The poor are ill-
situated and are kept in ignorance. The rich
and favored ones are haughty and austere. You
will recall with what austerity the clergyman
spoke to that little company of poor ones that
came into his church. It will be hard for the
men that are haughty and severe to become
meek and obedient. Concerning such the Lord
says: "And the high ones of stature shall be
hewn down, and the haughty shall be humbled."
(Isa. 10:33) But how will the Lord judge the
poor?

The Scriptures answer that he will lead the
poor and meek and will judge them in righteousness. "With righteousness shall he judge the
poor, and reprove with equity for the meek of
the earth: and he shall smite the earth with the
rod of his mouth, and with the breath of his

lips shall he slay the wicked. And righteousness shall be the girdle of his loins, and faithfulness the girdle of his reins."—Isa. 11:4, 5.

The meek are those who desire to be taught the right way. "The meek will he guide in judgment." (Ps. 25:9) That the trial and judgment day for the poor and meek will be a happy one is proven by the words of the prophet: "The meek shall inherit the earth, and shall delight themselves in the abundance of peace." (Ps. 37: 11) "Blessed are the meek: for they shall inherit the earth." (Matt. 5:5) The proud and haughty have spoken vain words and oppressed the poor. Of these God says: "The Lord shall cut off all flattering lips, and the tongue that speaketh proud things. For the oppression of the poor, for the sighing of the needy, now will I arise, saith the Lord; I will set him in safety from him that puffeth at him."—Ps. 12:3, 5.

The Devil and his representatives have oppressed the poor, but the Lord is a just Judge and he will justly deal with them. "He shall judge the poor of the people, he shall save the children of the needy, and shall break in pieces the oppressor. For he shall deliver the needy when he crieth; the poor also, and him that hath no helper. He shall spare the poor and needy, and shall save the souls of the needy."—Ps. 72:4, 12, 13.

Living First

The judgment of the people of the world in righteousness will begin with those who are living on the earth at the time of judgment. (2 Tim. 4:1) Not every one will have to die and enter the grave. Doubtless there will be millions living on earth when the judgment begins. There is a great deal of evidence showing that the judgment will begin within a very short time. The first thing for the people will be to bring them to a knowledge of the truth. God's great promise is that all the families of the earth shall be blessed. (Gen. 12:3) Such promised blessing means that they must have an opportunity to receive the great blessing of life which is the gift of God through Jesus Christ. (Rom. 6:23) No man can receive a gift of any kind unless he has some knowledge that the gift is offered to him. It is written: "Therefore, as by the offence of one judgment came upon all men to condemnation; even so by the righteousness of one the free gift came upon all men unto justification of life."—Rom. 5:18.

The reason that the people of the world have not been able to see the truth long ago has been and is that Satan the Devil, through his false teachers, has blinded the people's understanding. "But if our gospel be hid, it is hid to them that are lost: in whom the god of this world hath blinded the minds of them which believe not, lest the light of the glorious gospel of Christ, who is the image of God, should shine unto them."—2 Cor. 4:3, 4.

Because we are now in the day of judgment of the nations and of the preachers and of Satan's organization, those who are now earnestly searching for the truth will find it. When the government of the Lord, pictured as his mountain, is in full sway, and hindrances removed, then the Lord will spread a great feast of truth for the people and they shall have no difficulty whatsoever in learning of righteousness.

Those who are now learning the truth have the advantage of getting an advance knowledge and, by the light thereof, will be in line for the early blessings of the Lord. But in due time all shall have an opportunity to know the truth. The great feast of truth which God will spread for the people is represented in poetic phrase by the Lord through his prophet: "And in this mountain [government] shall the Lord of hosts make unto all people a feast of fat things, a feast of wines on the lees, of fat things full of marrow, of wines on the lees well refined. And he will destroy in this mountain [government] the face of the covering cast over all people, and the vail that is spread over all nations." (Isa. 25: 6, 7) As those living on the earth begin to partake of God's great feast of life and truth, they will rejoice and sing his praises. The judgment day for them will be a time of gladness.

The Dead

For many thousands of years the people have been dying. The great majority of them have died in poverty and have gone into the tomb in despair. They have been told by religious teachers, particularly the clergy, that their suffering on earth is but a small thing compared with what suffering awaits them in purgatory and hell. Some clergymen have actually told the people that if they would have their friends get money together and bring it to the preachers to say prayers in behalf of the dead, then

the preachers would pray and the dead would
have their time in purgatory shortened, but
that failing to thus get out of purgatory, they
would be sent on to eternal torment where they
would continue to suffer for ever. Such teaching
originated with the Devil. There is no such place
as purgatory, where those who have died are
suffering. There is no hell of eternal torment.
Hell, as used in the Bible, means the condition
of death, or the grave. Those who died have all
gone to hell. Even Jesus was in hell three days.
(Ps. 16: 10; Acts 2: 27-34) God raised up Jesus
out of death, or hell, on the third day. (Acts
10: 40) Jesus having bought the human race
by his own great ransom sacrifice, all the dead
"sleep in Jesus", and these he will bring forth
from the grave. (1 Thess. 4: 13-17) He said:
"Marvel not at this: for the hour cometh, in
which all that are in the tombs shall hear his
voice, and shall come forth; they that have done
good, unto the resurrection of life; and they
that have done evil, unto the resurrection of
judgment." (John 5: 28, 29, *R. V.*) "And have
hope toward God, which they themselves also
allow, that there shall be a resurrection of the
dead, both of the just and unjust."—Acts 24: 15.
When the dead are brought forth again in
human bodies similar to the ones had when on
earth, they will be given a fair trial. They will
first be given a knowledge of the truth, and no
one will be permitted to mislead them. They
will be taught what they may do, and they can
rely absolutely upon such teaching to be truth.
The awakening of the dead, and their trial, will
continue year after year until all have had an

opportunity to receive the blessings granted by
reason of the great ransom sacrifice.

Now the clergy try to hinder the people from
getting the truth. Working with their allies,
they have ordinances enacted by towns and
cities for the purpose of preventing honest persons from teaching the truth by bringing to the
people printed instruction concerning the Bible.
The Devil is the master mind behind that effort
because he does not want the people to have
the truth. When the judgment of the world begins and progresses during that period, it will
be a time of righteousness, and the people will
be delivered from false teachers and false
preachers and will be led in the right way.
What, then, will be the final result or judgment
upon the peoples of the world?

Sinners and Wicked

That company of persons that came into the
church building to seek shelter from the storm,
were they sinners or wicked persons? and is
there any difference between a sinner and a
wicked person? Is not God's wrath manifest
against all such? and was the preacher not right
in telling them that the wrath of God was
against them?

Even if they were sinners or wicked, the
preacher had no authority to pronounce God's
judgment against them. Had he known the truth
and told those people God's truth, and what his
judgment means, he might have done them some
good. On the contrary, he misrepresented the
Lord. There is a difference between a sinner
and a wicked person. God judges both by and

through his executive officer Christ Jesus. It is
well to learn the distinction between sinners and
the wicked, for then we can understand the
judgment of such.

Sin means the transgression of God's law.
(1 John 3:4) A sinner is one who transgresses
or breaks God's law. A person may be a sinner
and yet not be wicked. Let us first examine the
Scriptures concerning sin and the sinner, and
the judgment of such, and then give attention
to the wicked.

All the human race sprang from Adam. No
child was born to Adam while he was a perfect
man in Eden. It was after he had been sentenced to death and expelled from Eden that
Adam exercised the power to beget children.
God endowed Adam with the power to transmit
life to his offspring. Adam, under sentence of
death and being therefore imperfect, could not
beget a perfect child. Necessarily, then, the result was that his children were born imperfect.
No imperfect creature can keep God's law perfectly. The very moment that law is broken the
one breaking it is a sinner. The parents of the
children being sentenced to death, the children
would be imperfect and therefore sinners. For
this reason it is written: "Behold, I was shapen
in iniquity, and in sin did my mother conceive
me."—Ps. 51:5.

The apostle makes it clear when he says:
"Wherefore, as by one man sin entered into the
world, and death by sin; and so death passed
upon all men, for that all have sinned." (Rom.
5:12) Every child born of a woman has been
born a sinner, the only exception being the child

Jesus, who was born without sin for the reason
that he was not the offspring of Adam. If the
entire human race has been born in sin and is
still imperfect, how is it possible for them ever
to be saved and have God's blessing?

God made provision to redeem the race and
bring back all the obedient ones to himself. That
provision is by and through the sacrifice of
Jesus, his beloved Son. Adam sinned when he
was a perfect man, and was sentenced to death.
Jesus, as a perfect man, died as a substitute
for Adam. Adam was the father of the entire
human family. Jesus, by his death and resurrection, becomes the owner of the entire human
family. It is written: "Therefore, as by the
offence of one judgment came upon all men to
condemnation; even so by the righteousness of
one the free gift came upon all men unto justification of life. For as by one man's disobedience
many were made sinners, so by the obedience
of one shall many be made righteous."—Rom.
5:18,19.

It is therefore made clearly manifest that no
one could be reconciled to God and receive the
gift of life unless that creature had a trial or
judgment after learning of God's provision. The
entire human family, both the living and the
dead, belongs to Jesus, by reason of his great
sacrifice. The dead he will bring forth for the
purpose of giving them a knowledge of the truth
and a trial. He will first give those who are
living a trial. The sacrifice of Jesus provided
salvation for all, and all then must be brought
to a knowledge of the truth.—1 Tim. 2:3-6.

Do not all children that die before they reach

the age of responsibility go to heaven because they have not sinned? No. All children are born sinners, and no sinner can go to heaven. While it is true that a child is born a sinner, a child is not a wicked person. A child could not become wicked until he reaches the age of responsibility and learns of God's law. "Christ Jesus came into the world to save sinners." (1 Tim. 1:15) There were none others to be saved. "For all have sinned, and come short of the glory of God."—Rom. 3:23.

But did not Jesus say that all the children go to heaven? Is not that the meaning of his words: "But Jesus called them unto him, and said, Suffer little children to come unto me, and forbid them not: for of such is the kingdom of God." (Luke 18:16) That is the construction the preachers have put upon his words; but that construction is not right. God establishes his kingdom for the benefit of the people on earth. Jesus taught his disciples to pray, "Thy kingdom come. Thy will be done in earth." (Matt. 6:10) For a long while Satan and his angels have constituted the heaven or invisible power that has ruled the nations and peoples of earth. Now Christ will take charge of the affairs of men on earth and he and his associates shall reign for the benefit of those on earth. (Rev. 5:10) Referring to the reign of Christ, it is written: "The kingdoms of this world are become the kingdoms of our Lord and of his Christ; and he shall reign for ever and ever." (Rev. 11:15) That refers to the time when Christ takes over all authority over the peoples of earth.

Jesus was saying nothing about children's
being taken to heaven. In his words above
quoted he was addressing the clergy of that
day, who were proud and haughty and boastful.
He wanted them to understand that no one who
was proud and haughty and boastful would ever
be in the kingdom. He was comparing those
clergymen to sinners. They were more than
sinners, because they had some knowledge of
God's Word. To illustrate the matter of the
judgment in the kingdom, he called some little
children to him and then said to the clergy:
"Verily I say unto you, Whosoever shall not receive the kingdom of God as a little child, shall
in no wise enter therein."—Luke 18: 17.

A little child is teachable and obedient; and in
the time of judgment no one will have the blessings of the kingdom of God except he be as a
little child in this respect. Jesus was speaking
of God's kingdom, which is the kingdom of
heaven because it will be ruled by the Lord of
heaven. In that time many people shall come
from every part of the earth and sit at the feet
of Abraham and other like faithful men in the
kingdom and learn. "And I say unto you, That
many shall come from the east and west, and
shall sit down with Abraham, and Isaac, and
Jacob, in the kingdom of heaven."—Matt. 8: 11.

That will take place right here on earth. That
will be a happy time. Millions of little children
have died and gone into the grave, and they will
be brought back from the grave as little children. They will be gathered in groups and will
be eager to learn from the faithful teachers
whom the Lord will provide to instruct them.

The Lord announced the rule that must be followed then, by showing that each person who will have the kingdom blessings must be teachable, like a little child.

In that judgment all the sinners will be granted a full opportunity to be made clean and whole. The little children are among the sinners, and they and all others who have the teachable and obedient disposition will be judged in righteousness and, being obedient, will receive life everlasting.

Wicked

The wicked are those who are lawless, or deliberate law-breakers. The sinner is a law-breaker, but he is not a *wilful* law-breaker. The creature must know that there is a law before he could wilfully break it. Paul said: "I had not known sin, but by the law: for I had not known lust, except the law had said, Thou shalt not covet." (Rom. 7:7) And again, he said: "For until the law, sin was in the world: but sin is not imputed when there is no law." (Rom. 5:13) A wicked person is therefore one who has some knowledge of God's law and then goes contrary thereto.

Lucifer knew God's law. He deliberately broke that law and has ever since continued to break God's law. Since breaking God's law he has been known by the names Satan, Serpent, Dragon and Devil. He is the great wicked one. He is a degenerate from that which was once good. His course of action since has ever been hurtful. He is malicious, which means that he has no regard for the rights of others and is

fatally bent on doing wrong. God's decree
against Satan the Devil is that he shall be for
ever destroyed. (Heb. 2:14) That is and will
be the judgment against all who persist in
wickedness. "All the wicked will he [God] destroy." (Ps. 145:20) The Lord describes the
wicked when he says: "For the wicked boasteth
of his heart's desire, and blesseth the covetous,
whom the Lord abhorreth. The wicked, through
the pride of his countenance, will not seek after
God: God is not in all his thoughts. His ways
are always grievous; thy judgments are far
above out of his sight: as for all his enemies,
he puffeth at them." (Ps. 10:3-5) It is Satan
that has turned men into the way of wickedness.

One may be going in the way of wickedness
because of Satan's influence and then, seeing his
wrongful course, may repent and turn to righteousness. God is merciful to such, and for such
he mkes provision. It is written in his Word:
"Because sentence against an evil work is not
executed speedily, therefore the heart of the
sons of men is fully set in them to do evil.
Though a sinner do evil an hundred times, and
his days be prolonged, yet surely I know that
it shall be well with them that fear God, which
fear before him: but it shall not be well with
the wicked, neither shall he prolong his days,
which are as a shadow; because he feareth not
before God."—Eccl. 8:11-13.

Many of the clergy know something of God's
law and plan, and yet they pursue a wicked
course of persecution against those who are
honestly endeavoring to tell the people about
God's kingdom and the blessings coming. Such

clergymen are therefore wicked; and, if they persist in continuing in that course of wickedness, they will be for ever destroyed. But should they awaken to their danger and turn to the Lord and fear before him and seek his mercy, the Scriptures indicate that God will extend mercy to them. If a person is doing right and then turns to wickedness, God will destroy him. If he is wicked and then turns to righteousness, he shall live. God has announced his rule of judgment in these words: "When the righteous turneth from his righteousness, and committeth iniquity, he shall even die thereby: but if the wicked turn from his wickedness, and do that which is lawful and right, he shall live thereby." —Ezek. 33 : 18, 19.

In the day of judgment the Lord will make it clear for the sinner, that he may learn to do right and live. "Good and upright is the Lord: therefore will he teach sinners in the way. The meek will he guide in judgment, and the meek will he teach his way." (Ps. 25 : 8, 9) "The fool hath said in his heart, There is no God. Corrupt are they, and have done abominable iniquity: there is none that doeth good." (Ps. 53 : 1) "Then will I teach transgressors thy ways; and sinners shall be converted unto thee."—Ps. 51 : 13.

The Lord will not lead or teach the wicked; but if the wicked cease from his wickedness and turn to the Lord and seek righteousness, and do it, he will have the Lord's mercy. God has no pleasure in the death of the wicked. (Ezek 33 : 11) He will destroy the wicked for their own good and for the good of others. God is love. His mercy endureth for ever. (Ps. 136 : 1-8)

"The Lord is gracious, and full of compassion; slow to anger, and of great mercy. The Lord is good to all; and his tender mercies are over all his works." (Ps. 145:8,9) Every one, therefore, will be afforded a fair opportunity to know God and to do his will; and so long as there is an honest endeavor put forth to do right in obedience to God's commandments he will extend his mercy and aid.

There are millions of persons now on earth who know not God and who have no information concerning his means of salvation and their blessing. These are called heathen. They are very degraded and ignorant. The Lord Jesus died for them as well as for others. All the heathen must be brought to a knowledge of the truth. God's mercy will extend to them all; and if they embrace the truth, and heed and obey the Lord, the judgment concerning them will be the blessings of life everlasting.

The Evil

After one has been made fully acquainted with God's truth and been given a full opportunity to show his obedience thereto, if he then persists in doing evil he shall be put to death and shall not live. "All the wicked will [God] destroy." (Ps. 145:20) That does not mean that men will go to a place of conscious torment; but the evil shall be destroyed with an everlasting destruction from which there will never be a resurrection. (2 Thess. 1:9) Such will show that they do not appreciate God's goodness and the opportunity he gives to them for life; and that opportunity will be for ever removed.

The Obedient

Life everlasting in happiness is the greatest desire of man. The final judgment to be rendered at the end of the trial will be the giving of life everlasting to all those who obey the Lord. Life is the great gift of God through Jesus Christ our Lord. (Rom. 6:23) There is no other name given among men whereby man may obtain everlasting life. (Acts 4:12) The promise is that those who believe and are obedient unto Christ, the great Judge, shall not perish, but shall have everlasting life. (John 3:16,17) At the mouth of every one of his holy prophets God made promise that he would grant restitution blessings to those who obey him. (Acts 3:19-24) Restitution means restoring to man all that was lost by Adam's disobedience, which includes the enjoying of life everlasting in a perfect condition upon the earth.

Most of the poor of the world have been classed as wicked men and women. Many of them have not been nearly so bad, however, as those who have had the rule over them. It is true that many of the people have stolen and committed other crimes. Some of them commit theft in order to get food to live, and suffer imprisonment therefor.

It is also true that many of the rich have stolen on a much larger scale and have gone free. Wall Street, New York city, is known as the great stock market or place for dealing in stocks, securities, grain and other things. The men who operate there often begin with nothing and soon their holdings mount to the millions. They juggle and deal with what other men have produced, and grow rich in material wealth. Their conscience must hurt them at times, and they seek some relief therefor. At the end of the same Wall Street stands old Trinity Church. Its holdings amount to more than fifty million dollars. The clergymen who keep that church have reserved a space for the rich. At spare moments the stock gamblers rush in there to have some kind of prayer said to help them out. Those prayers do no good, however.

The clergyman is even worse than the stock gambler, because the clergyman claims to represent God but in fact misrepresents him and represents his enemy. Let it be conceded that both the clergyman and the stock gambler are wicked. Their evil course may have been induced chiefly by Satan the Devil. If in the time of judgment these hear that which is right and obey what is truth and righteousness, the judgment will be favorable to them. Concerning such it is written: "When the wicked man turneth away from his wickedness that he hath committed, and doeth that which is lawful and right, he shall save his soul alive. Because he considereth, and turneth away from all his transgressions that he hath committed, he shall surely live, he shall not die." (Ezek. 18:27, 28) It will be much harder, however, for them to stay in the way of right than it will be for the poor and meek.

Joyful Time

The judgment of the people of the world will be a time of joy to all who obey the Lord. Not

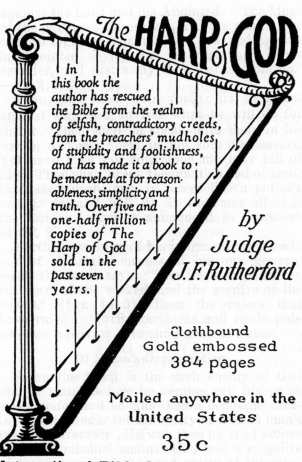

only will they learn that it is a time of deliverance from the oppressor's hand, but they will
then see before them the hope of life eternal and
happiness, with all the good things attendant
thereupon.

One of the names of God's organization, of
which Christ Jesus is the Head, is Zion. God's
prophet represents the dead returning from the
grave, and with them the living, the poor and
the exiles, coming unto Zion, which is God's organization. They come with songs of joy because they see that the time of the judgment of
the Lord has opened to them the way of blessings. The prophet says: "And the ransomed of
the Lord shall return, and come to Zion with
songs, and everlasting joy upon their heads:
they shall obtain joy and gladness, and sorrow
and sighing shall flee away."—Isa. 35:10.

Then they that hear and understand will rejoice in the words of Jesus: "Verily, verily, I
say unto you, If a man keep my saying, he shall
never see death." (John 8:51) "Whosoever
liveth and believeth in me shall never die. Be-
lievest thou this?"—John 11:26.

God made the earth for man. He made all
men of one blood to dwell upon the earth and
he fixes the boundaries of man on the earth. He
never intended that a human being should go to
heaven. "[God] hath made of one blood all nations of men, for to dwell on all the face of the
earth; and hath determined the times before
appointed, and the bounds of their habitation."
—Acts 17:26.

God has promised to make, and will make the
earth a real paradise as the everlasting home

of the obedient and restored ones. The desert
and the places that are desolate shall become as
the garden of Eden.—Isa. 35:1-7; Ezek. 36:
34-36.

\In the judgment the Lord will be entirely impartial. He has promised to restore the obedient ones and to give them a perfect home, and
he will carry out that promise to the letter.
(Isa. 46:11) He will not permit one man to
build a house and another to take it away from
him. Every man will then live in his own house.
(Isa. 65:21, 22) Men will not ruthlessly destroy
the trees and make the earth a barren place, as
they do now. They will cultivate the earth and
plant trees and make it a place of beauty and
glory. Every man will then own his own vine
and trees and will sit under them and enjoy
peace and happiness, and none will make him
afraid.—Mic. 4:4.

Let the poor and meek and distressed take
heart now and be of good courage. Remember
that the hardships and sufferings have enabled
you to learn to be sympathetic with your fellow
man in his weakness and that you will rejoice
with your fellow man in his blessings. The judgment day of the world will be one of gladness
to those who obey, and to them it will end in
joy unspeakable. With the wilfully wicked destroyed, and the righteous obedient, the result
of the judgment will be the end of death. Christ,
during his reign, will destroy all man's enemies,
including death.—1 Cor. 15:25, 26.

God's righteous government is likened unto a
holy city which brings everlasting peace, health,
life and happiness to the obedient inhabitants

thereof. Looking to the time of complete judgment and its happy ending, and for the encouragement of those who seek the truth, it is written: "I heard a great voice out of heaven saying, Behold, the tabernacle of God is with men, and he will dwell with them, and they shall be his people, and God himself shall be with them, and be their God. And God shall wipe away all tears from their eyes; and there shall be no more death, neither sorrow, nor crying, neither shall there be any more pain: for the former things are passed away. And he that sat upon the throne said, Behold, I make all things new. And he said unto me, Write; for these words are true and faithful."—Rev. 21:3-5.

When the young man who had followed the company of poor from the church learned of God's gracious plan and of his great loving kindness toward man, he rejoiced in his heart. He was thankful that he had gone to that church building on that stormy night and had there witnessed the unkind treatment of the little company of poor, because it had led him to search out the truth of the Word of God. He also learned that man's greatest privilege now is to take his stand firmly on the side of Jehovah God and to obey and serve him. He resolved then and there to go forth and tell his fellow man about the goodness of God and what is in store for the poor world in the day of judgment. He realized that to do so would lift the burden from some and make some sad hearts glad. He would also be singing forth the honor of the great Jehovah God's name. It is your privilege, dear reader, to go and do likewise.

politicians are proud and severe, and the clergy are arrogant, and all working together are oppressors of the people. Concerning such the Lord says: "For, behold, the day cometh, that shall burn as an oven; and all the proud, yea, and all that do wickedly, shall be stubble: and the day that cometh shall burn them up, saith the Lord of hosts, that it shall leave them neither root nor branch."—Mal. 4: 1.

The three elements forming the controlling power over the people are designated as the earth, and such are now in great fear and are feverishly preparing for war because of the things that they see coming upon the earth. Satan the Devil is therefore gathering his forces for the great battle of Armageddon. (Rev. 16: 13-16) These ruling powers well know that they have violated "the everlasting covenant" by shedding innocent blood, and God says concerning them: "The earth mourneth, and fadeth away; the world languisheth, and fadeth away; the haughty people of the earth do languish. The earth also is defiled under the inhabitants thereof, because they have transgressed the laws, changed the ordinance, broken the everlasting covenant. Therefore hath the curse devoured the earth, and they that dwell therein are desolate; therefore the inhabitants of the earth are burned, and few men left."—Isa. 24: 4-6.

Concerning those who have deliberately acted as Satan's instruments to oppress the people God says: "And I will make drunk her princes, and her wise men, her captains, and her rulers, and her mighty men: and they shall

a chance to learn the truth. (Rev. 20:1-3)
Christ, the great and righteous Judge, will then
judge the people in righteousness. Then the
people can have a hearing and a trial. When
Christ's kingdom of righteousness is in full
sway, then the judgment will take place as it is
written: "The Lord . . . shall judge the quick
[living] and the dead at his appearing and his
kingdom." (2 Tim. 4:1) Those living on the
earth will be the first ones judged. After them
the dead will be brought to life on earth and
be given a fair trial. The day of judgment of
the people, instead of its being one of great distress, will be a day of great joy to all them that
obey. It will mean the time of deliverance from
oppression, and the day of blessing. Concerning
that day of judgment the preachers have misrepresented God and have misled the people.
God never authorized them to speak. Now the
time has come when God will make known his
truth to his people in his own good way.

The Trial

Bear in mind always that God is just, and
his action always in harmony with his law. It
follows then that there could be no judgment
without a hearing or trial of the ones to be
judged, because God's law provides that such
hearing must be had. (John 7:51) It also follows that there could be no judgment of the
people without a judge; and, since the judgment work is assigned to Christ Jesus, the
judgment by Christ of the people could not take
place until his court is set and the due time has
arrived. Furthermore, there could not be a trial

of a person unless that person has knowledge
of and concerning his trial. The preachers
have told the people that all have their trial
and that their destiny is fixed at death. That is
not true. Only those who have learned of God's
plan and who have knowledge or could have
had a knowledge thereof have been on trial.
Some have been tried as individuals, and some
forming an organization have been subjected
to trial.

Take as an illustration that little company of
men and women who rushed into the church
building to escape the storm and who heard the
words of the preacher concerning their judgment. They were not on trial. They could not
have been on trial unless they had first heard
the truth. They did not hear the truth from the
preacher. They had heard it in no church building. They were threatened with eternal torment, which is not true. They heard nothing
about God's provision for poor humanity. The
preacher was not their judge and he had no
authority to single them out and speak in words
of condemnation or otherwise against them.
Satan, the enemy of God, has overreached the
preachers and has induced them to preach false
doctrines that have really blinded the people to
the truth.

Only those who have made a consecration to
do God's will and have received his spirit have
been led into the truth. That is exactly what Jesus said to his disciples, that "when the holy
spirit of God is given, you will be led into all
truth". (John 16:13) Until the second coming
of the Lord and his kingdom the poor of the